The
RAGGED
EDGE

A US Marine's Account of
LEADING THE IRAQI ARMY
FIFTH BATTALION

MICHAEL ZACCHEA and **TED KEMP**

CHICAGO
REVIEW
PRESS

Copyright © 2017 by Michael Zacchea and Ted Kemp
All rights reserved
Published by Chicago Review Press Incorporated
814 North Franklin Street
Chicago, Illinois 60610
ISBN 978-1-61373-841-2

Library of Congress Cataloging-in-Publication Data
Names: Zacchea, Michael, author | Kemp, Ted, author
Title: The ragged edge : a marine's account of leading the Iraqi Army Fifth
    Battalion / Michael Zacchea and Ted Kemp.
Description: Chicago, Illinois : Chicago Review Press Incorporated, 2017.
Identifiers: LCCN 2016032840 (print) | LCCN 2016056156 (ebook) | ISBN
    9781613738412 (cloth : alk. paper) | ISBN 9781613738429 (pdf) | ISBN
    9781613738443 (epub) | ISBN 9781613738436 (Kindle)
Subjects: LCSH: Zacchea, Michael. | Iraq. Jaysh. Battalion, 5th. |
    Iraq—Armed Forces—History. | Iraq War, 2003–2011.
Classification: LCC UA853.I75 Z33 2017 (print) | LCC UA853.I75 (ebook) | DDC
    956.7044/342—dc23
LC record available at https://lccn.loc.gov/2016032840

Typesetting: Nord Compo
Interior photos: All photos by Michael Zacchea unless otherwise indicated.

Printed in the United States of America
5 4 3 2 1

Better the Arabs do it tolerably than that you do it perfectly.

—T. E. Lawrence

CONTENTS

Part IV: Taji

AUTHORS' NOTE

THE NAMES OF SOME OF THE SURVIVING IRAQIS in this book have been altered in order to protect them and their families from retaliation.

FOREWORD

THE PUSH TO BUILD A NEW IRAQI ARMY was a struggle from the outset. I know. I led the effort.

On May 11, 2003, I was on my way back to Fort Benning, Georgia, after a short trip away. Since it was Mother's Day, I asked my wife, PJ, to pick me up at the airport so we could celebrate. On our way to brunch, I took a call from my four-star boss.

"Paul," he said—and this is how generals find out where they will serve next—"the chief of staff has selected you to go to Iraq and rebuild their armed forces." He gave me the name of the person who would be my point of contact once I arrived in Iraq and told me to report on June 10.

My wife asked what the call was about. I explained. PJ is the daughter of a Marine colonel. All she said was, "I would have expected the guy for *that* mission to already be there."

I had a month to prepare for deployment and to relinquish command of the infantry center at Fort Benning. I set out with the former undersecretary for policy at the Defense Department, Walter Slocombe, to design, man, train, and equip a group whose mission was to establish an army for a Middle Eastern country of thirty million people. My new command was called the Coalition Military Assistance Training Team (CMATT).

Somewhere in the bowels of the Pentagon, we found a short PowerPoint briefing that gave very broad guidance for the project. Essentially, it was a white sheet of paper. That was the extent of what was available as I set out to design, man, train, and equip the Iraqi Army.

The only hard guidance in the document was that the Iraqi Army needed to be representative of Iraq's population: 60 percent

Shiite Arabs, 20 percent Sunni Arabs, and 20 percent Kurds (who were mostly Sunni); it needed to be accountable to the Iraqi nation and under civilian control; and it needed to be defense oriented—meaning it shouldn't be designed to invade its neighbors. I knew I needed to learn anything and everything I could about Iraq and its people.

I had another problem that I did not yet appreciate at the time. My chain of command rose up from me through the senior US adviser for security and defense, Walt Slocombe, through ambassador to Iraq L. Paul Bremer to Secretary of Defense Donald Rumsfeld. At the time, I was a two-star general. The chain of command left me with no four-star general who could interact directly with the Pentagon for me or run interference at the top.

There are certain things that only a four-star general can accomplish within the Defense Department. I held a distant, two-star command whose mission was the most important in Iraq, but I was left in the position of negotiating with the Pentagon bureaucracy directly. Everybody could see that an insurgency was growing in Iraq, and no one in the Defense Department wanted to take ownership of the Iraqi Army mission. There on the ground, we began living through the consequences of Secretary Rumsfeld's decision to do no planning for the occupation of Iraq before the invasion.

Bremer was the leader of the Coalition Provisional Authority, which made him the de facto leader of Iraq. The press and the better-educated Iraqis called him the Viceroy of Iraq. He held great decision-making authority, and my next problem arose on May 23, when Ambassador Bremer dissolved the Iraqi Army. (Even though Ambassador Bremer gave the order, I am convinced that the decision to scrap the existing army was made at a much higher level.) The Iraqi Army self-demobilized, littering its installations with uniforms and random military gear of no value. Everything that was of value the departing soldiers or local civilians plundered. They stripped trucks, pulled the wiring from buildings, and made off with anything of street value. What was left of the Iraqi Army was completely destroyed, making the rebuilding effort that much harder. We also began to learn that while the Army's mostly Sunni officers were interested in continuing to serve, the mostly Shiite enlisted men were not.

I arrived at Baghdad International Airport on June 13 after hitchhiking aboard a UH-60 Black Hawk helicopter from Kuwait, courtesy of a major from the 101st Airborne Division. From there, I needed to get a ride to the Republican Palace in the Green Zone. The phone number I had been given for my point of contact was constantly busy. So I called back to Fort Benning and got my former aide-de-camp, Maj. Geoff Fuller, on the phone. He had just returned home from a run. He e-mailed my contact in Iraq, who dispatched a Marine colonel to get me in a civilian pickup truck.

That night, I was up at 3 AM, jet-lagged. I found a computer, e-mailed PJ, and decided to take a prowl of the Republican Palace. At about 5 AM, I ran into a two-man Army security detail at the main entrance. These were men I had met in Bosnia a few years earlier. They were in running gear and wearing pistols, and they told me they were waiting on Ambassador Bremer so they could escort him on a run in the dark Green Zone. At that point the ambassador showed up, asked me who I was, and invited me to join him. So off we went, at a fast pace, down dark streets I did not know, with two armed men shadowing us. The ambassador and I hit it off, and I realized I was now home.

A few hours later, I met with five great officers who were on loan for my mission from US Central Command. They were led by Col. Roland Tiso, who had taken over Uday Hussein's villa—a big, ostentatious stone-and-marble palace with an indoor/outdoor swimming pool. We set out to man, train, and equip the Iraqi Army and to build an infrastructure around it.

Our first tasks were to find a training base and, given the shortage of American and coalition military support, to award contracts for everything from teams of trainers to all types of logistical support. The first members of CMATT began to arrive June 20, and we slowly grew to some 250 men and women, civilian and military, from nine nations and all branches of US service. The most critical component was the actual, on-the-ground men who would train soldiers.

My former command, the infantry center at Fort Benning, was under no obligation to help me, but they volunteered to rapidly carry out a contracting process for finding trainers. The award went to Vinnell Corporation, a subsidiary of Northrop Grumman Corporation. In a great stroke of luck for all of us, retired Army lieutenant general George Crocker was assigned as program manager. General Crocker was invaluable to the mission, and he displayed personal and professional courage to take on a tough mission under austere and dangerous conditions. His team began flowing into Iraq on the Fourth of July, with the intention to begin training on August 1.

Other contracts were negotiated for logistical support for the nascent Iraqi Army, recruiting centers, refurbishment of the abandoned Iraqi Army base at Kirkush, and all the categories of supply. That included every material item that's required to sustain a soldier, because we had nothing to start. By the end of July, we had our first training base open at Kirkush, near the border with Iran.

We began with a thousand young Iraqi men and a number of former officers of Saddam's army who passed an exhaustive vetting process. Crocker and his team got to work. Conditions were hot, dirty, and raw, but training was underway.

Then, within two weeks, it became clear we had a flawed model.

There are three components to the creation of soldiers. The first is building them physically. The second is giving them the training they need to operate their equipment and function as a part of an infantry fire team, which consists of four men. The final component is what the British call the "moral component." It is a broad term, but essentially it means instilling the intangible attributes of the soldier—a sense of resilience, dedication to teamwork, belief in the chain of command, and belief in the state and their fellow soldiers. The first two components are pretty routine worldwide. The third, the moral component, however, varies dramatically from one culture to the next. It's relatively easy in

Western-style democracies. It is not easy for totalitarian societies. And only soldiers can impart that critical moral component. One of our big problems was that we had only four such soldiers: two two-man teams from Great Britain and Australia. They could not do it all. The Iraqi recruits viewed Crocker's civilian workers as technicians who could give training but who struggled to instill discipline. Vinnell did a great job training, but I needed soldiers who could perform drill sergeant duty.

But where to go for drill instructors? We needed to completely redesign the program.

In the early 1980s, the US Army embarked on an experimental program based on the British Regimental system COHORT (cohesion, operational readiness, training). The idea was that it was best to keep units stable for three to five years, with little or no personnel turnover. The guys who ran personnel hated it, but we in the field loved it. COHORT units started with a seasoned group of officers and noncommissioned officers (that is to say, sergeants) who came together for about two months of team building and training. Then they received several hundred new graduates of infantry basic training and taught them how to operate at the squad, platoon, and company levels. The result was extraordinarily well-trained infantry battalions.

We decided to try the COHORT model in Iraq.

We got word that Secretary Rumsfeld was coming to visit, and we put together a briefing to outline our plan to accelerate the development of the Iraqi Armed Forces in the face of a growing and increasingly violent insurgency. Our plan was to recruit enough former officers from Saddam's army for three new divisions and then to send them for two months of retraining in Jordan with the Jordanian Army—which was and is widely recognized as the best army in the Arab world. Simultaneously, we would recruit a like number of former Iraqi noncommissioned officers, and train them with the Vinnell team. After the officers and their sergeants were trained, we would bring them together, divide them into battalions, and give each battalion a thousand new recruits to train and develop.

It was the easiest briefing I ever gave. Secretary Rumsfeld, with Ambassador Bremer by his side and a host of generals at the table, listened to me. But then Rumsfeld stuck his finger in my chest. "Just don't make this look like the American Army," he said. I paused, because that was an odd thing to say. I assumed he meant that I shouldn't "gold-plate" the new battalions—meaning to spend a lot of money unnecessarily that yields few gains. I decided to tee up a little humor to defuse the situation. At that time, the US Army was in a fight with Rumsfeld, struggling to protect funds for a very expensive, very heavy artillery system called Crusader that it had had in development since the Cold War. Everybody knew Rumsfeld hated Crusader.

I turned to Walt Slocombe and said, "Sir, we have already removed Crusader from the equipment list for the new Iraqi Army."

The room was stunned. Nobody could believe I actually said it, and frankly I didn't know what was going to happen. After a long pause, Rumsfeld got the joke and blurted out laughter. I am convinced that that joke helped get our plan approved. Rumsfeld gave us his OK, and in one swoop he boosted my budget from $173 million to $2.2 billion.

Despite having the funds, obtaining equipment remained a struggle. A very understaffed contract team at the Coalition Provisional Authority built a comprehensive equipment contract that was overturned by a very overstaffed Department of the Army contract office after a losing bidder challenged it. We were forced to cobble together equipment purchases using a vast number of unrelated contracts.

Still, we put the first group of Iraq officers into training with the Jordanians in January 2004. Vinnell built an academy for non-commissioned officers at Kirkush.

I made a recruiting trip up north to try to get soldiers from the Kurds' long-standing Peshmerga militia, and while I was there I met with Kurdish leader Masoud Barzani. Over dinner I asked him for advice on integrating Kurdish soldiers into the new Iraqi Army. He replied that integration would sort itself out and that the friction between Kurds and Arabs was a Saddam Hussein creation that would not stand in the way of integrated units.

"The real problem," he said, "will be between the Sunnis and the Shiites."

I told him we were not seeing that problem.

"I promise that you will," he retorted.

In late March 2004, a Shiite imam based in Baghdad named Muqtada al-Sadr ordered his militia to increase attacks on Sunni civilians and begin attacking US and coalition forces. They nearly succeeded in cutting off a number of logistics and communications lines. The Green Zone crowd started stockpiling food. Meanwhile, the Marines started preparing for a fight in Fallujah after four Blackwater men were murdered there by Sunni militants.

Then disaster.

Our new Iraqi Second Battalion was in the middle of urban warfare training with a new ten-man Marine advisory team at a major base in Taji. The US Marine division commander asked if he could have the Iraqi unit perform checkpoint operations and secure the outer perimeter at Fallujah. I declared that they were trained to do that mission and agreed to see them there. I briefed the battalion officers on their mission and assisted them in the planning process. All seemed good to go.

However, while in their convoy en route to Fallujah, the battalion received harassing fire from Shiites on the outskirts of Taji. Civilians taunted them for being American supporters and for attacking Iraqis. The battalion's Iraqi leadership collapsed. The Marine advisers that were with the battalion had to take command of what was left of the battalion and guide them back to Taji. The next day, I got an e-mail from Tom Ricks, a military correspondent for the *Washington Post*, asking me about the "mutiny." We had a problem, and it was of my making.

When we recruited the new Iraqi soldiers, we had briefed them that they were joining to protect Iraq from foreign enemies. That was in fact what we were recruiting them to do. They were told that internal security work would be done by police forces that were part of the Iraqi Ministry of the Interior. But when the insurgency arose, and because the country was without adequate police, the Iraqi Army was suddenly needed for counterinsurgency operations.

We needed to reorganize the Iraqi Army on the basis of this very substantial change of plan. It was a gut-wrenching undertaking.

There was gallows humor around CMATT that we were trying to "build an airplane in midflight, while under fire." Twelve years later, I do not know if we ever had any chance to succeed.

Major General Paul D. Eaton (US Army–ret.)
Fox Island, Washington
December 4, 2015

ABBREVIATIONS, TERMS, AND ORDER OF INFANTRY

ABBREVIATIONS

AAV	Amphibious assault vehicle
CMATT	Coalition Military Assistance Training Team
CO	Commanding officer
DFAC	Dining facilities administration center, used for any dining room or mess hall
Gy. Sgt.	Gunnery sergeant
ICDC	Iraqi Civil Defense Corps
IED	Improvised explosive device
L.Cpl.	Lance corporal
MRE	Meals ready to eat, or packaged meals intended for consumption in the field
M.Sgt.	Master sergeant
NCO	Noncommissioned officer, or sergeants
NJP	Nonjudicial punishment, or a military hearing for misdemeanor infractions
RPG	Rocket-propelled grenade, or a shoulder-fired rocket with explosive
S-1	Administration officer, adjutant
S-2	Intelligence officer
S-3	Operations officer, Ops O
S-4	Logistics officer
SFC	Sergeant first class
S.Sgt.	Staff sergeant
WARNO	Warning order, or notice of an upcoming mission
XO	Executive officer, or the officer second in command

TERMS

billet	A designated duty station or assignment, also an individual soldier's lodging
irhabi, irhabeen	Arabic for violent criminal, criminals, used by some Iraqis to refer to insurgents
jundi, junood	Arabic for soldier, soldiers
lash-up	Military slang describing something rigged up or thrown together
mujanad, mujanadin	Arabic for recruit, recruits
musharaf, musharafin	Arabic for adviser, advisers
Peshmerga	The informal military of Kurdistan, Kurdish for "one who confronts death"

ORDER OF INFANTRY

platoon	A tactical unit comprising about 30–40 soldiers
company	A tactical unit comprising two or more platoons, or 100–250 soldiers
battalion	A tactical unit comprising three or more companies, or 300–900 soldiers
regiment	A tactical unit comprising two or more battalions, or 1,000–2,500 soldiers
brigade	A unit comprising two or more regiments, or 2,500–10,000 soldiers
division	A unit comprising two or more regiments or brigades, or 10,000–25,000 soldiers

Part I

KIRKUSH

1

BIRD DOG

THE CLOSER I GOT TO home, the more I felt myself coming apart.

On the last day of February 2005, I stared hard out of a speeding Humvee, eyes squinting beneath the brim of my helmet. My rifle was packed away for shipping. For the first time in a year, I was unarmed. The thundering vehicle quaked and rattled, the squeaks and squeals of thousands of dry steel parts protesting against our momentum. We tore down the one open road into Baghdad International Airport. The deadliest stretch of highway in the world. I trained my eyes on the scenery through the windshield. Rough roadsides flitted past. Everything wanted to be an IED: The carcass of a dog, ripped at by skinny canines still living. A dead mule, sideways and inflated like a black surgical glove. A smolder of ochre earth—I gazed at it, gripped the frame of a window. Why is that *heap* there? *Why is that there?*

The Humvee's shocks and frame yelped through the bouncing. The heat from the big American engine rose up through the seats and put our crotches on a slow burn. I removed my helmet, reached for the orange cooler of ice water we always kept inside, and poured a little over my head. An odor like shit mixed with grilled meat came through the open windows.

"Fuck," I said. The water cooled me, but only for a few seconds. "Just let me be smelling that for the last time."

3

Get me through this, and let that be it. Just let this be it. But who was I asking?

Pay attention, Michael.

Speed was our best defense. The road to Baghdad International Airport snapped past like a high-speed conveyor belt. We shot and bounded over it, on toward more of it. Always more of it. We bounced on our seats. Behind us, Iraqis floored trucks, trying to keep up.

This was my last convoy in Iraq. My final out. Every pile of dirt, every drift of garbage on the side of the road looked like an IED. Each seemed to bear the marks of our enemies' hands. And the country was full of garbage. I sat clutched by the anxiety of movement.

I tried to consider the men who shared the Humvee with me, a handful of the Americans I had led for months. Following us, in one SUV and two white Nissan pickups, were a squad of Iraqi soldiers and a handful of officers: my friend Ahmed Nu'uman, the quietly intelligent Mohammed Najm, my interpreters Arkan and Abdallah. I knew they were there but did not look back at them.

Zayn. For a moment I almost managed to focus on Zayn. *I hope you prayed for us today, Major Zayn.* And then something ragged and brown came toward us on the roadside to pass the Humvee, next to the death seat, and I couldn't think about anything until we had passed it. And we did.

Zayn had been my friend since the beginning. He'd taken me into his *tribe*, for fuck's sake. *This is ending,* I thought. *This is actually ending. It's been a year, and it's ending right now.*

But I couldn't attain that level of perspective on my own experience. I could not summon context. My mind was full of spiders, and they leaped and trembled and loosed themselves in silent bafflement into the open windows' hot gales.

Zayn had asked to ride in my vehicle, but we couldn't displace an American for him. It's hard to tell your friend, your brother, that someone else holds more tactical value than he does. It had been hard for me at the time, less than an hour earlier. *Fuck it. Let somebody else tell him,* I thought then. That old barrier, sometimes visible over the last year, sometimes not, had again come between us. He accepted it with grace. Again. Zayn took the SUV.

I should say good-bye. But the whole concept of "should" got sucked out the windows of the Humvee. So did everything else. It surprised me how quickly things drew away. *I have cared enough. I am done caring.* My calculus was brutal and irresistible: *I just need to stay alive all the way to the airport.*

The drive felt interminable, seeming to slow as we drew closer to Baghdad International, despite our speed. Finally, we entered the gates and crossed to the airport's far side. We piled from our vehicles into the staging area that would suck me up into the sky.

When the explosion came, most of us were out on our feet. Even at a distance of more than a mile, I felt its concussion ripple through my chest. A wave good-bye. *You're not out yet, Raed Zakkiyah.*

The wave came from the direction of buildings beyond the airport. Not the road. I knew: The blast wasn't planted on the highway. It was a vehicle-borne IED. Somebody just drove it to that place. The banner of some miserable life just came to its final unraveling.

The vehicle-borne IED birthed a brown-and-gray swarm of smoke, dust, and earth that unfurled upward and outward, pushing at the sky. It slipped out of earthen coils and showed itself to us, stretching. More than a mile away, it was like a giant rising directly before us. It loomed over me liked a cowled, deathly figure.

We were all silent for a few moments. Sergeant First Class Brown, whose knack for understatement never eluded him, spoke first.

"I am glad," he said, "that we dodged that."

We all agreed.

"Poor fuckin' bastards," said another American. "Poor fuckin' bastards."

Somebody spit onto the asphalt. The cowled figure kept climbing, uncoiling. It was looking at us.

I stopped myself and looked around. Arkan, my interpreter (or 'terp), a big man for an Iraqi, approached with his eyes on me. Mohammed Najm stood steady behind him, his uniform crisp by

Iraqi standards. Abdallah, another of my 'terps, kept a professional distance, hands clasped behind his back. Zayn had not left the SUV.

There was nothing to do about the IED. As always, time for reflection was limited. I still had to check in with the American manifest noncommissioned officer (NCO), show him my orders, and get my seat assignment on the plane that would carry me away.

The good-byes were awkward to the point of embarrassment. Even earlier that morning, while I was still in command, we never ran out of things to talk about, to joke about, pithy smart-ass comments to get a laugh, the 1,001 things that you say to run a battalion on a daily basis. But now, words dried up. We shook hands. We embraced. I glanced at the SUV. Zayn stayed inside. His shoulders shook; he hid his face in his hands.

That's the first time I've seen an Iraqi ashamed of crying. Zayn, I can't walk over there to you, my friend. I'm done, Major. It'll only make this worse.

He kept crying. *Christ, fuck it. Sever it all. Feel for a phantom limb later.*

We stood in front of a trailer; next to it was an improvised gateway that the others could not enter, at least not until it was their turn. The gateway led to the manifest NCO and my out-processing from Iraq. My gateway back to the world. The others said final farewells. I didn't hear them really, but I knew that's what they were doing. The Americans and the Iraqis boarded their vehicles and whipped around the corner of the trailer, out of sight.

In that instant, I inhaled, but it wasn't full or cleansing. Something remained clenched in me. My mind was nearly shattered. I didn't know what neurological lash-up was holding me together. I was waiting for a plane. The idea that I would be walking in the United States in a matter of hours was unfathomable. I no longer possessed context for that world. I might as well jump into a time machine to 1916. Or 1258. I tried to make myself *understand* that it was over. But I could not.

And anyway, it wasn't. Now I know it never will be.

I have written this memoir so you can understand the Iraq War as it really was, and as it really is. Because it is ongoing. If you're like most

Americans, really grasping the Iraq War will require you to rethink a lot of assumptions. Now, in the second decade of the twenty-first century, the United States is learning, to its shock, that the Iraq War didn't end as we supposed it did when we pulled out. Instead, the war birthed a wildly radical religious enemy that our country still fights. The administration of Barack Obama decided to go about that fight by encouraging Kurds and Arabs to work together and defeat that enemy for us. Now Donald Trump, still waiting to assume office as these words go to print, touts the benefits of having other people fight in Iraq or Syria. I've seen that strategy before. I lived it. The Bush White House wanted the Arabs and Kurds to "stand up" so "we can stand down." I was one of the very few military advisers who was to execute that mission. I am writing this book to illustrate, in the most personal way I know, that this strategy will not succeed now if we try it the way we did then.

I am in a unique position to know these things. As a US Marine Corps major, I led the small group of Americans who trained the first unit of the new Iraqi Army that managed to hold together through sustained combat. That unit was designed explicitly to include every major population group in Iraq: Shiite Arabs, Sunni Arabs, Kurds, Yazidis, and others. We fought the direct precursors—in many cases, the very same individuals—who later formed the so-called Islamic State, or ISIS. I intimately know the men who formed ISIS, and the Kurds and Arabs who now fight them. I killed members of the first group and commanded members of the second.

I do not idealize the Iraqis or Muslims or other Arabs. I also do not, like the sharpshooting hero of *American Sniper*, consider them "savages." At the root of Americans' misunderstanding of Iraq (and Syria) is a tragic, incorrect assumption that the Sunnis, Shiites, and Kurds of that region all want to be just like us. We think they want to be inclusive, pluralistic, merit-driven, and maybe even secular. They do not. They never will, and that's a hard thing for Americans, on both the left and the right, to accept. However, Iraqis also don't want endless war or theocratic tyranny in the form of the Islamic State. And we don't want terrorists from a barbaric caliphate only as distant as a commercial flight or a recruiting website.

I am not writing this book to present solutions to our ongoing war. I do not have them. Perhaps they exist, but they're not mine to give. I am a former Marine Corps officer who fought in the Middle East and Africa over a twelve-year career. I understand people, and I understand war. I understand enough to be disgusted by the stories Americans tell themselves about the Iraq War. I do not find our heroic Iraq War books and movies—almost none of which feature Iraqi characters—instructive on any level whatsoever. There *is*, however, a reality to explore, one our country both encountered and created. That reality is not going away. The American war in Iraq will not end with the current presidency, nor the next one, nor the one after that, unless we stop looking at the Iraq War as we wish to see it and start looking at it as it is, in all its awful and amazing complexity. We also need to look at *ourselves*, we Americans, as *we* really are. Otherwise, the conflict that we started in 2003 will be a multigenerational war.

I want you to have an unsparing look at the Arabs, the Kurds, ourselves, and our shared war so that we can form a starting point for real debate. I'm going to take you back and place you in that war with me. I want you to live my year in Iraq too. The lessons I learned there are as relevant today as they were then. I guarantee that parts will disturb you, no matter who you are or what your politics may be. That's as it should be. Everything you are about to read was real—the unflinching truth as I knew it. That's why I've written this memoir. It's my duty, and it's what I've got to give, to you and to my country.

The United States rolled into Iraq on March 20, 2003, with a total strength of almost 150,000 troops. The Army and Marines swept north out of Kuwait, up along the Tigris and Euphrates Rivers toward Baghdad. Forty-five thousand British troops invaded Basra in the south. Kurdish fighters from a militia group called Peshmerga—the name means "one who confronts death"—launched attacks with US Special Forces in the north. A sequence of Iraqi cities fell to the main American force: Nasiriyah, Najaf, Karbala, and finally Baghdad. The conventional fighting was over in about three weeks. On May 1, Vice

President Dick Cheney, one of the strongest voices in favor of the war, told a gathering sponsored by the conservative think tank the Heritage Foundation that the recent fighting was "one of the most successful military campaigns ever waged." He credited "a new American way of war." Later that day, President George W. Bush put on a flight suit, flew to the waters off San Diego in a Navy warplane, landed on the deck of the USS *Abraham Lincoln,* and stood before a giant MISSION ACCOMPLISHED banner to declare the end of major combat operations.

That new American way of war that Cheney spoke of came about largely through the political efforts of Donald Rumsfeld, the sixty-nine-year-old, Princeton- and Georgetown-educated secretary of defense. The so-called Rumsfeld Doctrine called for more use of technology in the military, heavier dependence on airpower, and a reliance on native troops who coordinate with relatively small groups of Americans. Rumsfeld's formula worked well to dislodge the Taliban from its strongholds in Afghanistan. Critics of Rumsfeld, both within the military and without, argued that the light American "footprint" his doctrine called for in Afghanistan was part of the reason Osama bin Laden escaped after the US invasion. Other critics, like US general Anthony Zinni, pointed out that the Rumsfeld Doctrine didn't address how a country like Afghanistan or Iraq was going to be *secured* and *occupied.* Zinni knew from experience: he trained the South Vietnamese Marine Corps in the 1970s and had just retired as commander of the US Central Command, which oversaw the Middle East.

But the Rumsfeld Doctrine carried the day, largely because the military thinking behind it fit neatly with the political thinking of most of the Bush administration. On the national security side, the Bush administration had adopted the confrontational ideology of the "neocons." On the economic side, it had adopted the belief that more of the US government should be privatized—including a lot of what our military usually did.

Most of the high-ranking members of the Bush White House identified with the neoconservatives, a group whose name the US news media like to repeat a lot without ever really explaining what it means. Neoconservatism concerns itself with the way the

United States projects power in the world. It calls for the active use of US military force in order to prevent geopolitical threats. If necessary, it calls for fighting to take place before threats arise. Generally speaking, neocons believe in the practical efficacy of military confrontation, they emphasize that the United States must be willing to act unilaterally, and they don't trust diplomacy. They also tend to exhibit a conviction that the United States is a power of good set in natural opposition to the powers of evil. They view the world in black-and-white moral terms.

Before the turn of the twenty-first century, many neocons had begun calling for the active promotion of democracy in places where it didn't exist—especially in the Middle East—on the grounds that established democracies rarely go to war with each other. In contrast, George W. Bush had campaigned for president denouncing so-called nation building as idealistic and impractical. But he changed his position as president, especially after the attacks of September 11, 2001. He followed the lead of Cheney, Rumsfeld, Deputy Secretary of Defense Paul Wolfowitz, and the other neocons surrounding him. On January 29, 2002, Bush first used the term "axis of evil" to refer to Iraq, Iran, and North Korea. The three nations didn't have much in common except, Bush argued, that they all wanted weapons of mass destruction. He singled out Iraq for his most threatening language, saying it was led by a "regime that has something to hide from the civilized world."

"I will not wait on events, while dangers gather. I will not stand by, as peril draws closer and closer," Bush said. Iraq would be the first point on the axis to feel American wrath.

On the domestic policy side, the Bush administration was influenced by conservative thought that called for lower taxes and a smaller role for government. That diminished role did not translate into less government spending, which exploded during the administration thanks largely to the Iraq War. But politically, Bush had run for president espousing smaller government and greater use of private enterprise to handle national problems. Libertarian-inspired, hands-off economic ideas proliferated in his White House.

Neoconservative and libertarian ideas don't necessarily work together. Neocons push for the use of military force to enhance the position of the United States and the power of "good," while, in contrast, many libertarian thinkers oppose military adventures beyond America's borders. The two philosophies managed to coexist in the Bush White House, however. And there's one man who epitomized the confluence of neocon hawkishness with libertarian small-government thinking more than any other. What's more, he's the man who put that ideology to the test in a real-life laboratory. His name was L. Paul Bremer. His laboratory was Iraq.

Paul Bremer was the administration's man on the ground, an experienced diplomat who became the commander in chief of Iraq starting on May 2, 2003. He worked in the Baghdad Green Zone, striding from palace to palace in a navy blazer with white pocket square and khaki combat boots, usually with an assortment of private security guards in tow. Bremer was a Connecticut native, a graduate of Yale University and Harvard Business School. He was given total authority over Iraq, whose government the United States had wiped out in the invasion.

Bremer ruled by decree. He wasted no time getting to them. Bremer's Order Number 2, issued May 23, 2003, disbanded the Iraqi Army and fired thousands of other government workers, ranging from teachers and engineers to clerks and museum curators. The decision instantly put half a million Iraqis, many of them experienced combat veterans, out of their jobs in an economy that was not producing new ones. Bremer next focused on blowing open the Iraqi economy. He removed restrictions from imports, disbanding tariffs, taxes, and even inspections on items shipped into the country. He ordered the privatization of two hundred formerly state-controlled companies. He cut corporate taxes to a flat rate of 15 percent, made it legal for foreign firms to own 100 percent of most types of Iraqi assets (except oil), declared that foreign investors would not be taxed on domestic profits, and made it possible for foreign firms to sign leases of up to forty years. He kept one of Saddam Hussein's economic rules: trade unions and collective bargaining remained restricted. On May 25, 2003,

standing near the docks at the deepwater port known as Umm
Qasr, Bremer declared: "Iraq is open for business."

Before the war, Deputy Secretary of Defense Paul Wolfowitz
told a congressional panel that the war would essentially cost the
United States nothing. Iraq's oil would pay for it, he said. It was
already clear before 2003 was over that things weren't going to
work out that way. The Bush White House in effect created a new
ad hoc wing of the US military for the wars in Iraq and Afghanistan that came entirely from the private sector. It was everywhere
in Iraq. And it was expensive. The country was swimming with private contractors of every stripe, from the United States and select
allies such as Kuwait. Never before had private companies, including highly paid mercenaries (called "private security contractors")
played such a central role in providing the actual personnel in
an American war zone. A 2013 study by the *Financial Times* based
on analysis of federal government contracts would find that the
United States spent $138 billion on private security, construction,
and logistics services over the ten years following the invasion. The
single biggest winner would be KBR, a subsidiary and later spin-off
of Halliburton, the company Dick Cheney left so he could run for
vice president. A 2011 study from the Commission on Wartime
Contracting in Iraq and Afghanistan would find that contractors
wasted or lost to fraud about $60 billion, which at that time came
out to $12 million a day. At some points during the war, private
contractors in Iraq outnumbered American troops.

Those contractors and those troops faced growing dangers.
On June 18, 2003, Rumsfeld blamed continuing attacks against
US troops on "pockets of dead-enders" who still hoped that Sad-
dam Hussein would return to power. A month later, President
Bush said, "Bring 'em on."

They did not turn out to be dead-enders, but they did keep
comin' on throughout 2003, in greater and greater numbers.
There weren't anywhere near enough American troops on the
ground to stop them, or even to secure much of the country
besides the Baghdad Green Zone and the oil fields. In the second
half of 2003, it slowly became clear that non-Iraqis were entering

the country to fight the Americans. Then it became clear that they were showing up en masse. In terms of who we were fighting, it had ceased to be just an "Iraq" war. A lunatic from Jordan named Abu Musab al-Zarqawi entered Iraq—either during or just after the US invasion—and, with funding from Osama bin Laden, started funneling fighters into Iraq through Syria that first autumn. He emerged as the de facto emir among foreign insurgents. Separately, Shiite fighters funded by Iran began fighting the Americans and the Sunni minority that previously controlled Iraq. Simultaneously, several domestic groups of Sunni insurgents rose to fight the Americans and the Shiite majority. In the north, the long-oppressed Kurds cooperated with the Americans but fought against both Shiite and Sunni Arabs. Almost all the groups involved in the war, besides the Americans, primarily preferred to "fight," if you can call it that, by using explosives to slaughter civilians from the other groups. Or to blow up Americans as they hurried in vehicles from place to place, trying to put out a thousand fires.

That was where the war stood when I got there.

On February 19, 2004, a letter arrived at my home on Long Island and activated me from the Fleet Marine Corps Reserve. It said that I had ten days to settle any outstanding matters of my civilian life and get myself to Quantico, Virginia. I was one of twenty Marines ordered to report to the Security Cooperation Education and Training Center at the sprawling base. All of us were certified as instructors or had prior experience as advisers overseas, in places like Haiti, Somalia, Liberia, Sierra Leone, and the Central African Republic. We were being called up, the letter explained, to train the new Iraqi Army.

We started in Virginia on February 29, the extra day of the leap year. I showed up in green woodland camouflage because I hadn't had time to sew my name onto my new desert cammies. The group at Quantico came from all walks of Marine Corps life, active and reserve, officers and enlisted men.

It was clear from the outset that the chain of command didn't quite know how to manage us. Regular Marines and Army soldiers are arranged in a straightforward, organizational hierarchy: Lieutenants lead platoons, and four platoons make a company. Captains lead companies, and four companies make a battalion. Lieutenant colonels lead battalions, and so on. Equipment and manpower are standardized for each level of the hierarchy. Each unit is allotted a specific table of equipment. It has a predetermined *billet* of officers and sergeants. Things may vary depending on a group's function, but for the most part military units have a preset order.

The twenty cocksure Marine advisers in Quantico didn't fit into the standard organizational design. We were to work in groups of about ten each, and attached to the hierarchy of the Iraqi military, not the US military. In practical terms, that meant foremost that we had no set table of equipment. We had rifles and the things we carried in our personal packs, but we weren't allotted ammunition, communications gear, or even rations. As in most bureaucracies, there was no system for addressing novel problems. Our unconventional structure fell outside the range of what the system knew how to fix—or even how to *acknowledge*.

We did, however, have a chain of command. As a major, I was going to be the senior adviser to an Iraqi battalion. Higher-ranking American advisers were going to advise the Iraqi Army at the higher brigade and division levels. I would report to a Marine colonel named Robert Abblitt, who would be advising the Iraqi colonels and generals at the Iraqi division level.

The Coalition Military Assistance Training Team (CMATT) was the name of the organization whose job was basically to start a national army in Iraq. CMATT's stated mission was "to establish the foundation of the Iraqi Armed Forces run by Iraqis." We were CMATT advisers. We were told explicitly not to engage in fighting except in self-defense. We were only to observe and guide Iraqi officers. Even those of us who had never advised foreign militaries—which was most of us—knew things weren't going to turn out that way. We expected to fight.

We trained for just two weeks. The program of instruction was a work in progress, to say the least. Remarkably little teachable intelligence had yet come out of Iraq itself, even though the

US military had been in control of the country for a year. Most of what we were taught was older material that had been written by the Saudis. As such, it focused on the things that Saudis worried about, such as a full-scale land invasion from Iraq. There was a general consensus that Saudi-centric information would have to do, however, because the Saudis were the only Arabs with whom the US military had real experience. I believe there was also a lazy assumption that Arabs were Arabs. If you knew Saudis, you knew Iraqis. That also turned out to be wrong. What we had in front of us didn't focus on the Iraqi people, culture, or geography, which was what we really needed. We did study maps of Iraq, some of which listed the names and locations of the nation's many tribes. We freshened up on combat first aid. We took a pistol course designed for "high-risk personnel"—handguns are short-range weapons, and as men who would be working among, around, and between Iraqis, we faced short-range threats. We also got to familiarize ourselves with the Russian-made AK-47 assault rifle, which was going to remain standard issue for the new Iraqi soldiers.

One of our guest speakers was the famous Marine Francis "Bing" West, who helped train Vietnam's army thirty years earlier.

"I will consider it miraculous," he said to us, "if none of you are killed or wounded."

I wrote down his words in my hardcover, general-issue notebook.

That was the extent of our instruction. We did not get language training. We received no cultural tips, except very basic ones: Iraqis, we learned, shook their head to indicate yes and leaned their heads back or nodded to indicate no. We learned a few things to avoid doing: the thumbs-up sign meant "You're a dick" to Iraqis, and the OK sign made with the thumb and index finger meant "You're an asshole." We got no guidelines on how to train the new Iraqi Army. We received no training course for them. We were not told how to do our job, because nobody knew how to do it. Americans had never built a Middle Eastern army from scratch in the middle of a war. The last Westerner who had successfully pulled off such a task—and he did it on a much smaller scale—was the British officer T. E. Lawrence (better known as Lawrence of Arabia) in 1916.

We flew from Quantico to Norfolk to Ireland to Kuwait. We were never on anyone's manifest. At each stop, we had to justify our presence. We made travel arrangements at each leg. We stopped men who were rotating out and asked if they could give us ammunition. They gave it to us. Standing on the tarmac, they handed over full magazines, even grenades. They were fully loaded, almost as if no one had planned to rotate them out of the country. But their invasion—and for most of them, their war—was over. Our group managed to get a flight to Baghdad International Airport. Then we took a civilian bus north. The dusty highway zipped past. Bedouins with their flocks set up goat-hair tents and lay down kindling as the night came in. We made our way to the critically important base at Taji, about twenty miles north of Baghdad. Taji overlooked the main road north from the capital and housed an airport that served as a conduit for equipment and supplies to the whole region. It was the most important logistics hub in the country.

I was a thirty-five-year-old US Marine Corps major whose job over the next 365 days was to nurture and strengthen a new army that was going to protect what we thought was a new country. We would build the military that would allow a free Iraq to stand on its own. Posttyranny. Postfactions. Postcolonialism. Postbackwardness. And post–its whole damned history. I was excited—thrilled is really the word—to be leading a group of smart Marines whose work lay at the very *essence* of the American mission in Iraq.

I knew that as a major I would be senior adviser in a group of ten, which was billeted to have three officers and seven NCOs. My rank, training, and experience had aligned with events to let me be a real part of history. Iraq was, at that moment, exploding. But I believed in the mission. I couldn't believe my luck.

The man sitting opposite me was a garden-variety Marine Corps major. Midthirties. A white guy with a ruddy darkness to his face after two weeks of Iraqi sun. Lean of build, almost to the point of being slight. Dark hair that was cropped short.

Behind the major, Alec Baldwin was glaring out of a TV screen, berating a roomful of morose salesmen.

"We're adding a little something to this month's sales contest. As you all know, first prize is a Cadillac Eldorado."

The major faced me. His back was to the screen. He had on *Glengarry Glen Ross* again. He always had on *Glengarry Glen Ross*. The movie was twelve years old at the time. It's about a real-estate sales operation that's relentless to the point of being dehumanizing. Alec Baldwin is the main hard-ass.

"Anybody want to see second prize? Second prize"—Baldwin produced boxed cutlery with a mocking flourish— *"a set of steak knives. Third prize is—you're fired."*

I had been in Taji only a week. The major, I had already noticed, liked to use the movie to get pumped up. He was senior adviser for a team of Marines that arrived at Taji just two weeks before us. Those two weeks were enough to make them literally the leading US military experts on working with Iraqis. My job was to learn from him.

After Bremer disbanded the old Iraqi Army, Vinnell, a subsidiary of Northrop Grumman, scored a $48 million contract to help train a new one. Vinnell had experience doing training work with Arabs, but only in a classroom environment—in Saudi Arabia, of course. Its new contract called for it to teach the green Iraqis how to do things like read maps and operate radios. Vinnell wasn't there to stand up an actual fighting force. That job, the equivalent of putting the Iraqis through basic training, was supposed to go to military instructors that a dozen countries promised to lend to the effort. In the end, though, of the 250 instructors who were promised, only four actually arrived—two Brits and two Australians. The civilian Vinnell workers, most of whom were former soldiers, tried to fill in the gap. They were unprepared, undermanned, and poorly supplied. Under orders from the Bremer administration in Baghdad, the Iraqi recruits were paid seventy dollars a month, which was low pay even for an Iraqi. When the first Vinnell-trained battalion came due to begin operations against the rising insurgency, more than half its soldiers deserted instead. That first training effort was supposed to have nine battalions in the can by the end of its first year. Instead, when I got to Iraq, it had none that could function as military units.

At the time, I blamed Vinnell. It was only years later that I learned about the 246 drill instructors who never showed up. When you're fighting in a war, what you know is limited by proximity and rank. Proximity determines what you can witness, and rank determines what's shared with you. I was in the dark on both counts when it came to the history of those first three useless Iraqi battalions that were birthed before I arrived.

The Marine senior adviser across from me had inherited a group of these barely trained Iraqis. They were proving problematic. But the more immediate concern for me, there in his office, was that I get up to speed as quickly as possible. I was "birddogging" the major—literally following him everywhere he went, watching everything he did, asking questions and helping where I could, so that I could learn how to do his job. Not that he had figured it out yet. He was running into unexpected frustrations and felt he should share them with me.

"You can't play in the man's game? You can't close them?" Alec Baldwin was leaning over a desk, berating a scowling Jack Lemmon. *"Then go home and tell your wife your troubles. Because only one thing counts in this life. Get them to* sign *on the* line *which is* dotted. *You hear me, you fucking faggots?"*

Two big problems really stood out with the partial, mostly untrained Iraqi battalion the senior adviser was trying to work with. First, both the soldiers and the officers showed a propensity for theft. They even stole things, he said, that they did not need and for which they had no obvious use. The other members of my nascent advisory team were out bird-dogging with their own counterparts, and already one of them, a taciturn New England staff sergeant named Todd Colwell, had busted a group of Iraqi officers as they tried to spirit away mattresses from an enlisted men's barracks. Their rationale for the theft, as best as Colwell could ascertain, was simply that it was possible to do. The Iraqis had never in their lives known what it was like to have superfluous goods of any kind. Most of them grew up in extreme poverty under an autocratic regime, and they believed instinctively that anything that could be obtained and taken into possession should be, no matter the circumstances, whenever the opportunity arose. They never knew when they'd need it. For many of them, this was a survival instinct, one handed down to them from a time only a century before, when they were nomads.

This trait also explained other things, like how the Iraqis always dropped their used water bottles behind on the desert floor during long marches. The idea of putting something that was still potentially useful into a trash bin was unfathomable to them. A plastic water bottle dropped in the desert, even an empty one, was not garbage. It was something that could prove useful to *the next guy*. Somebody wandering in the desert. Anybody. Maybe themselves or somebody they knew.

Another of the new advisers in my group, First Sgt. Thomas Reilly, was a tall Idahoan in his late forties. He had a complex background: The son of a US diplomat, he grew up in Afghanistan, Iran, Thailand, and other places in between. As a teenaged Marine, he had narrowly missed the end of Vietnam. He was a devout Christian and politically conservative, but his international upbringing gave him a patience and comfort level with the Iraqis that exceeded that of the vast majority of Marines. Reilly helped set up police lines of Iraqis, dozens of men standing abreast in the hot desert who walked slowly forward and picked up water bottles so they could throw them away. The Iraqi enlisted soldiers, called *junood* (singular *jundi*), didn't understand what they were doing or why. The Iraqi NCOs didn't understand why they were shouting out the orders to do it or why. Sometimes the advisers didn't explain why.

"These Iraqis," Reilly said to me, "have some tough habits."

Their second tough habit was even more difficult for us Marines to wrap our heads around: the Iraqi soldiers were having sex, and a lot of it, with each other.

At that time, I was devoutly Catholic. I followed Church teaching right down the line—except when it came to homosexuality. A lot of civilians will think it's ironic, but I credit the Marine Corps for making me more accepting of homosexuality than a lot of other Catholics are. More than one gay Marine had come out to me privately in the past. I was flattered, because it meant they trusted me. And to me, that trust was more important to the cohesion and good order of a military unit than somebody's sexual proclivities.

That said, it was hard for me to comprehend the Iraqis' attitude toward gay sex—or their attitudes and beliefs, for that matter, toward any and all sex. The Koran forbids homosexuality, and I asked some of the Iraqis about the apparent contradiction in their behavior. Everyone was praying five times a day, or at least going through the motions, but many of them were also involved in what the American senior adviser called "man sex." For the Iraqis, there was no contradiction. A homosexual act meant nothing, as long as one did not *identify* as a homosexual. To the Iraqis, *that* would be a problem.

The Iraqis had an expression that one of the interpreters shared with me: "Women are for babies, and men are for pleasure." Often when an Iraqi soldier spoke to us through the interpreters about another soldier he considered a friend, he held out his two index fingers. If he placed them alongside one another, they were platonic friends. If he placed one on top of the other, they were more than platonic. It was a casual way of clarifying things, and they did it without thinking about it. The enlisted men seemed to have sex with each other, and the officers seemed to have sex with the enlisted men on command, but it did not appear that the officers had sex with each other. That sort of fraternization (or domination?) was beyond the pale.

There in the American senior adviser's office, as he shared his observations with me over *Glengarry Glen Ross*, it became clear that he found the entire situation revolting. The major was a hard charger. He had recently been activated, like me. He had been a successful pharmaceutical exec in his civilian life back on the block. He liked to have things squared away, and he believed in his ability to make things so.

Appearances were important to the major, and he wasn't going to have any of this shit about Iraqi man sex, Arab cultural norms be damned. Paul Bremer had just published the new Iraqi Military Code (IMC), which was similar to the US Uniform Code of Military Justice. Homosexual activity was prohibited by the IMC on the grounds that rampant sex within a military unit, generally speaking, is not good for military order. But sexual activity was so pervasive in the Iraqi units that the IMC was unenforceable. That didn't stop the Americans from trying to change the Iraqis to fit our rules, however. It did not stop us then, and it was not ever going to stop us.

Behind the senior adviser, in his office, Alec Baldwin now was leaning on Ed Harris.

"You see this watch? You see this watch? That watch costs more than your car. I made $970,000 last year. How much you make? You see, pal: that's who I am. And you're nothing."

The senior adviser looked at me coolly.

"We have come across what I call a teachable moment," he said. He glanced into an open file on his desk.

"There's an Iraqi corporal . . . a corporal named"—he looked for it—"a corporal named Nawa'al. He refused an order and was insubordinate to a sergeant in front of the other junood."

The senior adviser explained that this Corporal Nawa'al had to be punished because he showed up his sergeant. Other enlisted Iraqis saw him do it. I agreed; punishment was necessary. But more than that, the senior adviser explained that he wanted to demonstrate to the Iraqis what real military discipline looks like. It was fairly clear that they didn't understand our version of it. Two weeks was a very long time for a military officer like the senior adviser to put up with failure among these Iraqi men who reported to him, these men for whom he was responsible, these men whose success or failure reflected upon him in the eyes of his own superiors. The senior adviser had had enough.

His plan was to put on an NJP—carry out a nonjudicial punishment. Such proceedings are like a snap hearing. They involve
direct questioning of the relevant parties, followed by a quick judgment by the officer in charge. They're provided for by article 15
of the US Uniform Code of Military Justice.

"We are going to put on a show," he said. His eyes locked on
to mine. A corner of his mouth curled. "We are going to put on a
show, man!" I could hear the italics in his voice.

"We're gonna show them *office hours*! We're gonna show how
it's *done*!"

The next day, in an air-conditioned room set aside for the
occasion, I bird-dogged the major's NJP.

Corporal Nawa'al was tall for an Iraqi, almost six feet, and
so gaunt that his joints seemed too big. A wisp of mustache
sprouted on his lip. He looked young, which meant he definitely
was young—I already had figured out that most Iraqis appeared
much older than they were. (The Iraqis also expressed shock when
we told them our ages. To them, most of us appeared physically
much younger than we really were.) The corporal's feral eyes
rolled across the room's many faces: Americans, big and of various ethnicities. The interpreter, an American of Egyptian descent
who spoke Arabic with an accent I'm sure the corporal couldn't
place. A handful of junood from the corporal's unit who waited
to serve as witnesses. Two or three Iraqi officers, half-lidded and
grim. The sharp-eyed American senior adviser, with a cut of smile
across his jaw.

The other party to the NJP, the Iraqi sergeant who had been
disobeyed, was dark, of middling height, and wore a uniform that
was too taut across his belly. His mustache lay thick and black on
his lip. He looked like he was in his forties, which meant he was
probably in his thirties. He cut a figure like a small-town cop who's
accustomed to scaring the local teenagers.

The senior adviser's show didn't go as planned. He questioned
the corporal, then the sergeant. They each took turns making
accusations against the other. All of this was in Arabic, of course.
The interpreter tried repeating everything for the Americans in

English, but it got harder for him as Corporal Nawa'al and the sergeant began making hurried counteraccusations while the Egyptian American was still translating the last thing that was said. The two men yelled directly at each other in Arabic.

"Now wait a minute!" shouted the senior adviser. "Tell the corporal and the sergeant that they will not speak out of turn! There is a procedure, and they will follow it."

The senior adviser looked at one of the Iraqi officers for help as the interpreter conveyed the message in Arabic to the corporal and sergeant. The Iraqi officer shouted an angry command at the corporal and the sergeant that none of the Americans save the interpreter could understand.

More questioning began of Corporal Nawa'al and the sergeant. It devolved into accusations sharper than before, recriminations more deeply heartfelt than the last ones. Generally speaking, the Iraqis did not hesitate at all to show their emotions. The corporal's voice took on an agitated pitch. The senior adviser's ruddy tan darkened closer to crimson. I caught two of the Iraqi officers cutting sideways glances at each other. One shifted in his seat. The senior adviser turned to the witness junood, who huddled like sheep in a pen. He picked one at random.

"You have heard the testimony of the sergeant," the senior adviser said to the first jundi. The soldier exhaled heavily as the 'terp relayed the senior adviser's words in his Egyptian American Arabic. "Is the sergeant telling the truth when he says that Corporal Nawa'al refused a direct order?"

The jundi shouted in animated Arabic, eyes flitting with anxiety from the 'terp to the sergeant to the Iraqi officers. He violently shook his head, and I remembered that that meant yes.

The interpreter listened for a beat and then spoke: "'Yes,' he says. 'Yes, of course the sergeant is speaking the truth. The sergeant would not lie.'"

"So you are saying that you witnessed Corporal Nawa'al refuse to obey a direct order. Is that right?"

The 'terp relayed the senior adviser's question. A pained expression announced itself on the jundi's face, and he flinched like a dog being forced to sniff its piss. Corporal Nawa'al, wide-eyed, said nothing, but raised his brows and waited.

"No, I did not see Corporal Nawa'al disobey orders," the 'terp said, following the jundi's words. "Corporal Nawa'al is a good corporal."

Jesus, I thought. The witness jundi was stuck between currying favor with the sergeant, a man who still held power over him, and the corporal, who was also his superior. He was afraid to criticize either of them. For all we Americans knew, there could be conflicting tribal loyalties coming into play too. The young jundi realized, and I realized as I listened, that he was damned if he did, and damned if he didn't. So he stated two things that ran directly counter to each other.

The other witness junood followed suit, doing the best thing given the power dynamics in the room, which was to support *both* of their superiors. Even if doing so was blatantly contradictory.

The senior adviser's frustration morphed into anger. He gave up on the witness junood and faced the corporal directly. We all stood in silence as he began shouting at the Iraqi in English. The interpreter tried to keep up. Corporal Nawa'al began shouting back in Arabic. The interpreter's desperate efforts capsized in waves of vitriol that bounced off the walls in two languages.

Then Corporal Nawa'al did something that stunned all of us. He reached into a pocket, produced his Iraqi military ID card, and held it up with one gangly arm for the senior adviser to see. He shouted angry Arabic directly at the American interpreter, whose eyes and mouth widened a little as he listened. Corporal Nawa'al slapped the ID onto a table, turned his back, and left me, the Iraqis, and the senior adviser behind as he strode out of the room.

"OK," the 'terp said. He faced the senior adviser. "OK. So, sir . . . the corporal says he quits. He is resigning, sir."

The senior adviser stood there in his khaki camouflage, staring at his interpreter without comprehension, as if this man who was supposed to guide his understanding had just spoken more Arabic to him instead of English. He had not prepared for this: the law said that the junood were allowed to quit the Army whenever they wanted. It was a promise made to new recruits so that they'd sign up for the job in the first place. The insurgents had already started blowing up lines of young men at recruiting stations. The pay was still shit. The American administration had to offer incentives to get people to volunteer. So they said they were allowed to quit if they didn't like it. Corporal Nawa'al had just exercised that right.

The Iraqi officers looked aside and consulted one another in low tones. The junood stared at their black combat boots. The American senior adviser had just gotten faced.

For Iraqis, the concept of public dignity is crucial to their sense of well-being and identity. Face was very real, and it was intensely guarded. Public shame was deeply feared and to be avoided at almost any cost. It appeared to me that this Marine, the senior adviser, hadn't been on the ground long enough to figure this out. He lost the encounter. In the Iraqis' eyes, this American officer had been shown up by a much younger and junior Iraqi. I don't think he realized how much damage that incident did to him as an authority figure.

A few nights later, I sat with my team of advisers in our quarters. I had put a system in place by which we always met at night before racking out. We discussed what we learned that day. Each man brought his own observations, and each man tried to soak up the others' contributions. We also discussed books we were reading: *The Arab Mind*, by Raphael Pitai, and *The Village*, by Bing West, the Vietnam-era Marine who had warned that we faced injuries or death. Quantico already seemed like a lifetime ago. The awesome task at hand was new for all of us, and it was becoming our world.

One of the men shared a story. A US Army adviser had boasted to him about how he had ripped the stripes right off an Iraqi sergeant's uniform in front of an entire formation of junood. We all agreed it was an idiotic move.

"This public humiliation, it's just not effective," Colwell said.

"Worse," Reilly said. "Badly counterproductive."

I did not know it yet, but I was experiencing for the first time something I would see repeated again and again in Iraq: the

Americans often said and did things that worked against our mission. It was going to be hard enough to get the Iraqis to decide to pick up Western values and start magically plugging them into their own society. It was going to be impossible if the example we provided wasn't worth emulating.

"When we get our battalion," I said, "we will treat them with the same respect as we would treat American soldiers."

The others nodded silently. I was glad to see it. We were determined not to repeat mistakes we had witnessed. There were very good advisers at Taji with those first couple of Iraqi battalions, and I wouldn't have wanted their job: they inherited Iraqis from the early training debacle who were already rotten to the core. But that said, for some reason it was the bad advisers who were carrying the day there. Nothing was getting fixed.

Just how badly those first battalions were broken would, within a couple of weeks, be illustrated to everyone in dramatic fashion. In the meantime, we bird-dogged along. The Iraqis and their advisers carried out road blocks, patrolled on foot outside the gates at Taji, and once carried out a cordon-and-search operation—essentially a raid on a target. It turned up no insurgents, weapons, or other contraband. Iraqis weren't yet being trained for actual combat while we were in Taji in those first weeks. No one had developed a training course yet. We were going to need one.

In March 2004, there were three new teams of advisers—mine and two others. Those three teams were tasked with raising up three Iraqi battalions. Even though they were going to be the first three US military–trained Iraqi battalions, we had numerical designations that made it seem like there was a bigger Iraqi Army out there than actually existed: we were the Fifth, Sixth, and Seventh Battalions of the Third Brigade, Fifth Division. The numbers made no sense, because, aside from us, the Iraqi Army consisted mostly of the three worthless Vinnell-trained battalions.

My group of advisers still stood at only seven Marines total, including myself, Colwell, Reilly, three other NCOs, and a blunt, hard-nosed captain named Kevin Hummons, who filled one of the three officer slots on our billet. Colonel Abblitt at division told me I could expect two more NCOs and one more officer in the coming weeks. In the meantime, we had to prepare to ship off to Kirkush, an abandoned Hussein-era base about sixty miles northeast of Baghdad and only twelve miles from the border with Iran. There, we were to link up with an Iraqi "officer cadre" that had just finished a round of training in Jordan. Those officers were slated to lead our unit. The raw, enlisted recruits would arrive later.

Those Iraqis would form a new unit called Fifth Battalion.

My job was to make them into soldiers.

2

KIRKUSH

ON THE LAST DAY OF MARCH, people back in the States started watching a televised loop. News pundits warned viewers about graphic content, and then they played it again and again. The footage came from a bridge over the Euphrates. Arabs danced and chanted between the bridge's overhead struts. Men flung their arms ecstatically. Boys clambered up green beams, intoxicated with joy. Overhead, the charred, broken bodies of men hung from ropes in the beams. Arms indiscernible from legs. Black, inscrutable carbon. Boys scrambled to bring bright faces near to them. The bodies were those of four American contractors from Blackwater USA. The men were ambushed during a supply run in a mostly Sunni region forty-five miles west of Baghdad. We watched on TV in Taji too. So did the Green Zone. So did the White House. US administrators and high-ranking officers immediately began a plan to retake control of that place. It was a city in the flat badlands of Anbar Province that I knew nothing about. It was called Fallujah.

We left Taji for Kirkush the next day. We had a battalion to build. I believed in my team. In addition to Hummons, Reilly, Colwell, and me, we had three sergeants who were all Marines. My plan was to have, along with Colwell, each of the sergeants advise an Iraqi rifle company. (As a battalion, the Fifth would include four rifle companies of roughly 150 men each.) S.Sgt. Alan Lindsay was a South Carolinian of about thirty years who loved NASCAR and had been stationed at Parris Island. S.Sgt. Matthew Stouder was in his early thirties, from Indiana, a former instructor at the Marine Corps Mountain Warfare Training Center. Sgt. Francisco Jenkins, also thirty or a little older, was from the Bronx and had been an instructor at the Marine Corps School of Infantry. Jenkins was up against time-in-grade limitations, meaning he needed a promotion. The Marine Corps uses a strict up-or-out system: if you don't advance in rank by a certain deadline, you're booted from the service.

The insurgency was erupting across Iraq. The word *IED*, for improvised explosive device, was entering the American lexicon. Daily, the bombs destroyed vehicles and killed soldiers and civilians. Iraqi truck drivers were refusing to take to the roads.

Nothing was available to take us to Kirkush. No helicopter, truck, or extra Humvee. Someone at Taji chartered a civilian bus for us. I couldn't believe the look of the thing. It stood out bright blue against the beige landscape. A hole gaped in the rear, where an engine hatch was missing. Cracks fractured the windows and mirrors. Its tires were bald and lumpy, like something from a cartoon. Even sitting still, the bus's wheels looked out of alignment. The Iraqi driver was a tough-looking little man who took no notice of us. He began a pot of tea over kindling, despite the eighty-degree heat.

"After we get our gear in this thing," Jenkins said, "we're all gonna have to push and jump-start it."

We laughed. But this was not how we imagined entering the combat zone. Marines go to the fight in vehicles with the words *assault* or *attack* or *combat* in their names. Terms like *high speed* or *low drag* or *heavily armed* contribute to deadly acronyms.

As we loaded our gear, I watched the driver. He squatted in the dry earth, leeward from the sun. His kindling took light and spit flame. He tended the boil and let his leaves steep. Not once did he look at us.

I wanted to understand him. To understand *them*. The wiry, brown man patiently worked his fire. Would our recruits be like him? In Taji, we bird-dogged Americans. In Kirkush, we were going to lead Iraqis. We were going to live among them now. The driver's clothes were Western but had a loose, discarded look. Half bus driver, half nomad. I wasn't watching a man working in a war zone out of devotion to high-minded principles. I was looking at a man who needed to feed his family. Or feed himself.

A US Army lieutenant gave us a briefing before we pulled out. He commanded four Humvees that were assigned to escort us. *Why not just let us squeeze in with them?* I wondered. *Never mind.* The lieutenant talked us through procedures for enemy contact, radio frequencies, and other precombat checks. We boarded the bus, rifles locked and loaded. We took firing positions around the interior. The bus shook to life and coughed smoke. Our muzzles poked out the windows.

Kirkush was less than a square mile of putty-colored, right-angle buildings that stood in brutal symmetry—a real-life Soviet-style ghost town. Sharp, windy desert ringed us like an orange-brown sea. Miles away to the east, over Iran, the Zagros Mountains piggybacked the sky on purple and white shoulders.

Down on the ground, we were doing a little heavy lifting ourselves. I strained my spine and walked backward, trying to feel my way over gravel through thick combat soles. Facing me, walking the same direction, was Captain Hummons, teeth gritting, thick shoulders straining, and a floppy cap shielding his brown pate from a sun that seemed to hate our guts. Gray-blue gravel carpeted the grounds, taking the heat and radiating it back up at us. Between Hummons and me stretched a black wrought-iron bed. Bedsprings twisted from the frame. An iron headboard was plated to one end. The thing had to weigh at least eighty pounds. It was one of nine hundred we had to get in place before our recruits arrived.

"Where the fuck they *get* these motherfuckers?" Hummons grunted.

Good question, I thought. It was hard to find an American Humvee in Iraq with this much armor. Sometimes decisions about materials get made by a faraway staff officer, and what seems like a good idea at that level isn't such a good idea on your level.

The unwieldy iron furniture was what we were given. So far, the frames and mattresses were practically the only supplies we had been allotted by Lowdes Corporation, a contractor that ran an office in Kirkush. I suspect that Lowdes was some kind of temporary venture that used an American-sounding name, because I have never been able to find any record of it anywhere since. American and Middle Eastern contractors often combined forces to jointly reap US government dollars.

We borrowed a truck from a North Carolina National Guard unit at the base. The vehicle could hold twenty beds. Seven Marines and six Iraqi laborers worked eighteen to twenty hours for two days straight. We loaded leaden beds into the truck at a Lowdes warehouse piled with frames and limp mattresses. We hauled them to putty-colored buildings we were making into barracks, muscling them inside and along stairwells. They were bunk beds. We swore as we fitted the black iron in place, one bed atop another. It hit ninety-five degrees outside and hotter inside.

We were on a tight deadline. My advisory team got to Kirkush on April 1. The Iraqis were going to join us in three waves: first the NCOs, who were already going through a sort of basic training with the two Australian drill instructors elsewhere at Kirkush. Then the officers were to arrive around April 7, coming in from a school set up by the Jordanians. After that, the untrained recruits, called *mujanadin* (singular *mujanad*) in Arabic, were coming in. Boot camp was to commence May 1.

We had very little time to set up barracks to house the men, arrange for the food to feed them, and secure sufficient water in a desert environment—three liters a day per man, which was less than US military guidelines but all that was mandated for the Iraqis. They needed boots, uniforms, toiletries, and field equipment.

Most of the buildings in Kirkush were unfinished shells arranged in square-shaped clusters called pods. Our Fifth Battalion pod had spotty water and sewer service—not a good thing when you're expecting nine hundred guys to show up. The pod's electricity was supplied by a single oil-powered generator that couldn't power all of its buildings at once. We had no computers. Because of the danger on the highways, nothing was moving. Kirkush's food was running out. Chow halls were empty. The contractors hired to finish the plumbing and power hadn't shown up. We had to figure out those problems before we could start our real mission: transforming a group of Iraqi civilians into a rifle battalion.

The Iraqi Army was going to be a critical force of security and order, which the country seriously lacked. That was the immediate problem. But it also was to stand as an important symbol of the hoped-for unified nation itself. Iraq was a country born at the end of a pen, drawn in arbitrary lines by the British and French at the end of World War I. Under Saddam Hussein, Iraq stayed in one piece through a policy of terror and intimidation that the dictator borrowed from Stalin's Soviet Union. The American idea was that Iraq would hold together as one nation because its people would share the gifts of democracy and free markets. The thinking went that, since they had never had either, they yearned for both. They would become like us, purely because we were giving them the opportunity.

The composition of the Army was critical to the "new Iraq" that America wanted to build, because in order for all Iraqi people to feel a stake in their new nation, they all had to take part in the order that supported it. American administrators decided that each battalion would represent the country's three major cultural groups: Arab Shiites, Arab Sunnis, and Kurds. Smaller groups like the Yazidis and Turkmen also would be represented.

Under Saddam Hussein, the Sunni Arabs commanded most of the power. In the new Iraq, everyone would have access to power, including the power of last resort that lies in an armed military. Iraqis would learn to work and live together. They would learn to respect rules and one another. They would share an identity. The idea was radical, but the new Iraqi Army was going to prove the concept. It was going to lead by example. The men of the Fifth Battalion would act in concert, and then the people of Iraq would

act in concert. Its successes would be Iraq's successes. The Fifth
Battalion was to be the new Iraq in microcosm.

I quickly learned the phrase *Leish makou kahrabaa?* It means, "Why
isn't there electricity?"

One day in the first week at Kirkush, I found myself asking
the question again to two electricity technicians who worked for
Lowdes. Mushtaq and Fouad were the first Kurds I met. Their job
was to keep our generator running. In fact, they lived with it. They
slept on bedrolls under an awning next to the machine, which
made a racket and leaked so badly that the two men lived in what
was almost literally a moat of oil—they had lain scrap boards in
the black, porridgy earth around them. The boards made a bridge
over the gravel and diesel muck so the men could get to the place
where they worked and slept.

Kurds are mostly Sunnis, but that is where their similarities
with Sunni Arabs end. They speak their own language and have
their own traditions. Some have light-colored eyes or hair. They
come from mountainous, northern Iraq, an unofficial, friendless
state they call Kurdistan. The Kurds have spent many centuries
fortifying themselves there against their neighbors, Arab and otherwise. They have a saying: "The Kurds have no friends but the
mountains."

Mushtaq was built like a linebacker, with a broad forehead and
wide-set eyes. He had dirty blond hair. Fouad was the opposite,
diminutive and dark. Some long-past accident left Fouad with only
his thumbs and two or three fingers on each hand.

Our efforts would collapse without electricity, so I tried to keep
Mushtaq and Fouad motivated. I got them a couple of beds—that
was one thing I had plenty of. I found a big wooden cable spool
they could use as a table. After I got them those rudimentary
things, they loved me. That's the word. The guys loved me. And
they worked like mules to keep that generator pumping.

Mushtaq reminded me of Lennie from *Of Mice and Men*. I
visited daily, and Mushtaq would pick me up and bear-hug me,
bringing tears to my eyes. I'm not a big guy, only five foot seven,

but I'm a United States Marine, and a man who doesn't like being picked up and hugged. But I never objected.

They didn't bathe. They had no vehicle. I began to suspect they were surviving on tea and crackers. Nobody had given anything to Mushtaq and Fouad, but they always shared what they had with me and always insisted that I sit down for a chat. They didn't understand my words, but they recognized the names of people and places. Mushtaq interjected, "Bush very good!" or "America! Kurdistan! Good!" with his index fingers extended alongside one another.

The first and only time I declined a cigarette from Mushtaq, he shocked me by bursting into tears. I was still getting accustomed to the idea within Kurdish and Arab cultures that it's OK for men to weep openly, even passionately. So although I wasn't a smoker and we were sitting on a lake of diesel fuel, I started accepting Mushtaq's cigarettes. I began to bring Mushtaq and Fouad parts of the care packages sent by my family: nuts, shampoo, vitamins. I took them cases of fresh water. Mushtaq lifted me off the ground, kissed my cheeks, and said, "Zakkiyah, very good!"

For the most part, that generator kept running. Our pod didn't have all the electricity I wanted, but it had more consistent energy than other pods, even some of the pods occupied by American troops.

The hard work of setting up a home for the Fifth continued. First Sergeant Reilly, a Marine's Marine, somehow got his hands on a Marine Corps leadership course for the Iraqi NCOs. He began modifying it here and there for a group of men we didn't yet know. He worked by flashlight after long days doing things like hauling bed frames.

We relied on a Marine Corps model to train the Iraqi Fifth Battalion's leaders. The Marine Corps emphasizes what it calls the intangibles—courage, honor, and commitment. Those intangibles go above and beyond technical training. In the US Army, enlisted soldiers are "specialists." They're radio operators or truck drivers or engineers. In the Navy, sailors hold specific jobs within the hive-like confines of a ship. In the Air Force, airmen specialize at tasks that range from fueling missiles to maintaining swimming pools.

In the Marines, there's only one specialty: rifleman. Every Marine is a rifleman. It's a philosophy that's taken so seriously that the Marines don't even have medics—all the medical first responders in the Marines are actually Navy sailors who are attached to the Marine Corps. We wanted to raise our Iraqi battalion the Marine Corps way. We wanted every soldier in the Fifth Battalion to possess a rifleman's ethos. The other two battalions in our Iraqi brigade, the Sixth and Seventh, were to be trained by the US Army. We decided the Fifth would be different: an Iraqi battalion with a Marine philosophy. And why not? There was nobody to tell us otherwise.

The Fifth Battalion NCOs were on the base already, so they moved into the pod first. Their Australian drill instructors had given them a more relentless workout over the last couple of weeks than most of them had ever known. I hoped they would feel relief arriving with the Americans. But as we helped them get settled into their spartan rooms and wrought-iron beds, they didn't speak to us any more than they had to. Most avoided eye contact. Few seemed to speak any more English than I spoke Arabic. It was still early going, but those first Iraqis near me were frustratingly unknowable.

A third of the NCOs were veterans of Saddam's army who had reenlisted with the new Iraqi Army. The other two-thirds had no professional military experience. The Kurds among them all claimed to be former Peshmerga, a militia revered by all Kurds as the heir of a warrior tradition that goes back thousands of years. Like the battalion at large, our cadre of NCOs was split into thirds—Shiites, Sunnis, and Kurds. The two highest-ranking NCOs held the rank of sergeant major. Their job was to schedule the activities of all the other NCOs, whose job would be to command and protect the welfare of their mujanadin. The Fifth Battalion was to have six companies: four rifle companies, one motor transport company, and one headquarters company that handled administration, supplies, and medical care and basically made things run. Each company got a building in the pod.

My plan was to hold nightly battalion meetings with all the advisers, interpreters, Iraqi officers, and high-ranking NCOs. The get-togethers would give us a chance to coordinate planning and share what we were learning. It would also give everyone a place to raise his voice about anything his unit needed. I decided to go ahead and start holding the meetings immediately, before the officers arrived.

I first got to know Sergeant Major Iskander at one of those meetings. He was designated as the S-1 for the Fifth Battalion, meaning he was in charge of administrative tasks like payroll. Unlike most of the NCOs, Iskander was very willing to talk to the Americans.

"Raed Zakkiyah, no good!" he said, singling me out by both my rank and name. He waved an unfiltered Iraqi cigarette at me. I looked at him, a little stunned. Iskander had an auburn tint to his hair, which told me he was a Kurd. And a jaunty Kurd, at that. He held a walking stick in his other hand. He wore high boots. His belt bore a black leather holster and a long scabbarded blade.

"No good!" he said again.

In piecemeal English, he complained that the NCOs lacked cleaning supplies. The NCOs' rooms were dirty. Barracks for the mujanadin, Iskander said, would be filthy when they arrived.

I was the boss. Iskander knew it. The sergeant major felt I was failing to provide.

Reilly was working with Iskander already. They were counterparts. Reilly was our S-1 adviser, so his job was to consult the Iraqi S-1. He must've seen my surprise at being upbraided by an Iraqi sergeant.

"This one's all right," Reilly assured me, patting Iskander on the shoulder. "Just wants what's best for his men." The tall Idahoan gave me a look that said to me confidentially, *I'll take care of it.*

For our personal quarters, we advisers chose the tallest building in our pod, a three-story structure at one end of our battalion area. We set up beds for interpreters on the second floor. We lived on the third. A ladder well ran from there up to the roof. A low wall, maybe two feet high, wrapped along the edge of the roof.

We chose the quarters for their defensibility. We had to think in extremis. If something went very, very wrong and we got into some kind of fight against the Iraqis, we could barricade the stairs, go up to the roof, and hold out there until we were rescued. Just like in that old Cary Grant movie *Gunga Din*. It was a remote possibility. We all memorized the plan. We kept water and rations on the third floor just in case.

We were dead tired at the end of the day, but I often stayed awake a little after lights-out. Sometimes Captain Hummons stayed up as well. He was trying to design a training schedule for the mujanadin, and he needed to have some of it completed before they got there. Otherwise, what would we do with them?

I studied Arabic words by flashlight, jotting down new ones in my journal. It was quiet at night. Without an immediate need for electricity, we had Fouad and Mushtaq shut off the generator. It was hard to stay up, knowing we had to rise at 5 AM, but I held on as long as I could. My eyes lost focus, and eventually sleep took me.

Still in the first week of April, we got word that the Iraqi officers would be delayed getting to Kirkush. The roads had gotten worse. Willing drivers were hard to find. Most vehicles weren't moving. Everything got pushed back. It was bad news, but it also bought us time.

A very important set of arrivals did manage to get through, however: our interpreters. A group of four got to us shortly after the last NCOs moved in.

Arkan Abdulrazaq was a tall man in his midforties. He had black hair but no mustache. His clean-shaven face was unusual for an Iraqi. Arkan found me while I was in one of the makeshift barracks with some of the other advisers trying to quantify how many of the sinks worked. It was strange to see a man in civilian clothes with a duffel bag. He introduced himself.

"Major Zacchea," I said, by way of introduction. "Michael Zacchea."

"Zakkiyah . . . ?" he asked. Zah-KEE-yah?

"Zacchea," I said. "Zah-KAY-uh."

Arkan had good language credentials. He spoke Farsi, Arabic, and English. That was a relief. When it came to Iraqi democracy, I would learn over the coming weeks that Arkan was a true believer. He was married and had a four-year-old son, and he dreamed of immigrating to the United States after the war.

I walked Arkan to the three-story building where he would be living with us. I explained our situation. We had no soldiers or officers yet. The NCOs were getting settled in. We didn't have a lot yet in the way of equipment. In particular, we lacked radios. Food shipments were still at a standstill. We were surviving on US-issued "meals ready to eat" (MREs), high-calorie meals that can be prepared over a simple flame and intended for troops in the field. I told him we'd be getting together for our regular battalion meeting that night.

"Of course, I will be there," he said, and dropped his bag. "It's my pleasure to meet you, Major Zakkiyah. You have an interesting name, has anyone told you that?"

"No," I said. "Nobody has."

"There is a word like that in Arabic. It means . . . something like 'charitable.' From the word for 'alms,'" he said, and hesitated for a moment. "It is a very good name to have."

The cast kept growing. Up until those days in Kirkush, my Iraq experience had been dominated by Americans: officers, advisers, contractors, soldiers, clerks, nurses. Iraqis formed the backdrop. I was coming to realize—to really internalize—that even before eight hundred or nine hundred raw Iraqi mujanadin rolled in, the set was flipping. Iraqis were drawing closer, surrounding me and the advisers. All other Americans were moving into the distance, becoming the background.

Then the officers started filtering in. Two here, three there, over several days. It gave us the chance to meet them individually. Their journeys from Jordan had taken circuitous routes and varying tolls. Some were exhausted. Very few of them, it seemed, spoke English. I found myself wondering why I had thought more would speak English. Communication—what could be more important for us? How long would it take me to understand these men?

The nightly battalion meetings, which we held in our empty chow hall, slowly filled with Iraqi officers. To my American ear, their names overlapped a lot: there were any number of Mohammeds and Ahmeds and Yusefs. I made sure to jot down names in my journal. The battalion's officer cadre was to be arranged in the standard American fashion. A commanding officer (CO) was the leader. His right-hand man was the executive officer (XO). Other officers managed discrete functions for the unit, just as they do in the US Army or Marine Corps: administrative officer, intelligence officer, operations officer, logistics officer, and communications officer. Each of the battalion's four rifle companies—the fighting parts of the battalion—would be headed by a captain or major. A battalion surgeon commanded the medics. Another officer was to command the motor transport company.

The commanding officer of Fifth Battalion was a tall, striking Sunni lieutenant colonel named Jassim Thammin. My early read on him was that he was alert but quietly aloof. He spent more time listening than speaking. His second-in-command, or XO, was a major and also a Sunni. His name was Ahmed Nu'uman, and he was clearly the more engaged of the two. His bearing was less rigid, and he immediately seemed more comfortable around the Americans than his superior did. Ahmed Nu'uman was young for a major, only about thirty years old.

Formal introductions took place nightly. The interpreters translated for the whole group or worked with individuals.

Everyone, American and Iraqi, was wary of the other side. A couple of the advisers carried hidden sidearms. When I wasn't sleeping, I wore my Beretta. The mission required trust, but I understood some of the Marines' cautious behavior. I even understood the wariness of the Iraqis. The United States and Iraq had fought two wars against each other over a little more than a decade. Jassim Thammin, the CO, had fought in both. Some of the Marines had fought in one or the other. We had been conditioned to think of each other as enemies.

For the Iraqis like Jassim Thammin who were veterans of the old army, the mistrust went beyond conditioning. They had been fed propaganda as well.

"Is it true—" an Iraqi officer began one night in English, before stopping himself. He turned to Arkan and said something in Arabic. I understood the word *musharafin* (singular *musharaf*). It meant "advisers." I watched Arkan's eyes widen slightly.

"Major Zacchea, the captain knows all of the musharafin for the battalion are United States Marines. He has a question."

"OK," I said.

"He wants to know, is it true that in order for an American to become a Marine, he must drink blood?"

I couldn't believe the question. Maybe Arkan misunderstood it. The advisers perked up.

"Drink blood?" I asked.

Another Iraqi officer spoke, and then a third. They all asked Arkan questions at the same time. Arkan said something back to them and finally turned toward me again.

"Major, the officers explain that they were taught that Marines are different from regular American soldiers. They want to know if it's true that you must kill a member of your family and drink his blood. In order to become a Marine."

The Iraqis watched me through narrowed eyes. The advisers gaped. Arkan chuckled a bit.

"Of course, I explained to them that this is nonsense," he said. "But they would like to hear it from you."

"No," I said, and I turned directly toward the Iraqis. I wanted them to see I was talking to them, not to Arkan. "No, we do not drink blood. I promise you none of us ever drank blood."

You don't have to be in a war zone for long before you draw powerful insights about the people in the new, alien land that surrounds you. I had been in Iraq for less than a month, but I breathed it, gave myself to it as inescapable, tried tuning myself to its rhythms. To my thinking, that was the best way to stay sane. One night, still in the first half of April, we Marines were in our quarters, racked out for the night. The recruits were going to arrive soon, and it looked like we would have things together in time for them. Everything was at least going to be functional enough.

US Army Major General Paul Eaton, a man we all respected and who was commanding the training effort across all of Iraq, had called all his advisers to the Green Zone for an early assessment. I was looking forward to it. All of us were looking forward to it: First, we were starving for guidance. Second, we wanted to air a grievance or two. Third, we hoped for good news when it came to materials and support. Last, we wanted an update on Fallujah. Idle talk abounds in the military, and there was a lot of talk about action coming in Fallujah, that mysterious town out in the western badlands. Eaton was our leader. I knew he would set things straight for us.

Up on the third floor, the advisers slept. Mushtaq and Fouad's generator buzzed in the distance beyond the window. A few of the Marines had a DVD of *The Matrix* on a tiny, lash-up entertainment system. The DVD player whirred along, and a little blue-green screen flickered in the dark pod. I thought about the idea in that movie that we're all operating within a great, interlinked grid, finding comfort inside a network that we don't see.

I took my eyes away from the small screen for a moment and reached into my seabag. I took out my journal and scribbled a thing or two about how, in a way, we Americans do live in a matrix. We have Social Security numbers and bank accounts and Internet passwords. We're all trapped there, even if we don't know or care. Then I wrote:

> *The Iraqis are free of any such thing—especially the Bedouins and the farmers out in the hinterlands—no ID numbers, no insurance, no banks, no registration, no time as we know it. They are both free, and not—because they are ignorant of so much, their lives have such a paucity of experience. They cannot do, or become. They just are what they are, and always will be.*

Just as Reilly and Iskander were counterparts as administrative adviser and administrative NCO, most of the Marines were going to have Iraqi counterparts they worked with closely. It allowed individual instruction for key officers. I hoped it would also create personal bonds between the Marines and Iraqis. It did, for all of us.

Not all of the advisers were in Kirkush yet, so I was filling in as battalion S-4, or logistics adviser. At a nightly meeting in the middle of April, I had my first meeting with the new battalion's logistics officer. He was a major, like me.

His name was Zayn al-Jibouri. I didn't know it at the time, but I was beginning my first true friendship with an Iraqi. And starting in that moment, I began to gain my first real understanding of Iraq itself, in all its complexities.

"I am the musharaf who will work with you," I said. "I'm your adviser." I pointed at him, and pointed back at myself.

"It is a pleasure to meet you, Major Zakkiyah, sir." Zayn smiled and shook my hand firmly.

His spirited expression and narrow features gave the major a vaguely coltish quality. Zayn had a rectangular face with high cheek bones and prominent nose. When he wasn't talking or laughing, he wore an open, careworn expression, and his eyes were small and almost black. He wore his hair short, like most Iraqi men. His mustache was trimmed rather than thick or bushy; it looked as if he had only a few days of growth. Zayn inherited probably the most difficult job in the battalion—logistics officers are charged with making sure their unit is properly supplied. I already knew how tough that was going to be for him.

I started my work with Zayn the next day, walking through the barracks with him, tallying the things that were broken, missing, or in need of maintenance. The list was daunting. Saddam Hussein hired Czechoslovakian officers to build Kirkush during the Cold War, but he never finished it. As a result, it was like a huge, abandoned construction site. Walls were unfinished. Window glass was missing. Sinks, showers, and toilets were partially installed, or broken outright. We needed to maintain a certain ratio of porcelain to personnel, but it looked like less than a quarter of our plumbing infrastructure was operational. Getting work orders filled was going to be a bitch.

Zayn and I got to know each other quickly. He was curious about my family. I explained that I came from a family of Marines, that even my sister was a Marine. He found that fact fascinating. I told him I had a fiancée back home. He asked about my religion, and I hesitated but decided to tell him the truth. I said that my family was Catholic—"*Catholiki.*"

His reaction surprised me.

"Ahh, this is good," he said. "Very good."

Zayn was devout himself, and it pleased him that I had religion. It did not bother him in the least that I was a Christian. Jesus, he told me, was the second most important prophet, after Muhammad. Zayn prayed five times daily, and I was to learn over the coming months that he did so without fail. He knelt facing south—when you're in Iraq, that's the direction of Mecca. He asked if I would like to join him and pray to Jesus. I thanked him but told him I would study my Arabic vocabulary instead. Zayn smiled, and crow's-feet appeared at the corners of his eyes.

Zayn was thirty-eight, married, and had four children. His family lived near Mosul, in northern Iraq. His extended Sunni family had more than one man in uniform. Zayn had cousins and brothers who had decided to sign on with the new Iraqi Army; another brother was the chief of police in Mosul. Zayn's tribe, the al-Jibouri, was the biggest in Iraq, with six million people. Mosul was more ethnically mixed than most of Iraq—Sunni and Shiite Arabs lived there in relative peace; Kurds and Turkmen lived there as well.

Zayn and I came from two worlds, but I found myself enjoying his company. One bright day we made our way over brown earth to the Lowdes building. We were scavenging for supplies, as usual, and we both dreaded the trips there. As we walked, he told me a story:

When Zayn was thirty-three years old, the chief of Saddam Hussein's army decided to hold an athletic contest. The best runners from the army were to compete in a twenty-kilometer race. The winner of the race would cross the finish line next to a podium holding Saddam Hussein and his brightly festooned generals. Zayn was very motivated to run. He was a strong athlete, and unlike most Iraqi men, he didn't smoke. Zayn hoped he might win a reward like a car, or an apartment in Baghdad. Those were the types of things commonly handed out for exceptional performance in the regime's army. The Iraqis even had a name for them: Saddam's Gifts.

Zayn ran the 20K race and won. He was ecstatic to finish in first place, right under Saddam Hussein's gaze. They held a little ceremony to congratulate the top finishers, with Zayn of course singled out. He was excited and nervous to meet Saddam Hussein. He wondered what his reward would be. Zayn approached the podium. Saddam reached out and greeted him with the traditional three kisses on his cheeks. Then Saddam stepped back slightly, looked into Zayn's hopeful eyes, and told him he would receive a great reward.

"I grant to you," Saddam said to him, "a year's worth of cigarettes."

I burst out laughing. Zayn burst out laughing. His crow's-feet made it seem like his whole face was smiling. His body shook. He held his hands to his eyes until the laughter passed.

"Can you believe it?" he asked me. He coughed out the words. "Can you believe, Raed Zakkiyah, how stupid was this Saddam army?"

He kept laughing. Zayn wasn't afraid to look at his own country and see the things that were unjust, crazy, or stupid. That's not easy for anyone to do, including Americans. That day was the first time I began to realize that Zayn believed in the idea of a new Iraq. He wanted to see his entire country become a place that was pluralistic, like his home of Mosul. He also wanted Iraq to be a place with rules, where people were rewarded for their merit. He thought something better was possible. He thought he could help make it happen.

The Fifth Battalion was a component of the Iraqi Third Brigade. That brigade had its own brigade-level American advisers. Its chief adviser was a hawk-nosed Army Reserve lieutenant colonel with a body that was all elbows and legs and sharp angles. He wore small gold-wire glasses and a toothbrush mustache. It was

remarkable to see an American officer with a mustache, much less
a little Hitlerian number. The lieutenant colonel was intentionally
marking himself as an eccentric in the conformist culture of the
US military. That could be a good thing or a bad thing. We called
him Ichabod Crane.

The lieutenant colonel was an earnest soldier who meant well,
but it seemed that his idea of advising was to focus his energy on
the Iraqi Third Brigade staff officers exclusively, not on the full
brigade as a top-to-bottom unit. The individual battalions didn't
interest him much. He had no vision of the brigade as an integrated whole. He was trying to get the Iraqi brigade leaders to
think like professional officers, just as we were doing at the battalion level. The lieutenant colonel left the battalion-level advisers
like me to our own devices. So we had little guidance, but we also
had plenty of leeway.

I once asked him for priority over the other two Iraqi battalions—the Sixth and Seventh—when it came to supplies. My
reasoning was that we were ahead of the other advisory teams in
the process of integrating our battalion—which was true—so we
should be better supplied, at least at the beginning.

"We have so little, it wouldn't make a difference anyway," he
said. And that was that. I couldn't believe his fatalism.

The lieutenant colonel called a meeting in Kirkush for all the
Iraqi officers and their American advisers. The Fifth Battalion pod
slowly was coming together. The advisers and their Iraqi counterparts, including Zayn and me, had all the plumbing and electric
checked and inventoried, if not exactly working. So we could spare
a little time for the brigade senior adviser. The lieutenant colonel's
idea was that he would introduce himself and his team, and then
each of the battalion advisory teams would introduce themselves.
It was supposed to be a show, a bit of military theatrics. He would
address the assembly of Iraqis and Americans. Then the Iraqi brigadier general who officially commanded the brigade would speak.

Our oily generator had apparently given Mushtaq and Fouad
more than they could handle that day, because the Fifth Battalion
pod temporarily had no electricity. Everyone from the Fifth, Sixth,

and Seventh Battalions gathered in the largest room of the only building that had electricity at that point, which was in the Sixth Battalion's pod. It was their kitchen and dining building, outfitted with many long tables and a smattering of chairs. For some reason, the room was equipped with a large-screen TV. Ichabod Crane stood in front of it with a dumpy Iraqi brigadier general who, for reasons I do not understand, wore leather slippers. A handful of young, enlisted American soldiers in the room nudged each other and snickered at the men.

The lieutenant colonel stepped up. Between the Americans and Iraqis, there were probably more than a hundred bodies in the room: my advisory team, the other battalions' advisory teams, and all the battalions' Iraqi officers, including Major Zayn, the stoic Lt. Col. Jassim Thammin, and his young, engaged XO Major Ahmed Nu'uman. The jaunty Kurdish Sergeant Major Iskander sat near the front. The interpreters were strategically scattered about the crowd.

"Can everyone hear me?" the American Ichabod lieutenant colonel asked and then waited for his interpreter to translate to the room. No one said anything.

The lieutenant colonel raised his brows inquisitively and, using his left hand, scanned the room from left to right with a thumbs-up sign.

The Iraqis murmured and shuffled. We advisers exchanged glances.

The lieutenant colonel's gesture had just said to every Iraqi in the room, "You're a dick."

Mistaking the uneasy sounds of the crowd for an affirmative answer, the lieutenant colonel plunged ahead.

"OK?" he asked, this time making an "OK" sign with his hand and scanning us right to left.

Again, more murmuring. A snort or two this time.

The lieutenant colonel's gesture had just told every Iraqi in the room, "You're an asshole."

On the rifle range, when a guy misses so badly that you don't know where the bullet went, we say, "No impact, no idea." That's what I thought about the American lieutenant colonel. No impact, no idea. That's all I remember about that meeting.

One day Zayn, the interpreter Arkan, a few advisers, and I shared lunch in our sparse chow hall back at the Fifth Battalion pod. Bare walls and hard floors magnified our voices. Torn plastic MRE wrappers crackled. Each man tapped into his 1,250-calorie allotment of spaghetti, cheese spread, and rice. "Play That Funky Music White Boy" was emanating from a tinny handheld radio.

Zayn started talking. He fumbled his English, though, and paused. In Arabic, he asked Arkan to expand on something for him in the advisers' language. Arkan did as asked.

Zayn immediately had all of the Marines' attention.

Zayn said that before he joined the other Fifth Battalion officers for training in Jordan, he had been a recruiting officer for the new Army, in Mosul. He had been signing up the very type of raw recruits—the mujanadin—that we were about to receive by the hundreds. He may have even recruited some of our own mujanadin.

Everybody stopped eating. Staff Sergeant Colwell, the no-nonsense New Englander, put down his knife. Colwell had been a drill instructor on Parris Island. He was clearly thinking what we all were: *Zayn can tell us what to expect. Zayn can tell us what kind of men these mujanadin will be.* It was like striking a vein of gold.

In the last year the US administration had changed its position on pay for the Iraqi Army. Whereas in 2003 it expected Iraqi soldiers to risk their lives for poverty wages, it was now offering recruits with no experience big money: almost 290,000 dinars a month, or about three times the Iraqi minimum wage. We knew the recruiting had gotten easier, but we had no idea what kind of men—or boys—they were bringing in. We peppered Zayn with questions: What were the qualifications? Who decided what the qualifications would be? How did the qualifications compare with Saddam's army (since Zayn had been in both)? The answers to these questions were hugely important to us.

"Zayn," I said, "tell us about the standards. Who's allowed to enlist?"

What he said blew our minds. Most of the requirements dealt with basic health, but they still told us a lot.

First was their age. The qualifying age was anywhere from eighteen to forty. But Zayn said it was possible that we would see mujanadin from outside that range.

Second was their weight: 50–150 kilograms. This would have been hilarious if it didn't worry us so much. Apparently, some American staff officer had signed off on that requirement without understanding that a kilogram equals 2.2 pounds. So a 150-kilogram recruit would be well over 300 pounds.

Third, Iraqi recruits had to have twelve teeth—six on top and six on the bottom. The requirement raised more questions: What happened if a recruit with only twelve teeth lost one? Would we have to discharge him? Or suppose his remaining twelve teeth were no good. After all, it's unlikely that a mujanad who had lost most of his teeth was going to have twelve left that were in good shape. And as far as I knew, the Iraqi Army didn't have any dentists who could make such a determination. Certainly none of the Marine advisers were qualified. I sure as hell wasn't going to stick my hands in Iraqis' mouths and start counting teeth.

Fourth, Iraqi recruits had to have all their fingers and toes. This requirement made sense, because leprosy was still a rare occurrence in Iraq. And it's contagious.

Fifth, Iraqi recruits couldn't have any "visible scars" greater than three inches long. I don't know why they qualified the word *scar* with the word *visible*. Regardless, I guessed that the standards makers didn't want anyone who had had major surgery. In the absence of enough medical personnel to screen recruits, that also made sense. Most Iraqis didn't have medical records in the way that Americans do. The Iraqi military, it seemed, sidestepped the problem by forbidding anyone with a big scar.

Sixth, each mujanad was supposed to have a blood test. Virtually every military in the world screens for blood diseases and AIDs. However, the Army didn't have the resources to give thousands of recruits blood tests. Zayn said recruits had to produce proof of a test themselves. I immediately imagined a situation when it would be less expensive for a recruit to obtain a good forgery than to pay a doctor for the real thing.

Finally, recruits had to pass a literacy test. In theory, Iraqis had compulsory education until the equivalent of American eighth grade. But Iraq was a poor country with a cash-and-carry economy. Young boys were often taken out of school around nine or ten to begin work. Obviously, that limited the pool of literate enlistees. Zayn told us recruiters got around the problem by assuming that if a candidate was responding to a recruiting ad in the newspaper, then he must have read that ad. That constituted sufficient evidence of literacy.

The Marines sat in silence for a moment, considering what Zayn told us. *So*, I thought, *that is the human material we'll have. That is what we'll form into a rifle battalion.* And really, how could I have expected anything different? We would take what the country could offer us. They would be men and boys of the land itself: poor, uneducated, desperate to support a family or to get ahead. Hopefully hardworking. Hopefully dreaming of a better future—not just for themselves or their tribe or their religion but for their whole country.

Zayn watched me take it in. He was silent. So was I. It was a lot to digest.

For two weeks I had been mentally treading over preparations for the battalion, all of which we advisers had formed on our own. Some tasks and plans were written down. Others existed only in my mind. Some rose to consciousness in the advisers' nighttime collaborations. I tried to turn over everything in my head. What had I forgotten? What was there that I could do, but which I had failed to do? What could I not do now, but could prepare to do later? Very powerful people were counting on us. At night in my barracks, pangs of anxiety struck like a burst of light, shocking me from near sleep. I sensed the awful flash of something missed.

At a certain point, I had to trust my efforts, trust all our efforts. I had to push those worries back a little in my mind. We Marines had a trip ahead of us. We were going to the Green Zone to meet General Eaton, and I knew we would get questions answered there. I could take some comfort in knowing that the most critical things were underway: We had decided on a Marine Corps–based leadership program, and Reilly was leading it. The basic training plan for the recruits was shaping up, and Hummons was in charge. The barracks were in serviceable condition. The Iraqi officers, NCOs, and interpreters were in place, learning new roles and thinking of the Americans in new ways—or at least that's what I hoped. We would leave them on their own while we went to meet with Major General Eaton.

All that remained were the mujanadin themselves.

3

GREEN ZONE

THE FIRST THING THAT STRUCK ME about the e-mail from Colonel Abblitt, my boss at the division level, was that he had sent it to me directly. I sat in the CMATT building in Kirkush, where they had working computers.

Abblitt sidestepped the normal chain of command. As division adviser, he should have communicated with me through the brigade-level adviser—Ichabod Crane. Abblitt was a conservative, by-the-book Marine. But he skipped Ichabod. He didn't even copy him. Abblitt opened his message with good news: the other three members of my team would be waiting for me in the Green Zone, rounding out a full billet of ten advisers. Then the bad news: one of the three new advisers outranked me.

I was being bumped from the senior adviser job.

I had been pestering Abblitt for a month and a half for a full complement of Marine advisers, but this was not what I counted on. My billet was designed to have a major—me, the team leader—plus two captains and seven sergeants. It wasn't turning out that way.

In the military, it can be hard to fill assignments. The Marine Corps has an informal policy called one up, one down that's designed to make it easier. One up, one down says that if you can't find a captain to fill a billet slot for a captain, you can go up one rank or down one rank and fill the position that way.

So for instance, instead of a captain, you get a lieutenant or a major. When there's an open slot, and the Marines need a body, they find a way to get one. Abblitt was telling me that he had gone one up to fill my team's opening for a captain. He found a major. That major, it turned out, had held his rank longer than I had. So technically, he outranked me. He was the new senior battalion adviser.

A funny thing about this development is that I knew the major, or at least I knew of him. His name was Curt Williamson. He had served with my sister at Parris Island, where he commanded a company of drill instructors. So I knew that he knew how to make Marines. Curt was rotating into Iraq from the Pentagon, where he was an analyst for the Marine Corps Plans, Policies & Operations command. PP&O acts as the Marine Corps' liaison to the Joint Chiefs of Staff and other branches of the service. The PP&O is big-time politics. Curt was a levelheaded, soft-spoken South Carolinian and a graduate of the Citadel. He also was a graduate of the Marine Corps' School of Advanced Warfighting—an alpha-male institution within an alpha-male branch of the military. Curt had accomplished a lot.

A good Marine officer takes orders and makes sacrifices. That's part of the job. That *is* the job. I certainly didn't push back against Abblitt or anyone else. But this was to be my command as an adviser, and Iraq was a very big stage. That April night in Kirkush I felt hugely let down, almost cheated by fate.

"It's the senior adviser who will get all the personal recognition," I wrote in my journal. "Just the word *senior* makes it so."

I felt sorry for myself. I began to beat myself up. I decided this was all happening because I didn't have political skills. Because I didn't promote myself. Because I couldn't play the game. I was too slow to recognize that the game even existed. I was a foolish idealist. Ultimately, it was political skills that mattered, I decided. That's how generals get made. Staff work, planning, research—all the things I was good at—none of them mattered.

But even in that journal entry, I was already laying the psychological groundwork that would get me past my self-pity:

"Why does it matter to you, Michael? Why is your sense of self tied up with the recognition, the game playing, of peers and seniors? Why isn't it enough just to be a part of it, and do it for its own sake? . . . Why must I endeavor to impress myself, and others, to satisfy some fake image of self?"

I decided I couldn't resent Curt Williamson for taking over as senior adviser. *You have to behave like a professional.* If I were him, I would do the same thing. He had the credentials. He was in the Pentagon. He was senior to me. And besides, I didn't have any choice. *For now,* I decided, *I will do my job and try to be glad for the opportunity.*

I walked back toward the advisers' building after dinner. It was night. Our trip to Baghdad was only a couple of days away, and I needed to square away travel plans back at my quarters. Computer time was still hard to get, so I was working off paper notes I kept by my bunk. As I approached our building at the edge of the pod, I heard quick footsteps on the gravel behind me.

"Excuse me, Raed Zakkiyah," said a voice. It was an Iraqi, speaking good English.

I turned. A solidly built man in uniform approached me. When he drew closer, I saw that he wasn't an Arab. Auburn hair showed below his khaki beret. His eyes were sky blue, made more so by their contrast with his ruddy complexion. He had a confident glint in his eyes and a Tom Selleck mustache. He stopped and saluted, palm facing outward in the Iraqi fashion.

"Warrant Officer Abdel-ridha Gibrael, sir. I was hoping I could meet you."

I told him of course, I turned back to my walk, and he continued with me toward the advisers' quarters. I had never spoken to this individual before. As a warrant officer, Abdel-ridha Gibrael wasn't a commissioned officer, but he ranked above enlisted men because he held some sort of specialized skill. In the US Army or US Navy, warrant officers are people who know how to pilot helicopters or take apart missiles.

"What's your job here?" I asked.

"Armory chief, sir," he said, crisply.

"I see. Well, hopefully we'll be able to get you some arms and vehicles to take care of eventually." This man would be in charge of my battalion's weapons. His job was important.

"You speak good English," I said. "Where did you learn?"

He said he learned in Kurdistan, where he grew up. Everyone in Kurdistan, he claimed, loves the United States. He said he also spoke Arabic in addition to Kurdish and English.

"Do you mind if I ask, Major—can we can step around behind the building?" He pointed toward the back of the advisers' building, which was on the outside of the Fifth Battalion pod. I didn't understand why he wanted me to go there with him. Then a group of Iraqis appeared around a corner about thirty yards away, laughing in the moonlight on their way back from chow. Gibrael looked at them warily. I realized he didn't want anyone to see us speaking.

"Yes," I said. "That's fine."

We crunched wordlessly over the gravel in the dark until we got to the back of the advisers' quarters. There we would be within view of the North Carolinians in the National Guard pod that bordered ours, but not within view of the Iraqis.

"The Arabs will like your name," Gibrael said.

"Yes, so I've been told. More than once."

"God gave you your name. No one can take it away from you, Major Zakkiyah. I hope you will bring good charity to the men."

"We all want to do our best, and we will. I hope you want to, too," I said. "I've never met an Iraqi with your name. That's a Kurdish name?"

"It's like the angel," he said. Gibrael took out a pack of cigarettes that had the color scheme of Marlboro Reds but were probably some Middle Eastern knockoff. He lit one. His hands were heavily calloused. "You call him Gabriel, I think, in your religion. But in our religion, he is not just a messenger. He is also a warrior."

I still didn't know what Abdel-ridha Gibrael wanted. We talked for a few minutes about the Kurds and the Arabs. Like most of the Kurds, Gibrael remembered the Ba'athist's al-Anfal genocide of the late 1980s, though he was only a teenager then. Saddam's army destroyed more than four thousand villages and killed tens of thousands of Kurds and other minorities. They poisoned civilians with mustard gas and executed boys and men. Gibrael told me that the youngest boys were spared, unless they were too big. Anyone who could fire a rifle was too big. It occurred to me that for the majority of the Kurds in the battalion, there was no way we were going to make them completely trust the Arabs.

Abdel-ridha Gibrael asked about my family. He wanted to know what state I was from. He asked about my religion and, like Zayn, was pleased by my answer.

"This is why you know the Angel Gabriel," he said, and gave me a smile of yellow teeth.

He asked what I thought of Iraq, and if I believed we would succeed. I told him that I believed we would. I told him that nothing would stop me from succeeding.

We paused again. I wondered if he was going to ask a question, make a request—anything. I felt like he had not arrived at his point. But it didn't seem he was going to. He was sizing me up, feeling out one of the Americans.

"I think you are right, Major Zakkiyah," he said, and saluted. "I hope we speak again."

"I'm sure we will," I said, and meant it. I hoped for it too.

I saluted back. Abdel-ridha Gibrael turned. He sang to himself in Kurdish as he walked away.

We got to Baghdad's Green Zone on April 23. One of the first things we noticed when we arrived there—a fortified, neighborhood-sized compound on a bend of the Tigris River—is that it didn't smell like the rest of Iraq. Aside from the heat, the most powerful and permanent sensation in Iraq is its smell. All of us advisers were veterans of multiple overseas deployments to third-world countries. It sounds bad to say it, but it's true: for the most part, poor countries smell the same. Take it from someone who fights the wars in the bad parts. Those places smell like a combination of shit, burning garbage, and roasting meat with spices. Iraq, especially in the cities, smelled that way. But not the Green Zone.

After getting settled into temporary quarters, the advisers from my team and others broke for the afternoon, left to our own designs until the following morning at 9:00. That's when we would meet Major General Eaton. A handful of us decided to wander around a bit and made our way to Saddam Hussein's Republican Palace. Everything was incongruously clean. The Americans had spared the palace from the air campaign the year before, and it remained surrounded by smooth roads, electric street lights made to look like gas lamps, and trees with long, green fronds. We walked in, and I didn't have to decide how to go about exploring the place. Its pathways seemed to draw at us, like a giant anaconda swallowing us in. Once-cavernous spaces had been transformed into a plywood maze of offices, cubbies, and hidey-holes. A human flood of rear-echelon pogues—Marine jargon for administrative types—scurried about in their warrens, sporting every uniform imaginable. Every age, color, nationality, branch of service, and bureaucracy seemed to swirl around us. We lost our bearings.

Many of the civilians, darting from room to room or milling over desk work, were sporting identical khaki pants and blue blazers. The outfit seemed inappropriate for a desert combat zone. I stopped a young Marine corporal who was passing by and asked about the boys in the sport coats.

"Bremer's brats, we call 'em," he said, leaning in a little to keep a lid on our exchange. "They're all Young Republicans. Big-time college boys."

Judging by their numbers, Paul Bremer and his people had recruited a small army of ambitious, like-minded young Americans to help the ambassador accomplish the huge tasks the Bush administration had set out for him. Their khakis and sport jackets, combined incongruously with their sand-colored combat boots, were an imitation of Bremer's favorite attire.

At one point I managed to break from the group and enter one of the palace's bathrooms. The opulence of the Green Zone commodes was already becoming legendary. The toilet was, as one might expect of a bathroom built for a tyrant, palatial. Marble climbed the walls. Not just gray marble but that reddish marble that looks fake but knocks real. Stalls rose in polished hardwood grandeur, festooned with gold-plated fixtures. I went to the sink. The water flowed. It was nice to wash my hands and face with hot water.

I stepped back outside into a clamor of purposeful voices. The palace walls stretched high and wide. I felt like a grunt. I felt like somebody who wasn't polished enough. That didn't bother me too much, though. I was getting a firsthand look at the great rear echelon of the "coalition of the willing."

That same day, less than forty-five miles up a broken highway to the west, Americans and Iraqis and a new wave of insurgents from outside Iraq were working hard to kill each other. They fought in a wide range around that bridge over the Euphrates where the mobs had hung the Blackwater corpses. Nobody there was thinking about history, neither the meaning nor the making of it. They had a mission, and I'm sure it was the only thing on their minds. Today, however, ten years after my time in Iraq, that fight up the highway has a name that historians use. Now it's called the First Battle of Fallujah, and it ran from April 4 to the beginning of May. Before the First Battle of Fallujah, it was still possible for some Americans, in Washington and elsewhere, to say that we were only fighting the last of Saddam's loyalists—the "dead-enders," as the neocons called them. But a new reality was becoming clear, like a Polaroid slowly taking gray shape on our consciousness. There was a real insurgency churning in Iraq, under its own power. The White House didn't call it by its name, but we on the ground knew what it was. Angry men were flowing into Iraq from all over the Middle East and beyond. By the spring of 2004, we were not doing a cleanup operation anymore. We were fighting an insurgency that had not existed until we sparked it.

But there it was, forty-five miles west. The morning we met Major General Eaton in a Green Zone conference room, men pulled themselves upright on Chinese-made card-table chairs. The floor scraped and yelped against the legs like a pack of hurt dogs. Other men milled about and greeted familiar faces. A podium stood front and center, with flags of the United States and Iraq behind. Men cleared their throats.

Among the attendees were the three new advisory team members that Abblitt had promised me. Gy. Sgt. Doug Webster was a Marine Reservist who worked as a court bailiff in Las Vegas, the son of a Marine father and a Japanese mother. S.Sgt. Anthony Villa was a Californian in his late twenties with a razor-thin mustache and a neck as thick as his head was wide. Villa was a trained armored-vehicle guy, so he knew mechanized warfare.

Finally, there was Curt Williamson. The major was a couple of years older than me, maybe thirty-seven at the time, with a square jaw and hair that had gone prematurely whitish gray. His eyes struck me. They were blue to the point of seeming almost violet. He introduced himself and shook my hand with an easy courtesy that I've seen in other officers from the south, though Williamson had mastered it—or had inherited it—to a greater extent than the others I'd known.

"Major Williamson," I said, and firmly shook his hand. "Good to meet you."

We were together finally, all ten of us, the group complete. In the same instant, I was no longer in charge. I tried to banish the latter thought from my mind.

At the time, there were probably a dozen American military and police advisory teams in Iraq. The room was packed. I greeted familiar faces from previous schools and deployments. The Green Zone was under daily mortar fire, and this room would have been a good target for the insurgents. It looked to me like all of the in-country US advisers were there, in one confined space. But then as I moved around the room, I slowly realized I was wrong—one group of advisers wasn't there. The ten Marine advisers we had bird-dogged at Taji weren't around. Not one of them.

"You see what I see? Or *don't* see?" Reilly asked. "Those Marines from Taji—"

"—aren't here," I said. "Yeah, I do."

A tall Marine sergeant major strode to the front of the room and faced the rest of us. Those of us still standing took our seats.

He welcomed us. He looked at a piece of paper on the podium. Major General Eaton had not yet entered the room.

"First," the sergeant major read to us, "I want to provide an update on the advisory team that was deployed in support of the First Marine Division, which is engaged in counterinsurgent activity in and around Fallujah. As you all are undoubtedly aware, the first three battalions of the new army, each about seven hundred men strong, were trained by Vinnell Corporation, beginning in July 2003. The first wave of US military advisers took over training of those troops in March of this year."

Then he got to the point: The ten Marine advisers we bird-dogged in Taji had been with their undisciplined, Vinnell-trained battalion for about a month when they got orders to lead their Iraqis to Fallujah to support the Marines and US Army troops there. But something went wrong. The story went like this: In transit, half the Iraqi battalion dropped out of the convoy. Some had worn civilian clothes under their uniforms; they shed their cammies as they fled. As the situation disintegrated around the Marine advisers, an angry civilian mob gathered. For some reason, the Marines were unable to radio back to Taji for help. The crowd grew larger and louder. Shots may or may not have been fired. The throng screamed in Arabic and demanded that the remaining Iraqi soldiers turn over the ten Americans. The Iraqi officers refused. The Marines escaped the mob but arrived at Fallujah with less than half a battalion. The two battalions that had remained in Taji saw half their men vanish overnight too.

The sergeant major finished reading. I tried to make real what he said. Just like that, the first four battalions of the new Iraqi Army had ceased to exist as functional units. Half of the men of the new army had deserted. Ten Marine advisers had barely escaped being handed over to an outraged mob. I thought of the charred bodies hanging from that bridge in Fallujah. I knew why that crowd wanted those Marines. I started asking myself serious questions. *Will we find ourselves in that kind of situation? Will we be as lucky as they were?*

What followed was a procession of American staff officers who all, through one choice of words or another, apologized for our lack of equipment or adequate housing. Ichabod Crane stood up from his seat in the audience, peered through his wire-rim glasses at a piece of paper, and read a litany of complaints to the staff officers who addressed us—each of them. He must have read the same list out loud six times. It made me uncomfortable. I was grateful that Ichabod Crane was speaking up, but it was an outright provocation to repeat his list again and again. People began to shift in their seats.

"You won't get everything you want," an adjutant to General Eaton finally said. I had a notebook with me and jotted down his words. "You won't get everything you need. Accept it and move forward. All we ask is you do the best you can with what we can give you."

Ichabod protested about a lack of manpower.

"There is no reserve," the adjutant said. "You're *it* until you're dead or you accomplish your mission. I'm not happy with you being unsupported. My job is not to be unhappy but to do something about it."

Major General Eaton came in. We snapped to attention as he entered the room, his head up, his jaw forward. The general looked as sharp as a bayonet. Not a terribly big man, he nonetheless was an imposing presence. He gave the impression of hardness, like he'd been carved from ironwood. He gave us leave to take our seats.

Chairs scuffled, then settled. The room was silent for a moment. At that moment, the sound of a distant explosion came muffled through the walls. The window frames shivered. It was a mortar hitting something, somewhere. The general stepped into the quiet after the explosion like a field officer of an earlier era, leading a charge into the breach.

"Gentlemen," he said into the silence, "we are operating at the ragged edge of our competence. And there is no assurance of our success."

He paused. We considered his statement. I realized for the first time that we were operating without a safety net. Taken along with the implosion of the first three Iraqi battalions, I realized that failing at our mission—unthinkable in US military culture—was a real possibility.

General Eaton gazed at us, a group of men at rapt attention.

"I have been given a mission by Ambassador Bremer and Lieutenant General Sanchez, not unlike building an airplane in mid-flight. You are the best your respective services could offer for this most difficult and dangerous mission. I understand that most of you accepted your orders on short notice, and with very little preparation and training. I share your experience, as I was given this mission eleven days before I arrived in Baghdad."

I tried to imagine the magnitude of the general's mission. I could imagine that Bremer, having disbanded the Iraqi Army and police during his first week in Iraq and then having watched the country's descent into anarchy, was jumping up and down on the general's chest every day, wanting Iraqi security forces up and running *immediately*. And now General Eaton had seen the first Iraqi Army units disintegrate.

"I am not satisfied with the level of support you advisers in the field have received from my command," he said. "We have sent you and your teams into the most precarious combat environment with less equipment and support than we would an infantry squad."

He skipped details about his workings with Bremer and the civilian leadership, that awful set of gears where military necessities grind against political imperatives, where need and utility clash with ideology and profit. But I could imagine how shitty that place was. I think a lot of people in that room could.

General Eaton did not bother with false promises. He was operating at the highest levels in Iraq, and what he was telling us was that he didn't have good news. If there were good news, he'd know about it. That day in the Green Zone would've been a very good time to share it. All he had to offer us was shared responsibility and encouragement.

"When you look back at the Iraqi Army and at this country, ten years from now, and you see your fingerprints and your mark, you will have something to be proud of," he said. "You will know that you made this army and were present at the foundation of this country."

He believed. I believed him. I think he made each one of us believe. Eaton wrapped up and had an aide hand out boxes of Thuraya satellite phones. He promised that we could call him at any time. And with that, he was done.

Or almost. Before he turned to leave, he looked directly at Ichabod Crane.

"Lieutenant colonel," he said, "you are dismissed."

Eaton walked out. He had just fired the brigade-level senior adviser. Everyone looked at Ichabod. He burned red. He had just been ended like a cicada stamped by a boot. Advisers shuffled away from him between folding chairs.

The exits made choke points. The room mumbled. Then I heard one of the advisers from another team, near and in front of me. He barked out a short laugh and turned to another officer, rolling his eyes, responding to something his buddy said.

"Well, we don't want to train the Iraqis too well, right?" he asked his friend. "In ten years, we'll probably be fighting them."

Daytime temperatures climbed to about ninety degrees, still cool by Iraqi standards. I took a couple of one- or two-mile runs while we were in the Green Zone. Throughout my deployment in Iraq, I tried to run most nights, usually in the desert. A quick shower usually awaited me afterward in one of several trailers equipped with stalls. Signs there warned "transient" personnel, myself included, to limit ourselves to a single five-minute shower each day. Returning to the palace after one of those quick showers, I found that the other advisers had already left for dinner. I set out after them. I had already taught myself a trick for whenever I lost my bearings in the palace: I simply followed the foot traffic. The human drift of uniforms and sport jackets took me, like water flowing downhill, to the dining room. A long line waited at that chamber, yet another cavernous space, this one filled with cloth-covered serving tables. Lights in sconces lined the wall. Chandeliers hung above. The place felt like a military wedding reception. I half expected a man in a tux to swing by and offer champagne.

I read the announcement board next to the chow line. There were general notices, threat-level declarations, base policies. Ads from people teaching Arabic to non-Arabic speakers or English as a foreign language. Notes from civilian contractors on their way back home, trying to sell stuff they didn't want to take with them: stereos, TVs, and DVD players. One listing advertised a wedding dress.

I was overwhelmed by the food choices. Beef, pork, chicken, lobster tails. A pasta bar. Potatoes baked, mashed, or fried. Steamed vegetables. Fresh fruit. Water, soft drinks in icy cans, milk, coffee, tea. Kool-Aid. Cakes, cookies, ice cream. All served by little men and women from Bangladesh or the Philippines, wearing white serving outfits, greeting us in English singsong.

I found an unoccupied table toward the back. I'd opted for steak and lobster, string beans, mixed peas and carrots, and a salad. I tried not to feel guilty about the men I'd left at Kirkush eating at the KBR chow hall. The kitchens at Kirkush were running by then, but the food was all varying degrees of fried. I'd just tucked in, and hadn't yet taken a bite when I was interrupted by a question.

"Major, can I join you?"

I looked up. The question came from an Air Force colonel in a desert tan flight suit. A cafeteria tray rested in his hands. A pilot's wings insignia announced itself on his uniform. He stood tall and lean, his skin as tanned as a penny loafer. He had a definite Texas drawl.

"Of course, sir."

The colonel sat down catty-corner to me. He said silent grace. Then he looked up.

"Nice dinner tonight."

"Yes sir, I'm pleasantly surprised," I said. "Much better than I expected, and way better than I'm used to."

The colonel glimpsed the name sewn into my camouflage blouse.

"How do you pronounce your name?"

"Za-kay-a, sir."

The colonel nodded. "That sounds like an Arabic word—did you know that?"

"Yes, sir. Every Iraqi I have spoken to has told me that."

"Where are you stationed?" he asked. "What unit are you with?"

"I'm here from Kirkush, sir. We're here for a conference. I'm an adviser to the Iraqi Army. We're about to start forming and training a rifle battalion."

He smiled broadly. "This couldn't have worked out better if I planned it," he said. "As a captain, I was an adviser to the Iraqi Air Force during the Iran-Iraq war in '86. Best tour of my career."

He had to have seen the surprise on my face.

"I had no idea we were advising the Iraqi Air Force then," I said. "I knew we were sharing intelligence on Iranian positions . . . I had no idea—no one in Quantico told us—that we had advisers on the ground in Iraq then."

"Sure," the colonel said, and took a bite of flank steak. "We lived on an Iraqi air base. We helped analyze air intelligence, target selection, plan air operations. I really liked working with the Iraqis."

I immediately thought of the raison d'être for our war, the one boiling around us: weapons of mass destruction. Only the month before, the chief US inspector for WMD had stated that he hadn't found any yet. I decided to try the colonel for information.

"Sir, do you have any ideas about the WMD? Where they might be?"

He looked at me sideways.

"That remains information not for public consumption," he said. He punctuated his statement with a long drink of cherry Kool-Aid, draining his glass. Kool-Aid, sweet, cold, with a slightly metallic tang, was a staple in the dining facility. Once I started drinking it on a hot day, I couldn't stop.

In the noisy bustle of the dining room, silence settled between us. He had volleyed the conversation my way. I bought some time, thoughtfully chewing a forkful of buttered lobster.

"Sir," I offered, "how do you fit into this lash-up?" The word is Marine jargon for something thrown together, an ad hoc organization. The Marines mastered the craft of building units from parts of other units, tailored for a specific mission. The Coalition Provisional Authority was definitely an ad hoc organization. We joked that CPA stood for Can't Provide Anything. For that matter, CMATT was ad hoc too.

The colonel gave a short bark that I took as laughter.

"Lash-up, huh, Major? I like that." Then louder: "I'm an adviser also. I work here in the palace. My boss is Ambassador Bremer."

I kept working the lobster. My mind raced. I'd dived into the deep end of the pool. I wondered if this might not be as random a meeting as I initially assumed. Was I asking the right questions? Was this an interview? Should I be asking any questions at all?

"Where do you come from, Major?" the colonel asked.

I began to feel that I was being interviewed, though for what I had no idea. Did they want to know if I was ideologically sound, the same way it seemed they vetted civilians for Bremer's staff? Or did the colonel merely want to know whether I was going to embarrass them: Did I have the mettle to hold my battalion together?

I gave him a brief narrative of my background and career. Raised in Suffolk County, Long Island. Catholic high school. Bachelor of arts in English and classical civilization at Notre Dame. Master's degree in organizational change at Hawaii Pacific University. Commissioned as a Marine officer in 1990. Deployments to Somalia and Haiti. Civilian work on Wall Street.

"How do you assess your mission?" he asked.

"Sir," I started carefully, "we're undermanned, underequipped, and we're out in front of the logistics curve. We're starting from scratch, literally from nothing. But we are approaching the training as we would approach Marine Corps recruit training, with an emphasis on the intangibles, and an ethos of *every soldier a rifleman.*"

The Colonel nodded, and asked me if I was concerned about what had happened with those first, Vinnell-trained Iraqi battalions. I was glad to finally get a somewhat military question. I told him the truth.

"Yes, sir, but I think we can do better." Based on what I observed during our two weeks with the Fifth Battalion's officers and NCOs, I did in fact believe that we could perform better than the advisers who had almost gotten handed to a mob on the road to Fallujah. Still, given the scant evidence I had, it was a brash statement, long on can-do attitude and short on details. I had really nothing to base my statement on save our team's faith in our Marine Corps training. But what alternative did I have? We could not fail.

The colonel nodded again.

"I think so too," he said. "My tour with the Iraqis was a great personal and professional experience. I enjoyed my relationships with them. I'm sure you will too, and you'll be very successful."

He rose for an after-dinner cup of coffee and asked if he could get me anything. I declined. The room remained busy, a swarm of uniforms, blazers, and food-service outfits. When the colonel returned to his seat, he sat down at a slight distance from the table, one leg bent over the other at the knee. I wondered if his body language was an attempt to get me to relax.

He asked who my reporting senior was. Who, in short, was my boss? I explained I had a dual chain of command, one through the Iraqi brigade, and one through Colonel Abblitt, the senior Marine adviser in the country. We made small talk for a few more minutes about administration in an ad hoc organization. I explained that Abblitt wanted the regular fitness reports of all the Marine advisers to go through him for review. When the Air Force colonel finished his cup of coffee, he stood. I stood as well. He offered me a piece of paper.

"This is my e-mail and Thuraya number. If you need anything, you let me know," he said. "And if you can, copy me on your reports to your Marine colonel."

We shook hands. He wanted to see the performance reviews on my individual advisers as I wrote them. I decided immediately that I was not going to give them to him. I said nothing. He held my hand for longer than a handshake.

"You know, Major, there are a lot of politicians and generals here in the palace—but you may have the most important job of any of them. Are you up to it?"

"Yes sir." Emphatic. Upbeat. Can-do.

"Good. And good luck. God bless. Stay in touch."

He released my hand and left me.

I took my seat to consider what just transpired. Then I decided I'd just been shown who was boss. I'd been vetted. I'd had a close encounter with the real authority in Iraq. It made me think back to those lit classes at Notre Dame. I'd just received tidings from an emissary—my own winged messenger.

The mujanadin arrived in Kirkush by the busload over five days, starting May 3.

It was good to be back in the desert. The Zagros Mountains watched us from their indifferent distance. There in Kirkush, getting back to the mission, at least we were in charge. Our destiny felt like something we could grasp and shape.

It sounds prejudiced and judgmental to say it, but I convey it as a simple sensory fact: the first thing I noticed about the recruits, when I really began to work among them, was their smell. People everywhere smell different from Westerners. It's only by being in a truly poor country that an American can even understand this. During the Vietnam War, the Vietcong became attuned to the odor of Americans, who bathed frequently (for soldiers) and smelled like American-made soap. Some Marines and soldiers in Vietnam stopped bathing so they couldn't be detected by their odor.

Like many people, the Iraqis smell like the food they eat: the earthiness of olive oil, the sweetness of chai, the sharp, hunger-inducing scent of grilled meat. But the Iraqis didn't bathe regularly, so their odors built up, becoming overwhelming to a foreigner.

In addition to adjusting to the soldiers' aroma, we Americans had to adjust to the sight of their teeth. They had grown up without fluoride in their water, and many of them had never regularly brushed their teeth. Almost none had visited a dentist. Think about how regularly Americans go to the dentist to avoid tooth decay and gum disease, and how quickly such afflictions can advance in the absence of dental care. Now imagine if paying for a dentist meant not being able to afford to eat. That was the situation for the average Iraqi.

It seemed like two-thirds of the recruits were named Muhammad. They were scrupulous about washing their hands, heads, and feet before praying. Already, Zayn and the young XO Ahmed Nu'uman had introduced me to this bathing ritual, and I found it distinctly refreshing during the long, hot days in Kirkush.

Major Williamson, Captain Hummons, Reilly, and the rest of us often walked among the mujanadin with an interpreter. Some looked like boys, others almost like old men. Most seemed to be in their twenties. They wore civilian clothes that ran the gamut from Adidas tracksuits to patched-and-mended business suits. We asked why they were there. We asked if they wanted to serve their country. Some appeared enthusiastic. More appeared intimidated and confused by being directly addressed by an American.

We learned a lot about each other over the coming days and weeks. The most basic cultural differences surprised us. Take toilet habits, for example. Iraqis relieved themselves in the Eastern style—squatting over a hole in the porcelain floor. They used water to clean themselves, never toilet paper. Abdel-ridha Gibrael, the Kurdish warrant officer, and Webster, the new Marine gunnery sergeant, one morning debated the merits of Eastern versus Western toilet habits. It was spur-of-the-moment conversations like this that slowly broke down barriers. Gibrael and Webster's debate drew chuckles from the Iraqis and Marines who were listening, and the two men began playing to the crowd. Each man loudly ridiculed the other man's toilet culture, complete with exaggerated, pantomimed mockery, and the Americans and Iraqis rolled with laughter.

Another thing we learned early about the mujanadin was that they seemed to think the toilets were good for throwing away garbage. They tossed things down the hole, stopping up the plumbing. We started finding cans of Coke, empty water bottles, batteries, clothing, and flip-flops in the toilets. The entire system clogged and overflowed. From the very first day, Zayn and I had to make runs to Lowdes to get plumbers to work through the muck and pull out whatever was lodged in the pipes. Some days, we had to call out the plumbers more than once.

Each company in Fifth Battalion was assigned to its own building in the pod. The two Iraqi sergeant majors—the lively Kurd, Iskander, was one of them—were supposed to schedule a duty NCO who was responsible for the good order of his company's building. Zayn and I walked through the barracks every day tallying a list of things that were broken or in need of maintenance. We usually had only about 25–33 percent of the sinks, showers, and toilets working at any time. The broken facilities overstressed the functioning facilities, and then the good, operating parts would break. The Iraqis were not accustomed to Western-style showers, and they regularly stripped the faucet knobs off their threads. No matter how scalding or powerful a flow of water became, they always wanted more, more, more.

Aside from our infrastructure needs, we faced other challenges. Most Iraqis didn't have bank accounts before the war, and none of them had accounts after the US invasion, because the country's commercial banks had all shut down. Most of the mujanadin were poor. To pay them, we had to send a small convoy to the Iraqi Ministry of Defense in Baghdad to pick up the payroll in cash. A pattern was going to develop: Immediately after every payday, the soldiers wanted to go on leave to take their earnings home. Paper money was safer when it was with their families than when it was hidden in their footlockers. The Iraqis worried intensely about being cheated out of their pay. In general, they expected to be robbed at any time. Arranging the convoy to get the cash from the Ministry of Defense required careful consideration from the advisers. To reduce the chances of a convoy stealing the payroll, we picked our most trusted officers and NCOs for pay runs. We tried to make each convoy group diverse as well. Kurds, Shiites, and Sunnis on a payroll run together were less likely to conspire as a group to steal the other mujanadin's cash.

Sometimes the most difficult tasks for us were also the most mundane. That's how it works when you have hundreds of soldiers to care for. Staff Sergeant Colwell, the no-nonsense adviser from New England, was the youngest of our group. He got the first really tough job.

Hundreds of Iraqis stood in a ragged single-file line that snaked out of a supply building. At the far end, outside and far beyond Colwell's view, the tail of the Iraqi line milled in the incandescent heat. Men who grew up in that heat waited patiently, idly chatting in Arabic and Kurdish. At the other end, inside the featureless interior, Colwell sat Indian-style on the concrete floor. An interpreter stood next to him. Behind him, towering stacks of cardboard boxes threatened to avalanche over.

In order to have "boots on the ground"—that term the politicians and TV news celebrities use instead of *infantry*—you need real boots. Colwell had boots, and plenty. Boxed up, with sizes marked on the outside. The boots were Pakistani-made, but flimsier than real Pakistani army boots, as if some US contractor had been duped into thinking he was buying actual military-quality gear. Our recruits waited. More than eight hundred Iraqi men stood in line to get sized up and fitted. Colwell took them, one by one, and fitted them out. Eight hundred Iraqis, 1,600 Iraqi feet, 8,000 rough Iraqi toes. Most of the mujanadin had never worn boots before. Tight-fitting, above-the-ankle boots are not typical footwear for a desert culture.

The Iraqis came forward, one by one, scanning the boxes the way a little kid peers at an aquarium full of fish. Colwell sat the men down, took each by one foot and measured. Then he turned to the towering piles of boxes and tried to find the right size, or close to it, and turned back. As he lifted men's feet by the heels, measuring them, he wondered by the look of those feet how some of the men could even walk. There is no podiatry in

Iraq. But they were the tough feet of a rough-hewn people. Colwell had already seen many of them playing soccer in the gravel and dirt, barefooted.

He quickly came to understand that, to many of the Iraqis, to be given something as simple as a pair of boots was to receive a great gift. Each man sat before Colwell in turn, awaiting his new shoes. Many men wore the rough, loose clothing of a peasant farmer—traditional garb known as a dishdasha but which the Marines had started calling a "man dress." Colwell tried squeezing a recruit's foot into a boot. When the first didn't fit, he pulled it off without a word and put it back into the box.

"No, no, please," said the mujanad. "Thank you, I take them. Thank you."

"They're too tight," Colwell said, turning back and skimming over the sizes on the boxes. "Let me get you another pair."

"No, good boots! I take."

"Wait, I need to get you into a pair that fits. You can't be out there marching in boots that are too tight."

The interpreter put a hand on the mujanad's shoulder and delivered soothing Arabic. Recruits often panicked when the first pair didn't fit, thinking they had missed a chance at new boots. Colwell got used to it. He repeated his fittings eight hundred times.

With the mujanadin on base, the chow hall stopped being a mostly empty room of NCOs who didn't want to speak. It turned into a boisterous chamber of Iraqi trainees who couldn't stop talking. I liked the change. It helped draw out the NCOs too. Little by little, they let down their guards. Officers and NCOs like Zayn and Iskander became at ease with the Americans, even friendly. It was a big deal to have Iskander on our side, because he quickly became the one guy in the battalion who was respected by officers and enlisted men, Arabs and Kurds, Shiites and Sunnis. More and more, I caught the other Iraqis watching our interactions from their plates.

The Iraqi NCOs never sat with the Iraqi officers. In terms of military culture, it was one of the first things we noticed about the Iraqis: they were much more rigidly hierarchical than we were. It was like a caste system. Other than when giving orders, the Iraqi officers never spoke to their NCOs. It made me think of the nineteenth-century class barriers of the British Imperial Army. Even the more easygoing officers like Zayn saw themselves as superior to their sergeants. And even the widely respected NCOs like Iskander behaved like second-class citizens around officers.

I mulled over those observations and a dozen other things, walking back to my quarters on another warm night, when I recognized Abdel-ridha Gibrael's voice behind me. He asked if he could join me, and I told him of course. We walked side by side and made small talk. I led us behind the advisers' quarters, out of sight, without being asked. He lit a fake Marlboro Red.

"I want to tell you something," he said, "but please, no one can know you learned this from me."

I agreed. He looked straight into my eyes and continued.

"It's about Lt. Col. Jassim Thammin."

He had my attention. Jassim was the CO, the head of the battalion.

"The lieutenant colonel has told the other officers not to listen to the Americans. He said we must just wait for a while, and eventually you will leave."

"You heard him say this?"

"More than once I have heard him say this, Raed Zakkiyah. He says just wait. He says that the Americans will leave and then things will go back to the way they were under Saddam."

I was stunned. Gibrael was telling me that the commanding officer of the Fifth Battalion was subverting our efforts to train it. Jassim Thammin was a Sunni. Could he really think the new army would return to being like Saddam Hussein's old Sunni-dominated army? Why would he expect the Shiites and Kurds to go along with that?

"Will the officers do what Jassim says?"

"Some. Most, maybe. For now. Not the Kurds so much." He paused. "I am here to tell you this because I hope the Americans will make a free Iraq," he said, his eyes taking on emotion. "And a free Kurdistan."

My head was swimming. I understood why Gibrael wanted our talks to be secret.

"And that is not all, Major," Gibrael said. "The officers and the NCOs, many of them speak English. Many of them good English, as good as me. But they pretend not to understand what you say."

"Does Jassim want them to do that?"

"It is because they want to be able to listen to you. They want the advisers to speak truthfully in front of them in English so they can learn about you. Many of them do not trust the Americans yet," Gibrael said. He took a drag on his cigarette and exhaled. "Also, I believe that they do this because it is a way to do what Jassim says and ignore the Americans until they go away. They must do what he says—Lt. Col. Jassim Thammin is the commander."

That night, I told Major Williamson about Gibrael's message for us. Williamson looked at me without expression; he was clearly deep in thought. I watched him wrap his mind around the possibility that at least part of our battalion command structure, including the CO, opposed our mission. If Gibrael was telling the truth, then some of the officers did not want any part of the new army we were trying to create.

"What do you think? Is he trustworthy? This Warrant Officer Gibrael?"

The flash in Abdel-ridha Gibrael's eyes when he spoke about his dreams for the Kurds had stuck with me.

"Yes," I said. "He's throwing his lot in with us because he thinks we can help the Kurds. But he's on board with us, in my judgment. He may be loyal to Kurdistan first and Iraq second, but he's with us."

Major Williamson paused. He nodded. He knew the Kurds as well as I did.

"Jassim's a Sunni Arab, right?"

"Yes," I answered. I knew his religion and I knew that he was an Arab, but I didn't know anything about which tribe Jassim came from. Neither did Major Williamson. We were going to have to learn more about that. Tribes are important, almost as important as family. We needed to know how many friends Jassim had, and how high they went in Iraqi society, before we made our move. We had to know who would align against us in a confrontation.

"I can see what Gibrael knows," I said. "Or maybe Zayn can—he's Sunni too. I trust Zayn."

"OK," Major Williamson said. "Not yet, though. Let me give it a think. Thanks a lot, Mike."

I nodded and turned away. I walked to my rack and found my pen. I wanted to get some thoughts down in my journal.

Then Major Williamson called over in afterthought.

"And hey, Mike," he said, "I hope you know that you can call me Curt."

4

HOW TRAINING WORKED

IMAGINE THROWING A DINNER PARTY for more than eight hundred people. Imagine creating the menu and arranging the delivery and preparation of all the necessary ingredients. Imagine finding the tables and chairs to seat your guests. Imagine finding a venue to shelter them comfortably from the summer sun. Now stretch your imagination a bit, and envision housing all those people. Their demands are legion, constant, insatiable. They need bedding, toiletries, plumbing, electricity, and transportation. They need rooms and lockers to hold everything.

Now imagine doing that not just for a night or even a long weekend but into perpetuity. Weeks on end. It's not one meal a day; it's three. Go further. Imagine keeping your guests busy. Every minute of their day must be scheduled, slotted, and filled; every minute requires buildings, rooms, stretches of outdoor landscape. And imagine that, people being people, you must smooth over life's disputes, petty or great. There are illnesses, minor and major. There are wardrobes and haircuts. There are things that break.

If you can imagine that much, you still have not imagined training a rifle battalion. Stretch your mind a little further. Imagine making each of your guests into a proficient killer who, critically, understands his role and responsibilities at the level of the full eight hundred people and his place in each subgroup of that and each subgroup of those subgroups and into further subgroupings, all the way down to himself and his rifle. You must teach him hundreds of individual skills and concepts, from dressing head wounds to land navigation to silent arm signals to the proper way he should challenge an approaching stranger when he's on sentry duty. You must teach him discipline. You must instill courage. You must build him into a person who can overcome extreme discomfort and privation. You must make him actually want to be such a person so badly that he will risk his life for it. And while you may want him to risk his life, you do not want him to die.

If you can conceive that much, bear with me and try to make your final push to Iraq in 2004. Envision that most of your eight hundred guests possess no functional English and are themselves divided into two primary language groups; that in any case, they are largely illiterate in any language; that as a body they are evenly split into three major ethnic and religious groups who harbor sometimes murderous animosity toward one another; that they hold dozens of competing familial and tribal allegiances that subdivide them further; that they spring from an economic culture that is fundamentally hierarchical and therefore encourages patronage, rapaciousness, and theft while ignoring rules and discouraging individual initiative; that they come from an autocratic political culture that has, in effect, permeated their entire culture.

Though your efforts are considered critical on the highest strategic and political levels, you will receive little material support. You will receive no outside guidance. On the contrary, you will often face animosity and obstruction from your own side. And finally, you and your guests begin your time together in a mutual distrust that you must overcome in order to face a common enemy that does not know mercy and is determined to slaughter all of you.

It was late April 2004. Kirkush. Most of the Iraqi officers and NCOs were on leave. The new Major Williamson, Hummons, and I huddled in an stuffy, sparsely lit, barely furnished room and tried to figure out how we would create our part of the new Iraqi armed forces.

Like Hummons and me, Williamson had gone through CMATT's largely useless program of instruction.

Our boss, the new brigade-level adviser who replaced Ichabod Crane, was a National Guard lieutenant colonel who had little experience with making soldiers. He had no staff to speak of and hadn't mandated a training schedule. The brigade's other two Iraqi battalions, the Sixth and Seventh, were both advised by US Army majors who had ideas very different from our own about the best way to create a fighting force. Between us, the other two battalions' advisers, and the lieutenant colonel at brigade, there was not going to be any agreement on how training would work. We had to just go it alone.

"Those Army guys want to teach combined arms for a desert environment," Williamson said.

"But we're going to be in an urban environment," I said. I knew the Fifth was not going to be carrying out large-unit maneuvers in the open desert. When we fought, if we fought, we would fight in cities, man to man, door to door.

The two Army majors' ideas included having the recruits fire as many rounds as possible during rifle training. They believed this would give their Iraqi troops a proper "feel" for their rifles.

"They don't need to be told to fire their weapons," I said. "They fire at the drop of a hat."

"We saw it at Taji," Hummons said. "A crescendo. One fires, they all fire, everywhere."

"Right," Williamson said. He paused without breaking eye contact with me. "It's got to be about fire discipline. And it's about an urban environment. And besides that, a challenge is going to be getting our guys *to* the fighting."

Here again, I agreed with Williamson. Hummons and I learned in Taji that most of the Iraqis couldn't drive. Or worse, actually—they did not know how to drive, but they believed that they did.

The schedule and design for most of the individual training packages fell to Hummons. He was the third officer on our team. Williamson and I would be plenty busy dealing with Fifth Battalion's labyrinthine links to the outside world: the adviser command structure, regular US military units, Iraqi officers, US contractors, and various Iraqi civilians, each of whom had his own demands and controlled one of our lifelines or another. For the first two months, Hummons worked on almost nothing except writing the training program. He based it on a standard Marine Corps program, except with longer days to compensate for a shortened calendar. Even then, the training would be stripped down by American standards. Hummons had written only two weeks of the program when the recruits arrived, so he worked overtime to stay ahead of them. It was a "work in progress" in the truest sense. At the end of the advisers' eighteen- or twenty-hour days, Hummons approached us for what he called a sanity check: Is this doable? Is that manageable? He wanted second opinions. It was guesswork. We also had to factor in translating everything into Arabic and Kurdish. Hummons turned especially to Colwell and Lindsay, the former drill instructors, and Jenkins, our former infantry school guy. As night fell on their own daily tasks, Colwell, Lindsay, and Jenkins rubbed their eyes and focused on the materials that Hummons put before them. Hummons accounted for every minute of forty-eight days.

Early on, we learned that even the simplest things were more difficult than we imagined. Case in point: jumping jacks. Most people in the United States have known how to do jumping jacks, a staple of the Western world's exercise regimen, from a young age. Here's something I learned in Iraq: a lot of people on earth don't know how to do jumping jacks. It's amazing how many ways there are to be terrible at jumping jacks, which Marines call side-straddle hops. Our Iraqi trainees had never seen jumping jacks before or moved their body that way. Americans forget how complex they are: Jump so that your feet land apart, and clap your hands above your outstretched arms above your head. Jump again, this time bringing your feet together while taking the hands to the thighs. To most of us, they are simple and natural. To the Iraqis, they were neither.

Americans in green physical training (PT) gear—usually Colwell and Lindsay—stood on dusty ground before their Iraqi charges.

The soldiers sweated in gray long sleeves and full-length trousers. By the end of April, the thermostat hit 100 degrees Fahrenheit most days. By the end of May, it was regularly 120. By the end of June, it sometimes exceeded 130 degrees. The instructors began their jumping jacks, counting off as they went along.

"One, two, three! One, two, three!" the Americans bayed out, giving their count in the singsong swing particular to drill sergeants. Their cadence came from bright mornings in San Diego, green lawns on Parris Island.

The Iraqis struggled. The men each tried something different. They hopped and clapped in separate rhythm. They clasped their hands above their heads and jumped, as if on hot coals. They slapped their hands together above their heads without moving their legs. They thrust out arms and legs like human starbursts. Some fell into the dust. Others, a minority, picked up on this strange new exercise and managed to stay in time.

Major Zayn never let me forget that the men were, in his words, "poor farmers." They were mostly uneducated. They had never had the leisure time to allow for "exercise." They knew work. They knew struggle. They knew how to survive in the worst economic, political, and social conditions. Their lives had been dominated by war: the long, pointless slaughter with Iran; the first war with the United States and its allies; Saddam Hussein's genocide against the Kurds—a third of the men before us, jumping, had been on one side of that genocide, and the other two-thirds had been on the other side—then another American invasion that had just ended; and now this new urban insurgency, which we Americans were sharing with them. These were hard men, and many of them had been beaten down by the circumstances into which they were born. They had never had time for something as pointless as jumping jacks.

Hummons skipped sleep and sweated the details of the battalion's training, page by page. The Fifth Battalion's recruits chased him the whole way in real life, in classrooms and out on the aluminum-sky ranges of Kirkush. But even Hummons, with his hard-charging determination, couldn't design every aspect of our fly-by-night program alone.

One of the most important elements fell to someone else entirely. Anthony Villa was a twenty-eight-year-old from Sacramento, California, who had grown up wanting to be either a teacher or a Marine. In Iraq, he was both. Like many of us, Villa hailed from a family of Marines. His grandfather, a brother, and more than one uncle had served in the Corps. He was an amtrac guy by training—he knew armored vehicles—and in Kirkush he took on the task of designing both a defensive driving course and, more critically, the Fifth Battalion's marksmanship course. He took Williamson's directive seriously. Like the Marines, each Iraqi of the Fifth would be a rifleman, would identify as a rifleman, first and foremost. Our ethos would become their ethos, regardless of their work assignment. You operate a radio? You're a rifleman. You drive a truck? You're a rifleman. You repair generators in the burning heat? You're a rifleman.

Villa was the rare type of American who had an intrinsic curiosity about other cultures and had found a job that would let him experience them up close. He brought his copy of *The Arab Mind* to Iraq and referred to it regularly. It was dry reading to most, but it interested him. He taught himself the Arabs' history, their culture, how different they were from us, and *why* they were different from us. Before he joined us, he was training commandos in Egypt and Qatar. He had never trained regular infantry before. He also had never experienced combat.

Villa's mission was straightforward: qualify each of the unit's eight hundred mujanadin to care for, safely handle, and effectively fire an AK-47 assault rifle. Make each man a rifleman. The marksmanship program would begin with what we Marines knew as grass week, move from there to classroom instruction, and finally to the soldiers' first foray onto the firing range with live rounds. Grass week was an expression from our earliest training. It involved developing familiarity with the weapon itself: handling it, training it on targets, and hour upon hour of dry firing. That meant no ammunition. To us Marines, grass week evoked the long, green ranges of Quantico or Parris Island, those orderly grounds half a world away. The term made less sense applied to Iraq's infinite stretches of desiccated earth. We joked among ourselves that we should rename it desert week or gravel week, but grass week stuck.

We lacked desks or chairs. The Iraqis, sometimes grouped by platoon, other times organized by language, huddled on the classroom floor. Villa was a dark, lantern-jawed Marine of powerful build. His almost six-foot frame rose next to big paper flip charts that he balanced on easels. Villa gazed over the pupils, his expression a mix of certitude and hopefulness. Four interpreters aided him: The Arabic speakers were Abdallah, a tall, soft-spoken man who had studied physics at the University of Baghdad; and Sala'am, a paunchy man who had been a captain in the old army. Two others spoke both Arabic and Kurdish: Jaf was bookish, openly atheistic and communist, and his face bore torture scars from Saddam Hussein's secret police. Najm was a small, precise man who had taught computer science at a Kurdish university.

Before classes could start, Villa and his 'terps prepared the flip-panel illustrations that would show their trainees the ins and outs of weapons that we wanted them to regard as extensions of themselves. Villa modeled each plate on the images in a Marine manual for the M16A3 assault rifle, which is an entirely different device from an AK-47. He drew them by hand, modifying them as needed. Time constraints meant Villa's charts had to be less thorough than the ones an American recruit would see. His pictures might portray something as basic as how to align the AK-47's rear sights with its front sights. Each lesson took almost a full day—usually the day prior—to design. Being civilians, with the exception of Sala'am, the interpreters themselves had to learn the points of weaponry that Villa wanted to teach. They debated the best ways to convey Villa's meaning in Arabic and two dialects of Kurdish, a process that itself required time. They bantered vibrantly in languages Villa did not comprehend. They reached consensus. They turned back to Villa for the next chart. Villa, Abdallah, Sala'am, Jaf, and Najm repeated this process again and again and again. Villa wrote out his flip charts in English, with simple numbered points such as "relaxation," "breathing," "bone-to-bone support," and "pull trigger slow and easy." The interpreters wrote the same underneath on each chart in three dialects. Of course, the written part of the charts helped only the portion of the battalion that was literate.

Villa taught in English, pointing at his illustrations and speaking deliberately. After a brief pause, the interpreters followed him in Arabic and Kurdish.

"Always point the muzzle of your AK-47 down when you're not firing," Villa said.

"Wajih fouehat silahak nahwa al ardh," translated the Arabic interpreters. As they spoke, Villa's thickly muscled arm gestured toward his hand-drawn muzzle on the chart.

The soldiers watched from the floor, some nodding in concentration, others expressionless, all of them silent. Many of them, especially the former Iraqi Army soldiers and the Kurdish Peshmerga, had handled an AK-47 before. Many had fought with one—perhaps even against Americans. None, however, knew how to handle a rifle the Marine Corps way. In the classroom setting, Villa slowly came to realize that the recruits were unwilling to ask questions in front of the rest of the group. Each was afraid to appear ignorant before his classmates. Abdallah, Sala'am, Jaf, and Najm figured out each soldier's individual dialect as classes proceeded. After Villa finished his part of the session, he watched the interpreters take soldiers by the elbow to one side or to a discreet corner. Questions were handled privately, in casual hand gestures and hushed tones. After a thorough run through with the individual recruits, the interpreters signaled to Villa with quick nods that everyone who needed to be spoken to had been spoken to. Then they proceeded. Villa looked out over his charges. He hoped they would soon be ready to go onto the range with real ammunition. They had to be.

My life during that time largely involved making regular rounds with a set of personalities, Arab and American, civilian and military, across Kirkush. Major Zayn always came with me. We spent a lot of time at the so-called Donut Building, which was the logistics and payroll center for Kirkush. It had the name because it was shaped like one, not because it had them.

The very concept of "commerce" in much of the Middle East includes embezzlement almost as a matter of course, to a degree that most Americans are incapable of grasping. It's not considered immoral. The Iraqis socially normalize theft the way the French socially normalize adultery. A few years hence, the US Government Accountability Office was going to report that 190,000 AK-47s and other small arms provided to Iraqi security forces by the United States in 2004 and 2005 had disappeared. They were just gone. On the ground, we knew why: transactions of every sort in Iraq involved misappropriation. I'm not saying this to condemn the Iraqis. I'm explaining that what Americans call stealing was part of the culture.

The Iraqis had formalized a supply request system, with different men assigned to separate, often minor, functions. The network was designed not so much to spread out the workload of distributing goods and disbursing funds as it was to allow as many individuals as possible in the supply network to touch those goods and funds. To touch the flow was to skim from it. Literally. A box of one hundred ballpoint pens would go down to ninety-five pens, then ninety, then eighty-five, then eighty, as more men in the supply network touched it on its way to the Fifth Battalion. We observed this happening. The same was true, incidentally, for crates of bullets.

For the men in power who controlled the supplies, to grant requests for items was to earn favors. To grant control over the flow of supplies was to earn undying loyalty. To the Iraqis, deprived all their life of material things, any reliable stream of goods was like a torrent of largesse. American support, in particular, seemed to them a wildly infinite deluge. US tax money became payments to Lowdes Corporation, then became seemingly random matériel, then became individual Iraqi enrichment. It strengthened tribes. It granted leverage. It created bonds. It provisioned loyalty. It was power.

As such, the network that managed it grew on its own. Cousins recruited cousins, tribesmen bestowed goodwill to tribesmen, coreligionists secured control for coreligionists. There was little in Iraq that operated on the basis of merit. The entire political and economic realms were based on patronage. In politics, the powerful bestowed gifts on supporters, and supporters in turn continued to give them power. It was a spoils system. In economics, theft was a cultural expectation. The Iraqis had a word for it: *baksheesh.* It meant everybody took a cut. Navigating the baksheesh was a convoluted nightmare for Zayn and me.

"I hate this byzantine shit," I said to Zayn one day at the Donut. We were standing around, waiting for papers to get stamped by someone.

Zayn smiled and cocked his head at me. "That word . . . byz—"

"Oh, right," I laughed. Zayn recognized the word from the Byzantine Empire.

"When we say it, we mean something's complicated," I said. "Hard to follow."

When Zayn laughed, it recast his entire face. His joy was effusive, and it always made me smile, sometimes in spite of myself. Most of the time I was mad at some clusterfuck or other and did not feel like smiling.

"I know this word!" he said. "'Byzantine!'"

"Maybe we should call it Iraqine," I said, wanting to see how far I could push the joke. Zayn laughed again and slapped my shoulder. I smiled again.

We sometimes found ourselves steered to half a dozen different Iraqi officers all over Kirkush, ferreting out rubber stamps. Sometimes even that wasn't enough. The Lowdes general manager, a man named Luay al-Obeidi, sometimes still refused requests. My linear American mind found the exercise maddening. And criminal. I had Marines and Iraqis working their asses off to keep a soldier-making machine fueled and running, and these guys were giving me the runaround.

With time, between Zayn's Iraqi wherewithal and my American authority, we got better at working the system. We overwhelmed

Lowdes with requests for cleaning gear, tools, TVs, office supplies, uniforms, ammunition, anything and everything, sometimes things we did not need. We turned in more requests than they had time to read. I crossed my arms and glared. Zayn yelled and gesticulated. We created so much work and pressure that they signed or stamped things just to get rid of us.

The Americans who controlled the flow of supplies sometimes were little better than the Iraqis. We had suspected that the battalion's uniforms, boots, and packs would turn out to be crap, and we were right. The uniform depot was run by another US contractor, KBR, which at that time was a subsidiary of Halliburton, the company run just five years earlier by Vice President Cheney. He was still a stockholder. Halliburton got a bigger part of the US government spending on the Iraq War than any other company, sometimes without submitting competitive bids. We Americans had our own baksheesh.

KBR's employees were often retired US Army supply sergeants. These men treated everything as if it was their own. They created a system whereby we could exchange gear up to five days after issue with no questions asked. Beyond that short time limit, however, we had to fill out a statement of loss that explained why gear was unserviceable. We had recruits going on their first forced marches out in the desert after KBR's return deadline and learning that they had been provisioned with garbage gear. Mujanadin had their seams split in the seat as they marched. I saw Iraqis literally walk out of disintegrating boots. Packs fell apart, spilling the recruits' modest field gear all over the sunbaked ground. The recruits wore green temperate-zone camouflage on their native, beige landscape. Their "camouflage" actually made them stand out more against the desert backdrop. It was what the Iraqi Ministry of Defense provided. Sometimes it helped us to laugh. But none of it was funny. Mujanadin used safety pins and duct tape to hold together sleeves and boots. One recruit finished a twelve-mile march through the desert in flip-flops without complaining. His feet swelled like they would burst the flimsy straps.

Still, the Americans denied our requests. One shop manager was a crusty former supply sergeant from Texas. He wore a drooping white mustache that bordered on silly. To my mind, he saw his primary duty as not to supply the coalition troops around him but to ensure that KBR's precious stores weren't pilfered.

"You don't want me to decide you ain't nothin' but a slicky boy," he told Zayn and me in a drawl. The term is an old one from the Korean War, one that quartermasters used to refer to Korean civilians who tried to survive by pilfering American supplies. To the Texan, just about everybody was a slicky boy. That included Zayn and me. He told me as much to my face when I showed up with requests to replace another batch of disintegrating uniforms: "Yep, just another slicky boy."

I knew it. I knew I was going to hear it from this fucking guy. Like I needed this.

"Hold on a second," I said in a clip. "I am not selling gear. I am not trying to get anything over on you. I am a major in the US Marine Corps. I am trying to accomplish my goddamned mission."

The man smirked behind his ridiculous mustache. He was a civilian. Like all the American contractors, he made a lot more money than I did. He did not care that I was a Marine major. As for Zayn, the KBR man had no regard for any Iraqi officer of any rank. But as the situation with our men's uniforms and boots grew worse—as it became obscene, really—and as KBR's lack of concern for my men became something I referred to as "negligence," my anger and sense of urgency started getting through. Even the Texas shop manager slowly learned to take Zayn and me seriously.

Other advisers dealt with their own bureaucratic obstacles. Villa had to submit written requests for time on the firing range. He repeatedly detailed time, date, unit, purpose, ordnance, number of vehicles, number of personnel, and more. But Villa jumped the hoops as needed. It was time, he had decided, for his riflemen to head onto the range with their rifles.

The Iraqis were eager, but they had bad habits. They thought about guns in a way that was radically different from the way Marines did. To them, the AK-47 was power, pure and simple. It was loud, reliable, and infused with authority. In the Middle East, a gun is foremost something that confers status. It is not a tool. The Russian AK-47, ubiquitous in the world's war zones, was the noisemaker at Iraqi weddings and funerals. It was the emblem of power for the armed men who came and went in Iraq, just as they had in the Middle East, with various arms, for centuries. The advisers' outlook on the AK-47 was different. It was the rifle of our adversaries, everywhere Marines fought. It would be fair to say that, as United States Marines, a big part of our normal job was to kill men who carried AK-47s. But there in Iraq, we took our philosophy toward weaponry and applied it to the AK-47. We would use our Marine Corps training to reintroduce these Iraqis to their own rifle.

Villa started his hands-on instruction without ammunition. It took place outdoors, on the wastelands of Kirkush. He taught the Iraqis how to take the AK-47 apart. Demonstrations came first. They watched his hands, then applied their own to the same tasks. He worked tirelessly, tediously, with groups and individuals. The translators shouted Arabic and Kurdish instructions, their voices rising in the new outdoor setting. Sergeant Major Iskander and his Iraqi NCOs watched Villa as well, memorizing his methods. Officially, the recruits belonged to them, not to Villa. But for now they deferred to him.

Voices seem small in the wide desert flats. It's the reason the Arabs spoke in what seemed to us such loud voices to begin with. There was no such thing as an inside voice among the Iraqis. Villa yelled over a landscape that tried to swallow his words.

"Insert the clip!"

"Hod al-rasas fi al-rashash!"

They obeyed. They learned. One mujanad. Then another.

"Let me see your firing position," Villa shouted.

"Khaleeni ashoof maskak li al-silah!"

Another. Another. The sun in its vicious arc pounded on them. The recruits learned from Villa how to fire; the NCOs learned from Villa how to teach. What had been one American instructor became several instructors teaching in the American fashion. They went through their paces.

Another soldier, and another. All eight hundred of our men.

Villa gauged their faces, watched their concentration. They needed to understand the AK-47 as a utilitarian device. A deadly tool, but a tool nonetheless. One seemed to understand, then another. Did they? Villa pushed them, reaching into his past, dredging up memories of American instructors who coached him on other fields, green fields, in the rites of weaponry.

Live-fire exercises would tell him more. The Iraqis had much to unlearn. They shot blindly around corners. They fired from the hip, rather than the shoulder. They sprayed bullets, rather than aiming shots. They thought of fully automatic fire as easier, more gratifying than controlled bursts of well-placed rounds. They thought of the AK-47 as some sort of bullet-spraying scepter. Villa needed them to think of it as an extension of themselves, of their very skeletons. Villa's hundreds of AK-47s remained set to fire one round at a time. Bullets were counted and rationed. Villa held the Iraqis accountable for each one. We learned quickly that some of them were likely to hoard bullets for sale on the black market. We had to keep track. Any round that went missing could come right back at us, loosed over Kirkush's walls like murderous rain.

Targets in black and white stood fifty meters downrange, a bank of brown earth behind them to catch the rounds. The American advisers, Iskander, and his NCOs strolled behind the recruits. The men lay flat and fired five times downrange. Targets were checked and rechecked. Villa wanted the mujanadin to worry about accuracy. It was how they were judged. Accuracy—where a bullet actually travels—had always been an afterthought for them. They needed to learn intent, concentration, specificity.

"Keep your focus on that target downrange, soldier!" Villa leaned over them as they lay prone on the ground, shouting at the backs of their helmets, hot breath over their scalps, merciless.

Afterward, they went through the vehicle program, another course of Villa's design. We knew they would be spending a lot of time traveling by truck across Iraq's endless flats. Villa taught them what to do when they got shot at: One mujanad handled the steering wheel. One sat in the passenger seat. When the bullets come at you, hit the brakes. Halt the vehicle. Return fire through the open window on the side where the attackers are. Send the other man out the opposite-side door. Second man follows, sliding across the seat. Get behind the engine block, return fire. Create distance from the vehicle—which is what shooting attackers' eyes will be drawn to—and take a new firing position flat on the ground. Act as a team. Cover each other. Villa ran them through their drills, screaming, shouting, as forceful a presence as the sun itself.

The 'terps, getting into the spirit of things, shouted when the advisers shouted. Control. Aim. Forget everything you thought you knew. It isn't the weapon that makes you powerful, it's your handling of it. And it doesn't make you "powerful," it makes you effective. It does not make you a man, it makes you an infantryman. Villa drilled on. That is the essence of military training: repetition. Drilling until it is second nature, a fluidity that happens faster than thought. They drilled on. We all drilled on.

We knew that one day soon we had to be able to look upon these men and honestly call them infantry. The new Iraq's infantry. Our infantry.

5

WASTA

IT'S AMAZING HOW FAR sharing a meal can go. Kirkush taught me the true meaning of the expression *breaking bread*.

Curt Williamson urged all the advisers to take at least some of our meals with the Iraqis. I started eating with the officers and NCOs, usually accompanied by Zayn. I began to enjoy the Iraqi food. Warm flat bread called *khubz* or leavened bread known as *samoon* accompanied every meal. Finely chopped cucumber was blended with tomato and onion salad. Sweet rice with jasmine or cardamom came in heaps. Raisins topped curry. Steam rose from roasted lamb or chicken, or a stew of lamb, tomatoes, and eggplant called *tabsi bathenjan*. The servers brought bottled water, a can of cola, and a piece of fruit. I amused the Iraqis by asking, "Aandek mileh?" (May I have the salt?) My Arabic made them chuckle. Every meal ended with a cup of chai. Several of the advisers acquired a taste for the scalding, sweet drink.

For the Iraqis, sitting down to eat with someone carried more meaning than mere sustenance. It went way beyond "chow." As we broke bread with them, we ceased being strangers.

Slowly I began to discern the divisions that separated the Iraqis from each other. The most obvious was rank. The officers strictly separated themselves from the enlisted men, to a degree much more stringent than we knew in the Marine Corps. Every expression, every gesture reinforced their separateness and their superiority. Their attitude toward the NCOs—those sergeants who acted as intermediaries between the officers and the mujanadin—was only slightly less condescending. The second-most-obvious partition among the Iraqis was ethnicity. The Arabs considered the Kurds inferior and their loyalty suspect. The Kurds considered the Arabs inferior and their motives dangerous. The Arabs spoke Arabic, and the Kurds spoke two dialects of Kurdish. The couple dozen mujanadin from other ethnic groups—Assyrians, Turkmen, and the like—clung to each other for safety. The toughest schism to detect—but probably the most dangerous—was the religious divide. The Sunni-versus-Shiite division of twenty-first-century Iraq made me think of the Catholic-versus-Protestant division of sixteenth-century Europe. The Sunnis and the Shiites split apart almost at the very beginning of Islam, in the seventh century, over a dispute about who should succeed the Prophet Muhammad. Each side considers itself the true Islam and accuses the other of apostasy. Fourteen centuries later, the dissension was just as real, right in front of me.

The fact that the Kurds were mostly Sunnis—and so had that in common with half the battalion's Arabs—scrambled things up that much more. We advisers had been taught about none of these rifts before we left the States. Probably nobody in the military knew to teach them to us. We learned on the fly.

Making things even more turbulent were a few basic facts about Iraq and our war. Most Iraqis are Shiites. But Saddam Hussein and his old power structure were Sunni. Both the Kurds and the Shiite Arabs resented the Sunni Arabs in a deadly serious way. Then there were our enemies, the insurgents. Most of them were Sunnis. But in the south and around Baghdad, they were usually Shiites who were allied with Iran. The two insurgent sects also were fighting each other. In some places, subsects were fighting each other. The Kurds were loyal to the Americans, but their Peshmerga warriors were fighting insurgents in the north without consulting with us.

That said, the Iraqis' bigotry seemed to evaporate when they dealt with each other one-on-one. Like prejudiced people everywhere, in the abstract, their words were a lot tougher and meaner than their face-to-face behavior. A Kurd may casually refer to Arabs as "rabbits," because they're good for hunting and killing, but then he'll be friends with an individual Arab. A Sunni may like saying that Shiites are wannabe Iranians, but then he'll greet a Shiite acquaintance with a kiss on both cheeks. Zayn, for example, was a Sunni, but he shared a room and was close with two Shiite officers: Mohammed Najm, a quiet, competent major from Karbala, and Aof Raheem, a brash, incompetent major from Nasiriyah. I stayed up with the three of them late nights, taking in everything I could. We sat on their scratchy wool blankets and talked about religion and the war and America, consuming sweet juice they called *aseer kokh*—I later learned it was peach juice—and chocolate-covered cookies. The Iraqis loved talking about politics and religion. They went on and on about those two topics more freely with the Americans than we Americans are willing to do with each other. The Iraqis were intensely curious about the United States. So we talked, long into the night. Outside, it was 110 degrees. Inside, they turned the AC down as low as it would go. My teeth chattered, and they laughed at me.

I needed to learn as much as I could. I felt rushed to learn. Military units need cohesion. They do not need baked-in discord. If we were going to overcome the Fifth Battalion's many partitions, we would have to do it on two levels: On a high level, we had to make them loyal to the concept of a unified Iraq where everyone is equal under the law. In other words, we had to make them Western. (Nobody back in the States had told us how to do that, either.) On a basic level, we had to work man by man, creating something cohesive between individuals that could supersede the cultural schisms. That meant building relationships between Americans and Iraqis, and building trust among the Iraqis themselves. We had to find the best, most committed leaders who could hold the battalion together. The ancient schisms weren't going away.

All the cultural barriers, all the mixed loyalties and ancient animosities, made one man perhaps more important than any other in the battalion: Sergeant Major Iskander, the haughty NCO who berated me for not providing cleaning supplies. Iskander was a Kurd, former Peshmerga, and the senior noncommissioned officer in the battalion. Here's what that means: Iskander was not an officer. He was an enlisted man. But he was the highest-ranking enlisted man in the entire battalion. So even though a young lieutenant may technically outrank him, he didn't *really* outrank him. Iskander moved easily in both the officers' and the enlisted men's worlds. He was revered by the enlisted men. He was "one of them." He watched out for them, and even better than most American sergeants major I've known, Iskander knew how to cultivate a perception among the men that he was their guardian. Even the highest-ranking Iraqi officers had to respect Iskander, whether they liked it or not. Some of them did not.

Older than his thirty years, with a voice deepened by unfiltered Iraqi cigarettes, Iskander was a slight but well-proportioned man, a couple of inches taller than me. He projected a regal bearing, with his beret and his sheathed dagger and his high boots. His name was a Middle Eastern form of Alexander—as in Alexander the Great, the Macedonian conqueror who swept through those deserts 2,400 years before the Americans.

Iskander was a survivor of Saddam Hussein's al-Anfal, the dictator's "final solution" to the Kurdish question. He joined the Peshmerga at fourteen. He lost brothers fighting against the old Iraqi Army. He lost cousins, nephews, and nieces to starvation and exposure. He grew up in camps and caves, hiding from the Sunni Arabs who led Saddam's military and the Mukhabarat secret police. Iskander and others told a story that he had once shot down an Iraqi Army helicopter with a rocket-propelled grenade. He had been tortured by the Mukhabarat, and he had a tremor in one arm from when the secret police smashed his elbow with a hammer. Sometimes the tremor got so bad that it was hard to ignore when I talked to him. Iskander was not afraid to stand up to the Iraqi officers or their American advisers.

He quickly became a sort of emotional center of gravity for the battalion. That meant everybody: Sunnis, Shiites, Kurds, Arabs, Yazidis, and Turkmen—they all counted on him to represent their interests to the battalion leadership. The sergeant major was a standout not just among the enlisted men but even among the Kurds, who demonstrated early on that they were the most dedicated group in the battalion. Iskander was critical for Curt and me if we were going to hold our unit together.

Iskander had what the Iraqis call *wasta*. It's a concept that we don't have a word for in English. But wasta is hugely important in the Middle East. It represents a man's influence, or clout. It means he can provide. Therefore, it means that he receives respect. Put roughly, wasta is a man's ability to lead, to get things done and to fix his followers' problems. In the movie *Lawrence of Arabia*, there's a famous scene in which the desert warrior Auda abu Tayi, portrayed by Anthony Quinn, explains what it means to be a leader of a tribe. The movie is fiction, but it's based on Lawrence's life among the Arabs. Abu Tayi was a real man, and he taught Lawrence that being a fierce fighter is not enough; a leader must also be a provider. As Quinn says in the film, "Seventy-five men have I killed with my own hands in battle. I scatter, I burn my enemies' tents. I take away their flocks and herds. The Turks pay me a golden treasure, yet I am poor. Because *I am a river to my people!*"

And "the people" roar their approval of Auda abu Tayi. Wasta is a leader's worth. If you can provide, then you have wasta, and therefore have the right to lead. If you do not have the ability to provide, then you do not have wasta, and are not worthy as a leader. Men who want wasta—and in Arab cultures, it's only males who can get it—understand that to gain status, they must provide. The art of Arab leadership is about accumulating as much wealth and influence as possible, by whatever means, and then selectively doling it out in a way that engenders loyalty without exhausting the trove.

Iskander didn't give a shit that CMATT headquarters in Kirkush didn't have cleaning supplies, thereby precluding me from delivering any. What mattered to Iskander was that I wasn't coming through. In his eyes, there was no excuse for not coming through, because I was an American, and every Iraqi knew that the Americans had more material wealth than they knew what to do with.

So why was I not delivering? To Iskander, I was not worthy. I did not have wasta.

I think it says a lot about the forethought that went into the Iraq War that my team of Marines, desperate to understand our Middle East of 2004, was dependent on a Hollywood epic from 1962 and a British war diary from 1916. But we worked with what we had. And we kept talking to the Iraqis. We kept talking to them and talking to them and goddamned talking to them. We stayed up late over cups of chai. We spoke in halting English over plates of cucumber. We broke bread.

Not long after the advisers began taking meals with the Iraqis, however, problems started, and the problems seemed related to the meals themselves. One of us would come down with diarrhea for two or three days. Soon after, another adviser would complain about stomach cramps. Then more than one of us would be hit at the same time. Abdominal pain became part of our existence, another discomfort in the life of an adviser. We laughed at our day-to-day maladies. Reilly, who got sick more than once, classified our intestinal afflictions into categories: the "Baghdad trots," the "Iraqi two-step," and "the lumpuckeroo."

"That's when it feels like your eyeballs are being sucked out of your head through your asshole," Reilly said, and we all broke out laughing. Reilly grew up a diplomat's son in Afghanistan and Thailand, and he knew what bad water or spoiled food could do to a person.

Then the Iraqis started getting sick in groups. As days passed, more and more soldiers were sick at any given time. And it stopped being a joke.

Curt and I decided that Captain Hummons was the right man to investigate the problem. He worked every day with the battalion's operations officer. The Ops O held responsibility for the day-to-day functioning of the battalion. At that time, the Ops O was one of Zayn's roommates, Maj. Aof Raheem. He was a member of the well-connected, Shiite al-Harbia tribe. He had been a lowly corporal in the old Iraqi Army. All the officers, American and Iraqi alike, suspected that the major had been promoted to his job and rank because of his family name. Or maybe by a computing error—some staff officer working an Excel spreadsheet in the Green Zone might have mixed him up with some unfortunate major who got made into a corporal.

As things were supposed to work, Hummons was to advise Aof, who in turn was to plan the battalion's training and schedule on his own. In truth, Hummons did the Ops O's job outright as much as he advised on it. All of us encountered that problem to some extent. We struggled to wean the Iraqis from dependence on us. Curt reminded us of what Lawrence wrote in his "27 Articles":

> Do not try to do too much with your own hands. Better the Arabs do it tolerably than that you do it perfectly. It is their war, and you are to help them, not to win it for them. Actually, also, under the very odd conditions of Arabia, your practical work will not be as good as, perhaps, you think it is.

At first we suspected our gastrointestinal problems stemmed from the food. The meat was rarely fresh. Refrigeration in Kirkush was nearly nonexistent. There were no food-quality standards or health inspectors in Iraq. Lowdes Corporation had a contract to supply food to the base. Lowdes bought cut-rate meats in Baghdad and transported them to Kirkush in filthy trucks. Shipments came once or twice a week, depending on how dangerous the roads were.

Hummons started by inspecting the Iraqi kitchen. Civilian Iraqis hauled in bloody lamb carcasses and turned them on spits. A Kurdish company that subcontracted with Lowdes provided the crew that prepared and served meals. The kitchen manager, a potbellied man with the unlikely name Barrakat Bebo Berbo, was related to most of his staff. Hummons assumed from the men's lighter coloring that they were Kurds. The platoon-sized crew, some thirty strong, scurried among ovens and pantries in bare feet. Hummons saw nothing wrong with the way the food was prepared, though. Regardless of the quality of the food, it was well cooked.

Captain Hummons began walking through the Iraqi barracks whenever the mujanadin were marching on the drill deck or training outside. The empty rooms lent themselves to careful midmorning inspections. Hummons passed set after set of double-racks—bunk beds—that stood in recruits' rooms, four to a side. Not even the buzz of fluorescent lights broke the quiet as he walked the aisles. We killed the power when the soldiers were not in the barracks. We needed to divert our electricity to the classrooms when they took instruction.

The captain realized he was seeing something again and again. It was barely discernible at first; he never would have noticed it, were it not for its repetition. They were tiny smears at eye level on the cement barracks walls, standing in relief against light-blue paint. Sometimes cross-shaped. Sometimes only a dot. Always less than an inch in diameter. Never in groups. Dark.

Hummons trained his eye to seek them out. He found more. Next to a bathroom mirror. Midway down a hall. On the back of a door. The type of thing someone would dismiss as random, were they not appearing so often. The "tick marks," as Hummons called them, indicated a human hand at work. They bore intent. Maybe even function.

Hummons asked Reilly to help him. They began talking to the Iraqis, looking for clues. They started with the interpreters. They moved from there to the NCOs and finally to the mujanadin themselves. Hummons and Reilly took men aside and, as discreetly as possible, asked questions: Do you know these marks? Have you seen them before? Who would make them? What is their purpose?

At first all the Iraqis denied knowing anything about the marks. But as Hummons and Reilly persisted, some of the shy, intimidated mujanadin began opening up. What they said seemed incredible. But it was repeated time and time again. The marks, the Iraqis told them, were human feces. They were made, they added, by the battalion's Yazidis. None of us knew what a Yazidi was. We gathered that they were some kind of subset of the Kurds. At that point, we didn't know if we had run into a bizarre cult ritual, or if someone was trying to sabotage the Fifth Battalion from within. We couldn't have large groups of men sick for days at a time. Sick men are casualties, just like men who are wounded. This was serious.

I went straight to Zayn. He twisted his face and told me the Yazidis were "devil worshippers."

"They are unclean," he said. The Yazidis, he told me, were from northern Iraq, in the mountains. They kept their distance from Arabs. Zayn explained that we probably had more than fifty of them in the battalion. Also, the contracted kitchen crew were not Kurds, as Hummons had assumed. "They also are Yazidis."

I dropped in at the CMATT building. The North Carolina brigade had computers that soldiers were allowed to use in fifteen-minute bursts for reading and sending e-mails home. They allotted a single machine for web browsing. That made it the only computer in Kirkush that could be used for Internet searches.

My impromptu investigation (on the 2004 Internet) yielded no details on Yazidis more recent than the 1930s, when a group of French anthropologists lived among them. I would learn that most of Yazidi culture had changed little since then. The Yazidi people number fewer than five hundred thousand. Most dwell along an invisible demographic fault line that lies between Kurds and Arabs near the Iraq-Syria border. Trapped between two tectonic plates of humanity, the Yazidis have been persecuted for centuries. They are not Muslims. They believe in one God, but they also revere an entity called Malak Ta'us, who is an angel. To devout Muslims, angel worship is a serious offense. The Arabs and Kurds also conflated the angel Malak Ta'us with the fallen angel, or devil. It all added up to a lot of hate for the Yazidis. (Today, ISIS militia slaughter, enslave, or rape Yazidis wherever they find them.)

After a dozen conversations with the Iraqis, Hummons and Reilly slowly arrived at a conclusion about the tick marks. It jibed with what I was able to find online. The explanation was bizarre to American ears: The Yazidis believed the marks scared off evil spirits. They were designed for spiritual protection.

I briefed the advisory team on the Yazidis at the evening meeting we always held before chow.

"The Yazidis have cultural habits that are resulting in the spread of serious bacteria into the barracks and the chow hall," I reported. "It does not appear, however, that the Yazidis are an intentional threat."

The Marines shook their heads and rolled their eyes. It wasn't that they had a problem with the Yazidis. It was that the whole episode, the unpredictability of it, the whole goddamned thing, reminded us of how little we knew about where we were. We had discovered an ethnic group that smeared shit on walls. And they were making the food. If *this* could happen, what the fuck *couldn't*? What else would we have to deal with? It underscored how ignorant we remained of our world. It reminded us how far we were from home. It was a distance measured in more than miles. We attacked problems. We figured out solutions as we moved. Challenges rose up and threw themselves at us from places outside of all context. Nothing in our experience could prepare us for these problems; nothing in our history could compare.

On a hot night in May, I relaxed in the advisers' quarters with a copy of Charles Tripp's *A History of Iraq*. A strange call came up the stairwell from down on the second floor, where the interpreters slept.

"Ex-squeeeeze me," the voice said, echoing off the cement walls. The speaker attempted a respectful shout. It was not the voice of an interpreter.

I set down my book and glanced at my Timex. Slightly after midnight. I had just returned from a meeting with the Iraqi officers. I planned to rise at 5 AM for battalion physical training, or PT. The other Marines slept.

I went to the stairs and looked down. It was Sergeant Major Iskander. I knew he didn't speak good English, but he had decided to skip the interpreters and speak directly to the Americans. He wasn't going to climb to the third floor, either. It was an American sanctuary, and all the Iraqis knew it.

"Junoodi mareethe!" Iskander said, trying to explain himself in animated Arabic. I knew enough by then to figure out what he meant: *Soldiers are sick.* Judging from his urgency, it was a lot of soldiers.

After lights-out, the management of sudden nighttime crises fell to whoever happened to be awake. At that point in Kirkush, I was getting by on about five hours of sleep a night. I didn't relish the idea of handling sick recruits with our less-than-meager medical resources. "OK," I said down to Iskander. "Hold on."

I awoke some of the advisers, but they were beat. Curt spoke without opening his eyes.

"You take care of it," he said. "You're the S-4," meaning I was the logistics officer.

I put on pants and boots, walked down the stairs, and gestured to Iskander to show me the problem.

Unpleasant is too weak a word to describe the scene in the barracks. Recruits lay curled on their beds, moaning and clutching stomachs. Room after room held stricken men. They ignored my arrival. In one bathroom, men hunched forward in their gray PT shorts and T-shirts, getting sick everywhere: on themselves, on the tiles, in their Middle Eastern-style toilets. The stench struck me like an eye-watering punch to the nose.

Iskander raised his arms, gripping an imaginary steering wheel, laying his palm on an invisible horn. He bleated out honking sounds. Throwing out English words in ones and twos, he mimed a plan of action. We needed to drive the men to the Kirkush medical facility.

I agreed. Iskander ran off to get the watch officer on duty, a reliable Sunni captain and first cousin of Zayn who bore the awkward name, in this new Iraqi Army, of Saddam Hussein.

We had a lot of sick men. Maybe fifty. Some appeared to be in danger of dehydration. Our "motor pool" at that point consisted of three vehicles: a two-and-a-half-ton truck we borrowed from the North Carolinians; an Indian-made Ashok Leyland flatbed truck, complete with right-side steering wheel, that we got from Lowdes; and a Nissan pickup with red racing stripes that we got from CMATT. Nobody awake was qualified to drive the deuce-and-a-half, and the flatbed would likely end up spilling stricken Iraqis all over the dirt roads of Kirkush. That left the Nissan.

Within ten minutes, the three of us were dressed. Saddam had the first load of soldiers, maybe a half dozen, pile into the bed of the truck. He squeezed into the cab with Iskander and me. Saddam seemed to be enjoying himself, smiling behind his thick mustache. Iskander had the wheel. We trucked the first group of mujanadin to a small Iraqi clinic on the far side of the base. The dry landscape of Kirkush was stamped with dogleg streets. It seemed we couldn't drive anywhere without making two rights and two lefts.

A half-dozen Iraqis staffed the clinic. Iskander, Saddam, and I jumped from our pickup to find none of them awake. We marched down the halls, banging doors until we roused them. They had a total of four beds and four saline IV bags. Our human cargo overwhelmed them. We decided to take the rest of our recruits to an American medical clinic run by the North Carolina Guard.

Iskander clambered behind the wheel. He blared the horn constantly, despite the absence of pedestrian or vehicle traffic on the road at that time of night. Headlights glared at full brightness. Our radio blasted a high-pitched, wailing Arabic song, the volume as high as it would go. That was the way the Iraqis were: they ran everything at full blast. These were men who grew up with nothing, and they took full advantage of everything when they could, as they could. The radio didn't distract Iskander, and I couldn't see how it was going to make his driving any worse. Saddam giggled like a joyrider every time we cornered, the tires sliding. Our human cargo groaned through the cab wall behind us. From time to time, Iskander slowed and called into the back to make sure no one had fallen out. They moaned. We moved on.

We arrived at the National Guard hospital. The American med staff, most of them women, launched into a full, mass-casualty drill: they tied on masks, broke out saline bags, and shouted to one another. Saddam spoke good English. I grew impressed with him as the night wore on. He took responsibility for the sick recruits, organizing the truckloads and recording their names in a notebook. After deliveries to the North Carolinians, he spotted a blonde American nurse and threw out cheesy pickup lines he must have learned from American television. She ignored him.

I didn't sleep that night. After we finished our many deliveries of sick men, the best thing to do was get out of the way of the North Carolina medical team. I asked a physician officer if she would convey a request to the Green Zone for me. There were US preventive medicine experts in Baghdad who could carry out an investigation. A request coming from the doctor was more likely to get a response than a plea from a Marine adviser to an Iraqi battalion. She agreed to help.

We got back to the Fifth Battalion pod at 6 AM, when the rest of the men were wrapping up their morning PT exercises. I briefed Curt. At 9:00, the Marine advisers and twenty or thirty Iraqi officers and NCOs gathered for our regular staff and commanders meeting. Curt sat at a long table with Jassim Thammin, the battalion CO. Reilly sat with Iskander. Hummons was paired with Aof Raheem. I was next to Zayn.

Several discussion items lay ahead that morning, but the mass food poisoning preempted the agenda. Hummons, who spoke first, got straight to the point. He didn't often temper his language, and as soon as his words came out, I knew they were going to make problems.

"So what are we going to do about these fucking Yazidians smearing their shit all over the walls?" he demanded.

Yazidians. He just made up a word, "Yazidians." My stomach dropped.

One NCO in the room, a sergeant major, was a devout Yazidi. He was the highest-ranking and therefore highest-profile Yazidi in the battalion. In an Iraqi culture that generally despised his people, and especially within a military culture that didn't trust Yazidis in its ranks, the sergeant major had to play the role of advocate. At that moment, he literally leaped to his people's defense, jumping up from his chair.

"This is not the fault of the Yazidis!" he screamed in English. His voice had a tattered sound to it. "Yazidis very, very good!"

The room exploded in shouts. It wasn't just the Yazidi sergeant major. Everyone, it seemed, was instantly yelling. We Americans still were unaccustomed to the Iraqis' mood swings, their habit of all shouting at once. The Yazidi sergeant major yelled at Hummons, at Curt, at me. Iraqi officers shouted at the Yazidi sergeant major. Other sergeants tried to restrain him. Some cursed Yazidis in general. Kurds shouted at Arabs. Men pushed at each other and swore violent oaths. The interpreters didn't bother trying to keep up.

Holy fucking shit, I thought. Every man in the room was strapped with a loaded sidearm. I stood from my chair involuntarily. The Americans were stunned. Hummons, startled by what he had set off, threw his eyes quickly from face to face.

The panic in the Yazidi sergeant major's voice and the fact that he was yelling in English told me that he was pleading with us, the advisers. He didn't want the Americans to despise him and his people as much as the other Iraqis already did. I looked at Jassim Thammin, the battalion CO. He sat, impassive.

Then Ahmed Nu'uman, the battalion's number-two man, snuffed out a cigarette and stood. The young major silently lifted his arms and calmly cast his eyes over the room. Right, then left, then right again. He said nothing but raised his brows. Men began to go quiet. One by one, they looked his way. The youthful but calm Ahmed Nu'uman was a problem solver. His practical nature was a refreshing counterpoint to Jassim Thammin's old-army authoritarianism. I never knew Ahmed Nu'uman to raise his voice, and he didn't then. He spoke in Arabic. Arkan interpreted for me.

"Gentlemen, let us remember where we are," he said. His voice was level and deep. His meaning was clear: this is a military meeting, not a bazaar.

And amazingly, that was enough. Just like that, the room calmed.

That was also the end of it. After calming themselves, the Iraqis decided on no further course of action to fix the problem. What they wanted to do about Yazidis wiping shit on the walls was exactly nothing. They didn't want to think about Yazidis. We Americans sat back, stunned by the emotions that had whiplashed through the room over the last three minutes. We slowly realized nothing was going to get done. The meeting ended.

I told Curt about the request for an investigation that I put in through the North Carolinians. The preventive medicine team arrived from the Green Zone the following day. Their report came two days after that. The primary cause of the outbreak, they determined, was a lack of hygiene among the kitchen staff. None of the Yazidis washed their hands before preparing meals. The dining hall also lacked washbasins that the recruits could use. A particularly galling problem was that no one had arranged living quarters for the kitchen workers. Like the electricity men Mushtaq and Fouad, the Yazidi contractor workers had no choice: they slept where they worked.

I commandeered a big empty room across a foyer from the chow hall. We designated it the living quarters for Barrakat Bebo Berbo's crew. Gunnery Sergeant Webster, Major Zayn, and I worked our supply connections. We scored wrought-iron single beds, mattresses, linens, and pillows from CMATT. We got personal lockers for the workers from the Iraqi brigade headquarters. From the KBR warehouse, I got my hands on thirty pairs of cheap Chinese-made sneakers.

"You must wear these in the kitchen when you're working," I told them, holding up a pair of the sneakers. "Always. If I see you without them on your feet in the kitchen or dining room, I will insist that Barrakat send you away."

The crew focused far more on the carrot than the stick. They were beside themselves with happiness that I brought new shoes. No one in Kirkush, maybe no one anywhere, had ever given them anything for nothing. They slipped on their sneakers and walked up and down their new quarters, excitedly showing them to one other, even though all the shoes were identical. They shook my hand and kissed my cheeks. Their gratitude moved me.

Next I tried to explain the concept of bacteria to the Yazidis. They had never heard of any such thing. They refused to believe that bacteria existed. They couldn't see them, and I couldn't prove their existence. Invisible, tiny creatures on their hands? Some laughed. Others inspected their fingers suspiciously. I watched them. We were in a part of the world where washing before prayer was a sacred responsibility, but washing before cooking wasn't considered. With Barrakat's help, though, and after much difficult translation about miniscule organisms that lived on their bodies, I got the crew to hear me out. At a new washbasin we had rush-installed in the foyer next to the dining hall, I demonstrated how to lather up with hot water and soap. From that day forward, a change came over the crew. Even though they were civilians, they began to consider themselves part of the battalion. They were proud. They strutted. All of us could see it.

We also established a small general store where recruits could buy cigarettes, toiletries, and sweets. The other two Iraqi battalions had similar stores. Our proprietor was an obsequious fellow named Mr. Subhay. When he came in, he wanted to charge outrageous prices. I insisted that he give me his price list, which I took to Zayn and Iskander, the two Iraqis I trusted most. They gave me fair prices for Mr. Subhay's goods. Zayn and I went back to him and explained that we were setting his prices. He complained that it wasn't fair—the other battalions weren't setting prices for their general stores. I explained that his store existed for the benefit of the battalion, not the other way around. I also explained something basic about American capitalism: soldiers from the other battalions would be free to buy from him as well, and they would likely do so in large numbers because he was going to be under-selling their own general stores. So his profit margins may tighten, I said, but he would more than make up for it in sales volume.

"And the best part is that I guarantee that no one, not me, not any Iraqi officer, will take a cut of your sales," I said.

A grin spread over his face, and his dark eyes glittered. He and Zayn decided the arrangement was fair.

We then arranged for barbers to visit once a week. At first the recruits kept their hair short, but not Marine Corps short. We took it as a major compliment when some of the recruits began emulating our high-and-tight cuts. To wear their hair that way was completely alien to their culture. To the Iraqis, the Americans' almost hairless heads and faces were a bizarre rejection of masculinity itself.

I didn't mean to do it, but I showed Iskander and others that I could, in fact, provide. We Americans could make good things happen. That impression grew as days passed without more men getting sick. It was like something silently blooming. I felt like they were thinking more and more: *Maybe there's something to this "bacteria" thing after all. Maybe the Americans know things worth learning. Maybe the advisers aren't all that bad.* I wasn't trying to gain wasta. And nobody ever came up to me and said, "Hey, Major Zacchea, congratulations on the new wasta." But by doing my job, I had gained some trust. So had the others: Curt, Reilly, Webster, and Hummons—all of us.

Sergeant Major Iskander looked over his men as they took their heaps of rice in the chow hall. I watched him watch them. His left hand rested on the pommel of his sheathed dagger. He absentmindedly patted his right hand against his thigh a couple of times and caught my eye as he turned. He gave me a curt nod and moved along. A swirl of uniformed mujanadin sought tables for their trays, and they wordlessly parted for him as he passed. He walked with a slow, easy authority. Never again did Iskander tell me I was no good.

6

THE OTHER SIDE
OF THE WIRE

WE STOOD TOGETHER, ZAYN AND I. June's sun fixed itself on Kirkush with something like rage, the temperature better than 130 degrees. Heat uncoiled up out of the road.

Zayn and I watched a platoon of American engineers bend and strain on the merciless wasteland. They toiled methodically, trying to make peace with the angry daylight. A crane screeched with a load of steel-reinforced concrete Jersey barriers, two feet by four feet each. It released the heavy weight onto hard-baked earth. The engineers were National Guardsmen from North Carolina. Razor concertina wire glittered above their rising barrier.

I had a hard time accepting the scene before us. The National Guard barrier wasn't designed to protect Kirkush from insurgents. It couldn't be. It was not on the perimeter. It was deep within our sprawling base. The concrete and steel was designed to separate the North Carolinians from their Iraqi allies. My men. Our Iraqi battalion and we Marine advisers were on the same side of this war as our National Guard neighbors. We were stationed on the same base. But we were not on the same side of the concertina. Our Iraqi battalion had just lost a confrontation with my fellow Americans that had lasted the better part of two weeks. In my mind, the National Guard's barrier rose as monument to their victory.

Iraqis made the North Carolina National Guard's leadership uncomfortable. That included the Iraqi men of Fifth Battalion. It didn't matter to the National Guardsmen that they were themselves foreign tenants on an Iraqi base. It didn't even matter that in the six weeks since we had moved into our jumble of three- and four-story concrete buildings opposite the Guard, no Iraqi had ventured over to the American area.

The showdown had started a couple of weeks earlier. A Guard officer delivered a complaint to Curt at a regularly scheduled base meeting. Our Iraqis, the officer said, had been leering at female American soldiers as the women ran in PT shorts on the streets of Kirkush. Curt brought that message back to the rest of the Marines. In turn, we warned our Iraqi officers: instruct your NCOs and recruits to avoid any behavior toward American troops, especially women, that could be interpreted as aggressive. In Kirkush, everyone carried firearms. Always. We didn't want anyone shot over a misunderstanding.

The irony pissed me off. The only real, verifiable incident between our two units was an embarrassment for the Americans. On May 14, shortly after we formed the Fifth, one of our Iraqi barracks got an uninvited nighttime visitor. The soldier, likely no more than twenty-one years old, wore a gray US ARMY T-shirt. He walked the halls, opening doors. When he saw Iraqis, he pulled down his black shorts to unveil an erection.

"This is my ice-cream cone," he said. "Does anyone want to lick my ice-cream cone?"

The Iraqi barracks-duty NCO didn't know how to react to something so unworldly. He ran for Iskander, who was equally unsure about what to do. Iskander ran to find a Marine—any Marine. In the meantime, he told his men to monitor but not to touch the American. Our young interloper realized his mistake. He bolted. The Iraqi recruits gave chase at a distance. The pursuing Iraqis were hesitant to get too close to the American. Generally speaking, Iraqis are very tactile with each other. We found, however, that many Iraqis were reluctant to have physical contact with Americans, even including us advisers at first. Americans made them uncomfortable.

Curt and the tall Idahoan Reilly joined the chase and glimpsed the American soldier running through the night toward the North Carolina brigade area. They caught up to him. The American protested his innocence. He was just out for some PT, he said, and was inspecting the battalion because he saw something suspicious. His eyes darted from Marine to Marine.

"They're lying," he said. "They were threatening me."

Curt and Reilly took his name. Later they reported the incident to the North Carolinians. The young soldier was shipped out of Iraq. There's no surer way out of combat than asking a guy to suck your dick. The hapless soldier got his transfer to the First Civilian Division—our term for an administrative discharge.

Shortly after that, the Guardsmen began building their barrier. I first spotted them from the window of my quarters, which faced the road between us. A squad of engineers laid up concertina wire that winked in the sun. I went downstairs, opened the door onto the desiccated expanse, made my way over, and asked the men what they were doing. The one who spoke gave a literal answer: "Putting up concertina wire, sir."

"Why?"

"Orders, sir."

"Who ordered you to put up concertina wire?"

"Platoon commander."

I got a name. I found the man in their engineer battalion building. A first lieutenant. I ordered him to explain what was happening.

"We're putting up a concertina barrier, sir," he said. Maybe he thought I'd gotten the "field-grade lobotomy" that soldiers say is given to anyone promoted to major.

"Do you realize," I asked him, "that your concertina barrier is effectively walling off my battalion from the rest of the base?"

"Orders, sir."

"Well, I'm ordering you to stop. And if you keep building it, we'll dismantle it."

They stopped. All that remained at the site afterward were the upright steel posts meant to secure the wire. That night, a group of our Iraqi supply NCOs uprooted them and took them away. Zayn may have instigated that. I never asked. Regardless, we could put them to use.

A few days later, as Zayn and I drove to the Lowdes building to cajole and threaten the contractors for equipment, we saw the Guard engineers back out in the sun with their crane and Jersey barriers. This time they had a captain with them.

I ordered the truck to a halt and got out. Zayn followed me with a coltish hop. His eyes seemed even more deep-set than normal under lowered brows. The truck caught its gears and hauled itself away. The Guardsmen toiled on as we approached.

"What the hell is going on here?" I yelled.

The captain protested but backed off. Once again, the engineers halted construction. Once again, they left their posts behind. Once again, our Iraqis liberated the posts.

For the next few days, there was an uneasy peace in Kirkush between the new Iraqi Army and the North Carolina Army National Guard.

Then, the Guardsmen were at it again. A major oversaw the work this time, sweating and suffering as overseer in the day's oven, even if not as much as the engineers methodically exerting themselves before him. The American officer, a big-boned, pear-shaped man, held the same rank as me. Naturally, neither of us knew which of us was senior. My stride was intentional, purposeful. Zayn saw that, read it off me, and set his lean gait to the same motion. In a way, it was he, not I, who represented the Fifth, though I would do the talking. The major glared as we approached. We drew up, and he leaped to the offensive.

"We erected some posts here, and they disappeared!" He spoke directly at me, without acknowledging Zayn. "Why'd you let the Iraqis take them?" He put his hands on his ample hips and loomed over me.

An old bit of military slang came to my mind: *Gear adrift is a gift.* My soldiers, I decided, had tactically acquired needed materials.

"Don't you think it's kind of irresponsible to leave your posts here for anyone to take? I would think your company commander would be more accountable for his materials. I don't blame any Iraqis for taking them," I said. "This barrier is offensive."

"I am supervising the erection of this barrier. We will leave our posts in place tonight. If they're gone in the morning," he said, "we will place armed guards here."

His fight was up. He wanted to go to war. Would he really place armed guards on this barrier? What would their rules of engagement be? Would they be authorized to shoot? He seemed to see erecting the barrier as a life-or-death mission.

"I'm going to have to talk to your battalion commander," I told him.

"You do that," the major said. "He'll tell you the same thing."

Zayn and I turned and left without responding.

Before darkness fell, Zayn must have told his NCOs to lie low. I'll never know. That night, our men stayed on our side of the barrier. Calm returned. Maybe the Guard major decided, over the next forty-eight hours, that he had intimidated us. Regardless, the peace was temporary. Two nights after I confronted the major, a group of Zayn's soldiers grabbed wire cutters and sneaked the couple hundred yards to the barrier. They cut down the razor wire. They added the wire and more posts to our supply-deprived unit's inventory of stolen goods.

After that, the North Carolina brigade went directly to Curt. They complained that the Iraqis were undoing their work and stealing materials. A South Carolinian himself, Curt calmed them through his patient self-possession alone. In turn, though, he ordered me to back off. He would speak to the battalion commander, he said. I passed along word to Zayn, who, in turn, passed along word to his fellow officers, including his superiors and the Iraqi NCOs. Another respite came. But I knew the Guardsmen were planning their next move.

Curt and I met with the brigade engineer, a lieutenant colonel. Curt reminded this ranking officer that the only verifiable problem between our units to that point had come about when one of his Guardsmen had solicited oral sex from several of our Iraqi recruits. No accusations of leering, unwanted advances, catcalls, aggressive behavior, or inappropriate contact blamed on our Iraqi soldiers had been verified by anyone. We felt the Iraqis we advised were more likely to be awed and afraid of American women than the American women under his command were to be afraid of the Iraqi recruits.

The lieutenant colonel, a man in his late forties, glared at Curt and spoke with slow intent.

"My brigade commander, the *brigadier general*"—he emphasized the man's rank—"requires continual position improvement," he said in a Piedmont drawl. "He has stated his number-one priority is force protection. I am the brigade engineer, and he has tasked me with securing our position. The purpose of the concertina barrier is force protection and segregation of American troops from Iraqi troops."

My jaw dropped. I don't know if I was more surprised by his desire for segregation or that he had admitted it so openly. To my New York ears, he sounded like an advocate of a separate-but-equal system from a south that isn't supposed to exist anymore. Here we were, decades later, in a Middle Eastern desert, fighting a war in which he and those "Iraqi troops" were on the same side.

Curt, the fellow Carolinian, was cooler than me, and quick with his riposte.

"Wouldn't your priority of work for force protection be the perimeter base defenses?"

He meant the defense of Kirkush itself, rather than the National Guard's position within it. The point was well made. Base defense at that time was contracted to a private security firm that employed Gurkhas, the Nepalese soldiers who traditionally serve the British Army. We, armed Marines and soldiers, worked for a government that was paying a corporation to protect us. And those corporations weren't doing any better a job of it than they needed to—or even *as much* as they needed to. Kirkush was at that time unfortified on two sides. The north and west perimeters gaped open to the desert that surrounded us. At any given time, only a handful of Gurkha riflemen in towers watched over those two flanks of the base, which stretched more than 1,700 yards each. The Gurkhas themselves seemed dedicated to their job, but, generally speaking, the tension between the professional soldiers and the professional mercenaries was profound. That tension was one of the defining characteristics of the war in Iraq, everywhere.

"I have my orders," the lieutenant colonel said. "This conversation is over."

Curt and I were dismissed. We'd been trumped by a brigadier general. And we'd lost this fight, unless we took the matter to Major General Eaton. But how could we? Eaton was overseeing the development of an army and police for all of Iraq, a mission the general famously described as "building an airplane in mid-flight." His job was a nightmare. The insurgency was exploding. Curt didn't like the idea of going to Eaton with an intrabase spat. It would be petty. Personal feelings aside, I had to agree with him.

The North Carolina Guard's decision to sequester its troops was unfortunate in more ways than one. The unit included many former Marines. They wanted to engage the enemy—they said as much to Gunny Webster when he visited on regular bartering trips, trying to scrounge supplies. Some suggested that we should pacify the nearby town of Balad Ruz. They were eager to conduct foot patrols and establish ties to the community. That wasn't going to happen. The brigadier commanding the North Carolinians chose a different course. I believe that he'd decided his chief mission was to have as little to do with Iraqis as possible. That mission, it seemed to us, even trumped trying to help win the war. Those Guardsmen limited their forays off the base to motorized patrols. They made drive-bys through Balad Ruz. They made stops at the mayor's office, which was really more of a small fort than a normal building. I suspected that the brigadier wanted to ride out his year in the desert as safely as possible and then go home. We saw the brigadier from time to time in a KBR-run chow hall. No one could miss him, a smallish man with a tight mouth and an odd gait that seemed like a combination of slouch and swagger. He wore aviator sunglasses, even indoors. Over the course of four months, I never saw his eyes.

Then there was his retinue: An aide-de-camp, an enlisted orderly, staff officers, and a half-dozen private bodyguards orbited the general wherever he went. I surmised that his personal security detail were all Blackwater employees. Indoors or out, they always arrived kitted up in body armor, wearing multiple magazines of ammunition. They sported black Ray-Bans or Wiley X sunglasses. Even for meals, they rolled up in "battle rattle." The entourage typically arrived at the KBR dining facility in armored SUVs. Once inside, they cut off the enlisted soldiers and officers waiting in line. The brigadier's security detail formed a cordon around the general. Mercenaries armed with M4 rifles took up positions around his table and at the facility's entrances and exits. No Americans, neither soldiers nor Marines, neither enlisted men nor officers, neither reservists nor active duty, were allowed to sit near the general. All this took place on the American side of the base, within the brigadier's own position.

Maybe he is a great leader, I thought at first. But then I wasn't seeing it. *Maybe he is good at his job.* But then I wasn't seeing that either. Maybe, I decided, he was a guy who realized his limitations in combat, a man who was scared of Iraq and Iraqis and who understood that he'd exceeded the utmost level of his competence.

I stood still in the yellow heat with Zayn.

On the other side of the razor wire, only feet from us, the lieutenant colonel and a captain supervised their engineers as they maneuvered heavy cement barricades into place. A massive pile driver thrust steel rods into the ground. The engineers lashed concertina to the posts. Never again would any Iraqi be able to dismantle their barrier. But we stood very close, unmoving.

Zayn wanted to believe something good, something positive that would explain things, but he couldn't come up with anything.

I knew he would convey all of this to the other Iraqi officers later. It would trickle through the ranks.

"I don't understand," he said, in a low voice. "Why here, in the middle of the base? Between us and them? This does not make sense."

I didn't look at him. For a moment or two, I thought silently.

"Do you remember when you all asked us if we ever drank blood?"

He shook his head, meaning yes.

"It's sort of like that," I said. "They have a lot of wrong ideas about Iraqis. Based on what they've been led to believe. They don't know you the way we know you." By "we," I meant the advisers, though there were still, at that early stage, one or two advisers I doubted.

I looked at him for a sign, to see if he understood. Zayn angled his head back and looked at me down his nose.

"Eeeee," he said. It's an Iraqi version of yes. I read his body language. Plainly, he was offended.

The Guardsmen had taken the same oath I had: to support and defend the Constitution of the United States against all enemies, foreign and domestic, and to bear true faith and allegiance to the same. Now we stood divided by concrete and concertina wire of their making, a massive barrier that cut off Zayn and me, cut off the men of Fifth Battalion and their US Marine advisers.

I felt Curt approaching before I saw him. He stood with Zayn and me and watched for a few seconds in his contemplative way.

"This is asinine, Mike," he said. "It's not worth it. Let it go." He left.

The confrontation with the Guard had become personal for me. Curt and I were both majors. I didn't interpret what he said as an order. I decided that what he said was friendly advice, from one Marine officer to another. I appreciated it. But I wasn't going to let the Guardsmen off the hook. They had won, but I decided I would stay there, in silence, as long as they did.

Zayn and I watched, not talking much. I wore a floppy desert hat and Wiley X sunglasses, the sleeves on my desert camouflage blouse rolled down to protect my arms against the sun. Zayn wore his chocolate-chip desert camouflage and a brown beret. The white afternoon light and hot breeze squeezed like a big snake. White salt stains streaked our uniforms.

"Zayn, you don't have to stay," I said. I spoke in a low tone so the engineers wouldn't hear. "This is an American thing. This is between us and them." An hour or so had passed. The sun was at its zenith, the heat at its most intense. "I'm not leaving, but that doesn't mean you have to stick around."

"No," Zayn said. And then just the single word for himself, one index finger pointing down at the ground: "Stay."

Four hours. That's how long Zayn and I stood in the furnace glare. We stood so close we could read the names on the soldiers' uniforms. Finally, the lieutenant colonel turned and left his work zone. He, too, had stayed out in the heat while we watched. He never acknowledged us. No one had.

Shortly afterward, the captain had his engineers wrap up for the day.

Before turning away, he saluted.

Part II

TAJI

7

SOVEREIGN

DURING WAR, THE DESIRE TO SURVIVE is often the only desire people have. Everything can get stripped away. There's no time for hazy ideals or principles. Whatever autonomy they have left, they will use to stay alive. Getting people to think and behave in new ways is a lot harder when others are dying around them.

In early June, the barbers at Kirkush all quit at the same time. One had turned up dead, bled dry, west of the base in Balad Ruz. The blood was warm when they found him, and floating in the puddle was a note warning in Arabic that this was the fate of anyone who worked with the Americans. The US and Iraqi bases attracted all types of Arab merchants and traders, and the insurgents hated these impromptu camp followers, whom they saw as supporting the US "crusade."

The barber's murder infuriated Zayn. Killing the innocent was an act of evil to him, a violation of the Koran.

"I will destroy them, these *irhabeen*," he said, referring to the insurgents. He never used the word the insurgents used for themselves—*mujahideen*, which means "holy warriors." Instead, he chose a term meaning "violent criminals."

Zayn and I were going over the training schedule with Captain Hummons and Maj. Mohammed Najm, who had replaced Aof Raheem as the battalion's operations officer. Mohammed Najm was a smart, reserved man, the Shiite from Nasiriyah who was close to Zayn. He smiled at his Sunni friend's rage.

"This Zayn," he said as he put an arm over his shoulder. "The Arab blood is strong in him."

Training continued inexorably, barbers or no barbers. We never had the option of slowing down. There was a war on. We needed to have the mujanadin through training before July, and our work was cut out for us. Classes that lasted only twenty minutes for Marine recruits took an hour or more for the Iraqis. The military principles we wanted the mujanadin to understand were even more alien to them than they are to the American teenagers who slouch up to Parris Island. The Iraqis were getting better about asking questions after classes, though, even if they preferred to do so in private. The 'terps patiently listened to each man's inquiries. Often the mujanadin wanted only to ask about America and Americans. They were curious about the advisers on a personal level. If one of us opened our wallet to show family pictures, they flocked to us like birds to bread crumbs. The Iraqis were especially interested in images of our wives, girlfriends, or sisters. In their culture, such images were taboo. They were amazed that we openly showed off the women in our lives.

Gunny Webster tried to use their desire to understand us to teach them about our views on society and soldiering. At one class he tried to make the mujanadin understand Western views on diversity. We felt that if the recruits were going to form the vanguard of a new, pluralistic Iraq, they should see how it works in another society. US race relations aren't perfect, but they're harmonious by Iraqi standards.

"Look at us," Gunny Webster said at one class. "Captain Hummons here is a black Marine. Major Zacchea is a white Marine. Staff Sergeant Villa is Hispanic. And I'm half Japanese. But we're all Marines, first and foremost. That's what diversity is all about."

Creating cultural changes is a very steep order, and we were trying to do so on an expedited schedule in a war zone. So we made up shortcuts. We held ourselves up as examples for them. There are notions that we take for granted in the United States, things that are so inherent to us that we think they're universal truths. We fail to even recognize that they are just our beliefs. Much of what we were trying to teach the Iraqis had no history or place in their world. I'm talking about things as elevated as the concept of peaceful diversity, and as mundane as not driving on sidewalks.

Many of them were desperately lost in the meritocratic military culture we brought to them. A sergeant named Hamid got a pistol and threatened to kill himself after his company commander told him he was being booted from the Army for incompetence. He squatted in the shade of the armory courtyard, dangling the weapon between his knees. Zayn and the warrior messenger Abdel-ridha Gibrael went with me to calm him. Hamid wept and explained his plight: He had held rank and privilege in Saddam Hussein's army. He was a warrant officer who was paid well and could provide for his wife and kids. In the new army, he already had been demoted to sergeant. Now he faced the added humiliation of being kicked out. It was too much; he said he would die instead. It wasn't my first encounter with the Iraqi concept of honor, but at that time it was the most extreme. The Iraqis knew authoritarianism. They had never lived in a merit-based society—they lacked any point of reference for the concept. Everything Hamid knew of the way the world worked had been overturned. Some guys adjusted faster than others. Hamid was unequipped to cope with the new rules. Listening patiently to the distraught man in the courtyard, Major Zayn told Hamid that he would intercede on his behalf with the company commander. Abdel-ridha Gibrael told Hamid that he could work for him directly. Hamid promised that he would turn himself around.

"Never again will anyone complain about me," Hamid said, tears streaming down his face. "You will see. I swear on my father's eyes, on my children's souls—you will be proud of me."

Zayn never looked away from Hamid's face as he gently but firmly took the pistol from his hands. Hamid let him do it. He kept weeping, promising us that he would be a good soldier. The crisis passed. In the end, Hamid remained with the battalion.

Some of the cultural attitudes we taught were specific to the military culture. We Americans worked to loosen up the Iraqis' strict sense of hierarchy in the ranks. It may seem strange for a Marine to be writing about a lack of rigidity as a good thing, but really, it's not strange at all. The Marine Corps' success depends on NCOs and even lower-ranking soldiers who take initiative in the field when there are no officers around to give orders. Sergeants also must feel free to make recommendations to their officers based on their own, hard-earned knowledge. Our flexibility and adaptability are strengths. The Iraqis had no notion of that. For them, everything was top-down. Speaking up was considered dangerous. It seemed like a giant leap for them to make. I wondered whether I would ever see an Iraqi NCO show the type of initiative we wanted from them. Would they ever stand up for what they believed were the best interests of the battalion? Those were big questions for me.

L. Paul Bremer, the Bush administration's handpicked leader of Iraq, went on television on June 28, 2004. Fifteen months after the invasion, the United States was ready to hand back Iraq's sovereignty. But before he left, Bremer wanted to speak directly to the Iraqi people and tell them things were great.

"I leave Iraq gladdened by what has been accomplished, and confident that your future is full of hope," he said. "A piece of my heart will always remain here in the beautiful land between the two rivers, with its fertile valleys, its majestic mountains, and its wonderful people."

Bremer put on his navy blazer and khaki boots, climbed into a big C-130 transport plane at Baghdad International Airport, and waved good-bye to Iraqi dignitaries. But he didn't fly away immediately. He waited aboard the C-130 until the press departed. After the cameras were gone, he slipped off to a smaller plane that the Americans believed was less likely to get shot down. They couldn't have the departing boss blown out of the sky on his way out, so they ushered him through the equivalent of an aerial back exit.

The inconspicuous, faster aircraft lifted Bremer out of Iraq, and out of his role in Iraqi history.

By the end of June, it was regularly hitting 130 degrees Fahrenheit during daylight hours at Kirkush. As tough as the daytime heat was, the swing between day and night temperatures was what really got to me. It plummeted to sixty degrees in the evenings. A seventy-degree swing every morning and every evening exhausted the body and wore on the immune system. The Iraqis grew up with it, but the Americans struggled to adjust, even those from desert states, like Nevadan Gunny Webster.

The season's brutality was perfect for the end of the mujana-din's training, however. We wanted it to be tough. For Marine Corps recruits, the final test of endurance, skills, and teamwork is a fifty-four-hour field exercise called the Crucible. It's exhausting mentally and physically, and it's performed under duress, with little food or sleep. It is, in a word, hellish. We decided to put the Fifth Battalion through its own Crucible.

The weather had Curt and me worried about heatstroke. How far could we push them? We didn't want dead mujanadin. At the same time, we were determined to drive them hard. We wanted the Crucible to be the toughest thing they'd ever experienced. We also wanted it to be more brutal than what the other two Iraqi battalions went through. We wanted the mujanadin of Fifth Battalion to carry in their hearts a certainty that they were *harder* than the Iraqis of Sixth Battalion or Seventh Battalion.

I contacted Lowdes Corporation days ahead of time to arrange shipments of ice, and got assurance that we'd have as much as we needed. Hummons, Curt, and I cut the schedule from the fifty-four hours of the Marine Corps down to forty-eight. We made sure that the men got eight hours of sleep the night before.

Reveille rang at 3 AM. Hundreds of men snapped into action at once. Everyone was all in. NCOs, officers, and advisers hounded small, squad-sized units of eight or nine mujanadin each, yelling, exhorting, pushing them through their exercises. The mujanadin darted in a green-and-beige swirl of camouflage uniforms, heavy packs, webbed helmets, and grim faces. They scarfed a breakfast of bread, hard-boiled eggs, and cheese. They took one liter of water each. It hit 110 degrees during their first nine-mile desert march. The terrain around Kirkush spilled out flat, scrubby, and hard. The Zagros Mountains rolled purple to the east. All the advisers were there—Curt, myself, the stern-faced Hummons, the tall Idahoan Reilly, the rifle instructor Villa, plus Gunny Webster, Colwell, Stouder, Lindsay, and Jenkins. The five civilian interpreters, none of them younger than thirty-three, stuck by our sides. American corpsmen from CMATT followed us in a truck, waiting for heat victims to fall out. Before the day's second march was through, the temperature topped out at 140 degrees. That is a kind of hot that most Americans will never understand. The Crucible was the pinnacle of the recruits' effort, and it was the apex of ours as well.

Each mujanad that first day had to complete twelve training stations—obstacle courses, fire-and-movement courses, marksmanship, first aid, land navigation, problem solving, and teamwork drills. We sang as we marched, a dark line of figures far off from Kirkush, crawling on a horizon that danced with heat. Over the course of that day, we gave each man three more liters of water. The advisers prowled among the mujanadin, talking to them, putting hands on them, looking for the confusion or dizziness that signal heatstroke. That night, the recruits got four hours of sleep on the hard-packed ground starting at 11 PM We rose as one at 3 AM. Then we did everything a second time. Over forty-eight hours, the mujanadin marched about forty-eight miles.

Lowdes never delivered the ice, of course. Curt yelled at me. He was gambling with the intensity of the Crucible—we all were. If the Iraqis had a command structure that actually practiced oversight, I'm sure we would not have been cleared to run the men as hard as we did. But we had no heat casualties. None.

When we told them it was over, the men shouted, screamed, howled. They clustered together and leaped again and again as high as their spent legs would lift them, a rifle in each man's right hand pointing at the blue sky. And like that, they were no longer mujanadin. Each man was a jundi—a soldier for the new Iraq.

I felt a palpable sense of history unfolding in front of me. Zayn clapped my back, put an arm around me, and shook my hand. I felt joy. We all did.

That same day, June 30, 2004, was the original deadline for the United States to return sovereignty to Iraq—the Americans had made the handover two days early and shipped Bremer out of the country in order to avoid insurgent attacks timed to the occasion. A group of caretaker leaders known as the Iraqi Interim Government immediately got to work. An interim prime minister, Ayad Allawi, took office. Allawi was a Shiite who at various times in his life had been a Ba'athist, a coup plotter against Saddam Hussein, and an expatriate opposition leader. Most important to the United States, Allawi was a University of London–educated secularist who believed in Western liberal values—open markets, separation of church and state, and democracy. The Americans and British still fought the war, but Allawi and his cabinet would run the government until national elections scheduled for early 2005.

I felt—we all felt—like we were on our way. There's no feeling like the realization that one's personal life story has merged with the great sweep of history. The new junood kept celebrating, even when we got back inside the air-conditioned buildings of Kirkush. They danced and clapped, chanting Arabic and Kurdish songs made by the strands of eight hundred voices.

Another milestone in June 2004 was the formation of Multi-National Security Transition Command-Iraq (MNSTC-I), which took responsibility for "developing, organizing, training, equipping, and sustaining" the Iraqi military and police. The White House recognized—belatedly and amid disaster—that security was a major problem that wasn't going to magically fix itself. Maj. Gen. Paul Eaton, the man who had led us as we struggled on the "ragged edge of our competence," rotated out of the country. The first commander of MNSTC-I was a newly promoted lieutenant general named David Petraeus. Petraeus commanded the US Army's famous 101st Airborne Division during its drive to Baghdad in 2003. He was a thoughtful strategist and a politically astute leader who early on had serious questions about what would happen to

Iraq after the United States toppled Saddam Hussein. Like Major General Eaton, Petraeus was a problem solver, not an ideologue. Over the coming years, Petraeus was destined to shape the military course of the Iraq War more than anyone else.

Ever since Major General Eaton's impromptu firing of the Iraqi Third Brigade adviser, Ichabod Crane, Curt had been playing a two-tiered role. He was advising Third Brigade, but he was also advising Fifth Battalion, which was *part* of Third Brigade. It was really two jobs. That meant I took on extra work as deputy senior adviser to Fifth Battalion whenever Curt was shuttling to Taji or managing the difficult Iraqi generals who led Third Brigade. That arrangement ended, however, when Petraeus showed up. The lieutenant general brought with him a number of like-minded officers he trusted, and one of "Petraeus's boys" was our new Third Brigade adviser, an Army lieutenant colonel named Rodney Symons. I first met Symons during one of his first visits to Kirkush to see his new battalions—us, the Sixth, and the Seventh. Symons struck me as mild mannered and patient—good attributes if you want to succeed as an adviser to the Iraqi Army. Symons was a Texan and a graduate of the University of Texas. He could slip from hard-charging to easy-going and back again without effort. Sometimes the Texas in him came out; other times he was all Austin.

Symons inherited a Third Brigade whose officers lacked command skills. His mission was to teach the brigade to operate on its own as an effective fighting force. He had to achieve that mission quickly. The Bush administration was beginning to feel embarrassed by an insurgency it had not seen coming and whose existence it had spent months denying. The White House put intense pressure on the men leading the training effort. Washington wanted the Iraqis in the fight.

"The Iraqis lead from the back," Symons said to the advisers, out of earshot of the Iraqi officers. "We lead from the front. The Iraqi officers have to learn to endure the same hardships that their men experience. As I see it, that's going to be the biggest shift they have to make."

"General Petraeus has made my mission clear," he said. "I am going to get this brigade into fighting shape."

Fifth Battalion had become an active military unit, and we were eager to start behaving like one. We finally got enough vehicles from the Iraqi Ministry of Defense—mostly pickup trucks—so that we could transport all the battalion at once. We continued training in Kirkush. The base was isolated from the worst of the war, but we knew insurgents were operating around Balad Ruz. We went on our first patrols there, taking out one or two companies at a time. We still awaited our first warning order (WARNO, in military shorthand). WARNOs are concise documents that lay out the particulars of a mission in advance.

Action was on everybody's minds. Curt and I talked about it at the end of the day in quarters with the Iraqi officers. Our late-night bull sessions with the Iraqis were friendly and relaxed. We ate sweets and drank chai. The meetings became a ritual that helped me unwind. I dedicated time to Zayn, his friend Mohammed Najm, the XO Ahmed Nu'uman, and others, even if it cut into much-needed sleep. Usually Arkan, the clean-shaven interpreter who wanted to immigrate to the United States, came with me.

We talked, and we learned about each other. Arkan spoke of a sister who lived in Canada, and how he would be close to her when he lived in the United States. Zayn boasted about his sons and laughed at his tales of Saddam Hussein's army. Many of the Iraqis' beliefs shocked me. Some of the officers believed the 9/11 attacks never happened, and that the Bush administration made them up as a pretext for invading Iraq and Afghanistan. They cited Hollywood special effects as proof of America's ability to fake the attacks. Others believed Jewish elements had carried out the 9/11 attacks as a way to get the Americans to shield Israel from mujahideen. They said they respected the Marines, but they thought we were being duped by Zionists. Those beliefs were all the more troubling because many of the Fifth Battalion officers were drawn from the minority of Iraqis who actually believed that a free, democratic Iraq was possible. From our perspective, these were the enlightened ones.

The Iraqis never got upset at me for asking pointed questions. They enjoyed debates. Sometimes we believed in diametrically opposite realities, but our conversations stayed civil. Animated at times, for sure, but civil. There were no forbidden topics. Today I look back on those nighttime chats and wish that Americans with opposing viewpoints were capable of the same open discourse.

"So wait a minute, Zayn," I said. "If, like you say, suicide is such a grave sin in Islam—"

"Yes, that's right," Zayn said, emphasizing his words with his hand and arms. "Because only God can decide when to end a life."

"OK, so if it's the greatest sin, then how do you explain the suicide bombers on 9/11 and here in Iraq?"

"They are not true Muslims," interjected Mohammed Najm, his jade eyes calm. "They are . . . The word in English is—" and he switched to Arabic to ask Arkan for guidance.

"Apostates," Arkan clarified.

"They are apostates. They are false Muslims. Shiite, Sunni, I don't care. They are all false and they will be punished by God."

"Is it the same for the suicide bombers in Israel?" I asked.

"Ahhhhh," they all seemed to say at once, before the young XO Ahmed Nu'uman spoke up for everyone: "Palestine is different. That one is a special case."

"What does that mean, 'special case'?" I asked.

Nobody had a good answer for that one.

No matter, for now, I thought, *we'll continue tomorrow night.* Or maybe I would stay up and talk further, one-on-one, with my warrior-messenger Abdel-ridha Gibrael, the Kurd with the perfect English. *Whoever it is, I'll keep them talking.*

Our WARNO arrived on July 20. It was a force-protection mission back at Taji, the base fifteen miles north of Baghdad that had been my first real stop in Iraq. Taji was an immense supply hub for the area around the capital. It was strategically critical to the war effort. It was under daily mortar and rocket fire. Our mission was to man half of the forty-four guard towers that ringed the sprawling, fourteen square miles of the base. We also were to set up an internal guard and rapid-reaction force for the base.

With change in the air all around us, Curt decided to shake up the Fifth Battalion leadership. Curt and I did not trust Jassim Thammin, the mostly silent commanding officer. Jassim was the one who told the Iraqi officers early on that they would just wait out the Americans; he still did not know that Abdel-ridha Gibrael had secretly informed us of everything. Curt acted against him.

The becalming, confident Curt Williamson had clout with the Iraqis on the brigade level, and he told the general in charge there that he wanted Jassim out. He wanted Ahmed Nu'uman, the younger and more engaged second-in-command, to take over as CO. Moreover, Curt wanted Ahmed Nu'uman promoted from major to lieutenant colonel. A major would not have the necessary wasta to get support for the battalion from the top-heavy Iraqi chain of command. The Iraqi generals gave Curt everything he wanted. Just about the time that Fifth Battalion was getting ready to mount its new fleet of Nissan pickups and deploy to Taji, the new Lt. Col. Ahmed Nu'uman took over as commander. I was very glad to see it. I trusted Ahmed Nu'uman.

We were scheduled to move the battalion to Taji on August 1, but the day before, we underwent one more change. Two advisers who had been critical to the formation of the Fifth were scheduled to leave. Captain Hummons, our brash third officer who wrote the training program, and First Sergeant Reilly, the tall diplomat's son who possessed a special patience with the Iraqis, both came to the end of their rotations.

Most American civilians don't understand how much of a challenge turnover poses in the military. People who work in the corporate world know about the concept of institutional knowledge. It was the topic of my first master's thesis. The idea is that what's learned by individuals in an organization has to be preserved over time so the organization still has that knowledge after those individuals leave. That's one of the ways an organization maintains its integrity even as the cast changes over time. Institutional knowledge is hard for the military, because units are perpetually realigning their personnel. For a Marine officer, being in one place for more than a year is a long time. Commanders shift in and out constantly at all levels. Others leave the military altogether. It's one of the greatest ironies of the military that group integrity is so important—literally a matter of life and death—but simultaneously so hard to maintain. No corporation would survive the leadership turnover that the military deals with. We were going to miss Hummons and Reilly, but that's how life in the armed forces works. New guys would come along, and we would get them up to speed. It wasn't going to be easy, especially on an advisory mission: each new adviser had to learn how to trust the Iraqis, and the Iraqis had to learn to trust each new adviser.

Taji is so vast that most of it isn't even occupied. Even though tens of thousands of US troops, Iraqi troops, and civilian workers lived there in 2004, the base had empty, dry expanses and scores of crumbling, abandoned buildings. Parts of it looked like something out of *Mad Max*. Traveling by pickup from one area of the base to another could feel like driving between small desert settlements. An entire air base with a mile-long runway lay in Taji's southwestern quadrant, along with a heliport named Angel Base. Taji was ringed by massive earthen berms that acted as exterior walls. The berms were literally pushed up out of the flat ground by bulldozers. Forty-four guard towers, like small houses on stilts, rose up behind the berms and peeked over them. Each was separated by five hundred yards or more from the ones on either side. Taji was really multiple bases within one larger base, because aside from Taji Air Base the facilities were split into American and Iraqi sides. Both armies had barracks, offices, and firing ranges. Some barracks on the Iraqi side had been built by the British in the 1920s. The American side had air-conditioned trailers, a swimming pool, a movie theater, a Burger King, a Taco Bell, and a Cinnabon.

Beyond Taji's perimeter, the region was fertile. The greenish-blue Tigris rolled lazily to the east. Irrigated by the river, onions, beans, palms, dates, turnips, and okra sprang up lush in all directions. The main road north out of Baghdad, Freeway 1, hugged Taji's western side. Fifth Battalion and its US advisers settled into multilevel barracks on the Iraqi side of the base in an area called Muntaqa Safra. Our area lay directly adjacent to the American side of the base.

August was a tough adjustment. The American plan for Taji was that it would become the central logistics depot for the whole Iraqi security apparatus. That put a big target right on our backs. If the entire army was going to be supplied through one centralized location, in theory that meant the insurgents could starve the whole Iraqi Army by strangling that one place. Insurgents crept through the crops beyond the berms and mortared Taji so often that it stopped feeling remarkable.

The insurgents' plan was to physically cut off the base and terrorize the Iraqi civilians who worked there. They blew up our sewer lines, and soon the backup formed a lake of liquid shit, directly in front of one of Taji's main administrative buildings. Our enemies set up roadblocks on a bridge north of Taji at a place called al-Muzerfa. Over the course of three weeks, they seized and beheaded almost two dozen truck drivers. They tossed the bodies into a canal. They also seized our food, water, and other supplies. We started literally shipping our shit from the sewage lake off the base via truck, which in turn got more truckers murdered, so we had to set up armed escort missions to protect the outbound shit convoys.

A brigade from the Arkansas National Guard had tactical responsibility for the area around Taji. The Arkansans had taken a number of casualties since April, and their supply convoys were meeting heavy opposition coming up Freeway 1. They were trying to work with a useless Iraqi unit from something called the Iraqi Civil Defense Corps (ICDC), which was a miserably trained, poorly equipped, lash-up organization that fell somewhere between a paramilitary and police. They weren't effective even as cops.

Curt and I, along with Zayn, the new CO Ahmed Nu'uman, and the Ops O Mohammed Najm, went to meet the ICDC. The ICDC men, uniformed in light blue, told us they got one week of "training." That meant they got uniforms and AK-47s, fired their weapons on a range, went to a class or two, and learned to stand in formation.

"We will never carry out any operations with that unit or any other ICDC unit," Curt said to us after we got back to Muntaqa Safra. Ahmed Nu'uman readily agreed.

We were still getting accustomed to the Iraqis, and they were still getting accustomed to us. Take sleeping habits, for example. The Athens Olympics were on that summer, and Iraq fielded a pretty good soccer team. Zayn always invited me to watch matches. The games came on at 12:30 AM local time, and I was usually up with the Iraqi officers anyway. Their normal cycle was to get up early, work until noon, eat lunch, take a nap during the day's worst heat, rise in late afternoon, eat dinner, then work until midnight. Zayn, Mohammed Najm, and the others were comfortable staying up until 2:30 or 3:00 AM watching soccer, then getting up a couple of hours later. The Iraqis were mystified by the fact that the advisers never napped; they couldn't understand how we lived like that. For the Americans, the Iraqis' penchant for midday shuteye caused endless irritation. We would run around looking for the Iraqi leadership in the afternoon, only to find them in bed. Despite Zayn's industriousness, more than once I found him sleeping under his blanket in the middle of the day, the AC blasting as cold as it would go.

Zayn was one of a number of Iraqis in Fifth Battalion whom I began to think of as true believers. He thought expansively, could see beyond his own country and even beyond his own era. It's a rare kind of intelligence, for anyone from anywhere. He had visions of Iraqis "becoming like the Americans." There were others who thought like him, to one degree or another—the interpreters Arkan and Abdallah, the Shiite Ops O Mohammed Najm, and the new Sunni CO Ahmed Nu'uman. Many of the rank-and-file junood were true believers too. The US administration thought that after we overthrew Saddam Hussein, men like Zayn would spring from the deserts and cities of Iraq and build a new country. I could see that such men were a minority. Still, there in the summer of

2004, with Iraq taking over its own governance, with a nonsectarian prime minister at the helm, and with Fifth Battalion part of a new, rising vanguard, Zayn still believed.

"I know there is hope for us," he said to me between sips of chai, while Iraqi soccer players in their green and white jerseys flickered on the TV screen. And Zayn's belief, more than anything, made me believe.

Zayn and I worked the same most days, grinding away at logistics issues. We fought a morass of problems stemming from ineptitude, mismanagement, and corruption. Somehow, it was OK. Zayn's good nature and his humor made the days pass more or less painlessly. Logistics work at Taji involved a lot more driving than it had in Kirkush because Taji was so much bigger. Zayn drove us in his red-striped pickup. He told me stories about his home in Mosul. He bragged about his car, a 1980 Chevy Malibu with 280,000 miles on it. He said his wife sometimes pushed it from behind so he could jump-start it. He said he played religious passages on the Malibu's stereo. Those same chants were coming through the truck speakers as Zayn and I drove about Taji. Even when we had no interpreter, we managed to communicate. We laughed a lot.

When I was a young officer in artillery school, I learned that you get the most bang for your buck by targeting enemy troops where they exist in big numbers. You call for artillery fire where the enemy is concentrated. The insurgents—irhabeen, as Zayn called them—instinctively understood the same thing.

Taji was vast, but the biggest troop concentration on the base happened three times daily, like clockwork. That's when men gathered at the base's dining facilities. Every mess had a routine, serving meals at the same time, morning, noon, and night. I continued to take most of my meals with the Iraqis, usually with Zayn, at the chow hall on the Iraqi side of the base. The Iraqis called it al-ma'atam, which means "the restaurant." The Americans called it the DFAC, which is what we call all dining facilities.

The Iraqi officers and enlistees still didn't eat together, so I usually took one meal with the officers in their mess and then took Zayn for another meal in al-ma'atam with the junood. The meat they had for dinner was sometimes shipped all the way from Pakistan, and it often was spoiled. The junood complained bitterly—led as usual by Sergeant Major Iskander—so Zayn and I thought it was important for the soldiers to see the two of us eating the same stuff. Over time, I persuaded the other Iraqi officers to eat with me at al-ma'atam once or twice a week. It delighted the junood to see their officers at their mess, eating the same meals and standing in the same lines.

On August 24, Zayn and I agreed to have dinner together. Later that night, Iraq was playing Paraguay. The advisers met at 5 PM at an administrative area known as CMATT Village for a regular meeting. It was always at that time that one adviser of the day handed off to the next adviser of the day. Our battalion was scheduled to eat at 6:30 PM. Most of the Iraqi soldiers would go to al-ma'atam, while a handful would pick up food to deliver to the junood doing shifts out in the guard towers. Zayn was supposed to come by and pick me up at 6:15 PM He showed up a little early in his striped pickup, just as the advisers were finishing their meeting. He came up the outdoor walkway on foot, offering his hand to a barking puppy the advisers had adopted. The Americans were breaking up and making their way to their own vehicles, car keys jangling.

The shock wave of an explosion struck us like an ocean wave. A massive black and gray spout shot up beyond some buildings, only a couple hundred yards away.

Everyone froze.

"Was that the DFAC?" Staff Sergeant Lindsay asked in his South Carolina accent.

The question galvanized us. Iraqi soldiers were gathered there for dinner, including some from Fifth Battalion. We sprinted to our trucks and sped toward the rising, gritty plume. Curt, Colwell, and Lindsay arrived first. The rest of the advisers, including Zayn and me, arrived right behind them.

It was the DFAC. The smell of curry mixed with that of propane and burned flesh. The explosion appeared to have come from the kitchen at the rear of the building. One of the new battalion trucks sat out front, shredded by shrapnel. Smoke and dust swirled over the ground like ghosts of the newly dead. In and around the dining facility, bodies lay torn and twisted. I passed a man whose face showed reddish-black and the white of bone. Others wandered, dazed, bleeding. Kitchen workers cried out names.

Zayn began shouting orders, organizing men to establish a security cordon around the area. More Americans and Iraqis converged from every compass point. Senior advisers to the base and Iraqi command structure arrived, looking grimmer than I'd ever seen them. American corpsmen swarmed the scene. Our Fifth Battalion surgeon, a captain named Adnan Naji, showed up with his medical platoon. They carried body bags. Adnan Naji set up a triage area, and he and his men began stabilizing the injured. Several were in shock.

Truck tires spit gravel as they tore out of the area with the wounded. Others took dead bodies up into their truck beds. The Iraqis began scouring the site for scraps of flesh. It was my first time seeing how seriously the Muslims took the flesh of the dead. They crawled on hands and knees, using pieces of cardboard to gather up every piece of human remains they could find so that it could be interred with the rest of the body.

I spotted Zayn. He had turned his security cordon over to the Iraqi NCOs and American military police. He sat in the driver's seat of his truck, the door open and his boots hanging out over the ground. I got close, and the Koranic passages sang in his tape deck.

He reached for my hand. I thought he was being sentimental, but I was wrong. He pointed at my boots. They were rimmed with blood and flecked with small bits of tissue.

"You must wash your boots, Raed Zakkiyah."

I almost gagged. He put his hand on my shoulder.

"I need a ride back to CMATT Village," I said, and went to the passenger side. The advisers were going to need to meet. "No dinner tonight, Zayn."

He nodded gravely. When he dropped me off at the administrative building, I told him I would meet up with him later that night.

"Insha'Allah," he said, nodding. *God willing.*

It was a suicide bomber. An insurgent—a young man in his early twenties—had managed to get hired in the kitchen. The blast killed four Iraqis and wounded eighteen, including five injured from Fifth Battalion. The attack was effective on many levels. Many Iraqi kitchen workers, fearing for their lives, immediately quit. The base was forced to shutter two of five dining facilities, including the largest, which was the one the bomber hit.

Worse than any of that, the attack prompted soldiers from across the Iraqi units to quit. We saw it when we formed up for morning PT the next day. There were too few men doing jumping jacks. We did a count. We lost 150 from Fifth Battalion.

They had the right to walk away when they wanted. They were granted that level of autonomy, and we knew that. But seeing the departures was a blow to the advisers. We were risking our lives, and some of us were investing everything—our beliefs, our careers, our senses of self-worth—into this effort to raise something from nothing. To see men turn their backs on us undercut everything we tried to do. For some of the Iraqis, seeing men like themselves blown to pieces in the chow line was too much. They wanted to live.

Over the course of a couple of days, I began to get past the disappointment. I decided the desertions would not endanger our mission. We crunched the numbers, and we could still do everything we needed to do with fewer men. We reorganized from four rifle companies down to three. Leaves were canceled. We redesigned the rotation of troops standing guard duty—fewer men meant longer shifts, from eight hours to twelve. That was no small consideration in August, when daytime temperatures were hitting 130 degrees Fahrenheit. Twelve hours was a long, long time to stand in an open tower, watching for more attacks.

I tried to focus more on the soldiers who had chosen to stay than on the ones who had left. Maybe desertion only washed out the weak hands, I decided. I drew on my experience from Wall Street and tried to see it as a market correction. Attacks were coming daily, guys were being wounded, and our enemy had demonstrated that he could reach out and kill us where we ate. So it was meaningful that most of the men were sticking with the battalion when the law granted all of them the individual sovereignty to cut loose whenever they wanted.

"Really, I'm not surprised some left, Mike," the new brigade adviser Symons said to me. "I can tell you no one at division is. I don't think you are, either."

And he was right. I wasn't.

I was surprised at what happened next, however. Many of those who deserted began to trickle back. The battalion's administrative officer, a captain named Mohammed Thyab, did a fresh count and told us we regained about half of those who had left. That wasn't something I expected. In the US military, deserters don't just walk back onto the base and ask for their jobs back. Mohammed Thyab, with Ahmed Nu'uman's blessing, fined the returning deserters as punishment. Two or three of them came to me personally, begging for leniency. I didn't yell at anybody, since technically, they had not broken any rules. But I was firm that I would not oppose the fines.

Around that time, I was at one of our regular meetings with the advisers, officers, and senior NCOs. Men gave reports, each updating everyone else on his areas of responsibility. Security changes after the bombing at the DFAC were a big topic of conversation. Everyone spoke in turn, the interpreters following along in translation. Then Iskander spoke. The cocksure sergeant major rose and stood bolt upright, his beret at a perfect angle. He spoke in Arabic for the benefit of the Arab officers. Arkan translated for me.

"I must bring to the attention of the battalion leadership a problem with the guards in the towers," he said. I thought he was going to report some sort of dereliction of duty. But instead, he did something amazing: he complained about the new rules the officers had made for the junood in the towers. Iskander said that the new system wasn't as good as it could be. Instead of the guards working in twelve-hour shifts that changed at 6 AM and 6 PM, it made more sense to rotate at midnight and noon. That way, each guard rotation experienced at most six hours of daytime heat, plus six hours of nighttime cool. Moreover, the dangers of guard duty would be shared equally, since most mortar and small-arms attacks were coming at night.

I perked up immediately. Iskander was suggesting a modification to the officers' orders. Then another NCO rose to speak, an Arab sergeant this time, and seconded Iskander's recommendation. Before the officers said anything, a third NCO followed. A few of the officers furrowed their brows and exchanged sharp looks with one another. But Ahmed Nu'uman, the young CO, raised a hand and effortlessly cut off any protest. He glanced at Arkan and me before he said, "The sergeant major makes a good suggestion. We will try his system. If it makes our guards more effective during this time of increasing attacks, then that is all that matters."

I listened in amazement as Arkan interpreted for me. He smiled as he delivered the translation. The senior NCOs did something that I was willing to bet had never been done in an Iraqi army before—maybe never in an Arab-majority army anywhere. They successfully protested a decision from the officers, on behalf of their enlisted men. In Saddam Hussein's army, such a suggestion would be insubordination. It would result in a bullet to the head. There in the battalion meeting, I watched the senior NCOs take initiative and devise a solution. Not only that, but their idea made sense. I was thrilled.

Maybe some of what we've been teaching these guys is starting to sink in.

They were operating in ways that were new to them. Just like I was. My optimism rose again. Despite horrified barbers and murdered truckers. Despite the bombing. Despite the desertions. Zayn was right: there was hope for us.

8

TAKING COMMAND

ONE EVENING IN EARLY SEPTEMBER, Curt said he was leaving the battalion.

"You'll have to take my place at these nightlies with division, Mike," he said. "The dailies too. "

The desert blackness pressed from the other side of the window pane. Curt had just returned from one of his regular meetings with the lieutenant colonel who advised the Iraqis at the division level. It was his nightly meeting, the big one with officers from division and all the units at Taji. His next meeting that night, the small one with just us Fifth Battalion advisers, was about to begin. He took me aside beforehand.

"They're moving me to deputy adviser for division," he said. "That staff over there is basically all Marines, and a lot of them are getting to the ends of their tours. End of September, a lot of them will be pulling out. They've asked me to step in. Better to go now while I can still watch them and learn the ropes."

I wasn't entirely surprised by the news, but that didn't make it less momentous to hear. Officially, nobody in Taji was supposed to be leaving, because we needed all the advisers we could get. But a lot of guys seemed to be heading for the exits. Every dimension of our life in Taji seemed to trip into flux at once. The battalion had been operational for two months, and the advisers who were staying faced a radically different job. We weren't raising a fighting force anymore.

We were leading a unit that would actually be fighting. That in itself required each of us to do some serious psychological recalibrations. The same obviously was true for the Iraqis themselves. Now, adding to this great confluence of change, Curt takes me aside and says he's leaving. "I'll let the others know at our advisers' meeting," he said.

Excitement, trepidation, and a dozen other feelings leaped through my mind like antelopes. I had wanted command all along. I had been disappointed when Curt first arrived and took command instead. Now it was mine, and we were going to be in for combat, maybe a lot of it. *If ever I would've really liked having Curt around*, I thought, *it's now*. He had schooling I did not—advanced warfare and more besides. Curt would not be far away physically, working at the main Taji administration building with other division-level Marines. But I alone would be in charge of Fifth Battalion.

The Marine Corps recognizes four levels of warfare: tactical, operational, strategic, and political/diplomatic. Curt and I were at the tactical level. Curt wanted to be at the operational level, making bigger decisions. I knew he would be good at it. Part of me thought he had the potential to be a general someday. Assaulting objectives with a battalion of Iraqis, rifle in hands, was not the most optimal use of his skills.

Back in April, I had questioned myself and my motivations. "It's the senior adviser who will get all the personal recognition," I wrote back then in my journal. I wanted the credit. I wanted to be the leader. It was a Marine Corps thing. Back in my first days in Iraq, one of the Green Zone generals had quoted Rudyard Kipling's "The Law of the Jungle." He meant to shore up our courage, to toughen us up. But all I thought about was the competition. The passage fit the world we officers made for ourselves:

> Now this is the law of the jungle, as old and as true as the sky,
> And the wolf that shall keep it may prosper, but the wolf that shall break it must die.

Now I was senior adviser. I knew more keenly at that moment than I had understood back in April: not only does the word *senior* bestow recognition for success. It also attracts blame for failure. It means full responsibility.

Gentlemen, we are operating at the ragged edge of our competence. I could still feel Major General Eaton's level gaze. *And there is no assurance of our success.*

So be it. For better or worse, I was where I wanted to be.

The third anniversary of 9/11 was still a week away when three new advisers came on board. They were not Marines. All were from the US Army Reserve—they had been pulled out of civilian life to fight in Iraq. Chuck Johnson was a blond, lanky captain in his midthirties but with a face that could pass for much younger. He wore wire-framed spectacles that accentuated a meticulous disposition. Johnson filled Hummons's billet slot for a captain. I wanted him to concentrate on security and base defense. That was a big job, because two of Taji's four compass points were the Fifth Battalion's to defend. The other two new men were NCOs who already knew each other: SFC Eric Warner was an affable hulk who had once been a promising outside linebacker. Now he was a forty-nine-year-old in an upright, six four frame. His size got people's attention; his clever, joking manner held it. He took over as administration adviser. S.Sgt. Richard Fryar, a powerfully built man with a Latin complexion and aquiline face, was a Bostonian who used every opportunity he got to let New Yorkers like myself know about the virtues of his city and the supposed superiority of its sports franchises. He was my new motor transport adviser.

Johnson, Warner, and Fryar were Army guys joining a Marine Corps unit. At first I could see that they felt a little tentative about working with Marines, who have a reputation in the Army for being either contemptuous or crazy or both. I would see that wariness about Marines, to one degree or another, in all the Army Reserve advisers who joined me over the course of my year in Iraq.

Colwell, Lindsay, Stouder, and Jenkins reached the end of their tours a few days after the new advisers arrived. They helped show the new guys the ropes a little, and then they were gone. Colwell had put his last Iraqi into combat boots. Curt transferred to division around Labor Day. Most officers and NCOs were getting their orders extended at that time, but among those who did leave was division senior adviser Colonel Abblitt. Behind the scenes, a lot of guys were jockeying to get on the plane with him. It's common in the military for officers to hitch onto a higher-ranking commander when he moves. That was happening at Taji, despite the intense pressure on the advisers to shape up the Iraqis. Or maybe because of it.

While we tried to realign ourselves, the insurgents kept trying to kill us. Taji's vastness made it impossible to seal them out entirely, and the insurgents began infiltrating snipers into the base. Scores of abandoned buildings flung across Taji's fourteen square miles allowed enemy gunmen to operate within our position, waiting for a clean shot on some unsuspecting American or Iraqi who thought he was safe deep within his own base. Our lone-wolf enemies slept during the day and sniped at night, lurking until they spotted solo vehicles or stray wanderers in the early morning hours. We operated on the assumption that Iraqi civilians working on base or Iraqi soldiers secretly working for the insurgency were helping the snipers with food and water.

Pretty soon it seemed like we spent every night chasing gunmen through ruined buildings, fields of garbage, sharp-edged junkyards, and dry plains of rusted vehicles. Night-vision goggles were of no use inside buildings, because they require ambient light to work. The interior of unelectrified buildings at night lacked even that. Every time it got dark outside, one or two of us led a squad of Iraqi soldiers, hunting gunmen for hours. Sometimes firefights erupted in the pitch black of giant abandoned warehouses. It was harrowing to fight in total darkness. Black factory walls amplified the vicious snap of AK-47s. Bullets reached out for us in the dark.

Even more than it was harrowing, though, it was exhausting. At daybreak we were dog tired but still had an eighteen-hour day ahead of us. Sleeplessness in turn made the night's fighting that much more surreal. It got hard to stay level. I had to stagger the men on the sniper hunts. On top of all that, we were almost always frustrated by a lack of results. We weren't killing snipers. With morning, we examined the scene of the fighting from the night before. The new, levelheaded captain, Chuck Johnson, proved particularly good at crime-scene work. Johnson had worked as a security expert for the retail chain Target back home. He found spent brass, rabbit holes where snipers hid their ammunition, discarded water bottles, and the blankets they used to warm themselves. He squatted in the dust and reconstructed the actions of men who had tried to kill us a few hours earlier. The snipers were well trained. They arranged paths to use as routes of escape, clearing trails through garbage, setting up makeshift ladders, and arranging themselves near blast holes that would let them slip through walls.

Outside Taji, the insurgents watched. They always watched; they were very good at watching. They monitored our routines, our initiatives. They discerned patterns. They sought vulnerabilities. They debated, I am sure, among themselves. And they were not stupid. A pattern emerged: We achieved a goal. Things improved in some way. Then the insurgents adjusted. We succeeded, they adjusted, we succeeded, they adjusted. They proved expert at devising new tactics to punish our successes. About that time, Fifth Battalion seized the bridge at al-Muzerfa where the insurgents ran their murderous roadblocks. Just like that, no more Iraqi truckers were getting shot in the head and dumped by the road. Our supply arteries pumped steadily back to life. Trucks hauled in fresh water by the thousands of gallons, brand-new generators and engine parts, rice and halal meat, and sweet-smelling, benzene-heavy Iraqi gasoline.

The insurgents adjusted. They decided to come at us head-on, to attack the very defenses we had built around us, with more than just snipers.

It was the type of fight each of us professional military men in Taji wanted, whether we were American, Iraqi, or one of the handful of other nationalities who were there. We were trained for wars of rifles, mortars, rockets, gunships, and artillery. We thought in terms of discrete units, mobility, and terrain. We were better at that kind of war than the insurgents were. When I say "we," I'm including the Iraqis of the Fifth Battalion. I knew the insurgents could not best us in a stand-up fight. The trick, though, was convincing my Iraqi soldiers of the same thing. We had the numbers, the training, the firepower. I could not let the enemy cow my men.

The insurgents started testing our defenses. Riflemen took shots at the guard towers from outside the perimeter. Rocket-propelled grenades (RPGs) exploded into our earthen berms. Small groups of men lit up sections of the wall with machine-gun fire. They hit us with drive-bys, like deadly boys in a street gang. They came at night, firing from the Tigris-fed fields of spinach, okra, and graceful date palms that flourished to the south. The insurgents were adjusting. Their new tactics created new worries for me. My great fear was a concerted RPG attack at night that would take out a tower and blow a hole in our perimeter. The western side of the Iraqi base bordered the American part of the base, so it was secure. Mercenaries from Lebanon protected the northern perimeter. The Fifth Battalion was responsible for protecting the southern and eastern sides—about half of Taji's forty-four towers—over an L-shaped perimeter eight miles long.

Here's how most of the Iraqi officers and all of the Marine advisers looked at it: we were guarding the lives of every American and Iraqi inside that base, and they were all counting on us to do so. I imagined worst-case scenarios. One was for insurgents to breach the perimeter, approach the air base within Taji, and take out a helicopter with an RPG. It was entirely feasible. The snipers already had proved that they could get in and literally live among us. I feared the same thing happening, but with more men making the infiltration. All told, Fifth Battalion was responsible for protecting a chunk of Taji that stretched across about eight square miles, with scores of structures. (When we were relieved of our security mission many months later, it was by an entire brigade with more than four times the manpower of the Fifth.)

So far that summer, we had lost a lot of helicopters. The official statement to the media was always that they had fallen out of the sky because of mechanical failure, but the truth is that the insurgents were shooting them down. One of those downed choppers was copiloted by a young American captain named Tammy Duckworth. She would lose both of her legs after the insurgents shot down her Black Hawk, and would later represent Illinois in the US Senate. The weapon that our enemies used to bring down her helo and others—the rocket-propelled grenade—was effective only when the choppers were low to the ground, taking off or landing. The insurgents had to get close. I knew it was one of their goals.

On the night of September 14, an Army staff sergeant named Helms was assigned as adviser of the day, teamed up with the Iraqi officer of the day, a young first lieutenant named Yousif Badr. (Helms arrived with Johnson, Fryar, and Warner, but didn't last long with us before rotatating out.) Helms's job that day and into the night was to supervise the Iraqi enlisted men and NCOs in the perimeter's guard towers. Badr, a quiet but attentive officer, was the official authority over the men on the line. Both men would be spending a lot of time on the radio with the towers. As night approached, Helms and Badr took their positions at what we called the guard shack, which stood alone about 550 meters within the perimeter, near the crook of the L. The guard shack gave Helms and Badr no view beyond the perimeter. The Iraqis in the towers served as their eyes. The Taji perimeter was immense. About 1,100 meters separated each of the guard towers. That's more than ten football fields between armed watch posts. If the insurgents wanted to draw close to the berms, they usually could.

Helms and Badr didn't like what they were hearing over the radio as the gloom seeped in. Men in the towers reported trucks rumbling in the distance, more than two miles away on the vast fields of date palms and okra. Through binoculars, the guards in the towers took turns watching the trucks deposit men into the fields. It was hard to tell at that distance, but it appeared that the men could be armed with rifles.

Helms and Badr reported back what the guards observed. I was at the battalion operations area, six klicks north of the southern perimeter, listening on a Motorola radio. As night took over, soldiers on the southern perimeter began to report that they were taking small-arms fire. The handful of men with night-vision goggles put them on, shouldered their rifles, and fired back. We had only one pair of goggles for every two towers. I listened to the men dutifully report back in quick Arabic. The Iraqis were not good at staying calm on the radio. Occasionally one of our own AKs cracked in the background during a transmission. My own Arabic had gotten good enough by that point that I could figure out a lot of what was being said. Translators explained the rest to me and the other Americans. From the sound of it, the perimeter guards were taking light probing attacks. Our enemies were testing us up and down our perimeter.

That changed. At last light, the radio crackled with reports that technicals—pickup trucks with machine guns mounted in the beds—were approaching in the southern distance. Or at least, the guards thought that's what they saw. The nighttime visibility was bad, and the vehicles were distant. The Iraqis in the guard towers didn't trust their own eyes. For three or four hours, an exchange of rifle fire continued, but no heavy fire came in. The idea of enemy technicals with machine guns ate at my stomach like a parasite. Other advisers began speeding south to the perimeter in ones or twos. I heard the big man Warner and the Bostonian Fryar check in over the net, saying they were heading to the towers.

At around 11 PM, it happened. Men in the guard towers began taking concentrated machine-gun fire. The insurgents were trying to take them out. The real fight was on.

I stood at battalion headquarters. The building, which housed the Fifth Battalion reaction force that we always kept on standby, was convenient to both the southern and eastern perimeters of the base.

"Oscar Four Zulu, this is Echo Six Hotel, how copy? Over." It was Staff Sergeant Helms, his voice crackling over the Motorola, asking for me.

"Roger, I copy," I said.

"We have one Whiskey India Alpha in tower four, over." One man wounded in action. "We also need more ammo here."

After a few short minutes, a group of soldiers burst into the room bearing a man on a stretcher. I approached him. His fellow soldiers had tried to staunch a massive flow of blood from one of his shoulders. He was a tower guard. The new battalion surgeon, Adnan Naji, came into the room and carefully pulled away the red dressings. The hole was big. I could see straight through the man's shoulder to the surface of the stretcher.

The time had come for me to assess things up close. I was already decked out in full battle rattle. I ordered that the Fifth Battalion reaction force be assembled and rushed to the perimeter. I left the room.

I strode out of the battalion building and spotted a Nissan pickup. The keys were inside. I hit the ignition and tore south over a dry, unpaved road, abandoned buildings flitting past my windows.

"Oscar Four Zulu, this is CMATT X-ray, copy?" It was Taji base operations. I recognized the voice of the CMATT sergeant major on the radio.

"Roger, I copy."

"Oscar Four Zulu, guards at the Cooke gate are taking fire. It's coming from the guard towers. Can you check on their situation, sir?"

Un-fucking-believable, I thought. Americans at a guard post within Taji were taking indirect fire from the insurgents, and they had assumed that it was the Iraqi soldiers—their allies—firing at them from the towers. Probably some full-bird American colonel had it up his ass that the Iraqis in the towers were a threat. CMATT should've known who was doing the shooting—the Iraqis had already evacuated casualties, and everybody listening in on the radio knew it. Instead of telling the Americans the real score, they wanted me to do it for them. Mistrust of the Iraqis poisoned many of the Americans at Taji. Most of them had never even been introduced to an Iraqi. I had a firefight on my hands, insurgents trying to breach our defenses, but first I had to swing by and explain to these Army soldiers who the bad guys were. I told the CMATT sergeant major that I would go to the Americans taking fire.

Four young American soldiers there had taken cover behind sandbags. They had their helmets on and their rifles at the ready. There was really nowhere for them to shoot, since the berms were too far away, and the insurgents were on the other side of them anyway. I stepped out of the Nissan and walked over to them.

"Be careful, sir!" one of them said. "We're taking fire from the towers. It's the Iraqis!"

"You are not taking fire from the Iraqis," I said, forcing myself to speak with a level tone. I pointedly remained in the open, showing them that I was not afraid of being a target. I stabbed a finger out toward the south, out over the berms. "The Iraqis are engaged with the enemy, who are attacking from outside. Any fire you took here was directed at those towers and came over the walls from insurgents in the fields."

The Americans looked at me and said nothing.

"We've had men badly wounded tonight. I know what's going on out there. I'm the senior adviser to those Iraqis."

A lean Army specialist stood silently in the darkness near me and peered south. Distant small-arms fire popped in the night, the high-pitched crack of AK-47s mingling with the heavier burst of machine guns. Even far away, I could tell that the shots had grown thicker, more frequent, in the last few minutes.

I spoke to a sergeant: "Call in to your CO and have him prepare a reaction force in case the insurgents get inside the perimeter. And close your interior gate. We're doing everything we can to hold them off. They want at the helicopters."

I looked at the young specialist. He looked at me. It occurred to me that maybe I shouldn't be doing this by myself. I decided I could probably use an extra rifle.

"You're coming with me," I said to him.

"Yes, sir." He quickly checked his M4A1 rifle and made a quick trot to my truck.

We ripped south through the darkness without headlights. I put in a report to CMATT X-ray over the radio. The black sky hung moonless. The Nissan jumped and lurched over uneven road, the front of the chassis sometimes cutting into the dry ground. I slowed as we arrived at the southern edge of the base. I turned east to inspect the huge earthen berm that the engineers were dozing up for us. High-pitched cracking sounds continued from the fields, closer now. Our guards responded all up and down the line, in front of us and behind as we prowled alongside the berm. The berm was not yet completed and was really several berms loosely joined together. Gaps opened onto the fields, making the earth wall like the top of some gargantuan, crenelated castle tower, open here and there for fire to come through. Construction vehicles, bulldozer tracks, and churned earth cluttered the perimeter road.

I couldn't see where I was going. I cursed myself for rushing there without grabbing night-vision goggles. I needed to see as much of the perimeter as possible, as quickly as possible. The terrain was slowing us down. It was risky to turn on the headlights, but I decided I had to take the chance. I wasn't going to be much help if I drove into the back of a silent bulldozer. I hit the lights. We edged ahead, behind a berm, between berms, back behind one. I examined the towers. I listened through the open window to the gunfire in the fields. It was definitely closer than two miles.

Suddenly I heard quicker, heavier bursts of gunfire, and I felt the rear of the pickup lurch, as if the bed was slammed by a wrecking ball. The windshield cracked.

"They're shooting at us!" the specialist screamed. "That's at us!"

I floored the accelerator, tearing forward to get out of the zone of fire. Bullets slammed into the truck's hollow body. We roared ahead, and the truck briefly went airborne over a ditch. We crashed, radiator-first, into a high berm. My helmet and body armor gave some protection from the blow, but they didn't stop my face from slamming into the steering wheel. I don't know if I saw stars or if I saw tracers. The blow was so intense that I didn't register pain. Dazed, bleeding from my nose and mouth, I foggily saw the specialist fumbling with his door handle.

"Get out!" he screamed. His torn voice had a sense of urgency born of mortal terror—he was probably realizing for the first time that he could actually be killed in Iraq. All of us, sooner or later, had that moment of realization, when our mind made the unexpected, horrifying leap from *This is unreal* to *No, this is as real as it gets, and it's for keeps.*

I pushed open the door and jumped into the ditch. The radiator hissed. I vaguely heard water dripping. The cooling engine clicked in the night. The truck gave me some protection from the distant *pop-pop-pop-pop* of insurgent fire. The specialist, exposed on his side of the cab, scrambled around the truck bed to join me. Bullets slammed with hollow thuds into the side of the pickup.

"We need to run to the tower," I said. My mouth was thick with blood. I spit, wiped my mouth on my sleeve, and saw the red streak there. Still stunned, I grabbed the young man by the arm, got up, and ran, half-stumbling, toward the tower. Our crash had made a lot of noise, and I knew we had to have gotten the attention of the men in the nearest guard tower. I knew, in fact, that we had probably spooked them. It was dark, and they couldn't see us.

"Awguf! Awguf etlaq alnahr!" I yelled, still running. *One of these Iraqis is going to shoot us while we run to him.* I was afraid they'd think we were insurgents who were attacking from behind. "Stop! Cease fire!"

They must have recognized my American-accented Arabic. They held their fire.

Five or six Iraqis scrambled down from the tower and tackled me as I approached. They surrounded the specialist and me, unexpectedly finding themselves in the company of Raed Zakkiyah. They pinned me down and ripped away my body armor. They threw out all manner of Arabic exclamations. Blood dribbled down my face. The Iraqis put their hands on me in the darkness, feeling for gunshot wounds. I was curious about whether they'd find any too. There were none. The specialist had not been struck either. I couldn't believe it.

The guard house was built on a long, low-slung building, and the tower rose from one end, overlooking the fields. Iraqis in the tower fired their AK-47s from behind a low wall of wood and sandbags. The specialist quickly joined them, firing his American rifle in short bursts. There was a lot of quick talk going on in Arabic. I still had my radio. I called CMATT.

"Get a platoon ready," I said. "I want the battalion to stand up three squads to reinforce the southern perimeter. We may lose a tower. They may try to breach. I want to be able to counterattack."

"Roger that," someone responded over the radio. "What happened up there?"

I told him about the crash.

"Are you all right?" It was another voice on the net, a lieutenant colonel who advised the Iraqis at the division level. "Do you need help?" He meant did I need medical help, personally.

"I'm banged up," I said, "but I'm all right." My voice was shaky in my own ears.

A volley of machine-gun fire ripped toward us through the night, and Iraqis responded all along the perimeter. CMATT X-ray came onto the net.

"Sir, what can you tell us?" I knew everyone from CMATT was there in the operations room back at CMATT headquarters, listening. Probably every American with a Motorola was tuned in, listening to the fight. I wanted to give a quick, calm report. I told him—told them all—that we were taking fire, but I would get back to them after I fully assessed the situation.

One of the Iraqis had night-vision goggles. I told him to give them to me. I gazed out into the night. It took a moment to orient myself, but forms slowly took shape in the distance, shadows in the goggles' soupy green light. Armed men stood around two pickup trucks, maybe four hundred meters away. They swiveled their mounted guns. The men firing the AK-47s sounded closer, but I couldn't see them. They would need to get within three hundred meters for AK-47 fire to be effective. Probably they were against the ground.

CMATT X-ray came on the net again. The sergeant major had a sortie of two Kiowa helicopters ready from Angel Base, the heliport area. The small choppers were armed with 22-mm rockets, and two ranged over Taji at all times, patrolling the sky.

Machine-gun fire tore out of the field of okra and onions, raking the tower and the berms around us. Those guns had to go. An excited voice on the radio reported in Arabic that the attackers had RPGs. My fear was that insurgents with RPGs would creep up under cover of the machine guns to within an effective range—seventy-five meters or so—and take out one of our towers. I remembered that Curt had once led a defense of the base against insurgents who fired volleys of RPGs at us. Were they testing us then for a major attack tonight? I had to assume the worst.

The CMATT sergeant major came back on the net: "Oscar Four Zulu, be advised that platoon is going to need fifteen minutes to arrive at your location."

I was stunned. "What the hell is taking them so long?"

"Oscar Four Zulu, they have to draw weapons and ammunition."

Shit. I told him I wanted the surgeon Adnan Naji to set up triage back at battalion headquarters. I needed a vehicle on standby to take any wounded from the berms to the base hospital. I expected it to get worse. I thought it would be that kind of fight.

More fire raked the southern perimeter. I climbed to the roof of the tower, above the sandbags where I would have the best visibility, holding the goggles to my face, as bullets sliced the air. The specialist joined me. I ripped off my helmet so I could use the goggles more easily. An Iraqi soldier, lying prone on the roof, tugged at my leg. He pointed to the helmet and tapped his head, trying to tell me to put it back on.

"CMATT X-ray, this is Oscar Four Zulu," I said into the handset. "I want those Kiowas."

In short order, the Kiowa helicopters came on station. I warned CMATT that the attackers had RPGs. CMATT would relay the warning to Angel Base, which would in turn warn the pilots. I feared a chopper going down, but then again, if the insurgents did have RPGs, they had not used them yet. We'd heard no explosions.

"Oscar Four Zulu, this is CMATT X-ray. Sortie needs guidance onto target. Can you mark it?"

"Affirm, X-ray," I said. "We can mark."

The Kiowa pilots wanted us to fire bright tracer bullets onto the technicals. From the air, our bullets would appear as a glowing, neon line against the dark earth. Where that line ended is where the Kiowas would fire their rockets. I asked around and found that the Iraqis didn't have tracer bullets.

I checked my own gear. I had three magazines of tracer rounds. I asked the specialist if he had tracers. He did.

I gave the specialist my night-vision goggles. I verbally directed him where to fix his gaze. He stared quietly. Then he spoke: "I've got them."

"Can you mark those targets?"

"Hell yes, sir."

I turned, put the Motorola handset to my head, and raised CMATT X-ray. I gave them my location. I gave them the direction and distance to the targets. I told them we would mark the technicals with tracers at my command. My message wound through the net back to the Kiowa pilots.

"I need you to put a steady rate of fire on that target until I tell you to cease fire," I told the young American soldier.

I waited a couple of seconds more.

"Fire," I said.

The specialist opened up with his M4.

I toggled the handset. "X-ray, we're marking target."

"Stand by," said the sergeant major. Another message wound its way through Angel Base to the helos and back again. "Affirm, they have the target."

The Kiowas let loose with their rockets. Their roar pierced the air over us, the sound like that of some huge, terrifying vacuum cleaner. I had never had one fly so close above my head before. The rockets tore forward and punctuated the night with percussive explosions out in the fields. They went off like a massive pyrotechnic fishnet flung out over our enemies. All along the perimeter, the Iraqis cheered.

Our attackers weren't done. After a pause, another volley of small-arms and machine-gun fire met the Iraqi's vocal celebration. Metallic ricochets erupted off a bulldozer behind our tower. The battalion soldiers put their heads down, stopped cheering, and answered with their own volley of fire. In the night beside and in front of me for hundreds of meters, determined Arab men were trying to kill each other. A young enlisted Arab from the Fifth next to me yanked a clip from his AK. It dropped, hollow. His fingers scrambled over his body, around the floor beneath him, desperate for another clip. Most of the Iraqis lacked what we called "fire discipline." They wasted ammunition. We were paying for that habit now.

I radioed Helms: "Echo Six Hotel, it's Zacchea. Get Yousif Badr to check on ammo levels for the towers. We have guys starting to run out."

CMATT X-ray came back onto the net.

"Oscar Four Zulu, can you provide bomb-damage assessment?"

Where there once had been a truck in my night-vision goggles, a white fire now spit in the night. I told him that much, or a version of it. CMATT X-ray said he could repeat the attack if we marked again. I agreed. In short order, a second volley of rockets was slamming the distant insurgents like a tidal blast.

I began pacing the length of the roof while bullets buzzed over the sandbags like killer wasps. I still had to deal with the insurgents who were on foot. I didn't know how many of them there were. I didn't know where they were. I could not guide rocket fire from one of the hovering Kiowas. In the meantime, a second technical was still active, loosing sheets of fire across our berms.

Still no big explosions up against us, though. Still. I contemplated something.

"CMATT X-ray, I don't think they have RPGs," I said. I waited a beat, thinking hard, *You'd better be right about this, Zacchea.* I toggled the radio. "We would've seen them by now. I think that was a false report."

"Copy, Oscar Four Zulu. First sortie is Winchester," said the X-ray sergeant major, using military shorthand to explain that the Kiowas were out of ammunition. "Second sortie is coming on station."

I took the goggles, spotted the second insurgent pickup, and gave the night-vision gear back to the specialist. The insurgents were committed to the attack; I had to give them that. If I had been them, I definitely would have aborted after the Kiowas blew up the first truck. I talked the specialist onto the target. He opened up again with his M4. The second sortie of Kiowas blasted it with two volleys of rockets.

Again, the Iraqi soldiers cheered. One jundi craned his neck up and cupped a hand to his mouth, spittle flying along with Arabic vitriol against our enemies. Again, angry small-arms fire answered from the fields. I wished my Iraqis would stop cheering.

The Kiowas gave their own bomb-damage assessment through to X-ray, and X-ray passed it along to us: two burning vehicles and eight bodies. The second sortie thundered back to Angel Base. A third arrived shortly after.

I realized that the dismounted insurgents, especially the ones who had come farthest forward to fight us at close range, were trapped. They could not escape by vehicle. They fought on. *These are al-Qaeda guys*, I thought. They're determined, more so than regular insurgents. The al-Qaeda fighters were always ready to die, in a way I could not understand.

More enemy rounds licked hot against the rolls of earth around us. The Iraqi soldiers called out to them in Arabic, taunting them. The insurgents yelled back, cursing the soldiers on the perimeter. Enemies screaming in the same language to one another.

I watched the fields, and then turned to the American specialist. "They're going to have to fight their way out," I said.

Over the next several hours, sporadic firefights flared up and down the perimeter. I remained on the tower, pacing the roof, directing the men, reporting updates back to CMATT. Adrenaline coursed through me. It was difficult to keep track of time, and the night seemed somehow both to move quickly and to drag on interminably. Finally, as the air warmed and the first rays of light crept over the Tigris to the east, it became quiet. Two trails of smoke snaked up from the vast fields. Twisted steel lay where they rose.

It was over. I called CMATT X-ray to let them know. They asked me to return for an after-action report.

The air conditioning tried to freeze me as I walked into CMATT headquarters. Even at night in September, it was still getting hot outside. I was soaked with sweat. As I pulled off my body armor, my desert camouflage blouse and trousers were rimed with salt stains. Flecks of blood adorned my filthy face.

Handshakes greeted me all around. The CMATT sergeant major, smiling, handed me a huge mug of piping-hot coffee. We spent two hours talking over the events of the night, sitting around the big table in our regular meeting room. I had not slept for a long time, and it was work for me to hold my head together. Adrenaline left me shaky. I was exhausted, yes, but I was thrilled. We agreed to do a patrol to see if we could find bodies, brass, any kind of battlefield intelligence.

What we found—or, I should say, what we did not find—stupefied us. No bodies. No blood trails. No bullet casings. Only the two burning hulks of what used to be pickup trucks, and, here and there, drag marks where the insurgents pulled their dead through the spinach and beans. We knew that the insurgents tried to retain their casings in order to melt down the brass for sale in the markets, but how many rounds had they fired? Thousands? We also knew that Arabs were generally particular about bodies and body parts, seeing to it that they weren't left behind. But no blood? Their ability to wipe out almost all trace of themselves staggered me. They had cleaned literally everything they could clean and hauled off literally everything they could carry, and they had done it all at nighttime, under fire.

It was 8 AM before I returned to our battalion area. It felt like home. The officers had formed up the battalion for my return. As I came around a corner into the men's view, they erupted into cheers. A big Iraqi sergeant pumped my hand.

"You are a hero, sir!" he said. "I tell you truly, the battalion sees you are a hero!"

I acknowledged the men with a wave, trying to exude the air of a professional Marine, but was also touched by the burst of emotion they showed me. Individuals stood out to me, beaming: Ahmed Nu'uman, Abdallah and Arkan, Iskander in his cocky glory.

I went to the motor pool and met with the Iraqi platoon that had been called to reinforce us during the night. Men smiled broadly at me. They had taken no casualties. I had called them there so we could visit the farmer who owned the fields south of the base. We needed to question him. He might have seen things the night before that would teach us something, anything, about the insurgents. He may have even interacted with them. CMATT loaned us a translator named Alia. We boarded four or five pick-ups and drove to the south gate.

A US Army master sergeant, a big-bellied, broad-faced American who reminded me of a country sheriff, waited for us there. He was to join us. His job was to report back to the US Army officers when we were done. We led the patrol out the gate and into the field. It was a bright, clear morning, but hot. The sun was merciless. The temperature would spike over 120 degrees later that afternoon, and there in the morning it was already over 100 degrees.

The farmer lived in a low-slung, one-story house of yellow-brown cement and brick. We didn't need to knock. He opened the door as the platoon dismounted from hot pickup beds. He strode toward the US master sergeant, Alia, and me with apparent purpose. Iraqi NCOs began shouting orders. Some of the platoon set up a perimeter defense. Others fanned out to search the farm's outbuildings.

The mustachioed, middle-aged farmer waved the sleeves of his dirty dishdasha and shouted in angry Arabic. He easily picked out Alia as our interpreter and began screaming right at him. He wasn't looking at me or the Army master sergeant. I kept my eyes on him but raised an eyebrow for Alia.

"He wants to know why we are here, Raed Zakkiyah," Alia said. "He asks why we attacked his farm last night."

I glanced at Alia as he spoke; I shifted my gaze back onto the farmer. If he wanted to have it that way, I decided he would have it that way. I was without sleep and in a bad mood.

"Tell this man that I will do the asking, and he will do the answering," I said.

Alia's Arabic translation silenced the farmer. I spoke directly to the man.

"Why did he let insurgents use his farm to attack us?"

The farmer remained angry, pulling at his salt-and-pepper hair and waving his arms as he spoke. It was then that, over his shoulder, something caught my attention: A line of young men began exiting the farmhouse, one by one. Two, then three, then seven, then I lost count. They approached warily. Even an Arab farmer wouldn't have this many sons. Two of the Iraqi NCOs saw the newcomers and trotted over, rifles ready. I saw no weapons on the young men, though that didn't mean none were there. They gathered around, getting close as Iraqis tended to, so they could listen to our exchange.

The Army master sergeant and I exchanged a look. The two Iraqi NCOs moved closer to the men, the muzzles of their AK-47s pointed at the ground but their fingers on the triggers. The young men stared the Fifth Battalion sergeants dead in the eyes, silent, studying them. I knew instantly: *They're memorizing their faces. They want to be able to recognize them later.* Every man there knew that's what was happening. It made me admire my Iraqi sergeants' courage.

"He says no one used his farm to attack. He says there were no insurgents here," Alia said. The farmer shouted. Alia looked at the farmer as he spoke, and his eyes told me that he didn't even want to translate the man's next line of accusation. "You are making things up, he says."

Again, I fixed my eyes on the farmer

"I did not make up the bullet holes in my wounded soldiers. I am happy to take him to my base so that I can show him those soldiers," I said. Alia followed me word for word in Arabic, not waiting for me to finish my sentences.

"Tell him," I said, "that if I find out he is lying to me, I will shoot him in front of his family here."

The platoon's first lieutenant stood at a distance with his back turned, directing junood about. He turned and saw the men who had gathered near me. He rapped one jundi's shoulder with his knuckles, and they came to my back.

The farmer and I continued our back-and-forth, the small crowd growing. The Iraqi lieutenant began questioning the young men with angry shouts. They all looked to be in their late teens or early twenties. The lieutenant told them to disperse. He demanded their attention: "Why are you here?" Alia listened to the exchange between the lieutenant and the young men.

"They say they are simple farmhands, laborers trying to earn some *floos*," Alia said to me.

Another sergeant approached, one of the men who had been searching. He said they had found nothing, not a single weapon. The lack of any kind of weapon at all was in and of itself suspicious. Every house in Iraq had at least one AK-47. Ever hear of a farm, even in the United States, that doesn't have a rifle somewhere?

Fresh hay lay strewn here and there where the ground was freshly furrowed, and when the soldiers swept the hay aside with their boots, they saw large indentations in the loose earth. Man-sized indentations. They also found a handful of brass casings. It was more than we found in the fields just south of Taji, but it wasn't enough for me to take the farmer into custody. I gave a signal to the lieutenant. He in turn nodded at his NCOs, and the men were ordered out. As a group, we made our way back toward the pickups. As we walked, the farmer mocked us in Arabic.

"He asks, Major, 'Where are the dead bodies? Where are the burnt vehicles?'" Alia was a professional. He translated even when we were done listening.

The Army master sergeant, who was walking away with us, turned quickly back to face the farmer.

"Who the hell said anything about burnt vehicles? Nobody said nothing about burned-up vehicles," he said. "How you know anything about burnt vehicles?"

Alia shouted the translation to the farmer, now several paces behind us.

The farmer looked away. He knew he had made a mistake. Some of the young "farmhands" turned away as well.

The Iraqi lieutenant, the American sergeant, Alia, and I walked back to the farmer. I stood close to him.

"I will spare your home," I said over a wind that had begun to blow, "but I will burn your fields." Alia translated, and without being ordered, some of the enlisted men, especially some I knew to be Shiites, began producing cigarette lighters and setting fire to the hay spread about on the ground. Taji is a mostly Sunni area. We didn't have to tell the men to do anything. They fanned along the edge of a field stitched with bean plants. Flames almost immediately hopscotched down the neat, thick rows.

"You must choose between us and the insurgents," I said to the farmer. Alia followed me word for word. "You can't play both sides against the other. The next time I have to come out here because insurgents are using your farm as a base to attack my troops, I will kill you."

I arrived back at my room in CMATT village around noon. I had not eaten for eighteen hours. I wanted to clean up and get lunch and sleep. I walked down to the shower room wearing my towel. The hard tile hurt my sore feet. As soon as the hot water hit me, my body seized up. That was it. I was out of gas. I collapsed to the shower floor. I rubbed my legs for a moment but then let exhaustion take me.

There I lay. The dusty streaks across my arms and legs broke ranks and made for the drain. I shut my eyes.

In the depths of heaviest fatigue, there's no room for politics, no room for self-doubt. That's one nice thing about it. Awake still, my mind was a blissful void. Forget gunfire and generals, rockets and helicopters, cultural chasms and phrases in Arabic. The water rinsed over me. I had room left only for abstraction.

Rudyard Kipling and his wolves. *Canis lupus.* Iraqis and their canine ways. Marines with their lupine rules. Flashing eyes and plaintive howls.

The perimeter was secure. The battalion had succeeded. I had succeeded.

There on the wet tiles, I reflected, and not for the last time: for better and for worse, I had gotten to where I wanted to be.

9

ABDUCTED

A CALM SETTLED OVER TAJI. It was short.

There was more than one of those dailies Curt had warned me about. Marines gripe about meetings just like working civilians do, and for the same reason: there's a lot to do, and we can't do it while we're in meetings talking about it. If I had wanted, I could have spent my entire day, every day, at meetings. One daily was the CMATT logistics meeting, which included representatives for all the base tenants—Iraqi and US units, plus contractors. It was hosted by a Major Gallagher, who advised Taji's commanders. The day after the firefight and my run-in with our farmer neighbor, three contractors were mysterious no-shows at the meeting. All worked for an outfit called Gulf Supplies and Commercial Services, a firm based in Abu Dhabi. They were helping transform Taji into a logistics depot. Two were Americans, and one was a Brit. Their names were Eugene Armstrong, Jack Hensley, and Kenneth Bigley.

It's impossible for me to pin down a single incident from Iraq that marked a turning point for my psychological health. That's partly because of the sheer volume of experience, which ranged from laughable absurdities to something akin to waking night terrors. There's also the mysterious apparatus known as our neurology, and the hard physical injuries mine took. There in the middle of September, I had in a short span worried about the murders of

161

truck drivers, organized defenses of Taji under fire, attuned myself like a Geiger counter for the wailing sounds of incoming mortars, sleeplessly chased ghost snipers, witnessed the chow-hall bombing, and slammed my head into a steering wheel. I knew pressure was building. But if there's a moment at which my self from before the war was severed from the self I am now, if there was an awful chrysalis, it was what happened to Armstrong, Hensley, and Bigley.

On September 16, Major Gallagher had an update for us. He said the men had disappeared on Highway 1 to Baghdad. "We fear they've been abducted by insurgents."

The room had questions. A CMATT sergeant major named Saxon, a square-jawed bull of a man, was especially concerned. He worked closely with the three men. Gallagher didn't have a lot to share with us, and what he said prompted more questions. The men had apparently traveled to Baghdad without any escort. That didn't make sense. Highway 1 to Baghdad was terrifically dangerous. As a main supply route for Taji, it came under constant attack. The contractors knew that. Sitting there listening to Gallagher and Saxon's exchange, I first thought, *This doesn't add up.* Then, *Were they set up by someone on the base?* And then, *Were they set up by someone in Fifth Battalion?*

The insurgents had preyed on Iraqi truckers serving Taji through August. The useless Iraqi Civil Defense Corps hadn't secured the area around us. Armstrong, Hensley, and Bigley knew how dangerous the roads were. They knew Iraqi colleagues and others who had been slaughtered. We all knew what happened to the Blackwater contractors who were hung from the bridge at Fallujah, and what had happened to Nick Berg, a contractor beheaded by Abu Musab al-Zarqawi that April. And Zarqawi's group wasn't the only one engaged in a cycle of kidnapping followed by ritual slaughter. Our enemies were disparate and often not even allied with one another.

These contractors were men I knew, men I talked with daily. Bigley's abduction would become a geopolitical event in its own right, as Tony Blair and the United Kingdom, followed by the Republic of Ireland, Yasser Arafat, and the Kingdom of Jordan made public pleas to spare him. Less was told of Armstrong and Hensley. Gene Armstrong was from Hillsdale, Michigan. He liked bass fishing. He had worked overseas before, but found himself in short-term jobs whenever he was stateside. He took a chance on Iraq. Jack Hensley and his wife ran a bar in Powder Springs, Georgia, but then ran into money problems. Jack worked three part-time jobs simultaneously—in a convenience store, as a substitute teacher, and in a post office—before he decided to risk the Iraq War. The men were emblematic of the American civilians in Taji. They liked the idea of making $120,000 or so, most of it untaxable, for a year of work overseas. But these were people who were even less psychologically prepared for Iraq than your average nineteen-year-old Marine, who had at least been told what to expect. When I think of the American contractors at Taji, I think of people like the hungry-looking woman who ran the CMATT laundry, a former waitress from East Texas who in a few weeks developed anxious, feral eyes. Most of them had no idea what they had gotten into.

I knew that Armstrong, Hensley, and Bigley understood the horrific fate rushing at them. Zayn and I visited the Taji supply warehouses daily, sometimes to get equipment, sometimes to offer something in trade, sometimes just to sit over cups of chai and chat with the Americans and Iraqis who worked there. Zayn and I had put in a lot of time to build rapport with the contractors. These were men whom Zayn and I had looked in the eye, negotiated with, joked with.

"What were they thinking?" Sergeant Major Saxon asked me one evening, his face red and deeply lined. He shook his head mournfully, as if already accepting the men's deaths. "What were they doing? I just don't understand."

I don't remember the words of condolence I gave Saxon. It's awkward offering sympathy for friends who aren't yet dead.

We were stumped. No one knew why they were on the road without security. We speculated that maybe their interpreter sold them out. But we also, it turned out, were operating in the fog of war. Good information was rare, and all information was hard to confirm. Through no fault of his own, Gallagher was wrong about the circumstances around the abductions. I would learn the truth about them years later. The three contractors had a house in Mansour, one of Baghdad's wealthier neighborhoods. At that point in the war, some Western civilians still lived openly in Baghdad. The men had been kidnapped from their beds. Coming so close after the firefight on the perimeter, people in Taji took the abductions as retaliation for the defeat we inflicted on the insurgents. Now I know the events weren't related. But from where we stood at the time, it seemed they had to be linked.

Over the next couple of days, the captives pleaded for their lives on TV. Their families, broadcast from the United States and Britain, pleaded as well. The insurgents threatened to behead a "prisoner" every forty-eight hours until their demands were met. Those demands were ridiculous. They wanted the release of all female prisoners held in Iraq by the allied coalition. The United States had only two female prisoners linked to the war, neither of them in Iraq. Great Britain held no female prisoners.

We calculated the contractors' life expectancies in weeks if they were lucky, days if they were not. On September 18, insurgents beheaded three Kurdish truck drivers. They posted the massacre on the Internet—a new media tactic at the time.

On September 20, I retired after the evening meal to a small room the Fifth Battalion officers set up as a sort of officers' mess. It was a ritual for us, a brief decompression before bed. I was happy Zayn was there. He had returned from leave the day before. He had already berated me for putting myself in danger during the fight on the berms. Among the officers gathered there were the CO Ahmed Nu'uman, the staff officers Mohammed Thyab and Mohammed Najm, a Shiite major named Hodi Jamaal and retired captain turned interpreter Sala'am. We sat in the pale-yellow room and shared sweet rice with raisins, spiced vegetables, and roasted chicken. An enlisted man served chai, and its smell filled the room.

We watched their television. They had somehow procured a big TV with a sharp picture. I already didn't like Al Jazeera for its anti-American editorializing and usually asked the officers if we

could switch to another channel. The officers' TV also picked up
Al Sharqiya and Al Arabiya, as well as the US-sponsored Al Iraqiya.
We sometimes debated the merits of Middle Eastern journalism.
Even the most neutral presentation included scenes that would
be censored in the West—images of dead children in the streets,
mangled people crying out from hospital beds—usually attributed
to "Zionists" or "crusaders." We were always hungry for news of
the war, but our interest was acute that night. We watched Al
Jazeera. It's an irony of fighting in a war that you're starved for
perspective on the conflict that's surrounding you. It's hard to see
the machine from inside.

We couldn't have steeled ourselves for what was coming even
if we had known about it in advance.

Al Jazeera aired a video. On the television, Gene Armstrong sat
in a nondescript room with flat lighting. Trussed, sitting on the
floor, looking miserable, looking scared. Only a few days removed
from the relative comfort and camaraderie of Taji. Five men, all
masked, stood behind him. A black banner hung on the wall
behind him.

And there was their leader, our enemy, Zarqawi, with his dis-
tinct, shrill voice.

The officers' mess went silent. No one ate. No one drank. No
one even seemed to breathe as it unfolded on the screen:

Zarqawi, shorter than the other men in the room, stood in the
center with Gene. He read a statement in Arabic.

"I will be so happy when your children and your people see
your nose turn red with anger over this," Zarqawi said in English.
"Now, Mr. Bush, we will make you drink from the same cup from
which you made our brothers in Abu Ghraib drink."

He casually pulled a knife from the waistband of his baggy
pants.

This, I realized, is actually going to happen. It couldn't be real.
But there he was on TV: Gene. He looked gray. He was blind-
folded in white. I couldn't watch. I couldn't not watch. I knew I
shouldn't watch. I knew already at that moment that I would never
be the same, would never be able to unsee what was coming.

Zarqawi bent one knee and leaned Gene to one side so he could get at his neck from a better angle. He pulled back Gene's head by his wispy hair. The knife sawed through Gene's throat. Gene made a sound somewhere between a scream and a moan, with a choke of blood.

To turn away would be to abandon him. He was going to die. I could stay with him, even if only at the receiving end of a TV broadcast. It was nothing, but what more could I do? What more could any of us do? Gene gurgled in his blood, aware of his own death, surrounded by men in black speaking a language he didn't understand.

Zarqawi balanced Gene's head on one raised palm. The body collapsed onto its stomach. Zarqawi lay the head upright on the body's back. The wrists were still tied there. Crimson engulfed the floor.

I couldn't stop the horrific speculation that flitted through my mind: *Did he still have awareness? Could he see his body? Was that the last thing he saw?* My eyes hurt. I wanted to burn them out. My head was down, my hands in my eyes, rubbing hard. The Iraqis around me made a tsk sound, as they did when they discussed the dead. Zayn put his hand softly on my shoulder.

"Praying?" he asked.

I grabbed Zayn's hand and looked into his face. I couldn't respond.

The interpreter Sala'am, a man of more refined sensibilities than most of us, was in tears. His rage was primal.

"*What is this!?*" he cried. "Where did this barbarism come from? This is not us—this is not Iraq! Who are these people? They are not Muslims! This is not our religion!"

The room became a spinning globe of screen and furniture and camouflage uniforms. I stood for a helpless beat and felt myself clench up in that awful space, which had abruptly become an eternal space, or which I at least knew was going to live as long as I did. I swallowed. Dry. I needed to be alone. The electric audio swirl receded down a hall behind me as I marched out at a half run, wordlessly. I made my way through the night back to the American quarters. I clambered to the roof. I sat in the dark, looking out over the desert. The occasional tracer round, fired as usual for who knows what reason, cut through the sky like a shooting star played backward.

Deep inside me, in a place I'd never known, something moved. I couldn't name it then, but it felt cold even in the stifling heat of that still evening. I didn't know its name. I imagined it like black ice spread over a still New England road. It lay like a cold, dangerous way of trespass. Now I know its name. Rage. It was rage. I never expected to feel it, to let myself feel it, to find myself fighting it. My war had been about anxiety and sometimes desperation, yes, but never about my heart. It never owned that part of me. I had never *wanted* to kill anyone. Then hate stuck in me, sick and irretrievable.

Two days later, Jack was dead. I couldn't fathom the despair he and Ken felt, knowing Gene was beheaded, knowing they were next, knowing what brutality lay in their future. I watched that video too. I couldn't not watch it. This time we braced for it. We knew what to expect. It didn't make any difference. Ken followed after that.

I was approached at my quarters a few days after the last murder. Two junood said I was wanted at Taji's front gate. Iraqi civilians often arrived at the base entrance, about two and a half miles from my quarters, to ask for me. Some wanted me to help them get jobs. Others hoped I could get relatives out of detention. This time the guards said only that someone had a message for me.

"No go, Major Zakkiyah," Zayn said softly to me as we sat at his desk. Arkan was with us, but Zayn chose to use English for emphasis. He always addressed me by my rank, no matter how many times I told him to just call me by my first name.

"Why not, Zayn?"

This time he spoke in Arabic for Arkan to interpret, still uttering his words softly.

"This is not people coming for a favor," Arkan said. "This is a message."

My face must have shown that I still wasn't getting it. The two men spoke in Arabic. Zayn looked into my eyes as he might have looked at an impatient child. He stood, walked to me, and pressed his hands on my shoulders, as if to keep me there. He stuck me to my seat.

Arkan said, "He thinks it may be a bomb. The insurgents will try to kill you because of the defeat they suffered." Zayn was saying I was a marked man.

"Oh, Zayn, come on. They don't even know who I am."

Arkan didn't translate for me.

"Arkan, tell him!"

A few of the Fifth Battalion officers had survived attempts on their lives. Somehow, I imagined the danger as impersonal. In my mind, the threat was directed at all of us, not specifically at me.

"Believe me, sir, if the farmers know you, the insurgents do too," Arkan said. "They know it was you who called in the air strikes the other night, and you went to the farm and burned it. They will kill you. They will pay to kill you."

I thought of the young men on the farm, how they had studied our faces. Then it dawned on me: Zayn was telling me I was a marked man. I had a bounty on my head.

Zayn ordered two junood to drive to the front gate and take the message for me. He reasoned it was an appropriate task for an enlisted man. Insurgents were unlikely to waste a suicide bomber on a mere jundi.

In short order, the men returned. They delivered a sealed envelope.

Zayn took it before I could. He opened the letter with a small pocketknife. His eyes narrowed as he silently read the Arabic script. He didn't want to translate it for me at first, but I suppose he realized there was no way around it. He handed it to Arkan.

"The message says, 'The infidel Zakkiyah will die like the other dogs,'" Arkan said. He dropped his hand to his side and looked at me.

"They will kill you," Zayn told me in English. He remained calm, almost serene. "You must be very careful—even with our soldiers."

The following day, during formation, Zayn strode to the front and addressed the battalion. His tone had changed radically. He yelled at the men in sharp slashes of Arabic, his upper lip peeled back and his gaze unflinching. I wasn't there at the time, but Sala'am later told me what he told the assembled troops.

"If any of you harm Raed Zakkiyah," Zayn screamed at them, "I will kill you all!"

10

"THE FIRST BULLET WILL BE FOR ME"

THE BEST MILITARY OFFICERS fixate on the problem in front of them while simultaneously remaining detached enough to discern what caused it. Counter the immediate crisis; take steps to prevent it from happening again. A challenge specific to military advisers is that the underlying causes of most problems come from a culture separate from his or her own. Problems spring from an alien context. We must navigate cultural complexities as we go. On top of that, it can be difficult to gauge whether we're succeeding or failing. Signals can be very, very hard to read. In Iraq, I whiplashed from optimism to pessimism and back, sometimes within twenty-four hours. It was like being a driver on a slick road, trying not to overcorrect as the skid comes on. I gripped the wheel as the course shifted beneath me. Off either side of that road lay failure or death, or both.

Shortly after Armstrong, Hensley, and Bigley were slaughtered, I gathered the advisers in a closed meeting. We agreed to two standing rules. We made a pact.

"First, we will do anything to avoid capture," I told them. "When I say 'anything,' I mean anything. That includes criminal acts. It includes sacrificing Iraqi troops."

They nodded silently.

"Second, we will each save one bullet for ourselves in extremis," I said. "If any of us realize we are about to be captured, we will not subject our families and our country to the spectacle of Zarqawi sawing off our heads on Al Jazeera."

Everyone quietly agreed. I wasn't breaking bad news to anybody. We all knew what would happen if we fell into the insurgents' hands. I was acknowledging a real problem, and we were agreeing on how to handle it if worse came to worst.

By the middle of September, seven of the original ten advisers were gone. Also that month, we got two more replacements. Both were active-duty Marines. One was a tough, no-nonsense master sergeant named A. J. Elesky. The other was named Brian Mulvihill, and he came from a family of Irish American New York City cops. Mulvihill was a captain, like Johnson, and the two officers would become a sort of yin-and-yang team. Where Johnson was rational and straitlaced, Mulvihill was tightly wound and emphatic. I was grateful to have two such different outlooks in my junior officers.

The Fifth Battalion was fully operational. We began regular missions around Taji. The junood kitted up in Kevlar and checked their weapons. Iskander snapped his walking stick against his thigh. The white pickups cranked like lawn mowers firing up in unison. Captain Mulvihill blasted Celtic punk—that was how he got fired up. For the rest of 2004, bands like the Dropkick Murphys and Flogging Molly performed the shredding, fiddling soundtrack of our war.

Has the shepherd led his lambs astray to the bigot and the gun?
Must it take a life for hateful lies to glisten once again?
'Cause we find ourselves in the same old mess, singing
    drunken lullabies.

We moved one or two rifle companies at a time, mounted in the beds of their Nissans. Sometimes we headed south in convoy down Freeway 1 toward Baghdad, sometimes north. Other times we dismounted in villages nearer to the base. We began to score small victories. On September 29, a Fifth Battalion rifle company running a tactical control point caught an insurgent holding 57-mm rockets. The next day, the same company carried out a raid with a Rhode Island National Guard unit and captured two more insurgents.

The irhabeen struck back. On October 3, they ambushed the Rhode Islanders, killing two American sergeants. The second was a medic they shot as he tried to rescue the first.

So we struck back harder. Two days after the American sergeants lost their lives, another Fifth Battalion rifle company, working alongside the Rhode Islanders, carried out a strike against a mosque and took twenty-two insurgents prisoner with no casualties. We delivered them to the Taji detention center, where they would be processed and adjudicated. Fifth Battalion also captured the biggest cache of weapons and IEDs that had been taken by anyone up to that point from the insurgency—hundreds of mortars, rockets, mines, rifles, machine guns, and more.

The mosque raid was led by First Lt. Mohammed Ahmed, who like my friend Zayn was a Sunni from Mosul. Just a year before, Mohammed Ahmed had been a paratrooper in Saddam Hussein's army. We were beginning to figure out that the officers from Saddam's army were usually the best officers in the new army too. It made it that much clearer how shortsighted Bremer's decision was to put all those guys out on the street. Mohammed Ahmed was allowed to join the new army. But many of Saddam's officers, blocked from the new army, were joining Zarqawi's fighters and other enemy groups. The green shoots of insurgency sprouted across the Iraqi dust, and Washington still wouldn't acknowledge their existence.

Operationally, that was the rhythm of our counterinsurgency war. We succeeded somewhere. The enemy succeeded somewhere. Everyone was out on the streets. It was almost like gang violence, but with bigger weapons. It was small units. The mosque raid led by Mohammed Ahmed involved only 87 Iraqis and 182 Americans. Fighting insurgents is nothing like the vast, army-versus-army warfare that the United States knew for most of its history. Violence in Iraq was low-level, historically speaking, but so widespread across

Michael Zacchea with Zayn al-Jibouri (left) and Abdel-ridha Gibrael (in beret), at Kirkush. Zayn became Zacchea's closest friend in Fifth Battalion, while Abdel-ridha secretly fed information to Zacchea about the Iraqi officers.

Todd Colwell, with an interpreter, fits an Iraqi recruit into boots. The New Englander Colwell fitted more than eight hundred Iraqis by himself.

Fifth Battalion recruits train outside at Kirkush.

Fifth Battalion recruits celebrate their completion of the Crucible, the brutal final two days of training at Kirkush.

Menhal Majid Hamid on the firing range. The Shiite major saved the battalion from a sudden meltdown before the fight at Fallujah with an impassioned speech in which he declared, "The first bullet will be for me."

Curt Williamson and battalion commanding officer Jassim Thammin march with the men of the Fifth. Curt would push to have Jassim removed as CO.

Curt Williamson (left) and Kevin Hummons (right) pose with Naufal Basheer, who was later kidnapped and murdered by insurgents while on leave.

Sergeant Major Iskander (left) was respected and trusted by all the enlisted men, Kurdish or Arab, Sunni or Shiite. Anthony Villa (right) gave the battalion critical rifle training.

Fifth Battalion forms up in convoy to make the perilous trip from Taji to Fallujah.

Fifth Battalion soldiers pose at East Fallujah Iraqi Camp days before the breach of Fallujah.

Amphibious assault vehicles take their positions north of Fallujah before the breach of the city.

November 8, 2004, predawn: soldiers from Fifth Battalion are packed into a Marine Corps amphibious assault vehicle minutes before the breach of Fallujah. The roofs of the AAVs are thinly armored, making them vulnerable to mortars.

Michael Zacchea and Fifth Battalion commander Sa'ad al-Harbia hours before the attack on Fallujah.

Mohammed Najm gives instructions to civilians in Fallujah. About ten thousand desperate, noncombatant civilians remained in the city during the fighting.

Carlos Forero with Iraqi boys who took shelter with Fifth Battalion during the Second Battle of Fallujah. The twenty-one-year-old Floridian served as Zacchea's driver, radio man, and sometimes bodyguard.

© Carlos Forero

The main prayer chamber at al-Hadra mosque in Fallujah. The holy place housed refugees, Iraqi troops, and Americans during the battle.
© *Andrew Brown*

Mike Suo poses with the bullet-riddled Humvee he used as cover during a firefight outside al-Hadra mosque. The Staten Islander received the Navy and Marine Corps Achievement Medal for his role in the fight.
© *Mike Suo*

Inside al-Hadra, a civilian refugee lies killed by a sniper moments before he could reach the safety of the mosque.

Mark Lombard (right) makes his rounds between the battalion's far-flung rifle companies during Fallujah.

Dead insurgents in the streets near al-Hadra mosque.

A typical street in Fallujah, wrecked by the fighting. All forty thousand buildings in Fallujah had to be searched by the Americans and their Iraqi allies.
© *Andrew Brown*

Brian Mulvihill, from a family of Irish American New York City cops, liked to blast Celtic punk to get hyped up before missions.

Fifth Battalion's Shiite commander Sa'ad al-Harbia (in khaki body armor) and his rival, Sunni second-in-command Ahmed Nu'uman (in black). The man over Sa'ad's shoulder is one of his orderlies.

From left: advisers Andrew Brown, Mark Faulkner, Chuck Johnson, and Richard Fryar in February 2005. By the end of Zacchea's tour in Iraq, he was the last remaining Marine in what had become an Army Reserve advisory team.

the country that it was impossible to track. In the first four days of October, suicide bombers hit Iraqi recruits near the Green Zone and in Mosul, killing twenty-two. A Science Ministry official was assassinated in Baghdad. One of our sister battalions, the Seventh, joined the US First Infantry Division for a three-day fight at Samarra. Meanwhile, American warplanes were bombing the insurgent stronghold of Fallujah nightly. Tens of thousands of civilians were streaming from the city.

The First Battle of Fallujah was an epic disaster. The White House abruptly decided to pull the Marines from Fallujah in the face of intense international criticism, as the battle killed civilians and destroyed parts of the city. It looked bad that no Iraqis were fighting the insurgents in Fallujah, only Americans. The Marines were ordered to hand the city to a supposedly friendly militia called Fallujah Brigade that was made up of former soldiers from Saddam Hussein's army. These were men who Paul Bremer had fired the year before. The Fallujah Brigade then handed Fallujah to the Sunni insurgency. Jubilant Fallujans celebrated what they saw as a great triumph over the US military. Our enemies seized equipment and weapons left behind by the Americans—just as ISIS would do, across Iraq, a decade later.

On October 4, the *Marine Corps Times* reported that Donald Rumsfeld was refusing to act on the recommendations of a study he had commissioned. The study called for more US troops in Iraq. Rumsfeld said the problem was that the military was not "efficient" enough. There would be no troop increase, he decided. He refused to drop his Rumsfeld Doctrine of warfare, no matter how badly it kept failing.

One morning in early October, as we were tallying the haul from Lt. Mohammed Ahmed's raid, a new face barged into our regular battalion meeting. The man was an Iraqi, thick through the shoulders and chest, shaped like a major appliance. He had ink-black hair, a mustache like the bumper of a tractor trailer, and an impossibly square head. He was not in uniform, but he clearly thought he belonged in the room. When he spoke, his voice was deep and loud and slightly slurred, like a person who's a little hard of hearing. Arkan translated for me.

"I am Colonel Sa'ad al-Harbia," he grunted. "I am now the commander of the Fifth Battalion. This is my unit. You are my officers."

The room was stunned. This was the first we'd heard of a new CO. I eyed Ahmed Nu'uman, the lieutenant colonel who had only recently taken command. His mouth hung open. He looked like a man who had been interrupted midsentence. This big Colonel Sa'ad walked heavily over to the two of us and showed us his orders. They were from the Ministry of Defense. They looked real. Just minutes later, like choreography, the chief of staff of the Iraqi First Division strode into the room and embraced Sa'ad like a brother. Specifically, a brother Shiite. They kissed cheeks while the officers and advisers watched in silence. The message was clear.

Sa'ad told us that he was a sheikh of his tribe, the al-Harbia. I knew about this tribe because some other officers in the battalion, including the incompetent former Ops O Major Aof Raheem, was from it as well. The al-Harbia were a big, influential Shiite clan from Nasiriyah, in southern Iraq. Sa'ad had been a paratrooper officer in the old army. He had fought against the Americans in Kuwait during the Gulf War. Before that, he fought Iran. In his days at Saddam Hussein's military academy, he was a competitive shot-putter.

I wanted to meet with Sa'ad privately as soon as possible. He agreed without hesitation. Maybe it was wishful thinking, I thought, but I felt optimistic about him. He had led men in combat. He certainly had a commanding presence.

"This battalion must have greater discipline," he told me through Arkan. "I will give them this discipline."

That sounded good to me.

"Our current CO, Ahmed Nu'uman, is a smart officer and a good problem solver," I said. "He's young, and the men respect him."

I updated him on all the officers, singling out Major Zayn and the operations chief, Mohammed Najm, as the best. I explained the important role the NCOs played in the battalion. I wanted to protect the progress they were making, as real decision makers who could stand up to the officers when necessary. I knew such an idea was going to be new to this big Colonel Sa'ad.

"We have a very good sergeant major, Iskander, who acts as the commander's adviser on enlisted matters," I said. "I think you'll find him and the other NCOs to be valuable assets to you."

Arkan gave it to Sa'ad in Arabic, and the colonel listened. He gave a noncommittal grunt before saying simply, "I understand soldiers very well."

My advisory team received its second WARNO on October 20. It was a big one: Operation al-Fajr—the joint US and Iraqi invasion of the biggest enemy stronghold. We were going to fight in the biggest operation of the war. Al-Fajr did not have its history-book name yet, but it does now: the Second Battle of Fallujah.

Officially, the WARNO ordered the advisers to prepare for an assault on an unnamed city. Unofficially, we knew which city it was. The order did not come as a surprise. We believed a fight in Fallujah was inevitable. We knew Iraqi units would take part. We knew the Fifth was one of the three best Iraqi battalions, along with our two sister battalions. We were practically a lock. I called a closed meeting with Captain Johnson, Captain Mulvihill, and the other advisers. The battle was still almost a month away. We did a basic mission analysis, and debated whether to tell the Iraqis now or later. Telling them immediately risked triggering a wave of desertions. Fallujah was a Sunni city. Would an order to take it make our Sunni soldiers depart? Might some go over to the other side with warning of our plans?

"We can go to the battalion's senior officers now, and then decide on the junood later," Johnson said evenly.

"And in the meantime, we dress rehearse the hell out of them until they can do it in their sleep," Mulvihill said, an edge of determination in his New York accent.

I liked it. The most important thing was to get the Iraqis started on the real work of planning and training, and that meant telling

Ahmed Nu'uman, the new Colonel Sa'ad, and the other senior officers as soon as possible.

The meeting with the Iraqi commanders went similarly, with the same debate at its core. Many officers said it was a bad idea to inform the troops so far in advance. Ahmed Nu'uman, who had just been bumped to second-in-command again with the arrival of Sa'ad, led this group. Ahmed Nu'uman was a Sunni. So were most of the others who took his side. They knew better than anyone how their fellow Sunnis would react to fighting in a Sunni city against a Sunni insurgency.

"The battalion is to be paid at the end of the month," Ahmed Nu'uman said. "That is when we are to go to Fallujah. The junood will leave us then. I am sure of this."

I understood Ahmed Nu'uman's point of view. I knew that if the WARNO told us to prepare to fight in Baghdad's Sadr City neighborhood, the center of a Shiite insurgency, it would be the Shiite officers who worried. As things stood, the Shiites mostly wanted to be open with the junood. Hodi Jamaal, the other senior officer from Sa'ad's al-Harbia tribe, led that group. Siding with Hodi Jamaal was a Shiite major named Menhal Majid Hamid. Like Sa'ad, Menhal was a veteran of the war with Iran. Menhal was an effective officer, but the advisers didn't trust him. We knew he had been imprisoned by Saddam Hussein for reasons that he could never explain satisfactorily.

Sa'ad, the gruff new commander, listened mostly in silence. The advisers were united in the conviction that we could not deceive the junood. Our own military culture called for open disclosure except when it endangered a mission. Sa'ad rubbed the stubble that grew on his face like black cactus needles and sided with his American advisers and fellow Shiites. That decided it.

"It's critical that we present a unified front," I said. "Not just to the Iraqi command structure and the American command structure, but to the junood. We must speak with one voice."

Arkan and one of the Kurdish-speaking interpreters translated for me, and something about the phrase I used—to "speak with one voice"—struck a chord. They didn't know the expression. Immediately, everyone nodded affirmation.

"Nettakalam bisaut wahed," they said. First one, then two, then everyone. "Nettakalam bisaut wahed." We speak with one voice.

We called a battalion formation on the dry parade ground. We explained that at the end of October, we would fight in a major battle. The Fifth Battalion was the hammer that would strike a blow for the future of Iraq. The phrase went out again to the men, "Nettakalam bisaut wahed," and I saw them react to it.

We speak with one voice. I saw the sentiment surge through them, as physical as a swell on the ocean, and then they were all shouting it:

"Netta-ka-lam bis-aut wa-hed! Netta-ka-lam bis-aut wa-hed!"

For a moment, I felt a rush of pride. I felt uplifted.

Then some of the Kurdish soldiers began singing and clapping and cheering something different, their own chant in their own language. They celebrated, but drifted into their own circles. Abdallah, the former physics instructor turned interpreter, was standing near me. I asked what they said.

"They say they are happy to go to kill the rabbits," he said.

I was confused.

"Rabbits," Abdallah said. "It is their word for Arabs. They want to kill rabbits."

Before I knew what hit us, some of the Arabs became angry. They tried to shout down the Kurds. Men began to push each other. Some used their fists. A flurry at the edge of my vision caught my attention, and I turned, stunned, to see my interpreter Arkan throwing a hard punch into the face of a Kurdish jundi. I couldn't believe it.

Holy shit. Arkan punched a guy? Arkan? This is going to turn into a fucking melee.

"Iskander! Get control of those men!"

The Kurd Iskander waded into the maelstrom, shouting and pushing at men. Other NCOs followed him. Zayn shouted over the din and separated jostling junood.

At that moment, Menhal, the Shiite major with the sketchy personal history, thrust himself into the center of the soldiers.

He rolled an oil drum into the crowd, turned it on its end, and climbed on top. Looking over the men, he cried at the top of his lungs, "Junood! Junood!" until they quieted down. Abdallah translated for me.

"Soldiers! Soldiers! Listen to me!"

Some stopped to listen, then more. The NCOs slowly reasserted control. Iskander and his sergeants shifted men and separated entangled companies.

"I have been a soldier for more than half my life!" Menhal cried. "I fought in Iran. I fought in Kuwait. I fought the Americans—twice! I have endured the same hardships as you, braved the same dangers as you. The enemy we face is no less dangerous now."

He turned out the pockets on his camouflage pants.

"I do not fight for money. My pockets are empty, like yours. My family is in danger, like yours. I will shed my blood like you. But I will be the first among you to engage the enemy, the first to shed my blood."

He had everyone. The battalion was silent.

"My wife will be without a husband—my children without a father! But the first bullet will be for me, if you follow me to Fallujah! The first bullet will be for me! *The first bullet will be for me!*"

The battalion roared. They leaped as one. Thirty seconds earlier, the battalion looked like it was disintegrating. Now the men chanted with Menhal, who raised his arms and threw back his head. The Kurds danced in ecstasy. Many men wept.

The first bullet will be for me! The first bullet will be for me!
And I was back. Uplifted.
The first bullet will be for me! The first bullet will be for me!
And I thought, *We will succeed. We will do this. I will deliver this battalion to Fallujah, and we will fight our enemies.*
The first bullet will be for me! The first bullet will be for me!
Nettakalam bisaut wahed.

The arrival of the Marine advisers Mulvihill and Elesky was a godsend, coming at a critical part of Fifth Battalion's new operational history. But the team was still at only eight advisers, right on the verge of the biggest battle of the Iraq War. And one of those eight, Gunny Webster, was due to leave on October 24. We got our last pre-Fallujah replacement almost by accident. Mark Lombard was a Marine in Taji working at the division level on something called Lessons Learned, a Marine Corps program that's designed to preserve that institutional knowledge we're always bleeding off as men rotate out. Lessons Learned officers observe operations and take meticulous records. They're part historian, part management consultant. They write reports that outline what worked and what didn't. The Iraq advisory effort needed men like Lombard—the Marines' last large-scale advisory efforts were in Vietnam, and we had lost a lot of know-how. In fact, we had lost basically all our know-how. We were starting from scratch, building that aircraft in midflight that Major General Eaton talked about. That said, Iraq was a war zone, Donald Rumsfeld was saying we weren't efficient enough, and the top-echelon US officers wanted everybody in the fight. Lombard, a reservist who got yanked from his wife and a job in the medical devices business to go to Iraq, was no exception.

"You're not just going to keep *diary* notes," a division-level adviser told him. "You're going to earn your *keep*."

Lombard was adviser qualified, so he was cross-decked to my team—they promoted him from captain to major and shipped him to me—just in time for Fallujah. I told Lombard that since he was now a major, I wanted him to be deputy senior adviser.

"I need somebody who can help me manage and plan in Fallujah," I said. "We'll need to oversee logistics, and we'll deal with a lot of demands—from the Iraqi command *and* the US command."

"Well," Lombard said, "at least now I know I'll observe the Iraqis under fire for Lessons Learned." He laughed and accepted my plan as easily as if I had just suggested what we'd have for lunch. Lombard, I was going to learn, took even the most harrowing things as if they were nothing at all. "That's gonna be the best damned Lessons Learned report of the war."

The Iraqi Seventh Battalion was still in Samarra, though the fighting there was over. That left the Sixth and Fifth to go to

Fallujah. Lieutenant Colonel Symons, the brigade adviser, told me that our sister Sixth Battalion, with its US Army advisers, would be attached to a US Army unit at Fallujah. Fifth Battalion would be integrated into a Marine Corps battalion.

"You're a Marine, Mike," he said. "You know how to work with Marines."

True enough. But what Symons had just told me was much more than which branch of the service we would be working with. I strongly suspected that the actual breach of Fallujah—physically invading the city under fire and confronting the enemy in urban combat—was going to fall more to the Marines than to the US Army. What Symons had just told me, or almost told me, was that Fifth Battalion was going to do something no US-trained Iraqi unit had ever done. We were going to enter direct, sustained combat in a large-scale battle. And it was not just a military role we were to play; it was a political one. The Bush administration wanted to put more of an Iraqi face on the fight against the insurgents. The Fifth Battalion was to be that face. We were already a living symbol of the new Iraq. At Fallujah, we were going to become *the* symbol, in the eyes of anyone who was watching.

Fallujah loomed. The new advisory team prepared. The new Iraqi commander established his authority. I was cautiously hopeful about the junood. Then a new crisis arose, with Iskander.

Sa'ad made no secret of his disdain for Iskander, who was a Kurd and a Sunni, and he had no interest in him being the battalion's sergeant major. He wanted the Shiite sergeant major named Kan'an to take his place. I knew Kan'an. He showed little interest in the men or their welfare. During the near riot a few days before, when Iskander brought order back to the battalion, Kan'an had behaved with utter indifference.

"I am quitting," Iskander told me. We sat in the dark outside, the two of us with Jaf, the openly atheistic interpreter with the torture scars. Iskander offered me a cigarette. I knew to accept it. His tremor showed in the match light. "I cannot go to Fallujah with Sa'ad."

I knew the Sunnis and Kurds had misgivings about Sa'ad. Ahmed Nu'uman certainly did, and already had told me as much. The Sunni Arabs and Kurds expected the Shiite tribal sheikh Sa'ad to favor his religious and ethnic brethren over the others. They also seemed to mistrust his tribe, the al-Harbia, specifically. Iraq was a Shiite-majority country, and that majority had been held down by the Sunni Saddam Hussein. Men of ambition like Sa'ad were gathering up strength around them as they had never been able to before. Now that the Shiites had access to the levers of power, the Sunni Arabs and Kurds feared them.

"I cannot have you leave, Iskander," I told him. "I just can't. You have to stay. If you leave, the Kurds will not fight."

"No. I will return to my home," Jaf translated. "I will go to my wife and my children. I can work. I can be a taxi driver there. I know people. It will be OK."

Iskander put his hand on my knee and drew close. Yellow light from a window nearby cast a shadow across his face, and I saw that his eyes were rimmed red. He switched to his best English.

"Since I was boy, I have fought. Fight with Peshmerga. My enemies wound me. They torture. I live with no home, like animal. I am tired, Raed Zakkiyah. I miss my family. I am *tired.*"

What could I say to that? What response could I offer? I believed Iskander. He had known a lifetime of suffering. I did the only thing that would do him justice.

"Thank you for your service, sergeant major." I reached over, and we embraced.

We sat straight again. Jaf drew on his cigarette in the dark and waited.

"I have no claims on you, certainly none on your wife or your sons. The battle will come with you or without you. But without you, this battalion will fall apart, Iskander. If you leave, every Kurdish soldier will follow you. They love you. I'll be left with the Sunni Arabs and the Shiite Arabs, and I'll go to Fallujah, but we will fall apart. Everything we have done over the last six months will be for nothing."

Jaf finished rolling out my words in Kurdish, acting them out with feeling and emphasis like a performer, as the Iraqi interpreters always did.

"You are the heart and soul of this battalion, Iskander," I said. "A few days ago, when I thought the soldiers would riot, the men didn't fall back into formation for Menhal. They did not fall back into formation for Kan'an. They fell back into formation for you. *You*, Iskander."

The sergeant major listened to Jaf repeat my words, got to his feet, and tilted his head back. He drew deeply on his cigarette and exhaled a tremendous lungful of blue smoke. He adjusted his scabbard, took his walking stick from against the wall, and walked away without saying a word.

Jaf looked at me in silence for a moment. I stubbed out my cigarette.

"Do not worry, Raed Zakkiyah. I do not think he will quit," Jaf said. "This is his way. It is the Iraqi way."

On October 24, I awoke into the still-dark morning, five o'clock, to the rudest shock I had ever experienced up to that point in my life: three-quarters of the battalion had disappeared.

PT was set for 5:30, as always, out in the predawn's relatively cool seventy or eighty degrees. I stepped out of the American barracks, made my way around the corner to the PT ground and saw a lot fewer men than I was supposed to. Most of the advisers were there, but only a quarter of my already diminished battalion. Of the 550 we had left, about 150 stood before me. It was barely enough of a battalion to even defend itself. We needed eighty-eight guys just to man the perimeter.

I looked at Mulvihill and Elesky, at Fryar and Villa. They were running to grab me when I came around the corner.

"What the fuck?" I said.

"They're nowhere to be found." It was Elesky. Or maybe it was Fryar. I can't remember—at that instant, my head lit up with anger, with anxiety. "The barracks are empty."

Instantly, I was banging through doors, glowering over quiet barracks, hoofing across open ground, stalking my way through row after row of empty racks. Some of the advisers and Iraqis trooped behind me. Others pushed through the doors of other buildings. Most of the junood were amazingly, inexplicably gone: about three hundred of them, it would later turn out. This was a secure base. *Where the fuck could they have gone?* It was as if aliens had swept over Taji, dematerialized hundreds of Iraqi junood in their beds, and beamed them up whole.

I needed answers. I needed explanations. I needed them immediately. The few Iraqi soldiers nearby watched me expectantly. My face flushed. I felt my pulse throb in my neck, decided very consciously not to focus on that any longer, and marched out of the room.

I tracked down the American who had been adviser of the day the day and night before. I struggled to restrain my voice from breaking loose into mad bellowing. Again, I don't remember exactly who it was. He was packing Styrofoam containers and plastic forks into his vehicle, preparing to take breakfast to the men on the wall.

"We've got problems," I said, "and I need to know what the hell is going on. I need answers. I need answers now."

The wide-eyed adviser vigorously scratched his head, as if trying to scrub recollection into his brain. He explained that he had done as all advisers of the day were supposed to do: he had toured the base perimeter once before midnight and once after. The second tour, in fact, had been only an hour earlier. He had not, he insisted, spotted at any time during those rounds a huge mass of humanity skulking out of the base. Desperation and frustration swam through my head like an awful drug, but I could see he was telling me the truth. I didn't have a lot yet, but I did have a timeline. They had to have disappeared between midnight and 4 AM.

Sala'am, the translator who had once been a captain, was scheduled to be the interpreter of the day. I was definitely going to be needing a translator. I burst into his room, yelling. Sala'am pushed his short, round frame up out of his rack.

"What is it, Major Zakkiyah?" he asked, his tone one of genuine concern. I don't know if he had ever seen me behaving as I was, not even under the daily shelling, not even after the big fight in September when I had nearly gotten killed.

I explained to him that we were missing most of the battalion.

"Come on," I said. He scampered up after me, clawing at clothing, pulling himself together. "We need to talk to Ahmed Nu'uman."

Sala'am and I barged into the XO's quarters as the day began stretching bright, hot fingers into the windows. Ahmed Nu'uman was sleeping. He rose quickly, eyes wide. I had seen a lot of wide, blinking eyes so far that morning, just not nearly enough of them. I repeated what was happening. Ahmed Nu'uman briskly buttoned his uniform, his eyes intense but focused on no object in particular, and started chain-smoking. The three of us made our way back to the barracks, finding them just as they had been all of that new, inexplicable morning so far: mostly deserted. A handful of the men who remained had entered from the formation ground. Sala'am asked the men what had happened, but none had good answers. They spoke softly, brows raised sheepishly, eyes roving from Sala'am to me, to Ahmed Nu'uman, and back to Sala'am.

"He says that the others left. In the night," Sala'am said, repeating some version of what would essentially always be the same story. "He says they just told him they were leaving, Major Zakkiyah, and then they were gone"

I pulled together the officers and NCOs we had with us, and Ahmed Nu'uman began giving orders. A few quick checks over the phone and radio with the perimeter guards and Iraqi military police who patrolled the base revealed no reports of men leaving base during the night, much less a horde of them.

We had a very big mystery to solve, and hell to pay—I knew already—as soon as this mass exodus came to light. I would not be able to delay reporting the incident to my own superiors, and neither would Ahmed Nu'uman to his. Still, it would be good to have *some* answers to pass along, to be able to deliver *some* report that would demonstrate that we were taking action. We got decisive.

Our first priority was to check on our current force-security situation, and Ahmed Nu'uman and I both knew it. *There's a war going on. We're attacked every day, and right now we don't even know if we have guys with guns in the towers.*

The two of us, along with Sala'am, clambered into my white SUV and tore straight for the defensive perimeter, about two and a half miles away. We ripped over the dry ground, my hands sweating on the wheel. Even on our approach, we could see there were too few men near the berms that formed our perimeter. A quick drive along a stretch of the line made it look as if about half of them had left. Despite Sala'am's entreaties, none of the remaining men had answers for us. No one had seen anything. A guard waved one arm toward the charred remains of the bean farm. Empty. He yelled down to Sala'am in Arabic, his voice a lilting apology.

"He says no one is there, Raed Zakkiyah." Sala'am's gaze locked on to me, watching, waiting, perhaps worrying. I could feel myself growing physically hotter, but it wasn't Taji's early sun that was pushing up my temperature.

I jerked the wheel, and we ripped over the dust toward the front gate. Getting there seemed interminable. As we drew near, an Iraqi military police captain—the job is only a title, because the Iraqis had no trained military police—watched us approach. I leaped out of the SUV almost before it stopped. Sala'am ran close behind, followed by Ahmed Nu'uman. I accosted the captain.

"Have you seen soldiers come through here? Did you see a very large group of soldiers come through here overnight?" Sala'am was flipping my shouted sentences into Arabic even before I had finished them in English.

"Yes," the captain said. They had.

"Well why the fuck didn't you do something?" I yelled. The Iraqis were very sensitive to Americans using the word *fuck*—they knew we reserved it for moments of real anger—and so I chose my language deliberately. Sala'am knew what I was doing. He even threw the English word into the middle of his Arabic translation.

"Why didn't you stop them?" I was livid. "Why didn't you at least fucking make a report to CMATT and get help?" Sala'am shouted as well, insistent, angry, my Arabic echo. I drew very close to the captain. He was taller than me, but I shouted, chin up, right into his bewildered face. For once, it was the American, not the Iraqi, who was the close talker.

He yammered. He stammered. His eyes darted, beseeching, over my shoulder at Sala'am, and at the mostly silent, glaring Ahmed Nu'uman. As the policeman's halting answer trickled out at me, I felt an overwhelming anger, a hatred not just for this captain but, for that moment at least, for Iraq and Iraqis and how desperately fucked up this entire country was, had always been, and always would be.

Sala'am spoke to me in a quick clip, rendering the man's frightened words.

"He says they threatened to kill him," Sala'am began. "What could he do? Shoot them? He says he didn't know what to do, Major Zakkiyah. Besides, he says they were not his responsibility"—and here Sala'am paused before continuing—"He asks, why didn't any of the battalion's officers try to stop them? Why didn't one of the American advisers?"

When he talked about the American advisers, I remembered, apropos of nothing, that it was Gunny Webster's last day. He was leaving. I was two advisers short. We were going to Fallujah. We were breaching the city with the Marines. I had a new battalion CO who didn't like Sunnis. I had a sergeant major who wanted to quit because he was tired. I had Shiites who wanted to kill Sunnis and Kurds who wanted to kill rabbits. And I lost my shit.

What followed was the first and only time I physically struck a member of the Iraqi Army. I am not proud of how I reacted. I gave the captain a quick, vicious leg sweep that put him on his back. I jumped onto him. I began pounding his face with my fists.

"That's why we have fucking gate guards, you fucking asshole!" *Bam, slam, smack, blam.* "That's why the fucking gate guards have weapons!" *Slam, crack, bam, smack.* "That's why you're a fucking captain! Do—" *slam* "you—" *crack* "understand—" *blam* "that? That's why you're a fucking captain!"

Ahmed Nu'uman and Sala'am leapt onto me, yanking at my arms, my shoulders, tugging me away from the military policeman. I hammered at his face, his head, his neck, but finally pushed off and away, letting Ahmed Nu'uman and Sala'am throw me backward. I staggered in reverse, like a drunk in the sand. My back found the steel side of the SUV. The captain moaned in Arabic. He wiped dirtied hands at his nose and mouth, at tears in his eyes.

I let myself sag against the SUV. My chest heaved. Ahmed Nu'uman stood over me, tears shimmering. Sala'am ran to me, knelt, and put his hands to my shoulders.

"It is not your fault, Major Zakkiyah," he said. "This is how Iraqis are! This is what we have become."

Don't worry. Again. *The Iraqi way.* Again.

And then the road twisted. Again. Over the coming three or four days, most of the junood who had left Taji returned. They filtered back in ones and twos. By October 27, we were back up to 444 junood total, which was not a full-strength battalion but was a lot better than where we stood on the morning of the twenty-fourth. The men, it turned out, wanted to see their families before we shipped to Fallujah. Some had material things they wanted in safekeeping. Others just felt like a break, and with large numbers suddenly on the move, they simply joined in. And of course, some permanently deserted to avoid the coming battle.

I decided, *Whatever happens, I'm taking a bunch of Iraqis to fight in Fallujah.* From that point until the battle, our lives were frenzied. Johnson and Mulvihill, Lombard and me, the NCOs Villa, Warner, Fryar, and Elesky, we all worked twenty-hour days. Administratively, it was a nightmare. The soldiers threw away their ID cards because they feared being captured with documents that revealed they were soldiers. So we got new ID cards made that looked different and told the junood they were "medical" ID cards. If you don't have it on you and you're wounded at Fallujah, we told them, you won't get medical treatment. They kept them. Logistically, the task of issuing new, combat-ready gear to each jundi was overwhelming. Getting vehicles in operating condition and allocating supplies and men to trucks kept us up at night. And all that had to be done as we simultaneously planned tactical training for actual assault. We coordinated with dozens of American and Iraqi officers. We already answered to two chains of command—the Iraqi Army and the American CMATT. We were about to start reporting to a third, because we were going into Fallujah alongside the regular Marine Corps. Much of what we had to do, we advisers did ourselves. Leaving big tasks to the Iraqi officers, we decided, was as likely to create new problems as to solve existing ones. We tackled issues without consulting them. It meant they missed a chance to learn from us, but it also meant we stayed on schedule.

One bright morning, Zayn and I climbed into a pickup, Zayn behind the wheel. It didn't turn over, and he tried the ignition a second time.

"You want me to get outside and push so you can jump-start it?" I asked. He got the joke and laughed.

Zayn was not going to Fallujah. Sa'ad picked him to command the battalion rear party, a complement that would stay behind in Taji and act as our presence on the base while the bulk of the unit was in Fallujah. The rear party would include only a handful of men. Basically, Zayn's main task was to make sure that no other Iraqi units came along while we were gone and stole our stuff. It said a lot about Zayn that the new CO, Sa'ad, trusted him to do the job. It didn't just mean that he thought Zayn would protect our equipment; it also meant that he thought *Zayn* wouldn't steal everything.

We began early morning drills, waking the junood with screams and shouts and telling them we were mobilizing. Vehicles roared into a convoy line. Dust rose around us. The men armed themselves, gathered equipment, and scrambled into the beds of trucks. Then we told the helmeted throngs to dismount and go to barracks. Drill over.

Iskander shuttled platoons back and forth, shouting over the rattle. Jaf had been right; Iskander had decided not to leave.

With each drill, the junood believed they were starting the real thing. We would not reveal the date for departing Taji in advance. We didn't want any jundi who was spying for the insurgency to know when the real deployment was happening. The way to Fallujah ran fifteen miles south to Baghdad, then thirty-five miles west into Anbar Province and the battle zone. We knew we could be ambushed along the way. We knew we were more vulnerable on the road than we were behind Taji's berms. A battalion in convoy, even an undersized battalion like ours, was a big, tempting target.

We had no idea how right we were.

Part III

FALLUJAH

11

THE ROAD TO FALLUJAH

DRIZZLE. A RARE THING.

The clouds came down, wet and close. They rode on gray-blue light. Throngs of helmets bobbed about, men unsure how committed they should feel to this rote drill, wary of getting faked out again.

I hoped my expression revealed nothing different to them than it had during dress rehearsals. Probably it did, to men like Ahmed Nu'uman, or my warrior messenger Abdel-ridha Gibrael. Certainly to Arkan and Abdallah. Engines awakened here and there into idle. A smell of diesel infused the damp air. Sa'ad cut a look at me under bushy eyebrows, then whipped his gaze back out over his bobbing charges. Iskander glimpsed Sa'ad sideways for a millisecond and then returned to shouting at his sergeants. Reflecting on it now, it's amazing how much shifted in those few hours. If my time in Iraq had a midpoint, that morning was it: We would not see Curt again; he dropped in from the Taji administration center to give a formal farewell to the men earlier that morning. Gunny Webster had made a grudging departure only a few days before. That left Villa and me as the last remaining advisers from the battalion's earliest, blind hustle. We tried to make something grow in the desert, and here it was, donning Kevlar, clambering onto truck beds. This thing we stood up was going into the biggest battle of the new century.

By 8:30 AM, most of the soldiers were aboard their vehicles. Many sat in open pickups. They seemed naked in the open air, exposed, their knees up against their chests. It remained wet out, around fifty-five degrees Fahrenheit. Men pulled balaclavas or kaffiyeh over their faces. They shivered as they hugged their rifles. I hated it, but the open trucks would have to do.

I had a lot of worries. A headache that started at my temples began stretching across my forehead. The idea of taking a hit from an IED bothered me. IEDs eradicate human bodies. They wipe them out. But if we took losses, it was critical that the right body be returned to the right tribe as soon as practical. In Iraq, as in most Islamic cultures, the rituals concerning corpses are sacrosanct. The Muslims believe that a human being takes out his or her body as a sort of loan. When you're dead, your corpse belongs to Allah. It's something that many Americans have a hard time grasping. Under most circumstances, giving corpses for medical research is forbidden. Bodies are bathed, enshrouded, prayed over, and buried with the face pointing toward Mecca. All those things are done as quickly as possible—preferably within a day of death. Failure to get a body back to its family and tribe promptly shows a serious lack of respect.

Warner, a giant among the Iraqis, tromped through the cool rain and checked each vehicle, verifying by name that everyone was seated according to our plan. He laughed, poked fun, teased with words most of them didn't understand. Each man lifted his medical ID for Warner to see. For the most part, despite Warner's disarming manner, tasks that morning had taken on a deadly-serious air. Fryar went through the convoy as well, doing last-second checks on trucks, reminding drivers and vehicle commanders about their drills, their training. Master Sergeant Elesky walked the line, checking weapons and ammunition. Mulvihill and Villa double- and triple-checked our communications gear. The Americans veiled our stress behind blank expressions and brusque commands. The Iraqis handled things differently: they let out their tension through their voices. As was so often the case, they all seemed to shout at once. Sergeants and officers tried to steer the mayhem with upraised arms and more screaming. Shouts met louder shouts.

Sixty-four vehicles made the convoy: one SUV for Sa'ad and his favorite officers; two Humvees for the advisers; five two-and-a-half-ton trucks loaded with ammunition, weapons, and communications gear; fourteen Hyundai troop transports, bursting with men, their packs, and their rifles and slung with sheet-metal armor we had welded in place; thirty-three Nissan pickup trucks, also with ad hoc armor and some mounted with machine guns; nine Indian general-purpose Ashok Leyland trucks. The men shouted, checked gear, and settled into their cramped mounts.

Our training taught us to maintain one hundred meters between vehicles in a convoy, which meant that our sixty-four moving parts would snake along more than three and a half miles on the open highway. That was if we managed to stay together. In addition, we were to be escorted by two shifts of American Humvees—from the Army on the journey's first half, and from the Marines on the second. I expected them to be armed with .50-caliber machine guns or Mk 19 automatic grenade launchers. The escort shifts would include five Humvees each, which wasn't anywhere near enough to protect the full, six-kilometer line. But seven combined Humvees were better than the two the Fifth had. Two Iraqi NCOs commanded the motor transport unit and had two trucks to themselves. They were to tend the convoy in motion, like roving mechanics. Their trucks held tools, spare tires, and parts. The battalion doctor, Capt. Adnan Naji, and one aide each drove Nissans that would serve as ambulances if we had wounded on the way.

My cammies clung cold. I barely noticed.

I wanted to walk the convoy line before we started moving. All of it. I wanted to be among the junood, to see their faces and let them see mine. Maybe I had become too jaded about them, I thought, because what I saw in their eyes at that moment in Taji was sincere enthusiasm. We were moving against our enemies in Fallujah.

"Entum jehazeen lil qetal?" I asked, again and again. I had practiced it. *Are you ready? Are you ready to fight?*

Vehicle to vehicle, I gripped hands, thumping junood on their helmets. They hadn't seen me walk the line like that during our fake-outs, and they slowly understood, I think, that this time it was real. They chanted. They cheered. I strode the ranks. Iskander followed close and snapped his palm against one leg. He screamed something sharp and determined in Kurdish and Arabic. A cry went up among the men. An Arab officer shouted for a response, and got a bellow from the men in their pickups. I didn't know what they were saying. I didn't care. They shouted with one voice. I spoke back.

"Ready? Ready for this?"

Each vehicle's passengers smiled and laughed as I approached. I had never been prouder as a US Marine Corps officer.

The Fifth Battalion, Third Brigade, Fifth Division of the new Iraqi Army, was ready. The advisers moved to their vehicles. I took my death seat and slammed the door. The convoy pitched forward, vehicles moving in turn, engines bellowing to life.

I was proud that we were going to hit our 9 AM mark. I wondered how Sixth Battalion was doing. They were to make the same trip to Fallujah that day. It didn't matter, I decided. I had more important matters on my mind. A wet gauze still lay over the day's lens, but the sun had come around on its circuit, and I bore that strange feeling of emptiness that comes from a full night without sleep. And loneliness. The day began without intermission from the day before. *God, look at this gray thing.* Time is all one unbroken stream after all. Sleep and night, they're illusions. Time is not a negotiator. It would not be offering appeals today. I was de jure adviser, de facto leader. Sa'ad didn't care as much as I did. Few of the Iraqi officers cared like I did. None of them believed that failure was impermissible. That was an American way to think. I saw failure as an impossibility, even as I was aware that it threatened at all times. It hung on me, biting at me, like a hateful, clawed thing.

I did not have to wait long for a mishap. The Army escorts stood by for us at the gate on the western side of Taji, US soldiers manning heavy guns atop the Humvees. As our train slowed and condensed, one of the deuce-and-a-halfs—our biggest vehicles—rear-ended the one in front of it. The collision wasn't light, something that bent a bumper. It hit hard. The radiator on the second vehicle was smashed. Worse, it slammed into the tailgate of the first truck, compressing all the communications antennae and other gear in the bed, crushing all of it. The crippled truck was hauling all our ammunition. In one awful stroke, we had destroyed our communications gear and lost one vehicle. We had not even gotten off Taji yet. I jumped out of my Humvee and trotted back to the wreck, muttering.

What the fuck. Jesus, what the fuck.

The headache crawled down into the base of my skull.

Fryar and the 'terp Abdallah came running from the rear, tore open the hood on the second truck, and leaned inside. A warrant officer named Abdelhodi climbed in as well. To one side, the driver stood, palms raised, aghast at himself as Iraqi NCOs berated him viciously. Abdallah told us the driver was claiming his foot slipped off the clutch. I could see on Fryar's face that he didn't believe it. Neither did Abdallah. Men crawled through the wrecked gear in the bed of the first big deuce-and-a-half while Abdelhodi, Fryar, and others tried to get a handle on the engine block of the second. The two groups of men rendered their verdicts to us. Neither went our way. Abdelhodi said he could get a third deuce-and-a-half emptied of less critical gear and transfer all the ammunition inside. It would take half an hour, he said.

Abdelhodi was right about how long it took. He had not calculated the great weight of the ammunition in the back of the new truck, however. None of us had. The dirt road had been dry the day before. This morning, it was waterlogged. The ground beneath the truck gave way as the heavy ammo went in. The new truck sank in mud to the axle. Abdelhodi organized men to do the filthy work of digging it out. Iraqis of superior rank watched him. But the problem was too much for him.

The Americans in our escort group tried not to laugh. Mostly, they succeeded.

I made my way to my Humvee and got CMATT on the hook.

"CMATT X-ray, this is Tango Three Lima actual, copy?"

"Tango Three Lima, this is CMATT X-ray, go ahead."

"We've had a collision with two deuce-and-a-halfs at the western gate. We're going to be delayed"—I cast a look over my shoulder at Iraqis rocking the truck in the mud—"until 0930. Over."

Mud-splattered junood rocked the truck. The replacement driver eased his clutch. The engine wailed. Time strode on. My head thudded. A vision leaped into my mind's eye of a jundi on the slick ground diving headfirst under a gargantuan tire before it rolled back again into the trough. The young American first lieutenant who commanded our escort stood with me, and I could feel him thinking something similar. I called Sa'ad over. I told him we were getting nowhere, that he should order the soldiers back to their trucks.

"Fryar," I said, and he came to me. "We need to get this situation unfucked ASAP. Get us a wrecker somewhere. I don't care. We'll use it to pull out this truck, and then we'll leave the wrecker so they can move the disabled one later."

I said nothing to the Army first lieutenant, but he tried to ease my anxieties.

"Not to worry. I completely understand, sir," he said. I appreciated what he was doing, but his words didn't help.

We finally left at 10:30 AM. All told, we didn't have to travel far—about forty-five miles. Our route of march called for us to head south on Freeway 1, roughly parallel with the Tigris. We would enter the western part of Baghdad and switch onto the Abu Ghraib Expressway at a big interchange. From there, we would head due west and pass Abu Ghraib prison about halfway between Baghdad and Fallujah.

My Humvee took the front of the convoy. The other adviser Humvee would ride last on our train of vehicles. I deliberately separated the two American captains and the two American majors. If one of the two adviser Humvees was taken out, the officers in the other would lead the convoy alone, and ultimately lead Fifth Battalion itself in Fallujah. Sa'ad's command SUV rode second in the convoy.

Elesky was driver for my Humvee. Chuck Johnson, reviewing the flat landscape through wire-rimmed spectacles, sat behind Elesky. Villa was above us, manning a .50-caliber machine gun mounted up top. He would have a wide view from there. I sat in the front passenger seat, which American troops called the death seat—it's closest to the right roadside, and IEDs are usually planted in the dirt on the side of the road. When an IED goes off, the guy in the death seat is closest. He will die. We always joked about it.

One of my jobs in the death seat was to monitor our progress toward Fallujah on the Blue Force Tracker, a GPS-based system that let me watch our progress across a virtual map almost in real time. It was cutting-edge tech in 2004. I also would work the radio, that most critical of lifelines that kept me tapped into everything around me. The translator Arkan, freshly shaven and with determined eyes set behind his hawk's nose, sat behind me. He manned a Motorola handheld. The 'terps were spaced strategically about the convoy. Arkan was dialed into Sala'am, who rode in Sa'ad's SUV. Sa'ad's vehicle was second in the convoy behind me.

Fryar insisted he would drive the Humvee at the rear of the convoy. The Bostonian genuinely believed himself to be the only man among us who knew how to drive for shit, anyway. On the back of the Humvee, a Massachusetts license plate blared out, RED SOX #1 FAN. A *Thomas the Tank Engine* toy sat on Fryar's dashboard. His nephew had sent it to him as a good luck charm. Captain Mulvihill sat in their death seat with the Blue Force Tracker and radios. Abdallah rode as interpreter with them, and Lombard was the fifth man. Above them, Warner squeezed his hulk into position to man a M249 squad automatic weapon (SAW—a military acronym rare in its poignancy, since that's what it does to everything it points at).

Ahmed Nu'uman rode second to last in the convoy. Sa'ad didn't want his Sunni second-in-command to have the status conferred by an SUV, so he forced Ahmed Nu'uman to ride in a pickup.

The convoy moved as quickly as the biggest trucks would go. Drizzle bleared the windshield. We proceeded smoothly at first. Civilian drivers pulled aside as we approached. I flashed looks backward again and again, checking the vast column roaring behind me. Iraqi flags snapped in red, white, and black. I felt the rush of our advance. Fifth Battalion was moving in force.

We approached the gates to Baghdad, at al-Shola. Low civilian buildings began to cluster and creep up at both sides of our passage until we were in the city. Uniformed Iraqi police waved us through a control point. On both sides of the street, small groups of Iraqis on foot assembled to cheer us. It said a lot that everyone, even civilians, knew why we were on the road and where we were going. *If these people know, everybody knows.* An observer may have concluded that the men urged us forward to defend their country. I decided that wasn't what was happening. Al-Shola is a mostly Shiite area. The civilians cheered because they knew we were off to fight Sunnis.

Four hundred meters beyond the police checkpoint, my Humvee drove beneath an overpass. The convoy began under it behind me. A minute passed.

Then a deep roar sounded to my rear, carrying through humid air, a new sound over the rush of wind in the Humvee window. The Motorola lit up in animated Arabic.

My fear was now real: an IED.

I radioed our escort, which had a couple of Humvees toward the center of the convoy. I wanted information, and immediately: How bad? How many vehicles hit? Elesky tapped the brake but didn't stop. I couldn't see the entire convoy. Arkan, working the radios in Arabic, didn't have straight answers. None of the Americans did either. I ordered a full stop for all vehicles.

The Army first lieutenant rose on the radio. His vehicle was at a distance ahead of the rest of the convoy. "Tango Three Lima, this is Romeo Two Whiskey actual. I recommend we continue forward until we're clear of this area."

Elesky yanked the wheel left and pulled us onto the roadside at a diagonal, signaling to the rest of the convoy to set up what's called a fishbone defensive position.

"Negative, Romeo Two Whiskey," I said. "We will halt in place."

The Iraqis followed Elesky's lead, alternately taking angles to the left and right on the roadsides, creating the fishbone posture. Up ahead, I watched the escort Humvee stop.

AK-47s began to clap up and down the line, like a popcorn popper coming on. Sa'ad's vehicle jerked to the right behind us. I dismounted and ran toward him. At that moment, the incompetent Maj. Aof Raheem leaped out of Sa'ad's death seat, rifle in hand. He was panicked, gripping the trigger. He sprayed bullets all over. I felt rounds hiss past me. They cut an arc at my feet. Shocked and infuriated, I ran straight at him. He kept firing. I struck the rifle from his hand with a hard blow.

"*Aof!* Goddammit! You're shooting all over the fucking place!" I clenched his lapel and pounded him into the ground. I hated him at that moment. "Show some fucking control!"

AK-47s popped all down the convoy. An immense plume of smoke and dust bloomed at the distant overpass. It was more like a hazy blossom than the dark, rising tower I had seen IEDs create in the past.

Suddenly, a shout behind me made me spin. Johnson had his back to me and was waving his arms at something up ahead. A vehicle rushed toward him, coming from the opposite direction we had been traveling. The big gray truck bore some sort of massive wooden structure on its bed. Its driver, apparently realizing at the last instant that he was barreling into a military convoy, slammed his brakes and swerved to stop short. But the road was slick—his truck got sideways on him and rolled onto its side with a crash. The ramshackle thing on back split and shattered, and what happened next was surreal. Thousands upon thousands of white-bellied fish spilled across the highway. They swept onto our boots like a mini–storm surge, skidding over the oily blacktop, coating the roadway from one side to the other. The overturned truck blocked two lanes.

Elesky worked the radios in the Humvee. Villa, atop the vehicle, swept the sights of his machine gun over the low buildings, vehicles, and gray-brown terra firma that surrounded us. He held his fire. Nothing to shoot at. Here and there, frightened civilians darted over the blacktop. Some were kids. Johnson took position behind the Humvee's engine block and looked for something to shoot. None of the Americans fired. The anxiety that coursed through me was unbearable. I needed information. Now, now, now, now, now.

I began running down the line in my boots and body armor. The Iraqis sizzled off bullets in every direction, but I saw no insurgents, no signs of incoming fire from off the highway. At least, that was the case in the part of the convoy I could see.

"Awguf etlaq nahr!" I shouted again and again, passing junood who pealed off rounds, seemingly at random. "Hold your fire! Stop, stop!"

The other advisers started doing the same behind me, slapping helmets and shoulders. I continued on, their shouts fading in the distance. Minutes passed as I ran. My lungs heaved as I arrived at the first medical Nissan. Half a dozen bloodied soldiers lay on foam mattresses that Capt. Adnan Naji had brought from the barracks. The battalion doctor worked precisely and with remarkable speed, tending to the men along with a handful of medics. I thought to look for Arkan, who was supposed to stick close to me. He was nowhere to be seen.

"Naji, what's the situation?" I shouted over a cacophony of AK-47s.

"I have six wounded, two badly, Major Zakkiyah," Adnan Naji said. His voice was even, though his chest ran with rivulets of rain and other men's blood. One of the medical pickups sat diagonally in the middle the road. Its tailgate was down. Its bed was smeared crimson. It looked like the wounded men had been brought to him.

"You haven't been to the IED?"

"No," he said. "But at least one vehicle was hit badly. I haven't seen it."

Suddenly an American voice chattered over my Motorola. I recognized Mulvihill's New York accent. The rear of the convoy. Thank God. Finally, information.

"Mulvihill: Zacchea," I said. "Go."

"Prepare for contact report," Mulvihill said, and I waited half a beat, my chest clenched. "We're engaged with insurgents. We have one at about three hundred meters firing from a rooftop. Warner engaging now."

The advisers in the Humvee at the back of the convoy, along with their translator, Abdallah, had seen the IED blow in the distance in front of them and thought the convoy would motor through it. An escort Humvee ahead of them pulled to one side, however, to engage insurgents who were firing in on them. Several vehicles halted. An instant later, the advisers' Humvee began taking shots too. Warner swung the big SAW and returned fire. A civilian sedan stopped nearby. Fryar jumped from behind his *Thomas the Tank Engine* good luck charm and grabbed two Iraqis, a mother and a young boy, and shouted at them in English to come with him. He got them behind the up-armored Humvee. They were horrified. Abdallah tried to calm them in Arabic. Fryar then ran back out and found a father lying protectively over two children in the backseat of another car. He grabbed them as well. The group ran in a crouch back to the Humvee.

Two or three minutes into the fight, insurgents at a second, closer position joined the battle. Warner spotted a man with an AK-47 atop a building at two hundred meters. The insurgent ignored the rear of the convoy, firing instead toward where the IED had exploded. He seemed to have tunnel vision. He didn't know Warner was watching him. Warner aimed, opened up with the SAW, and cut the man off the roof.

I began to worry that we weren't moving. We had been halted for only ten or fifteen minutes, but the longer we stayed still, the greater the likelihood that other insurgents would arrive, or random Iraqis would join the fight spontaneously. Iraq was armed to the teeth, and a lot of part-time insurgents wanted to brag that they had fought Americans. Our inertia invited a bigger fight.

I needed to get to the site of the explosion so I could make an assessment myself. Smoke and dust enshrouded the distant overpass. I turned to Adnan Naji. He hunched over wounded men. Some cried out. Others were silent. The cool drizzle permeated the mattresses.

I started running again. I arrived at the site of the blast a minute or two later. It was dry under the overpass. The blasted Nissan blocked the road. Shrapnel had shredded it from end to end, shattering glass, puncturing tires. Black scores marked the sheet metal hanging over the doors. There was no crater, no blast hole, but the overpass itself was pocked in a pattern that emanated from a clear center in the bridge's superstructure. I realized what I was looking at. Rather than bury the IED, the insurgents had strung it underneath the overpass itself.

I needed my motor pool adviser. Fryar responded to me on the Motorola.

"The vehicle hit by the IED is a kill," I said quickly. "We've got to off-load it, bump the guys who were in it. Medical has the casualties. Bring up a truck and get this thing moved off the road." Fryar acknowledged me.

I jogged back toward the front of the convoy. The firing had mostly stopped by now. Halfway back I spotted Arkan crouched behind a railing at one side of the road.

"Arkan, what are you doing?" He must have run with me part of the way from the front of the convoy before he gave out. "You have to stay with me! Do not leave my side, understand?" He sputtered apologies and took up behind me again, panting.

Fifteen more minutes passed back at my Humvee. Finally, Arkan gave me the word that Fryar's motor pool junood had finished bumping equipment and a couple of unwounded men from the blasted Nissan. Sa'ad gave orders over the radio to move. The convoy lurched back ahead, flattening a carpet of fish.

We approached the Baghdad–Abu Ghraib interchange. The drizzle let up. The Army escort peeled away as we ramped onto the highway toward Fallujah. Five Marine Humvees fell in with us. The Marines irritated me by riding as a separate body, out in front of the convoy. The road west from Baghdad was grim, more desolate, even forlorn compared with the road between Taji and Baghdad. Here the insurgents were more active, more brazen. The convoy slowed, snaking around craters that pockmarked the asphalt everywhere. The Humvee rattled where IEDs from months past had left ripples frozen in the concrete. And everywhere, dead animals: dogs, donkeys, other beasts. Villa and Elesky stared down each carcass, wary of IEDs. Black carrion birds flapped long wings and lifted away as we drew close.

On the right, the Abu Ghraib prison compound slouched toward us over the horizon. Picture the ugliest sort of flat, institutional architecture you can imagine. Multiple rings of chain-link fencing came into focus, set at intervals off a flat, long wall, the same ochre as the earth. Even the guard tower, elevated as it was, was impossibly wide and flat. Abu Ghraib was demented in its ugliness.

Something returned to my mind from an impossibly distant Notre Dame lit class:

Through me you pass into the city of woe:
Through me you pass into eternal pain:
Through me among the people lost for aye. . . .
All hope abandon ye who enter here.

My *Inferno*, I thought. Then I thought, *Stuff that shit. Keep yourself busy.* We passed along. The radio crackled in Arabic and English. Helpful little blips diligently made their way across the screen of my Blue Force Tracker, marking our passage within a tiny digital Iraq.

We had all fallen silent. My Humvee was less than a minute past the prison when Elesky spoke.

"Something's wrong," he said. His eyes squinted into his rearview mirror. "I think we're losing the convoy."

I tried my own rearview. My stomach dropped. The convoy wasn't there anymore.

"They're stopped," Villa shouted. He threw his voice down into the Humvee from his machine gun perch. He could see better than we could. "They've definitely stopped. They're a half klick behind us. Maybe more."

None of the possible explanations for the convoy halting were good. I grabbed the radio and tried to raise our Marine escort, to get them to slow down. Nothing. Arkan was unable to raise the Iraqis, either. I tried again. Nothing again. We could see the escort Humvees pulling away. Elesky crushed the accelerator. We pulled alongside the Marines. They didn't stop. I opened the door and screamed at them to stop. Villa did the same from above. They gave us wide eyes. After what seemed an eternity, they halted. I hopped out of the Humvee. Villa shouted an explanation.

"They've stopped back there!" he said. "We can't get anybody on comms!"

There in our new stillness on that forgotten road, we all noticed a new, distant sound: rifle fire, back at the convoy. Then the dull echo of an explosion.

There was a fight on. My battalion was fighting back there without me.

The escort Marines got their commander on the radio. I had seen him briefly: he was a first lieutenant, a guy probably in his midtwenties. I told him we had to go back. He declined to join us. He explained that his vehicles would hold their positions and wait for us. I was too pressed for time to argue with his worthless ass.

"Un-fucking-believable," I said. The door creaked and I jumped into the death seat. This was an Iraqi convoy, and our escort wasn't going to put itself in any more danger for it than it had to.

Elesky jerked the Humvee around and raced back toward the others.

About halfway there, we got Fryar on the net.

"We're getting hammered, Major," he transmitted. We could hear Warner's SAW barking in the background. "Heavy small-arms fire. Mortars too. Machine guns. Battalion's definitely taking casualties."

Arkan shouted into his Motorola and then switched to English for us: "The fighting is very heavy, Major Zakkiyah. Captain Naji reports many casualties."

We bounced over the rippled roads. I reached out and braced myself against the dash. Through the streaked windshield, mortars threw up chunks of earth around the battalion. Muzzles flashed. Machine guns hammered. A black tower of IED smoke rose into the sky. Elesky redlined the screaming Humvee. As we plunged forward, Villa opened up above our heads with his .50-cal. He blasted a distant tree line. He had no targets, but the foliage was the only place in our field of vision that offered attackers concealment. That's where they had to be.

We ground to a halt near Sa'ad's big SUV. Behind him, the convoy had more or less fishboned. I jumped and was running almost before we stopped. Arkan flung open his door and stuck tight this time. The soldiers had abandoned their vehicles and taken positions along a median, aiming at the tree line, lying in the soft earth as Villa had taught them to do. Sa'ad's hulking frame came at Arkan and me, striding, not running. He barked orders at a Motorola in baritone Arabic. The three of us crouched behind a truck. The Iraqi colonel said that, as best as he could tell, they had three vehicles hit, and extensive casualties. The attack had begun with another IED.

An awful terror flashed into my mind: *The battalion could be stopped here. This could be it.* A percussive explosion a short distance down the line punctuated the thought for me. But I clamped down the fear. *No.* That could not happen.

"We have to get fire superiority onto that tree line," I yelled to Sa'ad. All verbal communication on that road now involved yelling, was going to involve yelling for the foreseeable future. "We must get any casualties collected into trucks. We have got to execute a bump plan, and now."

I meant that the men and equipment from the three stricken vehicles had to get moved into one of our handful of empties. And we had to do that before three knocked-out vehicles became four, or five, or six. We would leave crippled trucks behind. No matter what, we had to advance to Fallujah. With Arkan's help, Sa'ad and I agreed that he would lead the defense of the convoy, and I would get everything bumped so we could move again. Sa'ad unfolded his brawny frame and began shouting orders at soldiers and officers alike. I told Arkan to get on the Motorola and tell Fryar's motor transport NCOs to rendezvous with us ASAP at the wrecked trucks. I ran down the convoy. Arkan chased me, shouting transmissions in Arabic.

Alongside me, prone soldiers fired into the tree line. Sound drenched the air: AK-47s popped; machine guns hammered; larger explosions split the sky at uneven intervals. As I ran with Arkan, I tried to calculate how many vehicles we could lose before we wouldn't have enough room for all the soldiers. The math evaded me. One thing I knew, however, was that the fight could turn into a rout if we lost a few more trucks.

For the second time in just a couple of scrambled hours, I came upon another impromptu Adnan Naji aid station. It was a bloody mess. Almost a dozen men lay on the ground. The poor guys wounded from the first fight crawled about, taking cover as best they could. Under fire again, the captain and his Iraqi medics knelt over fellow junood or jumped between prone bodies, feverish in their focus.

"We have many wounded, Major. I don't know, twelve or more. Some very, very bad. One we will lose for sure," Adnan Naji said, and gestured toward a man on his back, covered in blood. The man's face was intact, fixed on the sky. The top of his skull was partly sheared off above the eyebrows. But I recognized him immediately from his blue eyes. It was Abdel-ridha Gibrael. My warrior messenger.

Unbelievably, he was still breathing, staring. I looked into Abdel-ridha Gibrael's clear, dying eyes and tried not to fall in and measure what remained behind them.

Arkan shook his head and gave a "tsk, tsk, tsk." I quashed my rising grief.

"We need to get out of here, captain," I shouted to Adnan Naji. "Like, right now. I need to know if you can work on these men as we drive."

Captain Naji didn't respond. His eyes turned upward and behind me. I heard the *whomp-whomp-whomp* of rotors and turned. A flight of AH-1W SuperCobras came in toward us, level and low. Our escorts must have called them.

"We will if we must, Major Zakkiyah," Adnan Naji said. Blood drenched his cammies. He'd treated about twenty men in the last two hours. I heard the whoosh of rockets from the SuperCobras. Time held its breath, and then explosions wracked the woods in the distance.

"We must," I said, clapping his shoulder. Adnan Naji was already shouting orders to his medics as I turned to run farther down the line. Again I found myself marathoning past a parade of trucks. Arkan wheezed and struggled, but seemed determined to stay by me. Sporadically, bullets sizzled the air around our helmets. The worst feeling in the world: *It only takes one of those.* We clenched our jaws and bobbed our heads.

The three dead trucks were close together in the column. They burned orange and black, riddled with shrapnel. The roof of one cab had blown clear away. That has to have been Gibrael's truck, I thought. A fresh crater yawned. Fryar's motor transport sergeants had gotten to the wrecks before us and were busy transferring weapons and equipment into other trucks. They cannibalized whatever they could take off the blown-out vehicles. We stood very close to an overpass—the insurgents who triggered the bomb must have used it as a mark.

The IED was tremendous, and the attack was well coordinated. The explosive device had blown at a distance of about thirty vehicles from the rear of the convoy. Mulvihill, Fryar, Warner, and Lombard saw it explode in front of them, an eruption of truck parts and asphalt, followed instantly by a massive column of dense smoke that shot up like a writhing redwood. A great demon seemed to clasp their Humvee from below and gave it a single violent shake. They saw men in the air, soldiers from the back of Gibrael's pickup flying over the road. Seconds later, the sky showered mortars. In that area, a few insurgents—either bold or suicidal—had placed themselves closer to the highway in tall grass. American gunners in the Abu Ghraib towers joined the fight, blasting over the prison walls. The whole goddamned thing was surreal.

The fighting continued, but the firing from our own lines slackened, became more deliberate. That moment, catching my breath, was the first time I noticed something: the Iraqis were mounting an effective defense. The junood had calmed after their initial panic. I thought back to Villa's training of these men: Breathe. Aim. Kill a specific enemy. The junood's fire was controlled and discriminating. As strange as it may sound, I felt happy for an instant.

But this was still a kill zone.

"Arkan! Get Sa'ad. Tell him we'll be ready to go. He just has to give us word when we can pop smoke." Arkan looked confused. "He just has to give us word when we can *get out of here*," I said. Arkan nodded quickly and raised the colonel on his Motorola.

I don't know how long we were stuck there on that road, but it seemed like hours. I forgot to drink water. My throat felt like shredded meat. My head pulsed. I bit the valve on the CamelBak I wore and took a long draw of hot water from the tube. Arkan and I took off at a trot, back toward the front of the convoy. *This is why you've been running every night in the desert*, I thought. We came to Adnan Naji's aid station. He had almost finished loading the injured into truck beds. Abdel-ridha Gibrael's body lay in one. Looking at him, I knew he was gone.

The insurgents' fire remained deadly, but it slowed. Mortar and rocket fire ceased altogether. I didn't know what had done it. Was it effective return fire from the battalion? The rockets from the SuperCobras? Or had our enemies simply wanted to get in some quick hits and escape for another day? For all I knew, they were on their way back to Fallujah, a brief foray out of the city now complete. I wanted to believe that we had beaten them. I did believe. *Our enemies won't retreat anymore*, I thought. Not from Fallujah. We weren't going to let them.

Back at the head of the column, Sa'ad said he'd have the men ready to resume soon. I told him I was going to drive ahead to our Marine escort. We still could not raise them on the radio. All comms would have to be face to face. Elesky listened to my plan and got behind the wheel. Villa was still in his turret. We drove forward to find the Marines. They had to have seen and heard a hell of a fight going on. They had not joined us. I decided they would at least escort our medical trucks to the military hospital where the American forces were gathering.

Almost as soon as the Marine Humvees came into view beyond a small rise, we saw them straighten up on the road and speed away. They apparently thought we had the convoy right behind us.

"Fuck!" Elesky yelled. He was livid. Again he punched the pedal. Again we chased them down. Again we drew alongside. We got abreast of the rear Humvee.

"We have serious casualties!" I screamed through the open door at the driver. The broken asphalt whisked beneath us. "Goddammit! We have to go to the hospital!"

Adnan Naji's voice broke into the interior of the Humvee through Arkan's radio. It was as if he knew what I was doing, wanted to emphasize the importance of the situation to me, to Elesky, to Villa, to this bug-out Marine escort: "Major, we are losing casualties," Adnan Naji said. "We must get them to hospital."

"Arkan, copy Naji," I said. "Then tell Sa'ad to get the vehicles with the most serious casualties to the front of the convoy. Tell them ASAP. Now, now, now."

The Marine Humvees still had not halted. Neither had Elesky. I was still shouting car to car. I had to break it down Barney-style.

"We have trucks with casualties! Take them to the hospital! Do you hear me? *Take them to the hospital!*"

The driver gave a thumbs-up. Our American escorts slowed their Humvees. We slowed as well. After a minute, Sa'ad's SUV came up from behind and shot past us. A moment later, a Nissan roared past us at seventy miles per hour. Our eyes followed Adnan Naji in the bed of the truck, bent forward. I didn't know when I admired him more—stabilizing men under fire earlier, or there, his cammies flitting in a great whoosh of air, as he tended to a man from the back of a speeding Nissan.

The position set aside for Fifth and Sixth Battalions was called East Fallujah Iraqi Camp (EFIC). It was separate from the new American emplacement, called Camp Fallujah. EFIC on that overcast November 1 afternoon stretched in shades of brown along all its dimensions. EFIC was to be our home until we attacked the city itself. The flat landscape blended red and yellow. Black veins ran in rough horizontals. Berms rolled up out of the ground. Upturned earth next to firing holes lay like mounds of putty. Polluted haze rose from the city nearby and wafted above us the color of a smoker's teeth. To the west, where Fallujah lay three or four miles off, the sky had rusted. The Iraqis call Fallujah Medinat al-Masajid, the City of Mosques. Its low buildings lay beneath a tainted corona sky that was punctured by slender minarets. The blue-green Euphrates curled from behind the city, then flowed in our direction before slipping to the south.

We rolled in, ragged. One man killed. Sixteen wounded. Four vehicles destroyed. Trucks shot through by shrapnel and bullets. It had taken more than six hours to cover forty-five miles. A hazy orb of sunlight glowered high. It was hotter now but still fair by normal standards, only about eighty degrees. The rain had ceased.

My head pulsated. My voice was gone.

A platoon of thirty or forty Marines in combat bulldozers pushed around the universal brown, relocating it from places to other places, trying their best to make our new camp flat. They wired up generators. They set up portable toilets. The Marines obviously had not been there long themselves. Earthen berms lay along our northern, eastern, and western perimeters, but the desert still ran open to the south. I felt like I would never see a fortified position in Iraq that wasn't wide open on at least one side.

Another thing we noticed immediately was that our sister Sixth Battalion had beaten us there, despite having left Taji at least an hour and a half behind us. Their arrangement disconcerted me. Their empty vehicles were arrayed on the southern part of EFIC, near the open desert. But the men of the Sixth appeared to be setting their quarters about a mile away, in the northern part of the camp. I made a mental note. I'd bring it up, I decided, when I met up with Lieutenant Colonel Symons from Brigade.

A lot of work still lay ahead of us. I was disappointed to see that there were no tents for the Iraqis. We had no running water yet. If we had medical facilities, I didn't see them. Power wasn't running yet. Nothing was in place for waste disposal or hygiene. It wasn't as if the Iraqi Ministry of Defense didn't know we were coming. Only later would I learn that the US contractor tasked with building EFIC had backed out of the job at the last second after learning they had to sign a contract with the Iraqi interim government. They didn't trust such an arrangement. The Marines there at EFIC had to come in on short notice to do the job in their place.

I stretched. I was stiff. Men seemed grateful to jump down from their trucks. The second adviser Humvee pulled up as the last vehicles tailed into the camp. Fryar brought it to a halt, and Major Lombard walked over.

"Mike, I can take our wounded over to the Marine camp," he said. Adnan Naji had taken only the most severely injured directly to the US hospital at Camp Fallujah.

"And the body over to the morgue," he added. Abdel-ridha Gibrael. In the short time Lombard had been with the battalion, he had learned that the treatment of corpses was a serious subject for the Iraqis.

"Yeah," I said. One way you know a war is real is when you just let go of guys you knew and liked. "Yeah, get him out."

When Lombard got to the Camp Fallujah morgue with Gibrael's body, he explained to the NCO in charge that he was working as an adviser, and the body he had was an Iraqi, not an American. He wanted to place it into the morgue, he explained, but he would need it back later.

"And fairly soon," Lombard said. "But we just got here and we need to put it in the morgue for now."

"You want to come back and take it out?" the NCO asked.

"Yes," Lombard said. "He's Iraqi. It's important."

"Sir, I'll tell you right now that there's no way we're doing that. KIA are not withdrawn back out of the morgue. We have strict procedures—"

"It's not—no, you don't understand," Lombard said. "We just need to put him here for now. We don't need to ship him to Germany or anything."

"We don't do temporary storage, sir. I can take him if you like, but there's a procedure."

Normally, things rolled off Lombard like water off a duck. Nothing bothered him. But he had had a hell of a day. The Americans had devised no process for dead Iraqis, only dead Americans. So be it. Abdel-ridha Gibrael was dead, but there were wounded men, tired men, back at EFIC. We didn't even have tents yet.

"OK, OK," Lombard said, waving off debate. "What do you need me to sign?"

The body of Abdel-ridha Gibrael would have to wait for its proper dispensation. Lombard couldn't know that the corpse was about to itself become a threat to the Fifth Battalion. But we didn't have time to consider everything as well as we would have liked. The countdown to the breach was beginning.

12

BEFORE THE BREACH

NOVEMBER 1: SEVEN DAYS UNTIL THE BREACH

ROCKETS SCREECH AS THEY COME IN, splitting the sky on a low arc and sending men diving; mortars fall silently, tumbling from a high angle and shattering earth, air, and men. East Fallujah Iraqi Camp was within range of both being fired from the city. The larger American position, Camp Fallujah, was even closer. Marine and Army units poured into the area. Insurgents fortified themselves and watched from the urban blocks. They crept to the city's edges, fired big rounds one or two at a time, and then fled down rat trails. Their targets—the great hosts of Americans, Iraqis, and British—kept growing. We made no attempt to hide our intentions from our enemies: we were setting up outside the city in numbers, and once we were ready, we were going inside to kill them.

My priorities on the first day were to set up a defensive perimeter, establish communications with the Americans at Camp Fallujah, and get the junood into shelter. A Marine engineer told us that a rocket struck our battalion area only a couple of hours before we arrived. I fully expected us to take a hit that night. We had to prepare. Lombard set up our wounded at Camp Fallujah's combat surgical hospital. Mulvihill contacted the Marines and gave

215

them our status. Johnson set up a perimeter and internal guard. Fryar got the trucks in order. Other advisers hunted down tents.

As usual, a thousand little problems cried like hatchlings. I found the Iraqi Sixth Battalion senior adviser. I wanted to talk to him about the motor pools. It was a bad arrangement for Sixth Battalion to be at one end of the camp with our trucks and Fifth Battalion at the opposite end with their trucks. Looting was inevitable, by both sides. They may even start fighting, I told him. My counterpart did not care; he was beset by dilemmas just like I was. I took the problem to Lieutenant Colonel Symons, who took it to the Iraqi brigadier general who was in charge of both battalions. Things got fixed that way.

We held our first Fifth Battalion leadership meeting at 5 PM on the first day. All the US advisers and Iraqi officers were there. Dusk sifted in as we talked. Menhal, the Shiite major who gave the rousing "first bullet is for me" speech back at Taji, warned me that the junood were agitating for their pay.

"But I would not do it, Raed Zakkiyah," he said. "If you pay them, many will desert in the night."

I asked Sa'ad and Ahmed Nu'uman what they thought. We were about to begin a battle against a Sunni enemy, and I knew many of our Sunni Arabs did not want to fight.

"We have 440 junood now," said Ahmed Nu'uman, who was a Sunni and the senior officer I trusted most. "I would guess three hundred of them will fight with us in Fallujah."

Sa'ad grunted agreement but voiced determination: "I will fight, even if I am alone with six officers."

That was all well and good, but Sa'ad's personal bravado didn't help me with the problem at hand: I needed to deliver an intact Iraqi battalion that would fight next to the Marines. We all agreed that we ran the risk of losing big numbers of junood as soon as we paid them. We withheld their pay.

To keep an eye on the Iraqis overnight, Lombard and I arranged a watch schedule for the advisers. We would work in two-hour shifts from 6 PM to 4 AM, patrolling Fifth Battalion's position to make sure the Iraqi sentries weren't sleeping and no one was trying to sneak off. My shift was last: 2 AM until 4 AM. I also told Warner that I wanted a battalion head count and weapons count every morning.

In the middle of that first night, we took close machine-gun fire from a technical drive-by. No one was hit. We listened to the high, haunting sound of warplanes over the city. Explosions thudded in the black distance. The following morning, Warner gave me his first head count report: no desertions overnight.

NOVEMBER 2–3

Lt. Col. Michael Ramos bore exactly the sort of swaggering, resolute demeanor you would expect of a Marine who commanded 1,500 other Marines. Ramos was CO of First Battalion, Third Marine Regiment, which had shipped in from Okinawa to assault Fallujah. The Iraqi Fifth Battalion was going to attack with them.

Ramos rolled onto East Fallujah Iraqi Camp with two staff officers, there to meet Colonel Sa'ad. Ramos's First Battalion, Third Marines, had drawn a difficult set of tasks. It was one of six US battalions that was going to breach the city in the initial attack. Its Marines would be rushing in under fire and fighting door-to-door from the outset. It would fight on as long as it took to win the battle. And First Battalion, Third Marines, was the only American battalion that would be breaching Fallujah while combined with elements of an Iraqi battalion. That Iraqi battalion was ours. Ramos visited EFIC to meet Sa'ad because the two men's units were about to fight as one group.

Captain Mulvihill and I met Ramos and his two officers along with Sa'ad, Ahmed Nu'uman, one of the 'terps and a couple of Iraqi officers. I had never met Ramos before that day. He had a reputation in the Marines as a career ender. More than one American officer warned me to be on guard with him. Ramos, they said, burned through staff officers and company commanders.

He strode into Sa'ad's big tent. The Iraqis were always impressed with the military bearing of their Marine advisers; they were awed by Ramos. The Texan wasn't a big or imposing man. He was lean, with a narrow face that was almost avian at certain angles. But he knew how to enter a tent. Ramos graciously offered Sa'ad condolences for our losses on the road in. The First Battalion, Third Marines, had been in-country for only a couple of weeks, but already fifteen of its Marines had been killed when a suicide SUV hit a Marine convoy that had either broken down, gotten lost, or both. I never learned which. The day before we arrived, two more Marines were killed in a mortar strike. The Marines at Camp Fallujah were mad and restive and wanted to start killing insurgents. Sa'ad thanked Ramos for the condolences and played the role of cordial Arab host. We sat in a circle of field chairs.

I gave Ramos the Michael Zacchea infomercial on Fifth Battalion. I discussed our training, our experiences in Taji, and our fight from the day before. I gave him my most honest assessment of what our battalion could and could not do. Both the US and Iraqi sides agreed that we needed to get the Marines and junood training together as soon as possible. We knew the Marines and the Iraqis could gain mutual trust only if they worked together before the breach. We didn't know what the rank-and-file Marines were whispering among themselves about working with Iraqis, but I hoped to get some positive vibes flowing on the Lance Corporal Underground, as Marine officers call it.

Ramos listened to what I had to tell him. I felt good about that. I also felt comfortable with his two subordinate officers. One of them, the XO of First Battalion, Third Marines, I knew from Officer Candidate School back in 1989. The other, Ramos's operations officer, I did not know, but Mulvihill did. Ramos never took his eyes off me while I spoke. When I was done, he stood. He invited Sa'ad to the next planning meeting on the American side. Sa'ad eagerly accepted, showing more enthusiasm than was usual for him. I was already committed to that meeting. Ramos shook hands with Sa'ad and marched back to his Humvee. The commander of First Battalion, Third Marines, moved on flat ground with the resolution of a boulder crashing downhill. In all the time I knew him, I never quite figured Ramos out.

Afterward, Mulvihill and I tromped across the brown earth of EFIC, on our way to some logistics problem or other. The tough New York Irishman was blunt in his assessment.

"They're not thrilled to be working with us," Mulvihill said.

"Yeah," I said. "You're probably right. It doesn't surprise me."

Marines like Ramos came halfway around the world to kill bad guys in Fallujah. They didn't want to babysit a bunch of Iraqis. Some of the Marine units had already done training and small missions with local Iraqi militias that claimed to be loyal to the government. Those militias were headed by former Shiite generals from Saddam Hussein's army and were little better than armed gangs. I knew the Marines expected Fifth Battalion to be just more of the worthless same. There was nothing I could do about that until we had a chance to prove ourselves.

We kept pushing the junood, trying to keep them sharp. They stayed with morning PT—they had mastered jumping jacks by this point—and we carried out live-fire exercises. There was always more that could be done to improve our camp's defenses. The threat of mortar fire kept everyone alert.

For two days, Fifth Battalion's three rifle companies made trips next door to Camp Fallujah and trained with rifle companies from First Battalion, Third Marines. Two advisers went with each Iraqi company. The junood were accustomed to traveling by pickup truck, but the breach was going to be made in the Marines' big, heavy amphibious assault vehicles (AAVs). The AAVs had huge ramp doors that dropped in the back, and we worried some stray jundi would get squashed by one. We made them practice mounting and dismounting the vehicles. That meant packing them inside, driving them in a circle, stopping the AAV, and then having the soldiers surge outside and take positions with their rifles. Then again. Then again. The American camp had some abandoned buildings made of cinder blocks, and the junood used them to practice clearing rooms. The training and repetition were good things, but mostly we wanted the Marines to get to know the

Iraqis and vice versa. I wanted the Marines to see that the Iraqis of Fifth Battalion were professionals. I was relieved to see that for the most part everybody got along. The regular enlisted Marines seemed accepting of the Iraqis. They were younger than their officers and NCOs and didn't have the same anti-Iraqi biases built in from the Gulf War of the 1990s. The junood, in turn, clearly tried to up their games a notch when they had Americans at their sides. Many of the rank-and-file Marines had combat experience, but none had fought in a city before. The Iraqis actually had spent more time than the Marines searching indoor spaces, from our excursions around Taji. Nobody showed fear, but you could tell that most of the men, Marine and Iraqi alike, were apprehensive. Some of the junood still seemed to be coming to grips with what they were about to do. The very concept of close urban fighting is impossible to grasp until you live it.

"I will not shoot my brothers," one jundi told Fryar. "I will shoot only to frighten."

The staff sergeant from Boston squinted his hawk eyes at the young solider.

"What are you going to do when they shoot at *you*?" he asked.

"Still, I will not kill them," said the jundi.

"I bet you *will*," Fryar said.

Meetings with the Marine and US Army leadership were unrelenting. Staff officers gave briefings. Ramos and half a dozen other battalion COs listened, unblinking. Logistics officers talked about incoming shipments. An intelligence officer familiarized us with the physical appearance of Abu Musab al-Zarqawi and his top lieutenants. (None of Zarqawi's men were Iraqis.) A Navy officer gave updates on the dead and wounded. A meteorologist talked about the forecast. The 'terps Najm, Abdallah, Arkan, and Sala'am whispered translations, their chins hovering over Iraqi officers' green-and-gold epaulets. Arkan struck up conversations with the American officers whenever he had a moment, a broad smile on his clean-shaven face, taking every opportunity to learn more about Americans. It made sense. He intended to become one someday.

Fallujah was a Marine Corps operation. The man in charge of the battle, Maj. Gen. Richard Natonski, was a Marine. Four of the six US battalions that were set to breach the city—to invade Fallujah under fire and fight door-to-door—were Marine battalions. The other two were US Army. A handful of Iraqi units aside from the Fifth were slated to fight around Fallujah. A small Iraqi commando unit was supposed to take a hospital on the bank of the Euphrates opposite the city. One of our sister battalions, the Sixth, was south of the city, attached to a unit of the US First Cavalry. They were not going to make the breach. Our other sister battalion, the Seventh, was sixty miles away helping to secure the city of Samarra. Also at Fallujah were a handful of the original, useless Iraqi battalions that had been raised up by Vinnell Corporation. Since collapsing before the First Battle of Fallujah, they had been re-formed and given American advisers. Two of those battalions were going to follow Marine units "in trace," meaning they would hang behind them and do cleanup operations as the Marines churned south.

The role of the Iraqi Fifth Battalion became clearer over the course of the planning meetings at Camp Fallujah. The Fifth was the only Iraqi unit whose men would be mixed in with the Marines during the fighting in the city. We were not going to operate as a separate, whole entity at Fallujah. Instead, we were to be split up at the company level. Two rifle companies were attached to Marine rifle companies from First Battalion, Third Marines. Junood from the Fifth were going to storm buildings. In particular, a number of mosques lay in the sector that First Battalion, Third Marines, was tasked with taking from the enemy. It would be disastrous for perceptions in the Arab world if Americans stormed into mosques. It would be even worse to just blow them up. So Fifth Battalion was given the job of knocking down the doors of holy places and fighting inside. The third rifle company from Fifth Battalion was going to operate independently. Its job was to protect the supply route that fed ammunition, water, and food to First Battalion, Third Marines. That unit was going to operate without Marine

Corps supervision, so I put the levelheaded Captain Johnson in charge, along with Staff Sergeant Fryar.

The American and Iraqi officers gathered in a big tent around a huge sandbox that had Fallujah laid out in miniature. I brought all the Iraqi company commanders with me. We talked about what was to come. The first big battle-planning meeting lasted eight hours. One naval officer focused on the positives when it came to casualties, saying they had plenty of medics ready for us. Then he said that planners were forecasting 50 percent casualties for the US units.

"Look to the right. Look to the left. In forty-eight hours, one of those two men will be dead or wounded," he said.

The advisers gawked at each other. It's extremely strange to look at someone and think, "He'll be dead or wounded soon," and then realize he's thinking the same thing about you.

Comparisons to Hue City kept coming up. Hue was a brutal, monthlong battle in 1968 in which outnumbered Marines, US Army troops, and South Vietnamese held off an urban assault by a division of North Vietnamese. People talked about Hue so much that I got the impression some of them *wanted* another Hue.

Symons, who was there for all the planning meetings, warned me more than once that I was going to face command-and-control challenges in Fallujah after the breach. First, my Iraqi companies were going to be geographically separated from one another, by distances wide and hostile. That would make Fifth Battalion hard to coordinate and watch over. Second, I was going to be dealing with and reporting to *three* separate chains of command: the First Battalion, Third Marines, command topped by Ramos; the advisory command structure, topped by Symons; and the Iraqi brigade command topped by a Shiite general named Essa.

"But no matter what," Symons said, "don't forget that you report to me first."

To help with the command-and-control challenge, the Marines gave me two enlisted radio operators who would be the link between the Fifth Battalion advisory team and the Marines. Both were young lance corporals, and both had been in-country for only a month or two. Michael Suo was a twenty-three-year-old from

Staten Island, New York, who had requested a combat assignment. Carlos Forero was a twenty-one-year-old Floridian, an aspiring soccer player, and the son of a US airman. Suo went to Lombard; Forero went to me. Lombard and I had no idea how much of a gift these two would be to us. They were to be our radiomen, drivers, and constant companions. They were also going to turn out to be our personal bodyguards.

NOVEMBER 4

In Islam, the treatment of corpses is a serious business. The Koran tells of the Prophet Muhammad joining the funeral processions of strangers, including non-Muslims. The holy book mandates that bodies be ritually washed and buried in the ground without delay. It is important that the flesh not be allowed to "corrupt" before burial. I got the sense, though no Iraqi ever said it to me, that they believed the face the corpse had when it went into the ground was the face the spirit would have in the afterlife. Nobody wanted to have a fucked-up face for eternity. Quick burial was a nonnegotiable point for the Iraqis. The failure to recognize this was another shortcoming of the Americans' cultural intelligence, another misunderstanding that imperiled our mission.

I spent most of November 4 on the Marine Corps side of the temporary base, going over battle plans. I returned with Symons to the Iraqi camp in the pleasant, late-afternoon sun.

All hell had broken loose. It had been three days since I saw Abdel-ridha Gibrael die on the road to Fallujah, and his body was still in a vault in the US morgue. Abdel-ridha Gibrael had a cousin in the battalion, a young jundi who was one part soldier, one part class clown. He was a prankster and a cutup, and I never took him seriously.

I was taking him seriously now. Abdel-ridha Gibrael's cousin stood outside his tent on the open ground, wailing uncontrollably. He was rending his clothes and rubbing dirt all over himself. Other soldiers, Arab and Kurd alike, gathered and began to howl and weep with him. The group was growing and getting louder. A couple of NCOs tried to restore calm, but it was getting dangerously physical. Everybody was armed. There wasn't an Iraqi officer in sight.

I flipped. I couldn't have this—*not now*. In a sudden fury, I threw my rifle to the ground—an unforgivable thing for a Marine to do—and ran at them.

"Awguf! Awguf!" I screamed. *Stop*!

I threw myself among the men, pushing the junood apart. Symons stood by me with his arms outstretched. Iskander, charging at the noise like an angry mother hen, unleashed Kurdish vitriol on the soldiers in an attempt to get them in order.

"Get them in formation, Iskander!" I said. "Form up, form up!"

Iskander ordered the men to form ranks. Cords strained in his neck and spittle flew—I never had seen the sergeant major lose his cool like that. He was probably thinking the same thing about me.

The men slowly quieted under Iskander's imperious command. I ran to the officers' quarters. I tore away the tent flap and barged in. The officers, including the best ones like Ahmed Nu'uman and Mohammed Najm, were lounging around having chai. They had taken dinner, though I knew the junood had not eaten yet. And then it clicked in my mind: we haven't fed the junood; we haven't paid the junood; we are neglecting a Kurdish body; and as far as the junood know, that's exactly what we'll do to their own bodies if they die in Fallujah. I felt rage at myself for not dealing yet with Abdel-ridha Gibrael's body. I felt rage at the officers for absently eating dinner. I felt rage at the junood for their fickleness. I hated everything. The looming violence in Fallujah, my platoon of bosses from two armies, a forestalled payroll—all those pressures, multiplying each other—they bubbled over and erupted out of me like lava. I screamed at the officers in the tent.

"What the fuck is this? What is this bullshit?"

I grabbed leftovers, tables, mattresses. I threw them out of the tent flap.

"Have you fucking animals learned nothing in the last six months? Is this it? Is this what fucking happens when I leave for *eight fucking hours?*"

Outside the tent, I stomped the officers' bedding. I kicked their pillows and smashed their mess kits. Ahmed Nu'uman ran out through the flap and beseeched me to calm myself. I ignored him. Now the *American* was the crazy one. Some of the junood cheered. They had never seen an *Amriki* lose his shit before.

"Damn you! Damn your eyes and damn your fathers' eyes!"—this last one is a killing insult to an Iraqi—"This is my mission! Why do you think I'm *here?*"

Arkan appeared and began translating. He screamed along with me. It felt like my throat was bleeding. My voice began to crack. I had a vision of myself coming perilously close to a precipice. I could feel myself giving over to a gravitational pull that wanted to take me inside, and once I went there, I was not going to come back out. Words I memorized long ago, in a philosophy class, came to me: *If thou gaze long into an abyss, the abyss will also gaze into thee.*

Exhausted, I stopped. My chest heaved. All at once, I felt more embarrassed than infuriated.

Symons stood next to me, watching. I decided to speak first.

"Sir, we gotta get our shit together. I'm sorry you saw this."

The officers picked their bedding up off the dirty ground. Symons jerked his head toward the advisers' tent, as if to say, "Let's get out of here, Mike," and I walked with him. I could feel my face burning.

"I understand you used that display of temper for dramatic effect to take back control of the battalion," he said. Then he said he would catch up with me later. He wanted to find General Essa, the brigade commander. I was grateful for Symons's response. He was letting me off the hook. I knew it, and he knew it.

I found Lombard at the advisers' tent and told him that I did not care how he did it, but we had to get Abdel-ridha Gibrael's body out of here so it could be buried.

"This is deep cultural shit for the Iraqis, and if they see that the bodies of the dead are mistreated, they won't fight. They'll run. I need you to fix this."

"I get it, Mike," he said, and I believed him. Lombard usually laughed at his worries, but he didn't do that now. He was serious. "We have to do it. Nobody else will."

Later, I sat in the advisers' tent with Arkan. I was quiet. I didn't eat. An Iraqi soldier outside the flap asked for me. I went outside. It was a jundi runner that Sa'ad had sent for me. Sa'ad had not been there when I lost it at the officers' tent. The runner told Arkan that Sa'ad requested that I join him for dinner.

The Iraqi CO had commandeered one of EFIC's few permanent structures, a crumbling building with a partial roof, as his quarters. When I arrived with Arkan, a retinue of Iraqi generals was waiting for me. Sa'ad's boss, Brigadier General Essa, was there. So was Essa's boss, Major General Ahmad. Also there was a familiar face: Jassim Thammin, the tall, detached officer who had been the first CO of Fifth Battalion back at Kirkush. I saw from his insignia that the regally incompetent officer had somehow gotten promoted to colonel.

We exchanged pleasantries. Sa'ad had an orderly bring me water and a plate. Then he started in on me. As he spoke in Arabic, I saw anxiety rise on Arkan's face.

"The officers are greatly offended. They were at prayer, and you stormed in and upset them," Arkan translated. "The officers say you saw the Book and threw it to the ground."

I stared, speechless. Yes, I had let my emotions get the better of me, but this was complete bullshit. He was accusing me of disrespecting the Koran, which is practically a crime. I would never do that. Sa'ad was lying, and he knew I knew he was lying.

Sa'ad had me, and he knew it. I was the only American in a closed room full of Iraqi brass. These were officers who could squawk and make political headaches for my American bosses. All they had to do was complain. Sa'ad didn't wait for me to respond.

"The officers demand an apology," he said in Arabic while Arkan translated. I knew he was speaking for the benefit of the generals in the room. Arkan hesitated before he finished Sa'ad's sentence. "And it must be in front of all the men of the battalion. Or they will not fight."

Again, Sa'ad didn't wait for my feedback. He told an orderly to pass along an order to the battalion that the junood be formed up for me immediately after dinner.

Sa'ad, Essa, Ahmad, Jassim, Arkan, and I took silent bites of sweet rice and *khubz.*

Sa'ad was taking a gamble, but it was a good one. He needed to save face in front of his superiors, his officers, and his junood. He needed everyone to see that he called the shots. He needed to humiliate me. He knew that I could just refuse his demand. But he also knew that I feared failure, feared losing the battalion, especially now, right before the battle that was our moment of truth. I took a bite of yellow rice and knew I would do what he wanted. Sa'ad and I knew each other very, very well.

The last vestiges of afternoon stretched long and golden over the ad hoc formation area of East Fallujah Iraqi Camp. The Fifth Battalion's 440 junood, plus NCOs and officers, stood at attention in chocolate-chip camouflage and brown berets. The American advisers were there as well. Iskander formally presented the battalion to the officers, thrust out his chin, and saluted, palm outward. I strode up, Arkan at my side, to take my place next to Sa'ad in the front of the men.

"This afternoon, the battalion was in turmoil," I said. "I took decisive steps to restore order. I am working very hard to make sure that the martyr Abdel-ridha Gibrael, peace be upon him, is released by the Marines so we can send him to his family. I promise you it is my most important task."

I paused to let Arkan catch up in Arabic, then continued.

"It has been brought to my attention that I interrupted the officers while they were at prayer. It has been brought to my attention that the Book fell to the floor when I was interrupting the officers. I did not see that. It was certainly not my intention.

"You know me. You know the truth that I have always taken great care to observe the prayer requirements of Islam. Nor would I desecrate the Book, and you know I have spent many hours learning from you the teachings of the Prophet. I sincerely apologize for interrupting any believer at prayer. It was not my intent.

My intent was to address what I saw as a crisis of confidence and leadership in the battalion."

I began to let emotion come through. It was real. It was also useful.

"We have been through a lot to get here, on the eve of this great battle. The difficult training we went through, and then the hard days and nights in Taji. We endured great violence, and many soldiers left. Many soldiers left even before we came to Fallujah. Those of you who have come this far with me—"

I held my words for two beats before I continued. There was no sound.

"I am grateful to those of you who have braved everything we have faced together. I know what the costs are. I have not seen my family for eight months. There is no guarantee I will see them again. I understand what's at stake. I understand the risks."

I ignored the officers next to me and looked up, straight into the ranks of junood.

"This is why the Marine Corps sent me here. This is my mission. I will not let anyone stop me from accomplishing it. I will fight this battle. If it means I never see my family again, I will accept my death."

I turned to Sa'ad. Neither of us made any expression. I snapped a salute. He saluted back.

There was no reaction from the men. Only silence, and a setting sun. I walked away. Arkan accompanied me. He said nothing until we got out of earshot.

"That was very good, Major Zacchea," he said. Arkan clenched my arm and gazed at me fiercely. "That was very, very good."

NOVEMBER 5

Lombard came to me on the Friday afternoon before the battle and said, "Well, when I die, I'm definitely going to purgatory."

He told me the kind of insane tale that only happens in a war zone. Major Lombard felt confident that he could get the Marines to hand over Abdel-ridha Gibrael's body if he guaranteed to take care of it properly. After all, he was the one who signed it over to the morgue, and if he took it off their hands, he was solving a problem. They didn't know what to do with it, either.

Even once he had the body, though, he still didn't know where he would begin with the Iraqis. Will they want to ship it to his family? And if so, how will they do that? He had no answers, so he went where the wasta was: Sa'ad.

The truth of the matter was that Abdel-ridha Gibrael's body worried Sa'ad as much as it worried me. He didn't want to lose the men's loyalty over a burial issue any more than I did. If you can produce the body, Sa'ad told Lombard, then I can get it shipped to Kurdistan. Lombard sweet-talked the Marines into giving the body back. It was lying on a steel table in a sort of mortuarial holding pattern, and the Marines at the morgue knew that soon they were going to need that space for dead Americans. They handed it over in a black body bag.

Sa'ad met Lombard back at the Fifth Battalion area and introduced him to a man he called Abdel-ridha Gibrael's "cousin." This cousin was a mysterious little civilian with a long gray beard, dark brown robe, and traditional kaffiyeh headdress. He looked more Arab than Kurdish. He held a bag of Iraqi dinars that Sa'ad had apparently just given him—Abdel-ridha Gibrael's military life insurance payout. This robed cousin was going to take the body back to Abdel-ridha Gibrael's family for burial. The first thing Lombard thought was *How did this guy get onto the base?* Then he decided he didn't care how the little man got on the base, he just wanted to be done with the body.

The robed man was driving the oldest Subaru that Lombard had ever seen. The tiny, wheezing vehicle was supposed to transport the corpse, in the desert heat, all the way to the north of Iraq, through a war zone. All Lombard had to do was get the body into the Subaru.

Lance Corporal Suo, the new radioman working with Lombard, tried to help. They pushed. They twisted. They angled the body like movers trying to squeeze furniture through a doorway. But rigor mortis had set in, and the body would not fit into the

Subaru. Suo was an eager young Marine who was a little awed to be working so closely with an officer. He wanted more than anything just to be a useful guy to have around.

"So, Major," Suo said. "I know where I can get us some duct tape."

Lombard caught his drift. They hoisted the body bag to the top of the puttering Subaru while the mystery cousin watched them in silence. He didn't seem to object. They wrapped olive-green duct tape around and over the long black bag and then used more tape to seal it to the top of the car. The old man got into the driver's seat, and Lombard and Suo watched the body ride west toward the base exit, into the setting sun.

Once the body was gone, Sa'ad and I went straight back to work together. We never discussed the near riot among the junood, nor his fabricated Koran story, nor my "apology." The breach was drawing closer, and the battle transcended every other consideration. We had to work together. We had problems to solve.

"We must pay the battalion," Sa'ad said to me after dinner. "We cannot keep holding their money hostage."

Some Sunni Arabs were likely to leave after we paid them, and we knew that. Ahmed Nu'uman, the Sunni XO, put it to me differently.

"If we are going to be an army, we must treat them like an army," he said. "This must include regular pay."

He was right. We had to treat them like proper soldiers. That's what they were. Besides that, anyone who was around only to get paid probably wasn't going to be worth a damn once we got inside Fallujah anyway. We paid them that night.

NOVEMBER 6

The battle plan was set. US and Iraqi forces would carry out a feint during the day on November 7. That meant that all the troops would get into their AAVs and move forward to their prebreach positions just north of the city. We would sit there for a while, trading fire with the enemy. We wanted them to shoot at us. Then we would withdraw. The purpose of the maneuver was to gauge the insurgents' firepower and see their firing positions—the locations of mortars, rockets, and machine guns, which are easier to spot when they fire. Then, armed with that knowledge, we would return and make the real breach at night, in the early morning hours of November 8.

In the early hours on November 6, the day before the scheduled feint, Lombard woke me at 2 AM for my turn at watch. He was coming off his turn but stayed up to make my rounds with me anyway. We set out to walk the defensive positions, where the junood performed guard duty near the rough berms. Our base area was big to cover on foot, and the positions were spread far apart.

We found one abandoned. Then a second. Then a third.

That was enough for me. I had to operate on the assumption that our perimeter was completely unprotected. We forgot the rest of the positions and ran to rouse the other advisers. My heart pounded in my chest, in my ears. A terror squeezed me—a fear that we had a mass desertion of junood who had gone over to the other side. Would the insurgents overrun us while we were undefended?

My thoughts caromed in every direction. The soldiers had to have left sometime between midnight and 2 AM, departing in turn behind Lombard as he finished his rounds. What were the chances they would help the insurgents? Had they taken their weapons? I needed a head count and a weapons count. I needed to tell Sa'ad and get word moving up the Iraqi chain of command. I had to brief Symons.

The advisers woke the Iraqis, starting with the officers and NCOs. Immediately, it was clear that two officers were missing. One was a Sunni Arab named Ahmed Younis, whom none of us trusted anyway. When he joined the battalion, he had an apparent, recent bullet wound, and he was never straightforward with us on where he got it. No surprise that he was gone. The other departure was much, much more disturbing: Capt. Mustafa Hassan

Hamid, a Kurd and the CO of Second Company. That was one of the rifle companies that was going to advance with the Marines into Fallujah. Hamid had been to all the high-level planning meetings. He knew the entire American battle plan.

Warner approached me with his head count: We had 144 missing.

"But they left their weapons behind," he said.

Regardless, we had to operate under the assumption of an imminent threat. I put Mulvihill in charge of reorganizing our defenses. I had Forero get on the radio and make a report to Ramos's operations officer at the First Battalion, Third Marines: "Tell Ramos I'll be over to brief him in person once I have established facts on the ground."

Midmorning, Forero drove me over to Camp Fallujah. The day glared on us. Forero was behind the wheel of a new, up-armored Humvee that he had scored for us from a visiting Pentagon general. It was better protected than the one I had before. Forero was already proving his worth. But I had more immediate worries on my mind.

I stood before Ramos in the cinder-block building that served as his command center and gave him my report. Ramos's voice revealed nothing, but he was mortified. He looked at me, as we say in the Marine Corps, like I had a dick growing out of my forehead. I could tell what he was thinking: *Why the fuck am I dealing with this?*

"I'm taking you to brief Natonski," he said.

He walked me to the major general's tent, like a teacher taking a kid to the principal's office. I felt very small. I could not escape the sick feeling of someone who had been caught doing something wrong. *Was* there anything I could have done differently? My hands trembled. I wanted to be somewhere, anywhere else. But there was no way around this. I was bearing news that was critical for our mission. The best way for me to steel myself was to prepare my report in my mind. *You are a Marine officer. You deal with life-and-death issues. Deliver your report like a Marine.*

Maj. Gen. Richard Natonski, the man who commanded Operation Phantom Fury, the man who would take Fallujah, was a physically imposing Marine with a prominent nose and sandy hair that he wore on the longish side for a general. Two silver stars lay on each shoulder. He looked up with gray-blue eyes, surprised to see Ramos stride in with me. Natonski actually looked like a principal—from the 1950s.

Ramos and I saluted. I remained at attention.

"Major Zacchea has something to report to the General," Ramos said.

"At ease, Major," Natonski said. His voice was deep and calm. He waited.

"Sir," I said, "it is my duty to inform the General that an entire company of Iraqis from my Iraqi battalion deserted in the night. Our count is 144 missing, including two officers. One of the officers, Mustafa Hassan Hamid, was a company commander who attended the battle brief yesterday. He knows the battle plan."

Natonski slowly looked away, into some invisible distance. I looked straight ahead. It felt like he would never respond.

"How did this happen?"

I explained everything: how our watch rotation worked, when we believed the deserters left, the events of two days earlier with the near riot. "And we paid them yesterday. That may have been a contributing factor."

Natonski asked if anyone had seen the soldiers leave. I explained that no one had. I knew that Natonski knew that desertions were a chronic problem in the Iraqi Army. *Please, you've got to understand that we do our best, given what we're up against.*

The general was quiet for a few seconds.

"What do you think this means, Major?"

I cleared my throat.

"Sir, my best read on it is this: The soldiers left their rifles. I believe this means they did not switch sides but instead quit. We believe they took their pay and headed home. We have some experience with this. That's the most likely scenario.

"Captain Hamid is a Kurd," I continued. "He is a Sunni, but we doubt very much that the Kurds would make common cause with the Sunni Arab insurgents in Fallujah. They are implacable enemies. Captain Hamid is a former member of the Peshmerga.

I doubt very much that he had contact with the insurgency, or that he would or could sell the battle plans to the insurgents. They would likely kill him first. That said, the selling of the plans is the most dangerous scenario."

Natonski looked away again. Then he looked down at me. He was at least six inches taller than me, but he might as well have been six feet taller than me.

"It doesn't change our plans," he finally said. "It's a risk we can deal with."

Ramos and I walked out in silence. Ramos didn't say anything until we got to my Humvee, where Forero waited for us with his rifle and his radio.

"I don't want to see you again today," Ramos said.

NOVEMBER 7 TO PREDAWN OF NOVEMBER 8

On Sunday, Iraq interim prime minister Ayad Allawi locked down the country. He declared a twenty-four-hour curfew on Fallujah and Ramadi. He closed the border crossings with Syria and Jordan, and he shut down Baghdad International Airport. Then he flew into EFIC on an American helicopter to inspire the troops.

Allawi was a politician who knew how to behave in a Western way for a Western audience, and like an Iraqi for an Iraqi audience. Junood—especially the ones who were Shiites like Allawi—cheered as the prime minister gave them his prebattle address.

"The people of Fallujah have been taken hostage," he said in Arabic. Arkan translated for me. "You need to free them from their grip. Your job is to arrest the killers"—the idea of *arresting* people on a battlefield was a serious stretch, but I kept listening—"but if you kill them, so be it."

A jundi shouted back, "They will go to hell!"

"To hell they will go!" Allawi said.

The prime minister turned around to the American, European, and Gulf State journalists who had awaited his arrival. He explained to them that the city was more or less empty of civilians.

"There is a division between the Iraqi people and the terrorists," he told them. "We are after the terrorists. We are not after anybody else."

In the late morning, Fryar and his Iraqi NCOs got the motor pool revved up. For the second time in a week, the Fifth Battalion loaded itself into the beds of Nissan trucks. We weren't going far this time, just a couple of klicks to Camp Fallujah, where we would integrate with the Marines. We would make the attack with three hundred Iraqi junood. Ahmed Nu'uman's estimate of how many would fight had been spot-on.

With only hours to go before the breach, a young Iraqi second lieutenant named Iraq Abd al-Baqi was handed command of Second Company—a last-second replacement for the Kurdish officer who had deserted. Al-Baqi was a stern Sunni Arab officer from a prominent Saddam-era military family. He also was a Fallujah native. He told his new company that he wanted to take his city back from the false Muslim irhabeen who subjugated it. Master Sergeant Elesky and Staff Sergeant Villa, the advisers assigned to Second Company, punched al-Baqi's shoulder and told him they believed in him. We had four interpreters with us, and I decided that Abdallah, who was as good as Arkan but cooler under fire, would work with Second Company.

Things began to move very fast. At a final briefing at Camp Fallujah, Marine company commanders kept asking the more senior officers to clarify the rules of engagement. When could they engage? When could they not engage? What were the rules? The Iraqi officers listened in amazement: they were baffled by the idea of "rules" on a battlefield and bewildered by how seriously the Marines took them. Ramos finally lost his patience. "Look, I'm tired of this. If they have a gun, kill them," he snapped at everyone in the big tent. Then he added, "Unless they're trying to surrender."

Satisfied that we were ready for what was to come, Ramos gave his final address.

"Our cause is just. Our hearts are pure. This is good versus evil," he said. "Think about those Americans who were beheaded by Zarqawi. Think about the terror they felt as their heads were being sawed off in front of a TV camera. I intend to visit that terror on them tenfold tonight."

The fight was to begin. It started now. And so the world moved.

Eight thousand Marines and US Army soldiers were at Camp Fallujah, and all of them and all their vehicles acted at once, exploding rather than lurching into motion, like a violent kaleidoscope of unfathomable size and variety. Engines roared. Men shouted. Jet engines screamed overhead. Helicopters thwacked at the air and sent staccato shudders through the men below. American mortar explosions began to boom in the distance, toward Fallujah.

Each of Fifth Battalion's three rifle companies had two American advisers assigned to it. The advisers assembled their companies. Then we split the battalion. The Iraqi troops in their camouflage uniforms waited for a shout from Iskander, then jogged to their places with the Marines. The hosts swirled around them. Marine sergeants stuffed the men, American and Iraqi alike, into AAVs. Slow moving, twenty-seven feet long, eleven feet high, and weighing twenty-nine tons, each AAV was designed to carry twenty infantrymen. We packed in many more than that. Men pressed against each other, shut in under blue electric light, and hoped the armor would hold.

Forero and I climbed into our new, up-armored Humvee. It looked like it had just rolled off the assembly line in Indiana. Sa'ad and Arkan piled into the backseat.

Scores of AAVs crawled on their tracks, first to the north, then to the west, until they had positioned themselves due north of the city. A set of railroad tracks ran on a high crest of earth from east to west between the rolling AAVs and the city. It was too steep in most places for the AAVs to climb. They squeezed through a few navigable bottlenecks to get under and over the tracks. As the AAVs squirted through onto the other side, open to the city, the insurgents could see them rumbling over the desert like boats on land. They had never seen that before. They took aim at us. It was on.

The northern edge of the city lit up like a low constellation as the enemy gave fire. Rockets and mortars reached out for us, hoping to catch one of the lumbering AAVs. Great black spouts began to shoot up among the AAVs as the mortars fell among them. Still they crawled forward, willing targets charging to their assigned spots. The AAVs had stout armor on the fronts and sides, but only a light layer of steel across the top. A direct hit from a mortar falling from above would blast apart all the men inside.

Marine spotters, some bobbing atop AAVs, others scrambling over the sand in their boots, peered into the city with binoculars and called back coordinates on their radios. Within seconds, the US artillery responded to the enemy mortars, big shells howling overhead in great arcs. Fast-working Marine mortar teams, on foot among AAVs and the murderous, black geysers, set up their small artillery weapons and then hunched away from their mortars, fingers in their ears, as the tubes crumped out shells. A frenzy of black and gray explosions blew up in a line along the edge of the city, an impromptu forest of dark, deadly sequoia. The hard edges of Fallujah flashed in the smoke, backlit by explosions deeper in the city. Mortar smoke unfolded in strobes of white light.

The Marines drew within 650 or 750 meters of the city. It became clear immediately that the insurgents were more expert with their mortar fire than most of us expected them to be. You could see from the explosions that they were walking down individual AAVs, adjusting their fire and drawing closer to one chosen vehicle with each successive mortar. Their mortar crews were trained. One stationary AAV near me was missed by two hundred meters, then by seventy-five. I knew that AAV was packed with Marines. Somebody on board realized what was happening, and the AAV lurched backward finally. A third mortar blew apart the spot where the AAV had sat fifteen seconds earlier.

Finally, the radios crackled with the order to withdraw. The feint was over.

Most of the AAVs retreated to the north side of the crest, out of sight of the city. Night swept in. Squads of Marines on foot dug in on the exposed side of the tracks. Those brave souls would spend it out alone in their holes, lying between the two armies and watching the city. The rockets, mortars, and artillery diminished, then became sporadic. Back north of the crest where most of us came to a halt, men tried to sleep. Others climbed the high dune of earth to watch tracers shoot in and out of the city. Here and there, rifle fire winked white from the city's edge, disappeared, and then glinted from somewhere else. The Marines and Iraqis watched. *There they are.*

An unrelenting gale swept in from the north and west, passing through us and cutting across the city. My body was sapped of energy, running on reserves that came from some place that I had never tapped before. My mind was piqued to wakefulness by the scene before me.

The night sky scudded with blue-black clouds. All manner of explosive power arced in turn overhead. Invisible American artillery shells zipped in a high treble, went silent for a millisecond before impact, and burst low in the cityscape. Mortars coughed behind us, lobbing rounds. Other mortars came back in our direction. Rockets vacuumed at the high air on their way into Fallujah; RPGs tore the low air coming back out toward us. The four prop engines of an American AC-130 throbbed overhead as the big bird tilted and spit lightning bolts into the city. Digital radio nets crackled between the claps of machine guns. From within the distant city, my ears began to pick up on something bizarre, unplaceable. At first I couldn't identify it, but when the realization struck me, my hair rose on end: the rooftops of Fallujah fizzled with hundreds of tinny voices from the city's minarets. The mosques were beckoning the faithful to take arms against the crusaders at the gate. I could hear their numbers in the far black night, each calling out with its own song. They whispered like an electric hive.

We drew our Humvee close to the crest. I stood on the roof, facing Fallujah. The city was gilded with dozens of blazes. Lance Corporal Forero sat awake but with his eyes closed in the driver's seat, his rifle poking through the crook of the open door, the handset of his radio tucked into his helmet next to him. Arkan dozed, twitching, in the backseat. Sa'ad stood to one side and stared straight ahead, eyes hidden in black sockets.

This was our attack position. About 150 meters in front of us, the first line of Marines were dug into the hard ground. We couldn't see them in the darkness but knew they were there. To our left and right, a miles-long line of AAVs stretched parallel to the city's northern edge, noses facing south, waiting. Eighty or ninety meters separated each AAV from those to either side. Enough distance that each felt alone in the night. The schedule called for First Battalion, Third Marines, to move forward into the city after midnight. But no plan survives contact with the enemy, as they say, and this night was no different. Midnight came and went, and we still had no orders to advance.

Forero and Arkan rose from the Humvee to wait outside and stretch their legs. Sa'ad produced a small carpet, knelt facing south, and prayed under the black, lacerated sky. Every now and then, Forero updated me about something coming over the nets. Arkan translated the reports for Sa'ad.

Without warning, several large explosions rocked the ground around our position. Mortars fell all around us, the closest less than one hundred meters away. A 120-mm mortar found the AAV to our left. The shell crushed the AAV into the dirt. Its diesel fuel tanks exploded. The AAV was full of troops, American or Iraqi or both—I couldn't tell. I squinted into the night to make out the wreck and saw the figures of men spilling from the vehicle, flailing as the fire threw garish shadows across the ground. Some men were in flames. Silhouettes screamed. I saw a big Marine tackle a burning man and roll him to the earth. Forero's radio began to ring with alarmed voices, an electric echo of the scene before us.

Forero concentrated his attention onto the nets. I jumped down from the Humvee to take the handset and listen with him.

Neither of us wanted to look at the scene at the AAV. I needed to focus on the wider situation at hand, but it was hard.

"That was bad," I finally said to Forero under my breath. We stood close. "That's a lot of casualties."

Arkan overheard what I said to Forero. He rubbed one palm hard across his clean-shaven jaw and dutifully translated to Sa'ad, whose face showed no emotion. Sa'ad said something in Arabic.

"This is war. This is what happens," Arkan said. "Colonel Sa'ad says he has seen this many times, in Iran."

I didn't respond. Forero looked at me and looked back at the radio. The sound of weapons pressed at us. Then a voice yelled clear through the night from the direction of the burning AAV. I could not see the man, but I thought I recognized the voice of the sergeant major from First Battalion, Third Marines. He bellowed at his men. The words he said are the last memory I have from before we were on the streets of Fallujah itself:

"Listen up Marines! This is *it*! Do you hear me? I don't care who you are! I don't care how *hard* you think you may be! This is the *hardest* you are ever going to be *in your entire life*! This is it, *now*!"

13

CITY OF MOSQUES

WHEN THEY MADE THE BREACH at Fallujah, the mortars broke the earth and spewed rock, sand, and steel, skittering over the tops of the cans they stood in, the men in the compartments greeted by rattling, tumbling grit inches above their helmets. Their skulls. It was black. They had no windows. Man against pack against man against rifle against pack against man, in black. All packed, all together, for delivery.

Try to focus on the can's throttle, hear it gearing down, gearing back up. It jerks into motion, but don't worry: it's too tight for you to fall. The gears are better than the mortar blasts, better than trying to figure, there in the black, *How far away was that one?* The armor atop of the can was light. Better not to think of those men in the city with their deadly calibration, zeroing in, adjusting, walking each arcing mortar successively closer, each blast a little nearer to that thin roof.

Another blast.

Another, and much nearer. The disengorged earth skittered and knocked across the top of the can when the mortars came close enough.

They sat and idled. They waited. Twenty-five or thirty men waiting for that throttle. The four crew members coiled, grasping radios and weapons with slick hands. A man coughed, barely enough mobility to turn away from the next face. Mortars howled. Rockets screamed. The AAVs' .50-cals barked, close. Marine shells screamed high overhead, thudded into the city, splitting faraway streets. The places that awaited the men broke into pieces in advance of their arrival. The mortars kept at the men, walking down mobile cans. Before they made the breach at Fallujah, they were praying for just the chance to get outside and run through bullets.

I thought I understood urban combat. I had studied Stalingrad. I had followed Grozny. That knowledge mattered. It also did not matter. You don't really know anything until you live it. It's especially true of urban combat.

Six American battalions made the breach. We—the Iraqis of the Fifth, the other advisers, and I—were divided among the four companies of the First Battalion, Third Marines, on the eastern, left flank of the advancing line. In front of us lay the broken-tooth buildings of Fallujah's Askari neighborhood. We broke down this way:

Fifth Battalion companies	Advisers and attached Marines	Interpreters
First Rifle Company	Capt. Brian Mulvihill, SFC Eric Warner	Najm
Second Rifle Company	M.Sgt. A. J. Elesky, S.Sgt. Anthony Villa	Abdallah
Third Rifle Company	Capt. Chuck Johnson, S.Sgt. Richard Fryar	Sala'am
HQ Company	Maj. Michael Zacchea, L.Cpl. Carlos Forero	Arkan
HQ Company (supply)	Maj. Mark Lombard, L.Cpl. Michael Suo	None

Our objectives lay southward. The junood of the Fifth approached Fallujah's edge in armored vehicles. Then the AAVs stopped, the men dismounted, and they broke for the jumbled buildings and narrow corridors of the city on foot, under cover of night and under fire. The six main US battalions attacked from the north, abreast of one another. The plan was that as they killed insurgents and flushed others from the burning city, the American, British, and Iraqi units on the outskirts of town would kill those who fled. At any given time, Fifth Battalion's advisers were flung across the Askari neighborhood, far from each another, guiding their own companies of Iraqis alongside their assigned companies of Marines. Iraqi troops like ours were earmarked for taking mosques. The alliance stormed Muslim sites with Muslim men. About 10,500 Americans fought in and around Fallujah, as well as 2,000 Iraqi troops and 850 British soldiers—a battalion of tough Scots from the fabled Black Watch Regiment. We faced roughly six thousand enemies—nobody knew their precise numbers, probably not even the insurgents themselves.

Our enemies were of two types: One group was Iraqi and led by Abdullah al-Janabi, a fifty-three-year-old Sunni chief who had already fought the Americans once at the First Battle of Fallujah. The second was from al-Qaeda in Iraq—almost none of them Iraqis—led by Omar Hussein Hadid, a thirty-year-old former electrician who reported to Abu Musab al-Zarqawi. Our enemies knew the city intimately and were holed up in homes, mosques, factories, garages, slaughterhouses, garbage dumps, schools, clinics, and shops. And then, of course, there were the civilians who had decided, for reasons I could not imagine, to remain in the city. There were ten thousand of them, including children. Before the Iraq War came to Fallujah, the city's population stood at 250,000.

Fallujah, our battle, began the week after Halloween and ended five days before Christmas. Every building in Fallujah had to be searched. That was about forty thousand structures. The Second Battle of Fallujah was fought mostly indoors. The battle inverted everything American civilians think about warfare. Many Americans know the film *Saving Private Ryan*, which shows massive groups of men running outdoors in open spaces, yelling as loudly as possible. The Second Battle of Fallujah was about small groups of men creeping indoors in confined spaces, repressing sound as much as possible. A normal combat line of sight at Fallujah was five to ten feet.

The fighting was most chaotic in the first week, when it was still an outdoor melee. Bullets came from every direction. Imagine where your mind would go in a space where you can be shot at any time from any angle. It was impossible to protect every angle. Nobody was safe, and everyone fought—officers, senior NCOs, enlisted. Colonels knocked down doors and cleared houses. Sergeants major led assault teams.

My three bosses, Lieutenant Colonel Symons, General Essa, and Lieutenant Colonel Ramos, saw a broader battle than I did. Only the highest-ranking officers and their staffs, outside the city with their maps and communications gear, spread out in huge military tents, had a sense of the battle's totality. It's a great irony of warfare that the men who take part in the fight have no real sense of the battlefield they're a part of. They're immersed in whatever is right in front of them, every neuron firing into a sharp focus on the immediate. We would not see the forest for the trees; we would not see the Battle of Fallujah for its bloody streets and blasted bedrooms. Each person's ability to grasp everything going on is basically nil. So you stop trying. Or you don't ever. My team of advisers moved with their Iraqi companies, living street-by-street and house-by-house. Chance encounters with other advisers and friendly Marines allowed us to share information and slowly piece together a fuller image of our burning, reeking, superviolent world.

Fallujah had no zoning in the sense that Americans think of it, so residential, business, and industrial buildings were scrambled together. Many streets were exceedingly narrow and lined by buildings so close together that they were more like winding hallways than streets in the Western sense. Marines, funneled down narrow corridors, could not rely on the standard action drills we'd been trained for when we made contact with the enemy. Typically, platoons of Marines and Iraqis advanced in two parallel, single-file lines, one on each side of the narrow street. Men at the front of the lines kept their gun sights forward, scanning every doorway, nook, and window for movement. Men farther back in the lines trained their eyes upward, watching rooftops on the side of the street opposite. That way, each line defended the other from any attack from above. The last man in each line, his head constantly swiveling, guarded against attacks from the rear.

We didn't sleep for the first thirty-six hours. On the first day, my team picked its way forward in our Humvee. Lance Corporal Forero, nervous but keen eyed, sat behind the wheel. His radio remained in one arm's reach. I took the death seat and peered forward through the still-unbroken windshield. Colonel Sa'ad sat behind me, alert but unflappable. Arkan crouched behind Forero. Above us manning the .50-caliber gun was a Marine chief warrant officer whose name none of us would remember. The very first time I dismounted alone, to confer with a group of Marine officers, we came under fire. Forero hustled the vehicle into a good firing position and let our gunner open up. The big .50-cal roared at the *irhabi* sniper, and the incoming fire stopped.

Fallujah had its own light spectrum, which ran from tawny yellow to dirty russet, a beige filter that no color could penetrate. The broken city swallowed us. Men vied to kill each other. Soundless but for occasional shots, sometimes far off, other times on top of us; sometimes solitary, other times emphatic for minutes. Whole blocks broken and jagged like the horrified smile of a meth head. A place devoid of birds, except those that fed on carrion. Black gaps in ochre buildings that held the mark of death or dealt it. Insurgents fired shots and fled down greasy alleys. Others, the ones who thought an approving god would suck them to heaven, stayed solitary in the place they had chosen, and killed until killed. Everywhere, bodies sprawled. One, two, five on a block. Insurgents, coursed through by shock waves. Civilians with brains sniped away. I say bodies, though many barely retained human form. Split, ripped, blackened. Sometimes just charred pulp in a great bloom, with an intact leg and boot, or an arm and a wristwatch. Occasionally a Marine stopped to snap a picture. Everybody had

a point-and-click. It felt good to see our enemies divorced from
their living form.

The Marines and the Iraqis worked from building to building.
Power lines hung overhead in deranged tangles. The men took
turns being first through doors, through ruptured walls. Some
climbed roofs to fight in the urban canopy while others worked
below. Doors they couldn't knock open they blasted open. They
yanked doors with Humvee and chain. Squads entered central
arcades and tried to cover every corner at once. (You can't cover
every corner at once.) And always the same awful choices before
storming a building: Go from street up? Or from roof down? Each
posed loathsome contingencies. Men advancing from above fall
forward when they're shot, spilling down stairs. A squad advancing
from below meets grenades tumbling down stairwells. Our enemies
shot through floors and ceilings.

Shit announced itself everywhere, the odor curling around
corners, seeping through the Humvee windows. Sometimes burning shit, other times just shit deposited in an alley, spilled loose
from dead intestines. It snaked into our nostrils, planted itself
there next to our brains. It never left us. Rolling swarms of flies
skittered at our faces, took claim of us as if we were theirs. Oval,
like green-backed jelly beans. A blue, stumbling buzz that moved
from living man to corpse and back again, trying us out, finding
us living, shifting away with fat indifference. The best-fed flies on
earth. After a few days, I stopped swatting them from my face. We
became complacent, took them on like pilot fish. We held close
conversations with one another, the flies clinging at us.

Gold shell casings winked from the black streets. The spent
metal festooned whole blocks. They glared back at the angry sun,
defiant and hot and searing to the flesh. Waiting like shiny industrial ticks to embed themselves into the arch of a boot. Garbage,
filth of mysterious progeny, fled our approach in a dry wind. Shifting piles, half embers. Sometimes bigger things unfathomable: a
refrigerator mysteriously deposited in the center of an intersection,
the street around it ringed by a giant crimson asterisk. A blasted
Toyota, upside down, one wheel turning inexplicably. Candy bars

spilled in a trail along the narrow way where someone fled. A bicycle, entangled with an unspent RPG. Iraqis from the Fifth Battalion stalked up, consulted in muted Arabic over the strange display, and took the bicycle. The RPG stayed where it was.

And then there were the dogs. Not the beige garbage-dump scroungers common in the Middle East, but animals more wolflike. Bulky. Sharp mouthed. They prowled in desperate packs, their snouts smeared red like hyenas of the Serengeti. Abandoned by their masters, or wild to begin with, they survived by eating dead men. An impossible impression grew on more than one of us. The animals had begun to bulge bigger than normal dogs. As men killed men and corpses bloated in the streets, the dogs ate the men and seemed stronger and wilder.

Lombard and Suo, a few klicks away from me in their own Humvee, saw one running with a human leg in its jaws. Other beasts had their own horrific injuries from the artillery, running with entrails dragging. At one point Lombard and Suo spotted a man at a distance. He sat in the open on a curb, facing them. They squinted in on the figure and decided he was dead, but sitting upright. A low wall blocked the Humvee, so Suo got out to inspect more closely. Lombard took his rifle next to the big engine block and watched rooftops. Suo drew near to the man, and two things became clear at once: The first was that the man was definitely dead, because his face was gone. The second was that he was moving. The body jerked from the waist up, wobbling uneasily. Suo leveled his rifle at the apparition. As the lance corporal got close enough to see over the man's shoulder, he spotted a big, lupine dog. The animal's snout dug into the corpse's back, shaking the dead man's upper body. The dog stopped to gaze at Suo. It did not flee. The Marine did not shoot. He backed away, his eyes on dog and man all the way back to the low wall. The corpse's legs were clean skeleton. The feet still wore boots.

A constant throughout the battle was Lieutenant Colonel Symons's voice beckoning me on the radio. He wanted to know my position. He wanted to know my troops' disposition. He wanted to be briefed

on contact with insurgents. That was his job. I responded to him
quickly most of the time. Symons had warned me that I would face
command-and-control problems with the Iraqis broken into many
groups over so wide an area. He was right. We didn't operate as a
unit but as many piecemeal units, each with a couple of advisers. I
worked the radios with Forero and Arkan, perpetually updating a
mental map of where everyone was. A patchwork battalion, inexorably moving southward. Radios weren't always reliable. And of course
we had our normal challenges related to language. As for the other
advisers, they each led their own allotment of Iraqis but also had to
coordinate with the regular Marines they were attached to.

Those regular Marines were in town to kill insurgents. They
were not in town to make friends with armed Iraqis, even if they
had US advisers. Many of the Marine officers were not pleased
to have a unit of Iraqi soldiers tagging along with them. They
mistrusted the Iraqi junood, felt contempt for the Iraqi officers,
and couldn't fathom the professional motivation of the American advisers. The Iraqis weren't stupid, and they knew what the
Marines thought of them. The disrespect many of them felt made
it that much harder for the advisers to motivate them to do things
like charge into occupied mosques or keep advancing past half-
eaten Arab corpses. It made me extremely angry that there were
Marines who didn't respect what we were doing. I understood
where their attitude came from, and I wished their attitude didn't
infuriate me, but it did. We advisers were part of a strategic initiative. We were making an Army that would take over the fight
someday and help build a new society. But that was lost on some
Marines. Their attitude was that they were in Anbar Province to
kill bad guys. I got it; of course they were. But I hated their
lack of understanding that the advisers and Iraqis were doing an
important job too.

"Hang in there, Mike," Lieutenant Colonel Symons would say.
"We're all in the same boat."

The insurgents had set up their command-and-control structure largely within mosques. Their thinking here was twofold:
First, mosques were a natural choice for irhabeen who were

often religiously maniacal. Second, they figured—correctly—that the Americans would try to avoid destroying Muslim holy sites in the City of Mosques, since doing so would infuriate Iraqis and the wider Muslim world. We couldn't just *bomb* mosques. We had to *take* them. The Fifth Battalion, scattered about with the Marines, fought everywhere, not just in mosques. But the Iraqis' role in capturing holy places was critical because it stripped the insurgents of their chance for "crusader" propaganda. That job, more than anything, made the Marines slowly come to rely on us as the battle wore on. That role was also the reason the al-Qaeda insurgents, who, like the Marines, were foreigners who claimed to be fighting to build a better Iraq, began to deeply, deeply hate us.

Fifth Battalion's first-day objective was a mosque called al-Tawid. We had been up all night. The Marines set up a perimeter in the surrounding alleys and fought their own street battles, while the Iraqis, led by Sa'ad and me, struck the mosque. It was a long fight with rifles and machine guns. The insurgents blasted back at us with small arms and RPGs. We killed several before we finally claimed al-Tawid. Amazingly, we had none killed or wounded. That objective secured, we moved to the next. Late on the first day, Sa'ad approached me with Major Mohammed Najm, the smart operations officer who was friends with Zayn. Everyone was lit up with adrenaline. Everything around us had a brighter, sharper edge.

"Raed Zakkiyah, some of the men think we killed al-Janabi at the mosque," Mohammed Najm said through Arkan.

"At al-Tawid? Back there?"

Najm and Arkan nodded. Sa'ad peered at me under black rebar eyebrows. Some of Mohammed Najm's men had seen the body of an older man with a beard and thought they recognized him from television. Abdullah al-Janabi was a top Sunni leader at Fallujah, the man commanding insurgents who were real Iraqi nationals.

"Get me Ramos," I said to Forero, who immediately linked me to the tents and maps outside the city. I explained the situation, and Ramos told me to go back for the body. Mohammed Najm's men showed the way. When we got there, the body was splayed like a starfish. Rigor mortis had set in, and we couldn't fit him into the Humvee. I helped the Iraqis try to rearrange him, but we faced an impossible fit. It was as macabre as it was absurd.

"Fuck this," I said. "Break him. Break him up."

Every Humvee held a field kit with a sledgehammer. Major Mohammed Najm calmly took the hammer, lifted it over his head and pursed his lips as he brought it down. After a few minutes, we broke the body enough to fold it into the Humvee. For a while, everyone thought it was, in fact, Abdullah al-Janabi. Ramos gave an interview with the *Los Angeles Times* where he said the body appeared to be the insurgent leader. Years later, however, I learned that the body we broke up that day belonged not to Abdullah but to his brother, Thilab. Abdullah al-Janabi would be back in Fallujah, his city, fighting for ISIS and holding off the Iraqi Army, in 2014.

The second objective was a mosque called al-Mujahareen, which we took much as we took the first. Al-Mujahareen was low and beige, fronted by four narrow columns. A grassy yard was ringed by a wall that was just taller than a man. We all lived together for a little while: a squad from First Battalion, Third Marines, a platoon of Iraqi junood, the quietly competent Mohammed Najm, Colonel Sa'ad, Arkan, Forero, and me. Seemingly from nowhere, we were joined by a British lieutenant colonel who left his unit to get in some fighting.

"If they knew I was here, I'd face court-martial," he said, laughing. We call men like the British officer combat tourists. The lieutenant colonel had a Union Jack shoulder patch and a mobile phone that could make international calls. I told him he was welcome to stay. Forero unpacked his radio. He watched me at all times. He tended my gear as much as his own. I was the officer, the commander, and the more experienced Marine, but I was beginning to find his presence a comfort.

It was at al-Mujahareen that we encountered our first civilians up close. A family sought refuge with us. If it had been only men and boys, they would have worried me, but it was a family: a man, his wife, five children—three boys and a girl, plus an infant—and the man's parents. They claimed one of the mosque's small outbuildings. The girl, probably eleven or twelve, fashioned a broom from twine and twigs and swept the walkway in front of their new home. She wore a red gown and sandals. The father stood in his dirty dishdasha, a cigarette between two fingers and a tense look on his face. The boys wore bright red-and-blue outfits that were as mismatched as they were missized. As if by a miracle, Forero produced a soccer ball and cans of Pepsi. I never learned where he got them. Just an hour before, a sniper had come so close to hitting Forero while he manned the Humvee .50-cal that the hot, smashed round ended up inside the turret with him. His rifle slung over a shoulder, Forero kicked the ball with the boys. The Iraqi family was watching their city being blasted away around them. Bodies, burning buildings, torched cars, bombs, and feral animals had lay thick between that mosque and wherever they came from. They didn't know who to trust. They found us, a group part Westerners, part men in uniforms who spoke Arabic. That night and the next one, they threw in their lot with us. They would be the first of many. Beyond the open door, I spotted the mother inside her temporary home. I knew it would be an insult to look at her long, but I'll never forget the sight I caught in that one second: A mother, aged beyond her years, sitting on the floor in her gown, trying to calm and entertain her daughter. A baby wrapped up in her arms. The worry carved on her face will stay with me forever.

Our patchwork battle raged across northern Fallujah those first two days. We each lived it separately.

Lombard and his driver-radioman, Lance Corporal Suo, were close in the first few days to several explosive blasts that swept through their Humvee with hateful shock waves. Lombard trusted Suo implicitly, and Suo arrived at a place where he trusted three things: his radio, his rifle, and Lombard. Their first mosque was a larger one a couple klicks from al-Mujahareen. Lombard conferred with a group of Iraqis and Marines downstairs. Suo walked upstairs and found a US Army sergeant in the corner of a room, crying. Suo asked if he was all right. The sergeant told Suo that he had just lost a friend in a house nearby. An insurgent lying on a stairway landing wasn't really dead. As the American passed the man, he shot the US soldier in the back.

Another American in the room, a gunnery sergeant, seemed drunk with rage. He wore a sawed-off shotgun by a lanyard around his neck. The mosque's second floor had a mezzanine that looked down on the ground floor, where worshippers would normally lay out their prayer rugs. Civilian men, women, and children had begun to fill up the lower level, desperate for refuge. No plan was in place for dealing with them.

"If anything goes off down there," the angry gunnery sergeant said, "and I mean *anything*, you take this"—he handed Suo a grenade—"and you drop it down on those motherfuckers."

Suo held the grenade and stared silently at the man. Downstairs, babies cried and men spoke in hurried Arabic.

"I don't want to know shit about it," the American said. "I don't give a fuck."

For the battles' first three days, Captain Mulvihill and Sergeant First Class Warner took turns snatching naps that Warner described as turning his brain "one-third off and two-thirds on," but other than that, they didn't sleep at all. They never removed their body armor but found that if they hiked it up a bit, it would hold them sitting upright against buildings as they half-slept. The quick-talking Irishman and the hulking ex-football star got their first chance to rack out after their Iraqi company took their first mosque. The Iraqis from Fifth Battalion ran inside the mosque in the middle of a firefight, Mulvihill and Warner alongside. Marines came behind as a second wave.

Aged Islamic paintings, ornate with interwoven patterns, adorned the walls. The insurgents had hung rougher paintings on bedsheets from the ceiling: American flags were intertwined with snakes and Stars of David. The Iraqis swept the house and recovered grenades and AK-47s. Marine intelligence officers found an office with two computers. That was an amazing find—Iraq seemed to have almost no computers, and we couldn't even get one for Fifth Battalion. Mulvihill and Warner turned back to the mosque's walls. The interior of the building had been pretty badly shot up. The Marines went outside to set up a perimeter, and the Iraqis immediately set themselves to straightening up the place. Warner was surprised. He didn't think of the Iraqis as orderly people, but they eagerly tried to tidy the mosque and repair it where they could. Their second mosque was similar: a shoot-out, a charge inside, more weapons, and more damage. The Marines built their perimeter. The imam's office was in a small outbuilding. Warner walked inside. A set of bookshelves had tumbled down amid the shooting. A jundi with gray hair wept as he tried to put the books back onto the walls. Some of the texts had taken bullets, and small scraps of paper with Arabic script littered the rug. Warner knew his soldiers; most were from the rural class, peasants, functionally illiterate. The old jundi couldn't read the books. His hands trembled as he put them back in place.

14

RPG

NOVEMBER 10 WAS THE MARINE Corps' birthday. Marines, wherever they may be, take the day seriously. In the history of the Marine Corps, "wherever they may be" has included a hell of a lot of places, many of them extraordinarily dangerous venues for birthday parties. In Fallujah in 2004, the First Battalion, Third Marines, would be celebrating the same as the Marines who came before us.

Night came in. The dry air of al-Mujahareen's old courtyard was pleasantly warm. About a hundred of us stood together, faced by a sergeant major named Berg who as the oldest of us held the honor of master of ceremonies. After a minute of rowdy but good-natured searching, we ferreted out the youngest Marine among us, a teenaged private, and pushed him up front to stand with Berg. The oldest and youngest—it was all part of the ceremony. In the distance, machine guns rattled. Rifles popped. The sound of an occasional explosion thudded up against the sacred mosque walls around us.

Berg read from the Continental Congress document that commissioned our founding. In 1775, a Quaker innkeeper named Samuel Nicholas was made into a captain and told to raise two battalions of riflemen who would fight from Navy ships. Nicholas had no blueprint and no support. He made the rules as he went along. Berg then read from the Marine birthday address delivered by Gen. John A. Lejeune in 1921, three years after the War to End All Wars.

"In every battle and skirmish since the birth of our corps," Berg read, "Marines have acquitted themselves with the greatest distinction, winning new honors on each occasion until the term 'Marine' has come to signify all that is highest in military efficiency and soldierly virtue."

In the distance, beyond our walls: *Boom. Thud. Thack, thack, thack, thack.*

"This high name of distinction and soldierly repute we who are Marines today have received from those who preceded us in the corps."

Ka-whomp! Tak-tak-tak-tak-tak-tak-tak.

"With it we have also received from them the eternal spirit which has animated our corps from generation to generation and has been the distinguishing mark of the Marines in every age."

Whomp, whomp, whomp. Crack-ack-ack-ack.

Sa'ad caught my eye. He didn't understand everything we said, but he was a soldier. His hawkish countenance communicated a deep knowingness. Others looked on, silently respectful, exhaling cigarette smoke.

Berg stepped aside for Lieutenant Colonel Ramos. Upright and clear voiced, the commander of First Battalion, Third Marines, said that every Marine, alive or dead, wished he were there with us. Ramos's Hawaii-based battalion had gotten less time to prepare for Fallujah than other battalions there. He seemed to relish the chance to pump up his men's spirits. Some of those dead Marines Ramos spoke of had been alive that morning. *Yeah,* I thought, *I bet they would wish they were here with us.* I wished they were there too.

Men broke into MREs that contained lemon sponge cake—the Marine Corps' traditional birthday confection. We passed them around so everyone could have at least a bite. With water and Gatorade, we toasted the United States of America and its finest branch of service.

Then we did something that a lot of people, including a lot of people in the US military, would consider crazy. We all took part, officers and enlisted. Moved by the ceremony, heeding Ramos's words, and proud to a point of recklessness, we walked together from the mosque and boarded our Humvees. Forero took our wheel, and I settled into the death seat. Other Marines clambered inside with us. Men in desert camouflage scrambled for seats in other vehicles, playing a gleeful game of musical chairs amid the live fire of Fallujah. Two Humvees were attached to a US Army psychological-operations team—or psyops—and so were fitted with massive loudspeakers. Normally, the speakers would blast messages in Arabic, telling civilians to evacuate or warning insurgents to surrender. Engines cranked to life. We began to move, forming up in a long line. A psyops Humvee led the impromptu convoy, and the team hit their speakers.

Amid the sounds of war around us, some of it distant, some of it close enough to end our lives, the sound of a bugle blasted from the loudspeakers. A snare drum kicked in, and a full brass orchestra. Then the trumpets and chorus led the way. We played our hymn.

"From the halls of Monte-zuuu-u-maa to the shores of Trip-ohh-leeee . . ."

Crack. Boom! Crack-crack.

"We fight our country's baa-aat-tles, in the air, on land and sea."

Into the blackness of Fallujah. *Tak-tak-tak-tak-tak-tak-tak* . . . Picking our way among the craters and ruined buildings. We rode nowhere in particular, boasting to everyone who could hear: We are the Marines. We are in your city. We are going to kill you. This is the soundtrack of your annihilation.

"First to fight for right and free-ee-dom, and to keep our hon-ooor clean; . . ."

Trombones soared. I glanced at Forero. He gazed through the windshield, his eyes wide as if in terror, his mouth an open, ecstatic smile.

THOMP, whomp! Boom! BOOM! Outside the window beyond Forero's rapt face, a burning building slipped past, blazing out of control.

"We are proud to claim the tiii-i-tle of United States Marine."

We called out to our enemies. Teased them. Tantalized them. Serenaded them with our contempt. They spoke back to us, spilled fire into the sky, seeking out the music snaking near them. Neither side needed a translator for this conversation. Hot bullets reached blindly for us; mortars blew up streets, always one block off the mark. Missing us. *Wide right, you fucking pussies.*

We switched from the Marine Corps theme to another song. Then another. Our musical tour became a running battle. Men at the gun mounts of some of the Humvees began to let rounds rip from .50-cals. Marines fired rifles from open windows. It had been a terrifying couple of days, and we fought with fury. We held a firefight to blow off the stress of a larger battle. Of a larger war. It went on like that for three hours. Finally, spent, we returned to our temporary home at al-Mujahareen. Amazingly, we had no casualties. That night, we slept hard. We had a war to get up for in the morning.

The next day was the third of the battle, November 11. It was a sunny day, temperatures in the eighties, but the air hung thick with smoke. Stench rose out of the bodies that were bloating up and coming apart on the pavement. Marines still drew fire from every direction when they maneuvered inside the city.

We awoke to the sound of a big fight across the street. Charlie Company from First Battalion, Third Marines, held a building that stood a block north of the mosque. They were attacked. A handful of Marine engineers with a combat bulldozer got caught up in the middle of the shooting. A building collapsed in the course of the fight, killing two of them. The British combat tourist yanked tight his chin strap and ran with me to our roof. He put a cheek to the stock of his rifle and squinted over his sights. We returned fire. That battle went on for two hours.

After the fight, Ramos decided to move his battalion's operations center out of the mosque. Scouts found a building they liked a half mile away. Ramos's men formed up in convoy that afternoon and drove the half mile through the narrow, ruined streets of the city. I went with them, Forero driving.

There was no music this time. It was scarier during the day than it had been the night before. Refuse of every imaginable sort littered the ground, and we knew IEDs could lie hidden anywhere within the trash. Rocket-propelled-grenade attacks could wait around any corner or on any rooftop. Buildings had tumbled into the streets, blocking our way unexpectedly. Downed power lines got tangled into Humvees' antennae. As we broke free of the lines, they whiplashed back and sliced our gunners.

We approached from the east. We arrived near the building the battalion had selected and waited while a platoon of Marines worked to clear its courtyard and interior. I dismounted and advanced, leaving Forero with the Humvee. As I trotted off, Forero took a knee on the street next to the engine block, his rifle ready. A puppy bumbled out of nowhere and sat next to him.

An explosion ripped the air. Marines scrambled for cover. Rounds came tearing in. Irhabeen on the second floor of a building about 150 meters away opened up with a machine gun, onto the nose of the convoy. I jumped behind a wall and fired back.

A captain and two enlisted Marines huddled together just ahead of my position. Nut to butt, as they say. They gazed over the top of a low wall, up the street toward the insurgents. The captain looked back and saw me behind him.

"Cover us, sir!" he yelled.

I signaled that I understood. The Marines leapfrogged forward from cover to cover, approaching the enemy machine gun. They came to the end of a low wall. I watched. The captain peered around a corner. He and another Marine fired their M16s up at the machine gun. Bullets slashed the air and slammed the street around them.

Another Marine came running back toward me. "Sir, they need grenades!"

I had several.

"Cover me!" I yelled. The Marines began pouring fire into the house with the enemy machine gun. I broke loose and ran along the low wall toward the three forward Marines. Behind me, other Marines fired .50-caliber and M240 machine guns. The sound stabbed at my eardrums like a hammer on an anvil. I reached the three others. The captain had taken a knee. I peered around the corner over his shoulder. I could see the muzzle blast of the machine gun from a second-floor window. I passed a grenade to him.

"Cover me on three," he shouted over the din of the machine gun. The captain counted.

On three, we fanned out from the wall and fired up into the window. The captain sprinted to the house's exterior wall, pulled the pin, and tossed up the grenade. It tucked itself into the window. Perfect. A couple of seconds later, the room exploded. Smoke and flames belched from the window.

For a moment, there was silence. I signaled that we should withdraw, and the captain led us back out. I followed him, and the other two Marines followed me. The captain peeked back at us as we ran. I saw something deeply troubling on his face. His eyes bulged. I did not see what he saw behind me, but his alarmed expression sent electric adrenaline coursing through me.

"They've got RPGs!" he screamed.

I spun 180 degrees and leveled my rifle, seeking targets. So did the two enlisted Marines. Up the road, about seventy-five yards off, three irhabeen popped out of an alley and knelt. They faced us. One had an RPG launcher over his shoulder. He sighted in. On me.

My training guided my actions. It felt strangely comforting to follow the rote procedure that had been drilled into me: I gazed down the barrel and developed my sight picture. I took a man into the sights. I let out what I thought was a slow, steady breath. I squeezed the trigger, surprised when the rifle barked in my hands, feeling the recoil pop into my shoulder. The ammoniac smell of cordite enveloped me. I gathered myself to fire again, regaining my sight picture. I exhaled slowly, emptying my chest.

"Sir, get out of there!" It was another Marine. Somewhere. Far away maybe.

The insurgent fired his RPG launcher. I saw the muzzle blast. I heard the half scream, half roar of the round coming at me.

The round passed high and wide of my right shoulder. For a millisecond, I thought, *They missed. I can take another shot.*

Then the RPG round hit a wall directly behind me, and the explosion struck me from behind like an invisible bus. It rocked my head forward. My chin slammed my chest. The blast wrapped around me, the heat and the concussion lifting me, carrying me through the air. Flying, I slammed into the two enlisted Marines, knocking them to the ground. I tumbled on past them. My senses, my body lay just beyond my control, fluttering out of reach like a bright, blurry flag. A flash of scarlet showed itself on the dirty street. Shots popped from down the road, and I knew they were for me. Flecks of concrete stung my face from rounds striking the street.

Then men were bringing me to my feet. The Marines were moving me. We were running. *My feet are working,* I thought. *Sort of.* My mind processed things, but through a prism that made things so clear, and so quick, as to make them unreal. More blood here, on someone's uniform. Splashing on the ground under our heels. *One of us is wounded,* I thought. Or more than one of us. *If I've been hit, I can't feel it.* The Marines half dragged me back toward the Humvees. Up ahead of us, the Marines in their turrets blasted away, firing over our heads toward the insurgents.

"Whose blood?" Someone was yelling. "Is anybody hit?"

I found myself leaning against a wall. I thought, *I'm against a wall. I have cover.*

"No, no," men answered. "Negative!"

I said nothing. I readjusted myself against the wall. I turned my head and saw a lot of blood there. It was an outline of an upper body, on the wall. It looked like shoulders. I put my hand on one of mine. It came away crimson. I stared at it, dumb.

"Sir, are you hit?"

I felt wetness run down the back of my legs.

Then I was profoundly afraid, like I'd never been before. For some reason, the first thought that clutched me was that I had been hit in the kidneys. *The wetness on my legs is blood,* I thought. Blood mixed with urine, maybe.

"I'm hit."

My stomach dropped. My knees buckled. I sagged to the ground.

Then hands were grabbing me and hauling me up the street, into the courtyard of the new operations building. Forero came at a sprint from the Humvee. Men pushed and pulled me up a set of stairs. The bright light of day turned off. My dilated eyes tried to fix edges to the interior around us. Suddenly I was aware of Ramos. He was coming down the stairs as the Marines took me up.

"You hit?" he asked. He appeared genuinely surprised.

"Yes, sir."

He knitted his brow and put his nose to my shoulder.

"That's a million-dollar wound you got there. Looks good on you," he said. He punched me on my other shoulder. "Get patched up and get back out there."

Ramos clomped on down the stairs. The Marines took me to a room with a couch and lay me on my face. I dropped my rifle on the floor next to me. *Still got my rifle. Good.* Hands reached over me, pulled at me. Helmet and body armor fell away. A Navy corpsman came in and introduced himself. He looked at me with level eyes that were attentive without being alarmed.

"Where are you hit, sir?"

"I'm not sure. Shoulder . . . and I don't know where else." I noticed my voice was trembling. I took a deep breath, held it, blew it out.

I felt the corpsman untie and remove my boots, then my knee protectors. I was rolled to one side and my belt was undone, my camouflage trousers pulled off. Then my camouflage blouse. I was down to my socks, my green PT shorts, and my green T-shirt. I tried to relax and let them take control of me.

Forero and Sa'ad came in.

"We got them, sir," Forero said. His voice was angry, sharp. Then it turned tentative: "How are you?"

"He'll live." It was the corpsman.

I'll live, I thought. *I'll live.* I let out a long breath.

Sa'ad leaned over and put his hand on the back of my head, stroking it. Then he bent and kissed my cheek.

"I am very sad," he said, trying to use his best English. His eyes glistened. "I have seen your blood today."

I squeezed Sa'ad's hand. Everyone was quiet for a beat.

"Sir, would you excuse us?" The corpsman made it clear that it wasn't a request. He was talking to Sa'ad. The Iraqi colonel held my hand a moment longer. Forero gently guided him from the room. The corpsman went to work on my shoulder. He cut off my T-shirt, letting it fall to the floor. It was heavy with blood. He asked what happened. I related the story as I knew it. He probed my shoulder with what may have been tweezers. He said he was looking for shrapnel.

I told the corpsman I was afraid I was hit in the kidneys, that I had felt hot liquid flowing down my legs. He stopped working.

"You don't have puncture wounds back there, sir," he said. He bent over to my flak jacket on the floor. "Ahh, here you go. I found it. It was your CamelBak, sir. It was punctured. Look."

The soft bladder I had worn on my back was torn and empty. My water. That's what I had felt running down my legs. Water heated by the desert sun.

My wound could not be stitched, the corpsman explained, because it was "gaping." Instead, he packed it with a chemical coagulant. "QuikClot," it said on the package. He bandaged me over. He said I'd be sore and swollen for a week or so.

The corpsman sat down next to me and began to write.

"I'm filling out the paperwork for a Purple Heart, sir. We can send you back to the CSH." He wanted me to go to the combat surgical hospital.

"I don't want to do that. I'm concerned—" I cleared my throat and started over. "I'm concerned about what the Iraqis will think. I have to stay."

I looked at him to see if he understood. His face was attentive but noncommittal.

"I don't want them to see me leave the battle. I don't want them to think that—they can't think I'm leaving the fight without them."

"OK," the Navy corpsman said. He reflected for a moment and said, "I'm going to give you a painkiller and a shot to reduce the swelling. I want you to rest tonight."

He called in Forero, who gathered my clothes and equipment and helped me up more stairs to a room he and Sa'ad had staked out for the three of us. Forero had gotten his hands on mattresses and blankets and arranged them on the floor. The open window was screened with a curtain. Forero had begun to pile furniture and sandbags there. I knew he would finish his barricade after he got me settled. I was very glad to have him with me.

I lay on the mattress, facedown. My senses slowly made themselves mine again. I remained a little dazed, but I chalked it up to the last of the adrenaline running through me. My head ached. I didn't know it yet, but the new blow to the back of my head, coupled with the hard hit to the front of my head from the pickup steering wheel a couple of months earlier, had changed my life forever. I was never going to be the same. But that knowledge, and that personal struggle, all lay in the future. I had a different set of concerns there on my temporary bed in Fallujah. Lying there, I didn't even know I had changed. Maybe I hadn't yet.

Forero sat next to me. "Are you gonna be OK, sir?"

I turned my head a little to see his face and let him see mine. Behind him, Sa'ad walked up, his black eyes taking me in. They wanted to hear me speak.

"Yes," I said. "I will be."

15

AL-HADRA

I AWOKE BEFORE DAWN. Silence. No light on the other side of Forero's window barricade.

Then, a sound in the room's stillness. Quiet Arabic from the corner. I raised my head to look. Soreness in my neck. Sa'ad knelt on his prayer rug and chanted in a whisper. His block of a torso rose intermittently before bowing again.

Forero must still be asleep, I thought as I tried to roll to one side. My upper body—all of it, not just my shoulder—throbbed. My muscles were a stiff meshwork.

"How do you feel, sir?"

It was Forero. Awake after all. I felt hungover. I felt a cotton-mouth thirst.

"OK," I said, trying to believe myself. Forero would believe me—he was a lance corporal and would take my word as gospel. Or at least I hoped he would.

I touched my shoulder. Swollen, it pulsed against the bandages. It was wet again. I stood and tried to get my gear in order. Forero watched for a respectful thirty seconds as I tried using one hand to roll my bedroll and dress myself. Then he asked if he could help.

"Yes," I said. "Yes, you can."

Sa'ad finished his obeisance, stood, and wordlessly went to his breakfast stash. He kept it in a khaki satchel. Somehow he always had fresh *khubz*, the traditional Arab bread that most of the advisers had taken a liking to. He produced goat cheese and a glass jar of marmalade. I wondered, *How in hell does he get that stuff?*

Forero broke out MREs. I made coffee with a flameless chemical heater that came with our rations. I was phenomenally hungry. I had last eaten at dawn the previous day. The three of us sat on the floor and passed around our bounty. Sa'ad offered up a Muslim prayer.

"Bismillah, al-Rahman, al-Raheem . . ."

More than once already, Lieutenant Colonel Symons had reminded me that even though I was deployed with the Marines, he was still top adviser to the Iraqi brigade, which meant he was still my boss. And his boss was General Petraeus.

"You have to keep me happy," he said. I had been working hard to keep him happy. He continually sought me out for updates. He needed me to give him situational awareness. Meanwhile, Lieutenant Colonel Ramos made continually shifting demands on his Marines. By extension, Ramos made constant demands on me, the Fifth Battalion, and my advisers deployed with those Marines. The two sets of priorities naturally conflicted. I was caught between two lieutenant colonels. It wasn't a place I wanted to be.

That day was one of those occasions when demands would clash. The Marines of Bravo Company were going to assault our biggest objective yet, the al-Hadra al-Mahamudiyah mosque. Elesky and Villa's junood of Second Rifle Company would fight alongside them and storm the mosque itself. Villa would not be there, however; I had called in Mulvihill to temporarily replace Villa, who had gotten into a fight with an Iraqi lieutenant. Villa had discovered that the lieutenant was giving weapons away to his superior, a singularly useless Shiite captain the advisers had nicknamed Cartman, after the spoiled, fat kid on *South Park*. The captain was presumably going to sell the weapons on the black market. Villa confronted the lieutenant and got a kick in the stomach. Villa then knocked the lieutenant out cold. I got on the radio with Lieutenant Colonel Symons and told him we had to get rid of Cartman.

Symons backed me. The Iraqis usually honored our requests when we asked that officers be transferred out of the battalion, but in this case, Brigadier General Essa refused. Cartman was from a politically connected Shiite tribe from Basra. One of his relatives, Nouri al-Maliki, would become prime minister in 2010 and rip the country apart through kleptocracy and anti-Sunni bigotry. In the meantime, Cartman wasn't going anywhere. I had to sideline Villa.

The al-Hadra mosque sat on the east side of the main road, called Phase Line Ethan by the Americans, that divided the city in half. A little north of the mosque up Ethan, I had also called in Johnson and Fryar with their company of junood. Their job was to secure the flank of the assaulting force and to keep the road open to the north. The assault had multiple moving parts.

Using the Blue Force Tracker, Sa'ad, Arkan, Forero, and I drove north. Everyone was exhausted. Arkan's normally clean-shaven face had gone over to black stubble. I was supposed to meet Lieutenant Colonel Symons and Brigadier General Essa at an entry point to the city. They wanted to be there for the assault, and we were to guide them in. I couldn't stop looking at my watch. My stomach was rolling. Nausea had been with me for two days. My body armor shifted and ground itself into my bandages. Time had gotten away from us as we put our pieces in place, and we were drawing close to the fight's appointed hour. Marines had already started setting up a perimeter around the mosque to prevent insurgents from escaping. Soon the Marines and junood would advance south, first into a complex of buildings called the Islamic Benevolent Society of Fallujah, then on to al-Hadra beyond that. Al-Hadra means "the presence" in Arabic. It's a reference to poetic chanting practiced by the Sufi orders of Islam. The Sufi orders are contemplative and mystical. In America, we call Sufi Muslims "moderates." As we positioned ourselves to retake the mosque, it wasn't occupied by moderates anymore. Al-Hadra was an important symbol for the insurgents. They were going to fight for it.

Lieutenant Colonel Symons and General Essa wanted to be where the action was. I understood. But I looked at the Blue Force

Tracker. Then at my watch again. Blood was sticky down my back inside my shirt. I glimpsed the Blue Force Tracker again. It wasn't lying: We were running behind. We didn't have time to pick up Symons and Essa.

"Sa'ad, I think we need to get back," I said. The throbbing in my shoulder climbed up my neck and into my head. "We don't have time. We're close to H hour. We still have to drop in on Johnson and Fryar first."

Sa'ad grunted.

"Do you think you can make it OK with Essa?"

Sa'ad nodded.

"OK," I said. "Forero, turn us around." In addition to navigation, the Blue Force Tracker could also act as a text message system. I put one out to Lieutenant Colonel Symons apologizing for the change of plans, but explaining that I didn't have time to meet him.

Johnson and Fryar's stripped-down Third Rifle Company was at that point co-led by two first lieutenants. One was Mohammed Ahmed—the Sunni who led the successful raids around al-Muzerfa in September. The other was a Kurd named Bakr Saleh. The Arab Ahmed had been a paratrooper in Saddam Hussein's army. The Kurd Bakr had been with the Peshmerga. It was entirely possible that they had fought each other at some point in the last ten years—and it would have been a murderous ethnic fight. But for some reason, the two men defied the normal animosities that divided Arab and Kurd, and they worked together well.

Johnson and Fryar fortified a couple of houses along Phase Line Ethan. Their company's role was important. They needed to anchor a defensive position that protected the main force. But when we got there, many of the junood were taking advantage of what they saw as downtime. Someone had found ingredients for *khubz*. They baked bread and brewed chai. Someone had scored cigarettes, and every jundi seemed to have one between his lips. It was a great luxury for them to be in a relatively stable position with food and water. Many stood about in undress, doing laundry. Some wore flip-flops. Johnson, Fryar, and the two Iraqi lieutenants were occupied with other soldiers who were manning key defensive points.

The junood jumped at the sight of Sa'ad stepping from the Humvee. I shouted at the men. A fight was coming. The junood bent at a run for helmets, rifles, and trousers. Even with American advisers, an interpreter, and Iraqi NCOs present, the junood needed constant supervision. The battalion surgeon, Capt. Adnan Naji, was there with them as well. He insisted on a look at my wound. He carefully peeled back the dressings. I stood still for him. The nearest junood slowed down to tighten chin straps and lace boots. They watched us. I realized the simple sight of an Iraqi doctor caring for an American officer made a profound impression on them. What I could say for the soldiers there at Phase Line Ethan was at least they wanted to be there. The ones who didn't had already deserted.

We made it back to Elesky and Mulvihill before H hour. The commander of their Second Rifle Company was the last-minute replacement and Fallujah native Iraq Abd al-Baqi, who had already distinguished himself as the best small-unit leader in Fifth Battalion. The second lieutenant had a martial bearing, fierce eyes, and a black mustache. Once, he had told me that no matter what government was in power, he would always be an Iraqi soldier. Coming from a Ba'athist family, he was actually the very sort of soldier Iraq had too few of: a secular nationalist. Iraq Abd al-Baqi got command of the assault.

Only minutes after we arrived, Marine light armored vehicles opened up with machine guns on the low-slung buildings of the Islamic Benevolent Society of Fallujah. Marines of Bravo Company advanced on foot. Mulvihill and Elesky moved forward with their ex-physicist translator Abdallah, their determined Fallujan Iraq Abd al-Baqi, and the soldiers of Second Rifle Company. Automatic fire crackled at them from the mosque. Two hours later, with five wounded but none killed, al-Hadra was ours.

Al-Hadra al-Mahamudiyah mosque was bounded by alleys, homes, shops, and souks, including an apothecary, a computer shop, and a cigarette store. The mosque bore a great green dome.

A slender minaret stretched toward the sky. A fence of wrought iron and cement blocks enclosed a grassy yard. The junood dragged the bodies of insurgents they'd killed into a courtyard. There were almost a dozen; we kept them in a pile until we could get rid of them later.

Within al-Hadra, a central worship chamber enjoyed open air all the way from the ground floor up past balconies on a mezzanine level and into the hollow of the dome above that. The architecture was typical of holy places. The lofty chamber drew the eye upward and created the sensation of a greater, silent presence. Staircases climbed from the central room's four corners. Another spiral staircase snaked up the minaret, opening intermittently to rooms off the tower. This was where Sa'ad and the officers set up quarters. The junood found space on lower floors and in adjoining buildings. Adnan Naji positioned his medical team on the mosque's first floor. We advisers set up billets on the second floor, which had a low wall overlooking the cavernous central enclosure.

The mosque's central chamber began filling with civilians seeking shelter from the fighting. Most were men. They risked their lives just to get there. Eventually the refugees would number about three hundred, including families and many children. The advisers used sandbags to fortify second-floor windows and sections of the exterior wall that had been blown open. We kept a low fire burning in a fifty-five-gallon drum. It gave heat, brewed coffee, and dried socks. A radio rested on a table. Someone listened in on it, 24-7. Arbitrary plastic chairs sat about the room. In one corner, a two-and-a-half-square-foot "privacy tent"—basically a collapsible closet of plastic sheets and tent poles—was where we relieved ourselves in disposable bags. We had to operate on the assumption that insurgents were hiding among the refugees, so we designed both exterior and interior fields of fire. We blocked three of the central stairways and made the fourth defensible from the advisers' area. We designated an exit route to the roof. Just as in Kirkush, we squirreled away MREs and water on the rooftop.

The Americans of First Battalion, Third Marines, and the Iraqis of Fifth Battalion searched buildings for weeks after al-Hadra fell.

Homes stood in densely packed blocks. Their exterior walls, brick with a layer of mortar slathered over, almost touched the walls of houses adjacent to them. Grenades couldn't penetrate them. We had to frag individual rooms from inside. In Middle Eastern fashion, the houses often were built around an enclosed courtyard that opened to the sky. Even in wartime, I could see how those courtyards had served as inner sanctums for the families who had fled them. I saw how they had been quiet, peaceful contrasts to the streets. Some were beautiful, lined with the intricate geometrical designs that the Muslim world makes so well. They certainly were not peaceful spaces for the Iraqis of the Fifth Battalion or the Marines fighting with them. Iraqis and Marines who cleared courtyards found themselves surrounded by windows facing inward, toward them. To clear a house is to throw oneself headlong into the worst kind of uncertainty. Room to room to room. Most of the homes and businesses were empty of fighters; others bristled with insurgents—one in twenty, maybe. Some held huddling civilian families. It was like roulette, and the wheel spun once for each building in Fallujah. In the process of clearing them, we would end up destroying a quarter of them. We fought in stairwells, in narrow hallways, in kitchens and gardens and bathrooms. Men close enough to hear each other's desperate breathing blasted at each other with high-powered weapons. Fallujah was a battle between men who killed one another in small groups, taking each other's lives in ways that often could be described as intimate. Shots rang all the louder from being fired indoors and left survivors temporarily deaf out on the streets. The echoes of automatic fire hammered my head all day, all night, like a chisel chipping into my skull.

Most of the insurgents commanded by Abdullah al-Janabi, the man we thought we killed early on, were typical guerilla fighters. What I mean is that their mission was to attack and then melt away to fight again. In short, they didn't want to die. The second group, whose ultimate leader was Abu Musab al-Zarqawi, was from al-Qaeda in Iraq. They were foreign zealots: Syrians, Saudis, Libyans, and Chechens—none of them were Iraqis. The radicals wanted to die, and to kill Americans along the way. We had no way of knowing it at the time, but it was these men—often the same individuals—who years later would form ISIS. Abu Bakr al-Baghdadi, who is the leader of ISIS as I write these words, was arrested in Fallujah a month before I arrived in Iraq, but released. Abu Mohammad al-Adnani, who would later become the emir of ISIS in Syria, was one of the first foreign fighters to take up arms after the US invasion and was fighting the Marines at Fallujah.

On November 13, radioman Lance Corporal Suo stood by a thick rubber tire on his Humvee outside al-Hadra, body armor across his chest. The stock of his M16A4 relaxed in his left shoulder. A US Army captain stood with him. Ali Ghali, a dedicated Shiite captain who was popular with the advisers, was there as well. I wasn't there—Sa'ad insisted that he and I go to the Iraqi Ministry of Defense's temporary headquarters outside the city. His men had taken al-Hadra, and he wanted face time with the generals in the ministry. I told him he needed to oversee the construction of defenses for the mosque. He disagreed. He thought it was more important that he get credit for taking the mosque in the first place.

Behind Suo and Ali Ghali's position, columns supported seven arches on the facade of al-Hadra. We had held the mosque for less than twenty-four hours. Suo was waiting for Lombard. The major was inside, meeting with a group of officers. Another American sat atop the Humvee behind a big Mk 19 grenade launcher with explosive rounds. Over next to the mosque, a lone Iraqi soldier crouched against the wall. His AK-47 lay on the ground between his ankles. He was smoking.

Lombard came out from between two of al-Hadra's columns and trotted toward his Humvee. That's when the RPG came in.

Officers wore the same colors and gear as enlisted men. Somehow, though, the insurgents knew to target Lombard. It's likely that one or more of our men from Fifth Battalion had not bothered to desert because he was working with the insurgents, and he gave the irhabeen intelligence about the major. I'll never know.

Suo later related the whole story. The RPG sounded aerodynamic and clean when it came in, like something slicing through a giant, invisible tube. Nobody had time to hit the deck. The RPG struck between Lombard and the Humvee, only twenty feet from Suo. The blast blew the four standing men to the ground. Lombard screamed, grasping a leg that ran red below the knee. Suo thought Lombard's leg was gone. A black cloud swirled. A high-pitched, plaintive sound stretched like a taut wire from ear to ear through the middle of Suo's head. The young radioman's vision had gone blurry. Smoke stung his nostrils. The American captain began to frantically stomp his feet and pat himself down—arms, legs, chest, everywhere. Suo didn't understand what the officer was doing, so he did the same. Then he realized the captain was checking to make sure all of him was still there.

The captain was all there, but he'd been hit by shrapnel and took to the hard earth behind the Humvee. Ali Ghali, also struck by the flying metal, did the same. Suo was the only man outside the Humvee who was uninjured; shrapnel had hit the men to both sides of him. Suo realized then that they were taking rifle fire as well. It came from a rooftop across the street.

The mosque is being counterattacked, he thought. They may have more RPGs.

Suo dashed into the open toward Lombard. His job was to protect this major, this man who was important to the mission. He saw that Lombard's leg was not gone after all, but it was bleeding badly. Suo snatched up Lombard, grunting as the major shouted with pain. He helped the major get behind the Humvee.

Suo lay himself prone on the ground by one fat, black front tire and aimed at movement on a rooftop about a hundred yards off. He squeezed off rounds until the clip was done. Then he moved to the back of the Humvee where the spare jutted thick from the rear hatch and did it again, with a new clip. He kept changing positions. He didn't want to get sniped out. Above him, the gunner on the Mk 19 blasted the insurgents' rooftop with explosive rounds. Suo moved again. Then again. Once, he reached down for a fresh clip, and his hand pulled out his point-and-click camera instead. He snapped a picture or two. Then another clip, and back to firing. The fight went on for minutes (two, five?). Rounds slammed hollow into the Humvee. One hit near the gas tank on the side exposed toward the rooftop. The more the two Americans fired, Suo noticed, the less the insurgents fired. That was enough to convince him to keep doing what he was doing. The RPG's black smoke went gray in the air. Lombard had stopped shouting, but gave out long, low moans. The lance corporal crawled behind a tire, halfway beneath the Humvee. He took a deep breath and tried to take his time. His eyes scanned the rooftop, all the rooftops. Fire still came in. He tried to aim. Bone structure. Breath control. Make the rifle an extension of your body. Suddenly he became aware of a man standing over him. Suo lay partly between his legs. It was a huge Army sergeant.

"Stay there, kid!" the sergeant yelled, and he cut loose with a machine gun. The hot casings rained down on Suo, burning him through his clothes. A fear hit him that seemed absurd in the midst of a firefight, but that was real nonetheless: *What if a hot casing gets down the back of my shirt and I can't get it out?* Suo squirmed out from under the man's legs, back to the rear of the Humvee.

He looked back at the mosque. Americans and Iraqis, rifles raised, bolted outside to join them. They took positions and fired back. A light armored vehicle poked its nose from behind the mosque and drew itself into the open ground before the columns. The big machine had eight wheels. Suo and Lombard stared wide-eyed as the vehicle halted directly behind them and opened up with a 25-mm cannon and two .50-caliber machine guns, all at once. The vehicle fired directly over Suo's head. He felt the whoosh of the air as the huge rounds shot by. He saw the smoke that the cannon spit over them.

He hated the sound of the guns. *I've got to get out of here,* he thought. The gunner scrambled from the turret and helped Suo pull Lombard, the American captain, and Ali Ghali into the Humvee. Blood was everywhere. Suo hopped into the driver's seat and hooked the vehicle around to get behind the light armored vehicle. The Americans poured fire onto the rooftops. There was no more answer from the insurgents.

Suo realized, *We're going to hold them off. We are going to hold al-Hadra.*

He decided to just keep driving, to get his wounded men to a doctor. As he pulled away, his eye caught a glimpse of the jundi who had leaned against the mosque. The Iraqi had not moved. He squatted there, AK-47 still on the ground in front of him.

Squinting, he drew long on his cigarette and exhaled.

16

RULES OF ENGAGEMENT

BACK AT QUANTICO, they had told us our main rule of engagement: we were not to engage in combat except in self-defense. Even then, the rule was a joke. After that, Taji's insomniac snipers made it a farce. Then Fallujah's demented cityscape made it macabre. It got funny, all right. It got fucking hilarious.

Lombard was wounded on November 12, the day after me. Suo drove him out of the city, and Navy corpsmen stitched him up at a Marine aid station. From there, Lombard went by ambulance to the main base with two Marines who rode their stretchers as inanimate things. One of them died on the way.

Elesky was next. On November 13, he led a raid on a house. The interpreter Abdallah followed close behind him. Elesky opened a door, and it exploded. Shrapnel from a booby trap blasted his hands and face. A corpsman put forceps, bandage, and QuikClot to work. Fortunately, the explosive must have been misdirected. Elesky remained with Second Rifle Company. He never left for treatment outside the city.

A few days later, Sa'ad, Arkan, and I visited East Fallujah Iraqi Camp. It was bright out, an Iraqi autumn day that was neither too hot nor too cool. I had not been back to EFIC since the breach. Most of Fifth Battalion's headquarters company was still there. Forero drove, and another Marine lance corporal manned the machine gun up top. Marines and soldiers based outside the city were always getting permission to ride in our turret. Everybody wanted a combat action ribbon.

When Iraqis celebrate, they give themselves over completely to the joy of it. They clap and dance, their faces beaming. For a Westerner, even the very sincerity of that joy is a shock. It made some Americans uncomfortable. When Sa'ad and I rolled up, the HQ Iraqis who managed administration and supplies back at EFIC jumped in their boots, stabbed their AKs at the sky, and fell into chants. Thankfully, none fired into the air. They had heard already that I was wounded. They mobbed me, crying, "Asad al-Fallujah!"—the Lion of Fallujah. Menhal Majid Hamid, the major who gave the "next bullet" speech before Fallujah, clamped his arms around me, heedless of my injured shoulder. He gave me three kisses. The camp was a mess, with Porta Johns knocked over and hundreds of plastic water bottles littering the ground. The company had no plan for waste disposal. They still didn't have electricity. But their spirits were good.

They invited me into the ruined building they used as a make-shift office. I exchanged pleasantries with some of the officers over *khubz*, marmalade, goat cheese, and Saudi Arabian cola. The stench of feces and garbage insinuated itself everywhere, but it was no worse than the city and not much worse than me, since I had not showered for more than a week. I decided not to bring up the poor state of the camp with them; I'd do that later with Sa'ad. Mostly, I wanted to get to the advisers' tent so I could jump on a computer and e-mail my family and fiancée. I worried like hell about them worrying about me.

The American advisers' tent stood in ordered contrast to the rest of EFIC and the rest of Fallujah. Folded cots lined the interior. A generator was wired for electricity. Someone had scored a refrigerator. A table held a couple PCs. Seeing the Fifth Battalion advisers' heavy packs, which we'd intentionally left behind, tidy and unsoiled on our crisp, green cots, was like experiencing a mini–time warp.

Advisers from the Sixth Battalion sat inside, typing at PCs or watching TV screens. This was where they lived. Our greetings were perfunctory. Unlike the Iraqis, none of them knew I was wounded. They asked almost nothing about the battle. I felt my face flush, thinking about how easy it was for the men outside the city to insulate themselves from the inferno churning a couple of klicks away. A long nerve seemed to twitch inside my shoulder, igniting something voltaic up the back of my neck. A monotonous throb pulsed in my head.

I immersed myself in my e-mails. It soothed me a little. I barely noticed as the room emptied except for me and a US enlisted man who sat on radio watch at the other end of the tent.

"Excuse me, Raed Zakkiyah?" It was Arkan. His neck extended through the tent flap.

"I'm busy."

"Yes, sir. Of course. But the guards have someone who wants to see you."

I raised my eyes to my interpreter.

"You should meet him," he said.

I motioned to Arkan, who told two junood guards beyond the flap to wait outside. Arkan showed in a small, dumpy Iraqi man in a blue sports coat, frayed slacks, a dirty collared shirt, and sandals. He was unshaven.

"As-salaam alaikum," he said, and offered his hand.

"Who is this?" I asked Arkan.

"He is the mayor of Fallujah," Arkan said. "He says he has a meeting with the commanding general of the Iraqi Army, but the Marines will not let him onto the base to keep his appointment."

"What does he want? Why does he want to see me?"

"He has heard of you," Arkan said. "He says he knows you will help him."

I had not had a lot of contact with Iraqi civilian leaders. But I quickly took what I had learned about Iraqi military leaders, transposed those traits onto a civilian politician, and instantly despised this man in the tent with me.

"Mayor of Fallujah? What happened to your city? Arkan, ask him, 'How could you let this happen? This whole battle. Thousands of people are dead now.'"

Arkan relayed the message and took in the response.

"He says, 'I had no choice. The insurgents would kill me if I did not cooperate.'" The word *cooperate* blew on an ember inside me that went instantly incandescent.

"You had a police force! It was yours! Why didn't you arrest them when you had the chance?"

"He says the police would not obey him. He says they sided with Zarqawi."

"Why didn't you get help?" I looked directly at the mayor. "Why didn't you call Baghdad?"

The mayor tried to hold eye contact as he spoke in Arabic.

"He says there was nothing he could do," Arkan said. "He says they would have killed him."

"You let the people in your city kill those Americans on the bridge? You let them drag them out of their cars, execute them in the streets, hang their bodies from your bridge. Are they savages? Does the Koran allow people to burn corpses?"

The mayor looked down and away. He didn't answer the impassive Arkan, who waited, half-lidded. Finally, the mayor spoke without looking up.

"There was nothing he could do, he says. Zarqawi told him the Americans were Israeli agents. He says they would kill him if he interfered."

I must have had a physical reaction, because Arkan reached over and put his hand on my arm as I shouted: "I guess Zarqawi was lying, wasn't he? And thousands of people are dead because you were afraid."

I turned my back to the mayor and tried to focus on the keyboard and screen. There was nothing to see there, of course. *I can't get through to them. Nobody can get through to them. Nobody ever will get through to them. They can't be changed.*

But then, *No. Maybe I can.*

And then my rage flashed because I didn't know what I should think. I had not slept for longer than sixty minutes at a time for more than two weeks. With hate spilling loose in me like acid, I turned back one more time.

"In my country, we had a guy named Thomas Jefferson. During our revolution, he said, 'All that must happen for evil to triumph is for good men to sit idle.'"

It seems a little ridiculous now, but I meant it. I had to try something. I had to figure out what to say. I had to *reach* them.

I definitely reached Arkan. He repeated what I said, spitting Arabic, gesticulating sharply with his hands to emphasize the words. The mayor kept his eyes on the white dust of the tent floor. He was silent.

I told the mayor to wait outside, and Arkan escorted him out. I turned to the radio operator, who had heard everything we said but kept his eyes discreetly on his copy of *Maxim* magazine. I told him to get me Base Operations Command.

They told me that they knew about this mayor, that he'd been trying to get on the base for days. He was never going to be allowed access to anyone with authority. They said to send him away.

I went outside to Arkan. I was calmer now. I had to choose my words carefully. If I said, "Get rid of him," for instance, there was a good chance the Iraqis would kill him and dump his body in the desert. To them, that was within the rules.

"Tell the guards to escort the mayor off the base. He is not allowed in the American camp. We're not allowing him in over here on the Iraqi side, either. Make sure the guards understand that."

Arkan nodded and relayed the order to a jundi corporal. I returned to my e-mail.

Among the insurgents, we considered the snipers especially despicable. Not just because they were effective—and they were so effective that the advisers joked bitterly that they were much better marksmen than most of the junood. We hated them because they kept sniping the refugees. At the outset of the battle, there were no clear rules of engagement for going out and hunting for snipers after they killed civilians who sought our protection. Nobody designed a protocol for that. Add to that any person's natural preoccupation with staying alive, and it became easy to avoid risks beyond the bounds of the core mission. That is, of course, what the rules were designed for in the first place.

I returned to al-Hadra, bringing the headquarters company into the city with me. The extra seventy-five men or so would help man defenses at the mosque and the major intersection nearby while the rifle companies cleared buildings and assisted noncombatants. Civilians were still trickling into the mosque grounds, seeking the protection of their military and the Americans. Our enemies set men up to snipe them on the way in. Sometimes the refugees arrived at al-Hadra carrying one of their own with a new bullet in his face or chest. One time, a civilian man accepted water and food from Forero inside the mosque, bowed, thanked him profusely, stepped outside into the yard, and fell dead with a bullet to his head. The battalion doctor Adnan Naji, gray stethoscope around his neck, leaned over mustachioed men wearing bloody, shocked expressions. He saved some; he lost some.

This is war. This is what happens.

Early on at al-Hadra, it wasn't worth the risk to retrieve the bodies of civilians who were shot at a distance from the mosque. The snipers made it too dangerous. We got reports from the Marines that the insurgents were rigging corpses to explode when they were moved. The neglected bodies came apart in the sun. The stench was horrific. The admixture of flesh and shit and combustion that got into everything—our uniform, our pores, our food—never stopped being offensive; it got even more disquieting when it began to feel seductive. It was insistent, and it could pull you in.

Sa'ad, his officers, and the American advisers decided we needed to better organize the relief operation. At first almost all the refugees had been men, but increasingly women and children were showing up. The Iraqi officers scrounged, bartered, and pilfered to get blankets and nonperishable food for them. They also got them cigarettes. The refugees could accept only halal MREs. Kerosene heaters gave nighttime warmth in the prayer chamber on the ground floor.

Some of the American advisers caught on to a new scheme of Sa'ad's: he inserted himself into the flow of goods and made himself a gatekeeper, handing out supplies selectively in order to curry favor and boost his wasta. I confronted him about it and told him to stop. He casually said he would. That's the way it always worked with him. No shame, no anger. Whenever I challenged Sa'ad about one of his illicit arrangements, he dropped it without argument. Then he'd look for some new way to profit.

Letting Iraqi civilians into the mosque was a risk. We especially worried about the threat of suicide bombers. But it was getting colder—into the low fifties and high forties Fahrenheit at night—and we couldn't leave anyone outside. We set up a procedure for processing them. Iskander, his fists on his hips, organized a screening detail. He put some junood on a far perimeter. AKs at the ready, they ordered refugees to raise their arms and expose the folds of their clothing. Others on an inside perimeter patted down the men and boys. A queue of refugees formed, at times stretching a couple hundred yards. The noncombatants huddled in scarves and light coats, or with home linens draped over their shoulders. We kept the closest ones at a distance of fifty yards from the mosque itself. The junood didn't touch the women, even—or perhaps especially—the ones covered in burkas. The strongest graduates of Villa's rifle course manned the roofs to counter any snipers who tried to draw within range of the junood working their pickets out on the far perimeter. Inside the mosque building, enlisted Marines like Suo and Forero met the noncombatants just within the doors and searched them again. Other junood stood watch in the prayer chamber, where the processed refugees slept on a swept brown carpet among white columns. Immobile paddle fans and unlit chandeliers hung overhead. Once, an African-looking boy about eight years old walked up to Forero wordlessly and took the lance corporal's hand. He did not let go for ten minutes. Forero let him hold it. A Marine sergeant chewed out Forero for being too friendly with the civilians. I told

Forero his heart was in the right place, but the sergeant was right: it was important for us to be vigilant first and foremost.

A US Army psyops team brought gunpowder residue kits. These were tremendously valuable. The Iraqis had no notion that it was possible to use a simple swab to determine if they had recently fired a weapon. Suo and Forero began testing refugees within the mosque door, and then we doubled back and tested the men who were already living with us. It was eye opening. Two-thirds of the men came back positive, including many who had been with us for days. We detained them and sent most on to US military intelligence for questioning.

The ones who cleared the residue test—some of the men and all the women and children—were declared clean and allowed to stay at the mosque. By Fallujah standards, al-Hadra was safety. It was only later that we realized that Fifth Battalion was probably carrying out the first humanitarian mission of the Iraq War. You could see tension fall from people's faces after we rubbed their hands with our mysterious gunpowder test and then told them they were OK to stay.

"It feels," Forero said, "like I'm giving communion."

Midway through the battle, I was sleeping from about 9 PM to midnight most nights. While I dozed on the terrace level, the gunfire came and went outside, sometimes far, sometimes near. Women wept and babies cried in overlapping echoes below, beyond the balcony. Every morning, the bodies of more dead insurgents appeared on the streets, killed by the American infantry. After the fighting died down somewhat and we started clearing them, we recognized a couple of the bodies. They were men who had sought aid from us. We were saving innocent noncombatants' lives, yes. But we also were feeding insurgents. Regardless, a colonel at the regimental level ordered me to expand our food distribution.

Meanwhile, we continued to fight the enemy in the streets and in thousands of buildings. Regular Marine units were still storming houses and engaging in firefights. The Fifth Battalion was still clearing buildings and patrolling the streets, and that meant the advisers were doing the same. We were still spread out all over, even with Fifth Battalion HQ now in the mosque. More than half the advisers and Iraqi officers lived somewhere else on any given night. Forero and I roved in our Humvee, dropping in on the rifle companies to hand over supplies, share information, or gather intelligence. Lombard rejoined the fight, and he and Suo recommenced making rounds. We heard the *ponk-ponk-ponk* of bullets hitting the Humvees. You never saw the insurgents. It didn't seem worth it to try to spot them. In their Marine Corps training, Forero and Suo had been taught to dismount and return fire. In the real battle, it didn't work like that. The first time Suo hit the brakes after rounds came in, Lombard yelled at him like he was crazy.

All the enlisted Marines learned that the official rules of engagement changed constantly. Generally, the rules got looser—both officially and de facto. It got to where Marines opened up on anyone who ran away from them. They didn't wait to take fire. They didn't wait to see a weapon. Eventually, it came down to each Marine's decision for himself. Concepts of rules and rank slowly gave way to individual instincts, individual beliefs, individual perceptions. Some Marines never fired first, ever. Others always did.

The junood behaved better when they were operating jointly with Marines than when they were on their own. They looted habitually, and not just for food or cigarettes but also for personal valuables in private homes. If a Marine officer caught a US enlisted man eating a candy bar he found in a souk, he yelled at him. If an Iraqi officer caught a jundi taking a watch from a bedroom, he ordered him to hand it over and pocketed it. I should point out that most of the Iraqis were dirt poor and had never *seen* so much *stuff*. Even many of our better officers and NCOs, like Iskander, demanded "gifts" from junood who had acquired valuables, often under absurd pretenses. On at least one occasion, Iskander told soldiers to hand over booty because he wanted a gift for his mother.

"It's like they're an adolescent culture," Lombard said. "Which is ironic, because they're an ancient culture."

Early on, especially, all the advisers could perceive that the regular Marines felt sorry for us. I found that sentiment condescending and infuriating, and I'm sure other advisers did too. We were like the oil that eased the friction between two huge, radically different and immutable sets of gears—the Iraqis with their ancient customs and beliefs on one side, and the US Marine Corps on the other. What we were doing sometimes seemed next to impossible, but it was critical, and we did not need anybody's pity. The Americans who had never lived among Iraqis found Fifth Battalion perplexing. On the one hand, they saw junood who stole jewelry and slept on guard duty. On the other, they saw junood risk their lives in firefights and score massive hauls of intelligence from mosques. They saw interpreters like Abdallah, unarmed and in a sweatshirt, storm houses. They couldn't figure out what motivated these strange men.

The interpreters had an experience in Fallujah that was theirs alone. Again and again and again, they helped Americans interrogate prisoners and translated captured documents. They went everywhere their American advisers went, which meant that they, as unarmed civilians, faced more repeated danger than most of the individual Iraqi soldiers did. When an adviser led an assault on a building, it was always one of the interpreters who was second in line behind him. Sala'am, the former captain from Saddam's army, went on seventy-nine security patrols and searched hundreds of houses with Johnson, Fryar, and Third Company in November alone. He once administered first aid, under fire, to a jundi who was shot by a sniper. My interpreter, Arkan, interrogated twenty-four captured insurgents in the month of November. In one insurgent building, Arkan found a map that gave the locations of three dozen houses in Fallujah that the insurgents had stocked in advance with weapons and other supplies. American and Iraqi units hit the locations and took those weapons off the battlefield.

Sometimes it was the advisers who broke rules. It was part of my job to enforce rules. I filed a report on one of the advisers for using a flashbang—a nonlethal stun grenade—to wake up a group of junood he caught sleeping in a bunker. Another time, the same adviser destroyed a case of milk by firing into it with his Beretta M9 as an object lesson. For whatever reason, milk was wildly popular among the Iraqis. The Marines, watching the Iraqis gulp it down, began to call it fun-milk. The adviser punished a group of Iraqis by blowing away a shipment of fun-milk, firing his weapon within his own defensive position.

We all handled the psychological stresses differently. Our personalities became exaggerated. I felt a new, much more fundamental anxiety and desperation. Elesky got angrier and more impatient. Mulvihill wound himself up tighter. Lombard laughed more, and louder, at things that weren't funny. We saw the toll the battle was taking on the regular American troops. Once, after a full day of delivering supplies, sharing news, and getting updates, Lombard and Suo finished up at a medical staging area similar to the one that had processed Lombard just a few weeks before. Eight Iraqi medics there were always glad to see them—the Humvee's .50-cal provided security, and Lombard was a good connection for food and cigarettes. Lombard caught a nap, and Suo sat down to eat. About forty yards away, the Americans were running a station for receiving dead Marines. He described what he saw later: It was nighttime, and Suo watched two Navy corpsmen work there in the dark. *These are two poor guys*, Suo thought, *who signed up to sail ships but wound up in Fallujah.* Tracked vehicles rolled up out of the city, hauling bodies. The two corpsmen took out the dead, processed them, and then loaded them into special refrigerated Humvees that waited on standby. From there, the bodies went to the central morgue.

As Suo watched, the two corpsmen started arguing with each other. Still eating his MRE, he put on night-vision goggles to watch more closely. The corpsmen started screaming at each other over a body on a stretcher. Suo could hear what they said. One of the Navy medics recognized the body. It was someone he knew. The other medic wanted to load the body and be done with it. But the first medic refused. He didn't want to keep working. He wanted to be with the body for a minute or something—Suo couldn't make it out exactly. The second medic couldn't stand putting things off. One of the medics threw a punch at the other one. Suo got nervous. He looked at Lombard. The major slept hard. Suo looked back at the medics, who were on the ground now, hammering at each other and screaming in the dark. There didn't seem to be any Humvee drivers near the medics to break them up. He wondered if they were armed. He decided he had to run over to them. He stood, but at that moment, the two men mysteriously stopped screaming. A few seconds went by. They seemed to be done fighting. It was like they gave up on hurting each other. As if they somehow both realized the fight could only get them so far. The two medics stood, stumbled away from each other, and coughed and wiped their noses on their sleeves. And then, wordlessly, they returned to the body and leaned over together. They picked up the dead Marine, and loaded him into their refrigerator.

November 25, Thanksgiving, was cold, even by my New York standards. It hit the midthirties Fahrenheit and stayed that way for days. Neither the Iraqis nor the Americans were prepared for it. The junood received field jackets with sheepskin liners, one of the very rare instances where the Iraqi Ministry of Defense responded to their needs in a timely manner, as if the severity of the cold alarmed even the officials back in Baghdad. The advisers broke down desks and chairs and burned them in our fifty-five-gallon drum. We hung a heavy tarp over a window to hide the glow of the fire at night. The Iraqis managed to get the mosque's water running, which was a good thing, because they had been relieving themselves in holes in the ground without running water to clean themselves after. The water flowed, and the stench in the mosque lifted somewhat.

Major General Natonski, the commander of the First Marine Division to whom I gave my humiliating report after the EFIC desertions, decided that all the troops in the field would get Thanksgiving dinner. The logistical challenge of delivering a meal to every single Marine, US Army soldier, and Iraqi Army soldier in Fallujah was tremendous. Lombard, Mulvihill, and I went to our nightly staff meeting with First Battalion, Third Marines, to discuss that day's events, plan for the following day, and learn more about

Thanksgiving. I decided I wanted all the Fifth Battalion advisers, the Iraqis, and our attached Marines to have dinner together at al-Hadra. On a visceral level so insistent that I could not ignore it, I felt a need for us to give thanks.

Our delivery arrived at 7:30 on Thanksgiving night. It was moonless out. The Iraqis lined up for turkey, mashed potatoes, stuffing, and cranberry jelly. We also had juice, soda, and cans of walnuts. I was crazy hungry for it, my mouth watering after weeks of found scraps of food and MREs. In my mind, I was about to eat every Thanksgiving dinner I had ever had in my life. I ordered the battalion to eat in reverse-order rank: first the enlisted junood, then the NCOs, then the officers, then the US advisers. Typically, the Iraqis always insisted that the Americans eat before them. Their powerful Arabic and Kurdish sense of hospitality demanded it. But on this night, I explained that they were our guests. I moved with Arkan through the various rooms where the junood lived. The soldiers smiled as they munched down on turkey and cranberry, and I was eager for them to like it, but I had the sense that they would just as soon have stuck with their own food. They were polite. I found myself explaining the importance of the holiday. In our country, I said, this was a time for families to gather and give thanks for God's blessings. I intentionally played up the religious parts.

"I am thankful for you," I said. "I am thankful for your courage. I am thankful that you have stuck it out with your battalion."

Sa'ad asked me to eat with his officers, but I declined. I said I should eat with the Americans. He nodded and said he understood. Finally, the advisers got theirs. We lit a fire in an ammunition can. We huddled over cold stuffing and mashed potatoes.

"Gents," I said, "I just want to take a moment to give you thanks for all that we have. I am profoundly grateful for your company and your service. I am profoundly grateful, more than I can say, that none of us have been killed or grievously wounded."

And that was honest. It seemed miraculous that we were all still alive. We all knew it, but we never talked about it, and I think that acknowledging it made everyone want to speak. Every man in our small, flickering circle—Lombard, Mulvihill, Johnson, Elesky, Warner, Fryar, Villa, and me—said something about what he was grateful for. We used Ka-Bar knives as spits and warmed our turkey over the fire. We talked about this and that and nothing—conversation comes easy when you share hardship. It was the worst Thanksgiving I ever had, and the best. I would not wish those circumstances on anyone. I would not trade the memory of that night for anything.

The demands of the Second Battle of Fallujah did not lengthen any of the advisers' scheduled rotation. Villa, Elesky, and Mulvihill were due to leave. Their four replacements arrived just ahead of time, on November 27. Their names were Brown, Faulkner, Lowery, and West. They were all US Army Reservists, called out of their private lives for the war. It's hard for me to explain how difficult it was for a man who had been a civilian only weeks earlier to drop into the Middle East and begin managing Iraqis in the middle of America's worst urban battle since the Vietnam War. The four advisers—I call them that, though they did not know the job yet—arrived at al-Hadra mosque in broad daylight in the back of an Isuzu flatbed truck. They climbed the stairs to the second floor, trying not to stare at the unexpected crowd of Iraqi civilians living in the prayer chamber. True to his nature, Captain Mulvihill spoke quickly and wasted no time with pleasantries.

"This is our sector," he said. "This is where our Iraqis are fighting. We will introduce you to the Iraqi leadership in a few minutes. We need two of you to be here, and two of you will be somewhere else—a traffic control point."

He looked at them, waiting for volunteers. Sergeant First Class West had seniority, but said nothing. The other sergeant first class, Andrew Brown, answered: "I'll stay here with Faulkner, and West and Lowery will go to the traffic control point."

Andrew Brown, thirty-two, was a Gulf War veteran from Mechanicsburg, Pennsylvania. It had been fourteen years, but he remembered Iraq. S.Sgt. Mark Faulkner, at forty-seven, became the second-oldest adviser on our team after Warner. Faulkner started his military career with the Navy in 1978, and was an Army Reservist teaching military science at Niagara University when he got called to the war. Faulkner's first night, he drove Mulvihill to a 10 PM meeting with officers at First Battalion, Third Marines. He had never driven a Humvee before. They briefly got lost on the black streets of Fallujah. The next day, Mulvihill sent him on his first patrol with the Iraqis, without any other advisers. Faulkner was nervous about that idea, and said so. But Mulvihill reassured him.

"You'll be fine," he said. "They're Kurds."

Out on the street, Faulkner stacked up with his junood next to a building. The patrol was led by Iskander. The sergeant major seemed to actually grow more serene when he was on a mission. His hand tremor, which was sometimes so bad it debilitated him, ceased when he was outside the wire. Iskander, Faulkner, and a squad of Kurdish junood stormed the building. It was clear. The Kurds immediately started looting the place. Faulkner told them that they had to stop. His 'terp, the always cool Abdallah, relayed the message. The battle-hardened junood looked at Faulkner as if he had dropped in from another planet, which in a sense he had. The American looked back at these strange, armed men and wondered what he had gotten himself into. In general, Faulkner always played the straight man. He reminded me of a bigger, stronger version of Bob Newhart. He even wore half-moon reading glasses when he wasn't on missions.

"Just . . . Just go ahead and make sure you've cleared the whole house," he said. "And then you can . . . look around."

On December 1, we moved battalion headquarters a block north of al-Hadra to the Islamic Benevolent Society. It was the headquarters for a charity that had long since fled the city. The junood, their equipment, and our refugees occupied both the mosque and the Benevolent Society.

Cats swarmed over the grounds of the Benevolent Society. Dozens of them, orange, yellow, black, and gray, slipped around and under jumbled concrete and strewn garbage. The main thing we noticed about the Islamic Benevolent Society compound was that it was a lousy tactical position. Its main single-story cement structure didn't rise as high as the buildings around it. Even from the roof, visibility was limited. Chuck Johnson pointed out that an enemy insurgent who climbed to the top of an adjacent building could literally look down into the Islamic Benevolent Society's center courtyard. The compound was going to be miserable to defend if it came to that.

Just to the north of the shattered compound stood an ornate Arab mansion. Our first night, a jundi in the courtyard reported white glimmers coming from inside one of the darkened windows there, like a flashlight. Over the coming hours, others began to see it too. We couldn't have a mystery like that going on, so Mulvihill led Brown, Faulkner, Abdallah, and four junood to the abandoned building. They crept silently around the block. They breached a gate. The three Americans, Abdallah, and the junood quietly ascended a set of stairs, making their best estimate of which door opened onto the room with the mysterious window light. They stacked up in the hallway and threw in grenades. They burst in, ready to face anything. No one was inside. They saw where the light was coming from. A big mirror hung on one wall. It was reflecting ambient flashes from outside. They took it off the wall and left.

On December 2, I said good-bye to Lombard. He laughed and shook my hand and hopped a Humvee north out of the city. He had joined us officially just days before the battle, and now he departed as it was ending. His time with the Fifth Battalion aligned with the Battle of Fallujah. Before he left, Lombard nominated Suo for the Navy and Marine Corps Achievement Medal with the Combat V, which Suo received. Five days after that, Mulvihill, Elesky, and Villa rotated out. Villa was the last of the original advisers besides me. With the three men gone, I was also the last Marine. It was an Army Reserve team now. But I believed in them as I would believe in any Marine.

Fallujah remained dangerous, but the daily violence flagged. A nascent order returned as the Marines, US Army, and Iraqi Army took ground from the insurgents.

An old friend of mine, Marine major Scott Marconda, was a JAG officer—a military attorney—who worked as an adviser to Ramos. He was around Fifth Battalion more and more. He managed rules of engagement for the First Battalion, Third Marines. He also classified prisoners, looked into property claims from Iraqi civilians, and arranged work contracts with Iraqis as the fighting ebbed. He organized local workers to paint over insurgent graffiti, remove bodies, clean up trash, and bury corpses according to Muslim rites. Workers got five dollars a day for regular work, ten dollars a day for the unsavory stuff. Word got around, and Iraqi men began to show up asking Marconda if he had jobs for them. It was like a mini–economic stimulus package. At the start of each day, Marconda gave the men vests with yellow trim and gray reflective tape. They got paid when they turned their vests back in. That was his system for ensuring that random civilians didn't fake being on work crews. They tried anyway.

Around that time, First Battalion, Third Marines, caught workers from the Iraqi Red Crescent, the humanitarian aid organization, shipping uninjured men out of the city in ambulances. A local wealthy man let the Red Crescent use his property as a parking lot. It was packed with ambulances. They had already taken dozens of men out of the city by the time the Marines figured out what was going on. The Marines stopped a group of ambulances and did gunpowder residue tests on their uninjured passengers. They all came back positive. As the Americans took more and more of the city, our enemies were running out of places to hide. All the roads out of Fallujah were blocked. The Red Crescent started evacuating them under our noses so they could fight us somewhere else.

"They aren't ambulances," Marconda told me, just before the Marines shut down the Red Crescent operation. "They're buses."

The junood had not been paid since before Fallujah. Again, we agonized about payday. Sa'ad, Ahmed Nu'uman, and I had a meeting. Ahmed Nu'uman felt strongly that we should not pay the troops until we returned to Taji.

"They will see the money in their hands, and they will desert," he said.

As usual, we were to pay the junood in cash. Nu'uman argued that they would feel a powerful urge to take the money home to their families for safekeeping. Even if they only left Fallujah temporarily to drop off their pay, the whole thing would look terrible. "Think of the Americans, Raed Zakkiyah. What will they think when they see this?"

As usual, Sa'ad disagreed with his Sunni second-in-command. He said we should pay the men. I thought things through and sided with Sa'ad. Ahmed Nu'uman made a powerful argument, but I told him the greater show of leadership and moral prerogative was to take care of our soldiers. The American troops were being paid on time, and the Iraqis should be too. "We can't hold them hostage, promising a payday," I said.

The Shiite Major Menhal Majid Hamid, who had arguably already saved the battalion once, got the job to go to the Ministry of Defense for payroll. We gave him a truck. He was supposed to drive to Baghdad one day and return the next. But he didn't show back up at Fallujah. Another day went by, and we began to wonder if he was dead or if he stole the money. We finally reached the Ministry of Defense by phone. They confirmed that the major picked up the money on time. He never came back to Fallujah.

We ended up doing a delayed, partial payroll. Sa'ad said he wanted to meet with each jundi individually to discuss his pay. He said he wanted to be sure that no one "squandered" his money.

"That is a shakedown," the new sergeant first class, Brown, said to me, and I was surprised at how fast he was catching on. Brown had a cynical aspect to his personality that probably served him well in the US military and was definitely going to serve him in Iraq. We blocked Sa'ad from carrying out one-on-one interviews.

We continued operations from the Benevolent Society. The missions began to feel less dangerous, though I knew that feeling was in and of itself dangerous. We worked at keeping everybody alert and sharp. A US military group known as Civilian Affairs was supposed to get the electricity back on and the water running, but it wasn't happening. Moreover, they began sending us more refugees. A growing number came to us asking for food, blankets, and fuel. They were arriving on foot. The insurgents still had die-hard snipers who weren't giving up the fight, and the vicious assholes began setting up near the Islamic Benevolent Society and murdering the refugees in ones or twos as they tried to get to us over the trashed roads. It was militarily pointless for these snipers to be doing this. They were beaten. They just wanted to murder people.

I explained the situation to Civilian Affairs on the radio. We needed them to send fewer refugees our way, and we needed more supplies to feed and clothe the ones we had. Sa'ad stood by gravely and listened to the conversation. The American officer on the other end agreed it sounded like a problem. But it was not *their* problem. They didn't have the time or means, the officer said, to solve it for us. I decided to take a Humvee to the Civilian Affairs operations center and explain things face-to-face. They needed in-person pressure. Having an Iraqi officer with me would help, so I asked Sa'ad along. The Americans in Fallujah had all heard a lot of rhetoric by then about how our Iraqi allies were playing an important role in the battle. Generals were saying it. Trained spokesmen repeated it at press conferences and to embedded reporters. The Iraqis of the Fifth Battalion were critical to how the battle was being portrayed, all the way back to the United States. As their commanding officer, Sa'ad was a political symbol. It would be hard for the Americans to refuse him help.

As Sa'ad and I walked outside to depart, I spontaneously threw up. That was normal. I didn't slow down much. I was vomiting every day at that point, without warning or understanding, and moving past it as it happened.

Forero was waiting for us outside. He got behind the wheel. Sa'ad took the back. I climbed into the death seat. Another young Marine, whose name I never learned, was already up top on the .50-cal. We got onto the main east–west thoroughfare in the city, called Phase Line Fran by the Americans. It would take us straight to Civilian Affairs. The day was bright, the air pleasant. The tires rumbled. I was exhausted. I was mad. Nobody spoke. I decided that if we saw one or two civilians on the way back, we should give them a lift.

Then *ponk, ponk, ponk!* rang out against the side panels. Almost instantly, we could tell the direction of the shooting. I pointed. It was a three-story building, and close. Less than one hundred yards. We didn't usually stop when we were sniped at, but this time we did. We could tell where they were. Forero jerked the wheel, and the big tires scored the shattered pavement as we slid to a halt. I dismounted. Forero did the same. I took cover, aimed, held my breath and fired. Whiffs of concrete dust sprang off the building in my sights. More incoming rounds struck home on the Humvee—*ponk, ponk, ponk!*

"Marine," I said to the Marine in the turret. I felt oddly removed, low key. "Address that sniper."

The .50-cal detonated with sound as the Marine raked the building with bullets the size of carrots. Empty casings spilled over the Humvee with a sound like bells on a horse. The concrete building splintered and shredded at the machine gun's onslaught. A wall crumbled and thudded to the street, sending a bloom of white talc exploding in every direction. We stopped firing and waited. Soon, we spied movement through the powdery air. It was the sniper. He rose from the rubble, doubled over, and stumbled into a run. It was like a miracle to actually see one of them. There he was: the guy who just tried to kill us.

The Marine didn't wait for more orders. He made his rules. He opened again from the .50-cal. The upright sniper blasted apart and fell to the ground in pieces.

The machine gun went silent. Sa'ad stepped out of the Humvee. He wasn't armed—Sa'ad never carried a weapon. He put his fists on his hips and glared toward our target. Forero and I looked at the spot a moment longer and let our stocks ease down from our shoulders. The block's edges recrystallized as the white dust fell.

We got one.

The Marine up in the turret made a sound like a laugh, but not quite. More like a bark, or the caw of a crow. I looked back at him. He looked down at me. Bitterness and joy collided on his face like rapids spilling over each other.

"Just point 'em out sir," he said. "I'll fuckin' kill 'em."

Part IV

TAJI

17

BLOODED

THE TERM WE USE IS *blooded*.

It's military, all the way. Never heard it anywhere else. If your unit has been blooded, that means men around you have been killed or wounded by your enemies as you came up against them. Men who, at that moment, at the time of the blooding, shared an experience with you that no one, anywhere, will be able to know. A shared experience that was yours only. Together. Combat.

What kills men is also what makes battalions, what gives identities to the units those men fought for. The Fifth Battalion was blooded at Fallujah, and there was nobody anywhere who was going to take that away. When Fallujah was done, we documented fifty-eight insurgents killed by Fifth Battalion and 215 detained or captured. Two of our own were killed: Abdel-ridha Gibrael on November 2, and a private named Hussein Founi Abd Ali, who was shot by a sniper outside al-Hadra mosque. The Fifth was real. That's what Marines mean when we talk about esprit de corps. Fifth Battalion at that moment provided the sole proven model for the larger concept of a new Iraqi Army. At Fallujah, we earned a reputation among the insurgents, Iraqis, and Americans alike. When the battle was over, all three groups threatened Fifth Battalion's survival.

In the middle of December 2004, the Second Battle of Fallujah wasn't yet history. Nobody on the ground had the luxury of considering broader meanings. Nobody had time to think of "history." Of course, it didn't matter: Fallujah hadn't finished with history. Fallujah is a meteor that evaporates to black after searing the nighttime sky, only to flare again, and again, further down its falling arc.

In December 2004, the Americans were done with Fallujah. Black Hawk choppers torqued up, hacking at the low air and pulling away like tractor trailers that believed they could fly. An armored land armada arrayed itself on the dust, as profound as the earth under its wheels. Across dozens of square miles, unfurled American military power declared itself through a million permutations of steel and sinew and silicon, a new desert army with the nonchalance of a god. The god was done with Fallujah.

Dick Cheney said we broke the back of the insurgency. The insurgents who survived our onslaught had fled, though, and immediately, rumors started about where they were going. North of Baghdad this time, the rumors said, in Mosul. On the Tigris, 250 miles north of Baghdad. A place where our enemies would make themselves whole again. American and Iraqi whispers were saying "Mosul." That's where Abu Musab al-Zarqawi wanted to be. Maybe that's where he had been all along—we knew we had not killed him.

The Americans and Iraqis would be following the insurgents to Mosul sooner rather than later. National elections were scheduled for January 30. They would be the first real elections in Iraqi history—in Mesopotamian history, for that matter. They were only a little more than a month away. With Fallujah secured, the Americans wanted to secure the next-most-restive cities. They couldn't have RPGs blowing up polling stations. The pressure was to act, and to act now. Security in the country was worse than at any point since before the US invasion, and the Sunnis, in particular, didn't want elections until the violence was under control. But political forces in favor of a vote were going to win out: the White House needed a success. Ayad Allawi, who was appointed interim prime minister in June and wanted to be elected real prime minister in January, needed a successful vote too. Allawi was a Shiite, and everyone knew that a Shiite was going to win for the simple reason that there were more Shiite Arabs in Iraq than Sunnis or Kurds. In advance, the Sunni Arabs started declaring the vote illegitimate.

My main focus was on the Fifth, not Iraqi politics. I had a battalion whose numbers were nowhere near battalion strength. We needed new recruits. We had to train them. We needed the Iraqi Ministry of Defense to authorize new mujanadin and allocate them to us. Lieutenant Colonel Symons, that man who was the bearer of all news, good and bad, told me I could expect new troops back at Taji, but he warned me, "You'll get those recruits after we get your battalion berthed. That'll be our first challenge. If you want recruits, you need to have room for them. Things have gotten crowded back at Taji."

Warner crunched the numbers and gave me daily morning reports. Walkouts before the battle and casualties during it had reduced us to 288 enlisted men, NCOs, and officers. Including wounded, we had 319. Separately, Zayn's cohort back at Taji stood at thirty-two. The good news was that we had established a reliable core of soldiers—one created by a brutal, infuriating process of elimination, but a core nonetheless. The Iraqis who remained felt the same way about themselves. That nucleus of 288 gave itself a name: al-Insaharin. It translated roughly to "those who have been through the crucible." It referred to the Crucible at the end of recruit training, but the word had a new, more potent meaning as well: the crucible was Fallujah, and they had survived it. Al-Insaharin were the blooded foundation of Fifth Battalion.

Our plan was for half the battalion to return to Taji and then go on leave. The remainder would return to Taji and go on leave as the first group was finishing their leave. We couldn't send everyone on vacation at once. Our plan had to be approved by the Iraqi brigade commanders. Major General Ahmad and Brigadier General Essa sat in a tent at EFIC and listened to Sa'ad's and my plan. Subordinate officers stood by their table like waiters. Ahmad and Essa were old veterans of the Iran-Iraq War. Both were fat and bald. Both were shrewd men, political masters by necessity. They agreed to our leave proposal. But before Sa'ad and I departed, they had one more thing. The exhausted junood had been promised twenty-one days of leave before the battle began, but unfortunately, they said through Arkan, they had to reduce that number.

"We must resume our places in the towers at Taji so that the guards there now can go to Mosul," Arkan said. "They can give the men only ten days, Raed Zakkiyah."

Sa'ad slightly narrowed his gaze on the big, round generals. His thick eyebrows flexed for a moment. Then he acknowledged the order. We walked out.

The advance party left for Taji on December 14, rolling out of EFIC on the beds of the same Nissan pickups that shuttled them to Fallujah a month and a half earlier. They promptly went on leave. The second wave departed EFIC on December 21. Sa'ad, the remaining advisers, and I were to go with it. I thanked Forero for his service and shook his hand. Fifth Battalion trucks and Humvees kicked at the powder soil, and we left. We had no helicopter cover, and the Marines had us go out ahead of their morning IED sweep. I sat in the Humvee's death seat. I never looked back at the city. Not even in the rearview. My stomach rolled, and my tongue rubbed dry on the inside of my cheeks.

We arrived at a busier, more crowded Taji than the one we had left. New American advisers and new Iraqi recruits were living there. They were in the first stages of raising a new Iraqi Army division. They had taken the buildings in Taji that were previously home to the Fifth Battalion. People were talking about the coming Iraqi division as an "elite" force. I had serious doubts about how elite any of the new Iraqi Army was going to be. But the word must have sounded good to planners in the Green Zone and Washington. The new division was envisioned as a motorized unit that would respond quickly to flare-ups throughout Iraq, whenever they happened. The Bush administration was increasingly anxious to see an independent Iraqi Army. The insurgency was getting worse, not better. The war killed 848 Americans in 2004. A rising number of observant voices back in the States were beginning to say that the 2003 invasion and its MISSION ACCOMPLISHED banner had not been the "real" Iraq War. The real, grinding war against religious zealots who poured into Iraq from outside—the war that is ongoing and has spread to other countries as I write these words—was just starting.

While most of Fifth Battalion was in Fallujah, Zayn's rear party back at Taji was kicked out of our area, called Muntaqa Safra (Yellow Zone). Zayn tried to hold his ground, but he was only a major. He couldn't fend off the colonels and generals of this new Iraqi division who wanted our real estate. In general, when Iraqi units moved from one area to another, things disappeared. *Everything* went with them. Zayn's rear party was no exception. He let his group of thirty-two men take not just their personal gear but also the battalion's racks and lockers. The men stripped out light fixtures, plumbing fixtures, furniture—anything with possible resale value. Zayn's men moved their inventory into our new, much smaller Muntaqa Rasasyah (Gray Zone). What they couldn't store there, they sold in the open markets of Baghdad. The headquarters company of the new division inherited a Muntaqa Safra that was stripped and trashed. As Zayn saw it, nothing had come to us easy, and nothing was going to be taken away easy.

We shared Muntaqa Rasasyah with an Iraqi motor transport brigade—also a new unit—which didn't much like seeing Zayn move in with thirty-two men and furnishings for seven hundred more. The transport Iraqis were mostly drivers. They were older. They were not a combat unit. Their advisers were American NCOs and officers, all women. I tried to imagine the cultural tension between those male Iraqi drivers and their female American advisers. It wasn't a happy unit. The advisers gave up barracks space to Zayn's rear party, but they did not like it.

"More will come soon," Zayn told them, showing a toothy smile. "When they return from Fallujah."

Almost as soon as I got back, I saw we had other problems as profound as where we would be living. With part of the battalion away on leave, we suddenly did not have a full picture of *who was still in the battalion.* There was no sure accounting for who was alive, who was dead, or who may be a deserter. When junood went on leave, we had no way to track them. In 2004 Iraq, almost no one had a mobile phone. Most residences lacked landlines too. Our records of individual Iraqis' homes usually indicated only a city or village. If you wanted to reach someone in Iraq, you usually worked through a person in the same tribe who could convey a message. Working on only scant information, rumors began to weave their way through the battalion like a black embroidery: stories of soldiers who had been abducted or murdered, or who had been threatened and quit. There was no way to ascertain the veracity of any of it.

Zayn sat with me in my new, spartan quarters. Christmas was still a couple of days away. My wound remained bandaged, and blood thumped through my shoulder hard and dully. The dumb ache pulsed up into my head, like it didn't want me to forget.

"We know for sure of Naufal Basheer," Zayn said. Naufal was a veteran jundi who had fought in the Iran-Iraq War and had been wounded several times. "He is dead."

Zayn lay one hand on my forearm and planted the thumb and forefingers of his other hand into his eye sockets. "Two junood saw him. From his tribe. The insurgents took him, and then . . . they put his head onto a pole, Raed Zakkiyah. On the road to his village."

There were more stories, most unconfirmed. Most involved men who for one reason or another stood out in the battalion. Two of our company commanders were rumored dead. Even if only half the tales were true, it was clear to me that the insurgents were targeting individuals. They were among us. We had insurgents in the battalion. That much we had known for a while. And even with the battalion down to a fraction of its former size, the insurgents with us had stayed with us. They weren't going anywhere. And there was no easy way to identify the motherfuckers.

"They know our victories. They know what we have done, that the battalion fought hard in Fallujah," Zayn said, dropping his hand from his face. His eyes were rimmed red. "They know much about us, Raed Zakkiyah. We killed many of them. We fight for Iraq. Now they must kill us. They will kill as many of us as they can."

We had come through Fallujah. The Fifth Battalion had seen more combat than any Iraqi unit, and for a longer duration. We fought for a new Iraq that the insurgents hated and were determined not to let come into existence. To our enemies, our very existence was an affront. We were a symbol of their failure. We were real. We had been blooded. To the insurgents, breaking us was a critical mission.

The Fifth Battalion's official table of organization strength called for 757 men total, including officers, divided into four rifle companies, a motor transport company, and a headquarters company. Even without factoring in the number of men we were unlikely to see again after leave, we were down to three rifle companies that were more like small platoons of 30 soldiers each, a truck company of about 60 men, and a headquarters company of 120. The HQ and truck companies experienced fewer desertions because they were less dangerous than the rifle companies. Muntaqa Rasasyah wasn't big enough to house a full battalion. I needed space for us to grow in. Without the space, I could not get the new recruits I needed. Without new men, Fifth Battalion was a battalion in name only. Sa'ad and I decided on a strategy. It became our two-man Taji modus operandi: I worked the US chain of command, and he worked the Iraqi chain of command. Sa'ad said he would speak directly to the Iraqi Ministry of Defense in Baghdad. With luck, one of us would succeed at getting what the battalion needed.

The Marine major who oversaw Taji had been around only since August, but he was already on his way out, rotating somewhere else so a new guy could come in. The new guy was going to be a US Army colonel. The Marine major was sympathetic to my request for more space, but he wasn't in a position to help.

"There's no way I can do that for you. Your battalion isn't even manning base defenses yet," he said. "I can't recommend giving you the space and resources you want when you're not even able to contribute."

I tried the CMATT logistics officer—also a new guy. More space, he said, was a nonstarter. He didn't even have tents for us. It was a simple matter of capacity. There were more soldiers at Taji than Taji had buildings to put them in.

Joseph Heller made military logic famous in his book *Catch-22*. Military logic really is just bureaucratic logic, the same systematized thinking that runs the Postal Service or your local Department of Motor Vehicles. Except the DMV doesn't have heavy artillery. Military bureaucracy is more obscene than other bureaucracies because there's a lot more at stake. That's what Joseph Heller was writing about, and at Taji I found myself living an intractable, epically bullshit problem: I couldn't get the space because I didn't have the recruits, and I couldn't get the recruits because I didn't have the space. The system had gone as rigidly immobile as a rusted lock.

OK, I decided, *progress has to start somewhere, somehow. If I can't get the space until I have the recruits to fill it, I'll go ahead and push for recruits without the space for them.* I decided to approach the senior adviser of the new Iraqi division that had taken over so much of Taji. He was actively bringing raw mujanadin into the base.

The new American advisers to the new Iraqi division were anxious to show progress. Their political bosses demanded it. They were under intense pressure from the White House to quickly forge a new army. The advisers were Marines, flown in from Okinawa. They bought into the idea that the new division was going to be the best, the tip of the spear, the A game. None of the advisers like me who had been in-country for a while believed it was going to look that way, but such ideas weren't spoken aloud.

The senior adviser to the new Iraqi division was a full-bird Marine colonel. I visited him in his office, hoping he could help with my catch-22. Marines have an expression for officers like the colonel. We say that they're in the Corps on the "athletic scholarship." He was physically imposing, hard bodied, and his uniform was immaculate, no matter what he was doing. All the other advisers were sweat rimmed and salt stained. Our uniforms were hand sewn where concertina wire had snagged us. My contempt for the colonel was automatic. He sat behind a desk, crisp desert camouflage bulging over his chest. He was not sympathetic to my recruiting needs.

"Why would I help you?" the colonel asked. He was blunt partly because he was a Marine, and partly, I believed, because he wasn't good at talking. I sensed that he wrestled with the language. "You aren't even part of my division!"

"I understand that, sir, but I'm caught in some circular logic," I said. "I can't get troops because I don't have space, and I can't get space because I don't have troops. I have to go ahead and tackle one problem to fix the other. And seeing as how you're now engaged in direct recruitment of new Iraqi troops, I hoped that—"

"Major," he cut me off. "Maybe if you shape up your . . . battalion up, maybe if you start to act like soldiers—get them to act like soldiers—and then learn how to do more with less, then you can stop asking for resources." Or something like that.

The Scholar Athlete gave me a strident glare before continuing, as if my inability to see his words as self-evident was a failure of my intelligence.

"Maybe if you concentrate on accomplishing the missions you're given, then people will be more inclined to give resources to you!" he said.

"Sir, my battalion just returned from a mission. In Fallujah." I repressed a potent desire to add, "Where a big battle just happened." I wanted to scream at him that we had come from seven weeks of constant urban combat. We had, in fact, recently accomplished *a big fucking mission.*

"The *other* battalions don't have this problem!" he said. "*They're* not coming to me asking for things! Why aren't the other battalions complaining? Tell me *that*, Major!"

This wasn't going to work. I told him I understood and thanked him for his time. But I was not dismissed. He became more serene. "Major, I know you have problems. With housing your battalion, I mean. Taji's a lot more crowded than it used to be."

"Yes, sir."

"But there's a way you could relieve some of your berthing problems for now—and help the broader mission."

I said nothing. *He's angling at something.*

"That battalion of yours saw action in Fallujah. Just like you said! I have a mission to stand up my new division," the colonel said. "It's an important mission."

"Yes, sir."

"There are a lot of people who would be very grateful if we could take some of your experienced infantry and . . . *sprinkle them* . . . around."

Again I said nothing, but he must have seen my face go blank. He was talking about taking apart Fifth Battalion. He was talking about taking the men I had trained and plugging them into other units. Everything came together for me at that moment. The quickest way for him to build a division was to cannibalize a battalion that was already trained and insert its junood into the new division. *My junood.*

"No, sir. I don't think that would be a good idea," I said. "The Fifth Battalion has built real unit cohesion. It did so under fire in Fallujah. They have real pride. They have a name for themselves—al-Insaharin. It means—"

"Al-what?" He looked at me sideways, as if I had said something frivolous, possibly subversive, in the midst of a serious conversation.

"Al-Insaharin. That is the name they gave themselves. What it means is—"

"Major," he cut me off. He did not want to hear about my Arabic word. I knew his mindset. The Marine Corps has an old expression from World War II and before, coined to refer to Marines who spent too much time in China or the Philippines and who got too close to the locals: going Asiatic. I sensed a judgment that wafted over the colonel's desk like a sharp odor—I was too close to the Iraqis, too close to the unit I built.

"We have a *mission* here, Major," he said. "We will *succeed* at this mission. We've got a *division* to build. You think Mosul is going to surrender without a fight? Experienced combat troops are critical!"

I felt a panic that threatened to teeter over into a despair. I suppressed my emotions. I showed him nothing.

"Sir, I understand the importance of building an effective fighting force. But trying to do so by dismantling the core units that have combat experience is not an effective way to do that. Sir."

The colonel reddened. He knew as well as I did that in Marine Corps doctrine, the battalion is considered the core tactical unit. When commanders look at units on a battlefield map, their Marines are arrayed in battalions. Young, rising officers in the Marine Corps make or break their careers when they reach battalion-level command. The colonel's and my shared Marine concepts strongly supported the idea that a successful Iraqi Army should have strong battalions as its building blocks. The Fifth was one. We could not dismantle it. The colonel reclined behind his desk. He never took his eyes off me.

"No matter," he finally continued. "These are decisions to be made by our Iraqi counterparts."

Yes, I thought. *Officially, that's true. But you and I both know that they're going to do what we tell them to do. And if you don't know that, then you haven't seen the ball since the whistle blew.*

"Yes, sir," I said.

I went to Lieutenant Colonel Symons. He was sympathetic, as always. He told me he would do what he could about barracks and recruits. He took interest in what I told him about the colonel and his novel approach to unit cohesion. I got the impression from Symons that it wasn't the first talk he'd heard about "reorganization" of his battalions. The political landscape had shifted while Symons and I were away, and he had two battalions besides the Fifth to worry about.

On top of all that, we were coming up on two high-level events scheduled for Taji. On January 3, there would be a top-to-bottom review of the fight in Fallujah. Big names were flying in: an array of generals, plus US ambassador to Iraq John Negroponte. Then on January 6, there was a holiday called Iraqi Army Day. Units were going to parade for an international crowd of military and civilian VIPs. Politics were becoming a bigger and bigger priority in Iraq, and we all felt it. The country's first elections were still on schedule for January 30.

"We left one Taji in November," Symons said, "and returned to another Taji in December."

I asked Sa'ad to push Brigadier General Essa for fresh troops. American battalion advisers regularly reported unit head count up to the brigade advisers. On the Iraqi side, Sa'ad was supposed to keep his superiors updated on battalion strength through the Iraqi chain of command. Sa'ad told me he would work channels to get us replacements. Sa'ad made another trip to Baghdad to talk to the Ministry of Defense. The road to Baghdad was dangerous, and Sa'ad showed dedication by making the trip to meet with officials face-to-face. Or at least that's what I thought was going on.

I felt a massive hammer slamming again and again onto a white-hot anvil. It was the same hammer that had been ringing for months, even before the RPG blew up behind me. But lately the blows took on a merciless, metronomic quality. They told me that I was leaving Iraq in a few months. They warned that Fifth Battalion was running out of time to reconstitute itself. The hammer told me that the thing I risked my life to build was close to being annihilated. I feared an abyss that couldn't be possible.

I began to feel breakable. My armor, abraded. It became difficult, then next to impossible, when I called my fiancée, to bring words out. More than once, I fell down in the middle of the day for no apparent reason. The daylight slashed my eyes. I threw up meals. Moment-to-moment anxieties settled like bright mercury into fissures that Iraq had cut into me. It hurt worse than it ever had, worse than when Gene Armstrong was desecrated. Worse than when Abdel-ridha Gibrael gazed at his dying sky.

I still think of 2004 as a year without a Christmas. Or maybe it was the first year that I stopped giving a shit about Christmas. I wasn't having it. I was revolted by the Christmas bullshit at Taji. KBR ran a dining facility there, and the Americans filed in lines while Pakistani and Filipina food workers ran around in little elf hats, smiling like idiots and slopping food onto trays. Tinny Christmas music piped into the dining room. I hated them. I hated it. I hated the soldiers laughing in line. I hated the Americans feeling jolly and bold at their tables. I hated the women from the Philippines wearing their clown outfits. I hated the Muslim Pakistanis saying "Merry Christmas" when they didn't know what the words meant. I hated the fat KBR executives who ordered elf hats. I hated the stray Iraqi officers who laughed with the American officers, angling for advantage, flashing their yellow teeth over plastic trays.

It was not their fault. The American reservists had not asked to spend the holidays in a gargantuan kill zone. The Filipinas had not asked to be made into ridiculous cheer merchants. The Iraqis had not asked the Americans to blow the shit out of their country in the name of a bright-eyed nation-creation mission. It wasn't their fault. It wasn't their fault. Even then, I knew that it wasn't their fault. But I was mad, and people stayed away. People saw me waiting for my cranberry sauce, and they instinctively avoided me. I know I wore rage as plainly as I wore a uniform. I wouldn't have wanted to talk with a guy like me either.

It was cool out in Taji, not cold like Fallujah. The humidity settled into my joints. I rubbed them at night while I watched movies with the other advisers. Everybody got care packages from family and friends when we returned to Taji, and DVDs were a big gift. DVDs were new. DVDs were technology. DVDs were America. The sergeants Faulkner and Brown who joined us in the middle of Fallujah set up a TV with a DVD player. We watched war movies: *Saving Private Ryan, We Were Soldiers Once,* and the series *Band of Brothers.* I preferred some of the comedies, especially the Will Ferrell movies *Old School* and *Elf.* Andrew Brown could watch the movies and make wiseass remarks along with Will Ferrell in an understated way that made me crack up. It was good to laugh. The white-blue light flickered at night, and I wasn't there anymore. I loved not being there. The DVDs gave us entry into the quintessentially American act of disappearing completely into a screen's glow.

Some of the Iraqis picked up that something was wrong with me. Sa'ad, Ahmed Nu'uman, Zayn, my interpreters Arkan and Abdallah—they knew. Others could see my anger, too, but I think they didn't feel they should speak to me about personal matters. That's all the war was anymore: personal.

"It is wrong that you are here, far from your family," Sa'ad told me. He was due to go on leave, but before departing, he dropped by my quarters with a small Christmas tree and sweets. I knew enough about the political beast in Sa'ad to recognize that his gift was meant to keep things good with me, but it was a serious gesture on his part, and I appreciated it. A Shiite Muslim gave me a Christmas tree in Iraq. I gave him candies and a pair of Wiley X sunglasses.

Zayn came with gifts as well. He picked up pastries in the city—"the best in all of Baghdad." In a gesture that stunned me, he also gave me three dresses to pass along to my own family: one each for my mother, my sister, and my fiancée. These were three women he was never going to meet. Even more amazing was who had picked the dresses out: Zayn's wife. She never left home. She never went out. But he took her to Baghdad because he didn't know what an American woman would like. She didn't either, of course. But the gesture genuinely humbled me.

Like Sa'ad, Major Zayn was slated to go on leave. I didn't want him to go. I feared for his life. Someone among us in the Fifth was betraying other members of the battalion, and everyone knew how close I was to Zayn. His friendship with me made him a target. Leave was his right, though, and I didn't ask him to stay. Before he departed Taji, he checked in with me. He was as worried about leaving me behind as I was worried about seeing him go. At least, I think that's what was going on. We didn't talk about things like that. Instead, he spoke about the Christian holiday.

"Jesus is a prophet for us as well," he said to me again. We walked in the cool of evening. A kitten we had brought from Fallujah and named Jundi trotted over the dust, keeping up with us like a dog. "Second only to Muhammad."

He was trying to relate to me, to express some solidarity with what he thought were my religious beliefs. He was doing it for my sake, and I knew it.

"It is hard for Muslims to understand why a man would die for others' sins," Zayn said. "Even if he was a great prophet."

The Muslims didn't believe in original sin. The Adam and Eve of the Koran are different from the Adam and Eve of the Old Testament. The Koranic Adam and Eve bear full responsibility for original sin, alone. As far as Muslims like Zayn were concerned, there was no human stain for Jesus to die for. I turned my head to get a look at his face. He was staring straight ahead as we walked.

"It's hard for me to understand it too," I said, and it was. It felt good to utter it, though I could tell from his expression that Zayn was confused by my words. I did not explain myself to him. Lately I could feel my religious upbringing falling away. And I wasn't conflicted about it. It didn't involve him. It didn't bother me.

Just before the New Year, Warner stood up before me like the big former outside linebacker that he was and reported that a group of Shiite officers were overreporting the Fifth Battalion's payroll numbers.

Warner's latest head count to the brigade advisers was 288 junood. That was the real number. Sa'ad and his closest officers were reporting a battalion head count of several hundred more than that to their own superiors. As a result, the Iraqi government was paying the Fifth Battalion as if it had more soldiers than it actually had. It all came together. That frozen lock clicked, and the tumblers worked for a moment, and something opened up. The numbers flowed through Sa'ad to the Ministry of Defense, and the money flowed back through him to the battalion. Sa'ad's crew was pocketing the difference between the junood we had, and the junood we were being paid to have. And we were not earmarked for new recruits because the Iraqi Ministry of Defense believed the Fifth Battalion had more troops than it actually had.

"Ain't that a bitch?" Warner said.

New Year's Day came.

I wanted to confront Sa'ad, but he wasn't in Taji. He was off to Baghdad again, visiting the Ministry of Defense. He had been making the trip more and more, each time risking his life on the highways. It was always "for business." Before, I thought he was trying to get us more recruits. Now I had no idea what his so-called business was. I also had stopped caring, except about one thing: I had to hold the battalion together. Sa'ad could run his rackets. That was fine. But not if they endangered the Fifth.

The second wave of the battalion started trickling back in from leave. Again, it was difficult to ascertain who was late to return, who had deserted, and who was dead. The insurgents netted a few more lives while the second group was going and coming. The commander of one of the rifle companies, a major named Ali Ibrahim Hussein, who had been with the battalion since the beginning, was shot in the head at a Baghdad gas station. The biggest soldier in the battalion, a corporal named Muhammad Ahmed Yusef, was abducted in Baghdad and murdered. Yusef was six foot six—a giant among the Iraqis. We always had trouble finding uniforms that fit him. The advisers joked with Corporal Yusef, calling him Ahmed the Giant, after the wrestler André the Giant. He laughed and bowed and loved the attention. But his size made him stand out, and the insurgents went after the easy-to-spot target.

First Lieutenant Mohammed Ahmed, the officer who shared command of Third Rifle Company with the Kurd Bakr, told us an amazing story. He was from Mosul, which was swarming with insurgents who had fled Fallujah. Murder flashed in the streets unpredictably. Mohammed Ahmed returned there, to what was probably the most dangerous place on earth for an Iraqi soldier to visit at the turn of 2005. Mohammed Ahmed's family and fiancée told him that strange men had appeared at their home with a message: he had to quit the army, or he and his family would be killed. The first lieutenant laid low. One night, he ventured out to see what the night would show. He came across a corpse in the street near his house. A man, about the same size as himself. He dragged the body home, where he had a handheld torch. He burned the face off the corpse. He planted his Army ID card into one of the dead man's pockets. He dragged the body back out onto the street. There were no more threats, no more strange visitors. When his leave was over, he left Mosul by night and rejoined us in Taji.

The battalion seemed threatened from every angle. The insurgents murdered junood. The new American colonel wanted to "sprinkle" Fifth Battalion's troops into his own division. The Ministry of Defense was not giving us recruits, because the battalion's commanding officer was reporting a bigger battalion than actually existed. CMATT—aka MNSTC-I—either could not or refused to give us enough space to live.

The greatest threat, though, came last. After one of our countless nightly meetings, Sa'ad, now back from Baghdad, asked me outside for a word. An explosion of stars hung overhead.

"It is about the new commander of the new division," he said. "The Kurd." He was talking about the counterpart to the new American colonel, the Iraqi officer tapped to lead the elite division. "He has taken some of our soldiers. A number of the Kurds. He says he will take more."

"What?" I was livid. "Of all the things we've run up against—"

Sa'ad cut me off. He explained that the new division commander told him he did not need approval from the Ministry of Defense to take Kurdish soldiers from the Fifth Battalion. He had direct authorization, he claimed, from the chairman of the Iraqi Joint Chiefs of Staff, a man named Gen. Babaker Baderkhan Shawkat Zebari. Babaker was a Kurd, a former Peshmerga who joined the new Iraqi Army the year before, as Saddam's regime was burning.

I knew this would kill the battalion. It would kill the whole idea. If nothing else ended us, this would. Disproportionately, our best troops were Kurds. Most of the good NCOs were Kurds. We had to put a stop to it. I told Sa'ad that he had to take this news to the Ministry of Defense directly. I knew he had to have some sort of inside relationship going at the Ministry of Defense by that point. "You have to go directly to the top," I said.

Sa'ad furrowed his rebar eyebrows. He shared my anger. Or did he? I didn't know anymore. What reason did I have to trust Sa'ad? Why should I think he would have the battalion's interests in mind? And then I realized it was just as likely that he was happy to be rid of the Kurds in the battalion. He was always trying to marginalize them. He resented Sergeant Major Iskander, who was loved even by the Arabs.

"I will speak to the Ministry," Sa'ad said. "I will see what the generals have to say." He gave a curt nod. His immense, Lego-like frame melted into the night. To where, or to whom, I had no idea.

A stray white tracer discharged into the night sky. I didn't move. I was standing in Taji, but I had arrived at a place where I never thought I'd be. I no longer trusted anyone.

18

LION OF BABYLON

THE NEW YEAR CAME and went and might as well have not.

Lieutenant Colonel Symons listened carefully while I explained to him what we had learned: Sa'ad, probably with a group of top Shiite officers, appeared to be overreporting battalion head count and taking money paid to ghost soldiers. I suggested we request a full audit of Fifth Battalion payroll from the Americans and Iraqis at the Ministry of Defense level. That was a level higher than Sa'ad and me. Symons agreed he would make it happen. "I'll let you know what we find out," he said.

I was having Sa'ad investigated behind the scenes, but I wasn't going to stop working with him. My main goal was to get Fifth Battalion back up to strength. That's what the audit was really about: demonstrate to the Ministry of Defense and everybody else that we don't have the manpower that they think we do, and maybe they'll give it to us. Separately, I wanted to convince Sa'ad that Fifth Battalion needed to take on more responsibilities. We will get more resources, I decided, if we're more indispensable. Thoughts of Mosul hung in the air over Taji. The new, elite division was going to become operational and enter combat there in the far north of Iraq. Fifth Battalion was going to stay behind, but I said we should go ahead and take over perimeter defense at Taji.

Sa'ad didn't like the idea. He argued that we didn't have the manpower to man the towers and operate an interior guard. He was right. We didn't have the men we needed. In fact, he was more right than he knew, because I had not told him that I planned to begin operations beyond the perimeter: patrols, traffic checkpoints, and raids. I believed the best way to protect Taji was to project a presence *outside* Taji. Johnson, Warner, Fryar, Faulkner, and Brown believed the same thing. But I told Sa'ad none of that yet. I needed to get him on board just to put the Fifth into operation.

"We're going to have to take those towers, ready or not," I said to him. "The new division is pulling out. But after we take the towers, they're more likely to listen to us when we say we need more troops."

"Insha'Allah," he grunted, and looked away. The response could mean anything.

"This Mosul offensive is going to happen sooner rather than later, Sa'ad. We need to do this."

Sa'ad was an Iraqi, and he thought like an Iraqi. And he didn't like the idea. He didn't see how it was beneficial to take on more responsibilities before we were offered more men. To Sa'ad, it felt like giving something for nothing, which was anathema to his entire world. Everything in Iraq incurred a debt or exacted a price. My idea didn't suit his political instincts.

I left the idea alone—for now.

January 3 was a Monday. It was time for our post-Fallujah briefing. All the senior American and Iraqi officers gathered at a Taji administrative building that people called the White House. About a hundred people stood along the walls of a conference room. Zayn and I were shoulder to shoulder against the back wall.

A long table sat front and center. Seated there were General Zebari, the Kurdish chairman of the Joint Chiefs of Staff, and all the big Iraqi generals, including the top commanders from Fallujah, Major General Ahmad and Brigadier General Essa. American generals were present, rows of stars on their shoulders. The solemn, bald John Negroponte, in a suit and red tie, carried himself with ambassadorial gravity.

Most of the conversation in the room that day was about the battle—the results, the numbers, what had gone right, what had gone wrong. We had cleared the city. We had killed around fifteen hundred insurgents at a cost of ninety-five Americans, eight Iraqis, and four British dead. Zarqawi got away, but we were going to kill him too. Next they shared some high-level coordination on Mosul, which we all knew was the next fight. The men at the long table said volunteers continued to pour in for the army, with four thousand Iraqi men currently in basic training—*No surprise there*, I thought, since the pay was great and they could walk away whenever they liked. Iraqi police forces had doubled in size over six months to fifty thousand men. The figures cited were all huge and all pointed in politically desirable directions.

General Zebari from the joint chiefs spoke longest. Zebari had a gray, balding head, a gaunt face, and a long, straight nose that made him look like a Kurdish version of Montgomery Burns from *The Simpsons*. He discussed the urgent need to secure the country during the coming election. He emphasized that the Iraqi Army, with help from its American friends, was going to do the job successfully.

As we listened, Zebari went to the topic I most dreaded and most opposed. He said Iraqis had distinguished themselves at Fallujah, and the new units of the growing army could be bolstered by "reorganization." He meant breaking up Fifth Battalion, of course. There was no one else he could mean by "distinguished," and no other action he could mean by "reorganization."

Idiots, I thought. I felt my face going flush. They wanted to push new units into the fight as quickly as possible. The presence of five or six battle-experienced junood in a whole battalion of new troops was not going to magically make green soldiers better. The battalion is the basic unit of warfighting—why did they want to take us apart? *The insurgents were not able to destroy the example we have made, but these assholes will.*

I had heard this talk before, of course, from American officers trying to find a fast route to raise the elite division at Taji. They were under intense political pressure to show military results. The White House was desperate to cover its own ass in the wake of a well-planned invasion that was turning into an unplanned occupation. I knew the Americans' motivation. But until that day, I hadn't heard reorganization talk from the Iraqis. And because of that, I had never shared my fears with the Fifth Battalion's officers.

That included Zayn. We glanced at each other at the same time, standing with our backs to the conference room wall. I will never forget the look on his face. It was unguarded, totally vulnerable. He let the mask drop completely, and I glimpsed a despair that I understood right away he had tried to bury for longer than I could know.

"There's no hope for us, is there?" he asked. It was less a question than a declaration. A moment of sudden lucidity.

I was immediately overcome with shame. I was afraid I had failed him. I had failed Zayn and everyone else. The fear and pain in my friend's eyes made me realize that Zayn had allowed himself to believe the mission would work. The war would end in victory. We would march in the vanguard of a new nation. There in that room, when we should have been basking in the victory at Fallujah, he changed viscerally. I was watching him puke out his hopes that anything good would come of the war.

In the past, I had poked fun at Zayn that he was the last honest Iraqi. He had joked back that I was the last honest American. There in the conference room, I stared at him, mute, and felt that we were wrong. We weren't the last honest men. What we had in common was that we started as true believers. Now our shared belief was dying.

January 6 was Iraqi Army Day. The holiday had been around for years, with parades and speeches and feasts for the troops, even since before Saddam Hussein. Ayad Allawi decided to keep the holiday intact in the New Iraq. After all, its political symbolism was more important than ever. The Iraqi government wanted to showcase the

Army as an example for the whole country. Allawi and the Americans picked Taji as the place to do it.

Anybody who was anybody was on the guest list: interim prime minister Allawi, US ambassador John Negroponte, and Iraqi defense minister Hazem al-Sha'alan. The commander of multinational forces, General George Casey, and the commanding general of multinational security transition, Lt. Gen. David Petraeus. The British and Australian ambassadors. All the Iraqi generals, including Ahmad and Essa. Even present was our old Fifth Battalion CO, Jassim Thammin, the man who eight months earlier was telling his officers to "wait out" the American advisers.

Security was tighter than I had ever seen it at Taji, which was saying something for a place that faced shelling and rocket attacks every day. Sa'ad, Arkan, and I arrived at 9 AM. A review of the troops from the new Iraqi division—the Scholar Athlete's people—was set for a 9:30 start. The sun shone warm. Iraqi guards patrolled in ascots, leggings, and berets of blue, green, and red. I thought of the junood of Fifth Battalion, with their drab brown berets like the caps of mushrooms. American military police in body armor directed traffic. Most of the military and civilian glitterati weren't there yet, but their advance security men, often mercenaries, listened to earpieces and scanned the grounds through wraparound sunglasses. Reporters moved from short interview to short interview with their cargo pants and notepads. TV crews ran equipment checks. Then, of course, there were the Iraqi soldiers, smoking cigarettes and joking with each other.

Sa'ad worked the early crowd, giving politicians three-kiss greetings. He seemed to know everybody's names. He insisted on introducing me to each person, with Arkan translating. I was not interested in meeting most of them. I couldn't keep track of who was the assistant minister of this or the deputy minister of that. The hawk-faced Jassim greeted fellow officers in his detached way. I couldn't help but remember Abdel-ridha Gibrael, telling me Jassim's secrets behind the barracks in Kirkush.

I said hello to Americans I knew, exchanging small talk about their corners of the war. Most asked me about Fallujah. Sa'ad,

Arkan, and I wandered next to the cement parade deck. An Iraqi band tuned up, playing preceremony music. They were awful. They reminded me of a bad high school band in their gray uniforms, red epaulets, and gold braid. They even marched out of step.

I kept a close eye on my watch. It was getting close to 9:30, but the big VIPs still hadn't arrived. At exactly 9:28, I heard a rising sound. It pierced the sky like a huge, awful vacuum cleaner. People looked up, wondering what it was. I knew what it was. I dove behind a Jersey cement barrier. I broke fingernails trying to claw down into the asphalt. I heard the massive, metallic *SLAM!* of the rocket striking asphalt. It sounded like a car accident. But there was no detonation, no shock wave.

After a couple of seconds, I stood. I didn't see Sa'ad or Arkan. Men in a dozen different uniforms tentatively rose from the ground. A few were bleeding. Pickup trucks raced in. The rocket had planted itself right into the parade deck. It was big—its diameter looked like 157 millimeters—jutting at a sharp angle from the cement like the trunk of a black, windswept tree. Miraculously, it failed to detonate. A few men bled, and I reasoned that they must have been hit by flying metal. The rocket, I realized, must have come in at too low an angle to detonate. It freaked me out a little. If it had exploded, it would have killed dozens and wounded hundreds.

Sa'ad and Arkan found me. Men ran around, seemingly without purpose. Shouting erupted everywhere. Sa'ad and I helped where we could but mostly stayed out of the way. At a building behind the parade deck, we came across Sergeant First Class Brown, our operations adviser, coming at a run. He heard the impact and had just narrowly missed being hit by a careening, up-armored pickup truck.

"Nobody killed, it looks like," I said. "None of the VIPs here yet, either."

Brown was serious and alert, but he chuckled under his breath.

"Well, that's something," he said, suddenly a little amused. "The VIPs haven't shown up because they moved the parade back to 1030 hours."

I took it all in. Sa'ad did too. The insurgents' intelligence and capabilities were truly amazing. They knew precisely where and when Allawi, Negroponte, Casey, and Petraeus were all supposed to gather. They were able to hit that exact location with a 157-mm rocket. But they got their firing angle wrong. And they were an hour early.

"Somebody must've left them off the memo for the time change," Brown said.

We waited another forty-five minutes. American and Iraqi troops scoured the perimeter. The band dusted itself off, short a few men. People generally calmed down. Then the real superstars started arriving. Sa'ad saw Major General Ahmad, who insisted on taking my hand and dragging me to Defense Minister Hazem al-Sha'alan for an introduction. I was flattered but didn't understand why he was going out of his way. I greeted Sha'alan with my limited Arabic.

The parade began with a brassy blare from the band. For what seemed like hours, they played. Armored vehicles crawled in circles around the parade deck. It was like some absurd, slow-motion NASCAR race. Iraqi infantry units from the new division joined the carousel on foot, falling out of step as they tried to march at a funeral pace. A lash-up PA system shrieked out names of units and their COs in Arabic. The advisers—starting with Brown, I'm sure—began to laugh under their breath. Our Iraqis saw their advisers chuckling and began to do the same.

Mercifully, the carousel ended. The Iraqi leadership wanted to use the opportunity to hand out awards. It gave the big shots a chance to engage in military ceremony, to show they were a real army. It also let them demonstrate their benevolence, to exhibit their wasta. They announced promotions among the Fallujah veterans of Fifth Battalion. Sa'ad, the man whom I suspected was committing fraud against his government and his army, was promoted to brigadier general. The crowd applauded dutifully. I did too. Ahmed Nu'uman, the Sunni I wanted as Fifth Battalion commanding officer from the get-go, was going to remain XO—second in command. Most of the officers who got promoted were

Shiites: Major Hodi Jamaal, from Sa'ad's al-Harbia tribe, was made a lieutenant colonel. Mohammed Najm, the friend of Zayn who oversaw operations, was elevated to lieutenant colonel and made co-XO, alongside Ahmed Nu'uman. Militarily, having two seconds-in-command was awkward, but the structure made sense to the Ministry of Defense or Sa'ad or somebody—who knew?

The unlikely but effective Kurd-Sunni duo who headed Third Rifle Company—Bakr Saleh and Mohammed Ahmed—were both bumped from first lieutenant to captain. Ali Ghali, the Shiite captain who was wounded with Lombard during the counterattack on al-Hadra mosque, was promoted to major. The battalion surgeon, Adnan Naji, was deservedly made a major as well.

The speeches started. The most important speaker was Ayad Allawi, who was at that time campaigning and deal making to become the country's real prime minister. He stood at the podium. Allawi was a balding man whose reserved Western suits stood in contrast to his expressive face. The sixty-year-old could switch into instant gregariousness. In style and manner, he reminded me of an American big-city mayor.

A translator moved along with Allawi, speaking through the pauses. Like all the politicians, Iraqi and American, he put everything he said in the context of Iraqis' new freedom from Saddam Hussein.

"Building an army is a long and difficult mission," he said. "Iraq has been liberated of Saddam, who turned the army into a tool of repression."

Our enemies, he told us, targeted the security forces because they feared an effective, better-equipped army. I agreed with that. Allawi warned that the attacks would likely get worse as the January 30 election drew closer. I agreed with that too. Allawi said Saddam's last followers had formed a bloody alliance with "criminals, murderers and terrorists who are the enemies of our people and our progress." The election would go ahead on schedule, he said.

Next, Hazem al-Sha'alan took the podium. Sha'alan was defense minister. Like more and more of the people running things, he was a Shiite. He had a corporate look to him. Before the

US invasion, he had, like Allawi, lived in London. Sha'alan had been in real estate. He spoke, through a translator, at length. I began to drift away.

I was pulled back to the scene by the sound of my name coming from Sha'alan's mouth. All I heard was "Zakkiyah." I had no idea why he said it.

Sa'ad pushed me forward but said nothing. I began to feel a very intense kind of self-consciousness, like something out of a wild dream.

"It's an award, sir," Arkan said. He smiled and gestured at the podium. "They want you to go up."

I looked toward the front and made my way forward. The crowd was silent during my walk under the springlike sun. I stepped up to Hazem al-Sha'alan. He smiled with his mouth shut under a neat mustache and slender-framed glasses. He clasped my shoulders and kissed me three times.

"On behalf of a grateful Iraqi government, and for your leadership and service to the Iraqi Army, I present to you, Raed Zakkiyah, the Order of the Lion of Babylon."

An aide gave al-Sha'alan a certificate and a box. He turned back and gave them to me. The box was open, lined with burgundy velvet. Inside was a gold disc inscribed in Arabic and English. The crowd applauded.

"Shukran jazilan," I said—"thank you" in Arabic—figuring that was appropriate. I was still stunned to be standing there. He reached out to shake, and I awkwardly tried to shift the items to one hand. Then I was ushered along to shake more hands, a whole sitting line of ambassadors and generals. Among them was John Negroponte and finally Allawi himself, who beamed as he kissed my cheeks.

"Thank you for your commitment to your battalion," he said.

When I got back to my seat, another speaker was starting behind me. Sa'ad and Arkan came forward and hugged me. Arkan said he was proud of me. Two Marine lieutenant colonels nearby shook my hand, as did other advisers within arm's reach. I was still having a hard time processing what had happened.

Allawi's speech on Iraqi Army Day in Taji was reported by
the US news media as an afterthought. Most reports back home
on the war didn't go into ceremony. The events of note almost
always involved Americans or Iraqi civilians getting killed. There
was plenty of that going on, and other bad stuff besides. The same
day Allawi spoke in Taji, nine US troops were killed by a roadside
bomb in Baghdad. Two Marines were killed back in Anbar province, near Fallujah. A French journalist disappeared in Baghdad.
American troops were accused of forcing two civilian Iraqi brothers
into the Tigris and laughing while one of them drowned. Eighteen
Shiite workers from the village of Bayda were found dead in Mosul
after going to work for a mysterious "contractor" who lured them
with promises of jobs with the Americans. The workers were all
shot in the head. The head of police in a Shiite neighborhood
in Baghdad was gunned down in an ambush. The leader of the
Iraqi Communist Party was found strangled at home in Baghdad,
his hands bound with steel twine. The day before Allawi spoke,
the Baghdad governor was assassinated in his motorcade. Abu
Musab al-Zarqawi, the Jordanian terrorist we tried to kill in Fallujah, claimed responsibility for the hit. In the two days leading
up to Iraqi Army Day, a total of fifty civilians had been killed in
suicide attacks across Iraq.

When our celebration was over, I was eager to show the disc
to Zayn. He didn't get a promotion, because he didn't go to Fallujah. But I wanted to let Zayn know that I credited him for many
of our successes. His quarters served as both office and personal
area. I walked inside and showed him what Hazem al-Sha'alan
gave me. The certificate was in Arabic. Zayn read it silently and
opened the box. His eyes grew. He whistled long and low, and I
chuckled at him.

"This is gold! Real gold!" he said, trying the heft of it in his
hand. "A kilo!"

It said so on the certificate, he explained. I was surprised.

"Wow," I said. "That's pretty cool."

Zayn put the box on his metal desk and grabbed my hand, which was something he did when he really wanted me to pay attention.

"No. You no 'stand," he said. "Listen. This is a kilo of gold. If they learn about this, they will kill you to steal it. Kill you! 'Stand?"

A kilo is more than two pounds. That came to $13,600 in 2005 gold prices. I didn't know who "they" were, but I figured he pretty generally meant anybody. And he was serious.

"OK, you take it," I said, and pushed it toward him over the desk. "Take it to your family. You can keep it."

When I walked into that room one minute earlier, I hadn't planned to give it to him. But now I found myself serious about it. He could keep it safe back at home, with his wife and his father and his tribe.

A stubborn look spread across Zayn's face as he pushed it back at me.

"Nooooo," he said, vigorously nodding his head. "That would not be honorable."

"But you could just hold it for me. You can keep it to remember me."

Zayn pulled his head back, elevating his chin in a gesture of flat refusal. "Nooooo. Give it to your son when you have one someday, Insha'Allah."

More than a decade later, I would go to appraisers with that Lion of Babylon disc that Zayn and I thought created a threat to my life. It turned out to be made of brass, with a thin veneer of gold. It's worth fifteen dollars.

Maybe Sa'ad was riding an emotional high from his new promotion to brigadier general, but for whatever reason, that same day, he agreed to tell his superiors that Fifth Battalion would immediately take over perimeter security. I think the political calculus began to make sense to him. Yes, we seemed to be giving something for nothing, but it would strengthen our bargaining position for more troops. We'd gain the most leverage at that moment, when the new elite division needed to teach its soldiers to fight insurgents. It couldn't train them if they were up in guard towers.

Sa'ad told two of his bosses, both brigadier generals, that Fifth Battalion would take the perimeter on January 8, only two days away. I told the new American colonel the same thing.

"But I need bodies," I said to him.

The next day, we were offered seventy-five fully equipped and trained junood. We could pick them up on January 11.

"But you have to go to Kirkush," the colonel said, "and get them yourself."

The joint American-Iraqi audit of the battalion's pay records came back soon after Iraqi Army Day. It found that every level in the chain of command, from the Iraqi Ministry of Defense down to Sa'ad, was skimming from the top. They were doing the same thing with battalion payroll that the Iraqi supply network did with bullets and ballpoint pens: every hand that touched the goods, took from the goods. Each hand in the baksheesh skim took about 10 percent of what it touched, standard. From hand to hand, it added up. The auditors did not recommend a course of punishment for the perpetrators, and as far as I know, none ever came down. But we purged 150 ghost soldiers from our personnel rolls. Financially, the damage had not been too bad—the battalion was never paid in full while we were inside Fallujah, so the embezzlement network had only been able to steal from two pay periods total.

The audit also helped us further demonstrate that we had too few soldiers to man the base perimeter. Up to that point, it was easier for the Iraqi Ministry of Defense and the American advisory structure to argue that we did not really need fresh junood because our manpower situation wasn't as dire as Symons and I were making it out to be. They were wrong. We proved it and exposed the Ministry of Defense's wrongdoing in one dramatic sweep. They stopped pushing back. It didn't hurt that I had just become the first American to receive the country's highest military honor, direct from the hand of their presumptive first-ever prime minister.

Fifth Battalion took the walls as scheduled, all forty-four guard towers circling Taji. Johnson, Fryar, Warner, and Brown worked to get the new seventy-five junood up to speed starting on January 11. Faulkner, now the logistics adviser, quickly shifted gears from the confusion of Fallujah to the politics of a major coalition base. He bribed Iraqis with cigars and cans of Coke to get supplies for our new troops.

With our battalion numbers still light, we kept off-base operations simple: traffic control points, foot patrols, and the like. Johnson, Warner, and Brown all agreed we had to keep the junood busy doing something besides standing in towers. We didn't want them to take on rust. We wanted them out on their feet. The Iraqis were much more at ease with work outside the perimeter than they had been before Fallujah. They were better at it than any Iraqis I had ever seen. After Fallujah, straightforward tactical work was easy for them.

Shortly after we recommenced patrols, the decision came down from the Iraqi generals: Muntaqa Safra, the Yellow Zone that had been our home before Fallujah, was returned to us.

On January 19, the battalion received 147 more trained junood. Another 200 followed shortly after. They dismounted trucks and sat in cross-legged huddles, their billed caps and chocolate-chip camouflage so identical in color to the earth around them that they looked like they had sprouted from it.

19

IRHABI

AMERICANS ARE CONDITIONED TO BELIEVE there's a neat, dramatic structure to everything—movies, TV shows, sports, and even history. We like thinking that things have a beginning, a middle, and usually a happy ending. We applied that structure to Fallujah. Unequivocally, we *had* won the Second Battle of Fallujah. We wanted to believe, therefore, that we had reached a *turning point* against the insurgency—as if we had just fought Midway, except on foot and in the desert.

The Iraqis picked up on this need we had for narrative order. The officers questioned me about it during our late-night talks. They thought it was silly. Zayn, Mohammed Najm, and Ahmed Nu'uman criticized Americans for believing that everything has a happy ending. At first I couldn't even grasp what my friends were talking about. Now I understand. It's almost neurological for us. We have it implanted in our brains from *Sesame Street* on, and we will instantly believe a narrative that we find *pleasant* to believe. The American leadership said Fallujah was going to be a climactic battle, and we believed it was, even those of us who fought there. But it wasn't. Fallujah didn't fit the structure we wanted to impose on reality. Iraq didn't fit the narrative. It wasn't going to, ever.

On January 13, I was in bed before midnight. Jundi the cat slept, balled up in my armpit. I was in my sparse quarters in the advisers' building. Beyond my closed door, I heard light footsteps out on the cement floor of the common area where we kept a desk, a table, chairs, a coffee maker, a microwave, and a TV. Soft knocking came from my door.

"Major Zakkiyah?" It was Zayn's voice. "Major Zakkiyah?"

I rose and answered the door without turning the lights on. I glanced at Zayn in his chocolate-chip camouflage with green-and-gold epaulets and gestured him inside. He walked in and flipped on the light. I cleared my uniform off the metal chair where I had thrown it and sat on my bed. He took the seat.

"This is very important, Major Zakkiyah," he said, sitting close. He put one hand on my arm and looked at me. His eyes were fixed and grave. "You 'stand?"

"Nam, aftehamet," I said. Yes, I understood.

"A soldier came to me this evening," he said. "He needs to speak to you."

Soldiers often wanted to speak with me. They always said it was important. But I didn't say anything. I was still half asleep.

"He says there is irhabi in the battalion," he said. "He knows who is this irhabi."

Irhabi. An insurgent. That woke me up.

"OK," I said, "we need to have an interpreter here for this conversation." I didn't want any chance of a misunderstanding. I thought about the translators. Arkan was trustworthy, but he wasn't as level as Abdallah. I asked Zayn to go get Abdallah.

Zayn was back in a few minutes with Abdallah, who despite the late hour and unusual request was his usual, imperturbable self. I had dressed. We met in the common room and stayed quiet so as not to disturb the advisers, who were in their individual quarters down a hall. I looked; all their doors were closed. Abdallah and I sat next to each other in chairs opposite Zayn.

Zayn said he was approached secretly by a jundi named Omar who worked in the armory. Omar told Major Zayn that he knew of a plot being led by another enlisted man in Fifth Battalion who was working for the insurgency. The irhabi was a former deserter who had gotten back into the battalion by threatening to expose an officer's family to the insurgency. Once reinstated, the irhabi began offering bribes to some junood and threatening others. He had tried enlisting soldiers who guarded the battalion armory, and may have approached soldiers elsewhere at Taji. At least two Iraqi soldiers had begun conspiring with the irhabi. Omar claimed to Zayn that he was not part of the plot himself but was pretending he was so that he could expose it.

The plotters had two goals: First, they wanted to steal a cache of weapons the battalion had captured in Fallujah. Second, the irhabi wanted me dead, along with as many of the other advisers as possible. The irhabi was offering the armory guards a cut from a bounty put up by the insurgency: $25,000 for Raed Zakkiyah, dead.

I said nothing. That was more money than some Iraqis make in a lifetime. I thought about the note that showed up at the gate back in September: "The infidel Zakkiyah will die like the other dogs."

You must be very careful—even with our soldiers.

"When?" I asked.

Zayn spoke. Abdallah translated: he didn't know when, and the soldier Omar was saying he didn't know yet either. But he would know soon. The plot was in motion. I decided I needed to talk to this soldier Omar directly.

"This is very dangerous for him," Zayn said. "If the others see him come here to you, they will kill him."

"Come up with a normal reason to order him out of barracks first," I said. "Then bring him here. Bring him now, when no one will see you."

Zayn left. Ten minutes stretched, and I paced the room. Abdallah sat on his metal chair, watching me. Questions bounded through my mind like startled deer. How deep did this go? Which Iraqi officers could I tell? How would the advisers on my team, especially the new ones, react? How was I going to bring my superiors into this? The answer to each question affected all the others. And there was the simplest, worst question: Who could I trust? Who in fuck could I trust anymore?

When Zayn walked through the front door of the advisers' building, I recognized the soldier with him. I had seen him in the armory. Omar was small with round features. He was nervous. He looked at me with big dark eyes and stroked his black mustache.

Zayn closed the door. Omar took a metal chair. Zayn asked the questions. As Abdallah translated, I watched Zayn restrain a rising anger. Omar detailed the plot. They planned to load a vehicle with stolen weapons, kill the advisers in their barracks as they slept, then flee Taji. As I feared, it had the potential to be a bloodbath.

I wanted minimal bloodshed. The first thing I decided was the fewer Iraqis who were told about the plot, the better. I would never be able to control their reactions. Someone would act on his own, either with the plotters or against them. Then I decided I would tell the advisers about the scheme to steal weapons, but nothing about assassinations. The truth is I thought there was an outside chance that one or two of them would respond to the threat on their own too. On Taji, everybody was armed. The possibilities were wide-ranging, and not good. I wanted zero shots fired on our base. I decided everything would happen on a need-to-know basis.

I dismissed Omar. He left, and it was Zayn's turn to pace the room. He was brimming with indignation, raising his arms and cursing in Arabic. I tried to calm him by asking questions. Did he believe Omar's story? Zayn's reaction alone showed me that he did. And I believed Zayn.

I swore Zayn and Abdallah to secrecy about the assassination part of the plot. No one, including the advisers, could know. They agreed. I think both were surprised that I was asking them to keep information from the Americans.

I called the other advisers into the room. They entered in various states of dress, rising from sleep or music or DVDs, surprised to see Zayn and Abdallah in the room.

"Gentlemen, we have a situation," I began, and explained what we knew about the weapons plot. The advisers listened in total silence. They all knew we held a huge cache of weapons from Fallujah. The weapons were under twenty-four-hour guard in the battalion armory. Fifth Battalion seized a lot of weapons at Fallujah. I filed a report that detailed twenty mines, ninety-two hand grenades, 219 AK-47s, more than 135,000 rounds of 7.62-mm ammunition, 614 RPG rounds, 1,124 82-mm mortar rounds, and more than six hundred artillery shells. During the battle, I called in US engineers to carry out a controlled explosion of captured weapons. I planned to do more. But after Thanksgiving, a group of Iraqi generals became incensed that I was destroying the munitions, which they saw as war booty. They believed they had a right to it, as personal property. The generals complained to Symons, even demanding that I be relieved of command. Symons explained to them that that's what Americans do with captured weapons: we destroy them. And besides, he told them, General Petraeus would never consent to having me removed. My position was safe. But my controlled explosions created unneeded tension between senior Iraqi and US officers right in the middle of a major battle. We could not turn the weapons over to the Iraqi generals because we feared they would sell them back to the insurgents. So I was ordered to hold the weapons rather than destroy them. At the end of the battle, Fifth Battalion ended up driving half a dozen five-ton trucks full of insurgent weapons back to Taji. Until we were let back into our area, Muntaqa Safra, that's where the weapons stayed: in the trucks. It made a serious security headache. We used Iraqi guards full time to watch over the weapons, and American advisers part time to watch over the Iraqi guards.

Back in the common room of the advisers' building, the Americans sat or stood in silence, absorbing the turn of events. Eric Warner spoke first, and his usually good-natured tone had turned deadpan.

"Why don't we arrest them right now?"

"We can't charge anyone yet," Johnson said. The taciturn captain was trained as a military policeman as well as an infantryman. "It's all accusations."

Abdallah ran everything we said past Zayn, rushing through the Arabic in low tones. Brown asked me what I thought. I said I didn't want gunfire on the base, and I wanted to keep the number of Iraqis who knew about the plot to a minimum. What I did not tell them yet was that I had decided to keep developments from our own chain of command, including Symons. I didn't want to face the embarrassment of raising an alarm with senior American officers only to have nothing happen. Also, I did not need formulaic, idiotic questions from higher-ups, like "Did this happen because you failed to motivate the Iraqi leadership?" For now, I told the advisers we needed more information. "We still don't know when, or if, this thing is going to happen."

We agreed to tell Omar to keep playing along with the plot. Our goal was to catch the conspirators in the act. Our plan had risks. We would have to give the plotters continued access to the armory. We would have to put faith in Zayn to stay on top of Omar and monitor developments very closely. He would have to focus on the plot to the exclusion of everything else, and he'd have to do so without raising suspicions among the plotters or anyone else. Zayn had to know when the conspirators' plan was about to go into action, and then we would have to react quickly, at a time not of our choosing.

We went around the room. One by one, the Americans all signaled agreement.

"Zayn?" I asked. "You'll have to manage this without direct help from us. If they see Omar speaking to an American adviser, they'll think something is up."

"Yes," Zayn said in English. "I will do it."

The time came two nights later. Zayn strode into the advisers' building with Abdallah. They said they needed to talk urgently. We closed the door to my quarters.

"It will happen at 4 AM."

I told Zayn that I needed to talk to the other Americans alone. It was already 10 PM. He agreed to come back in an hour.

The advisers agreed we would leave the building two by two over the next couple of hours, so as not to arouse suspicion. We would stay in contact on handheld Motorolas set to an internal channel that only the advisers used. We looked at a map. The advisers' building fronted a road. As you walked out of the building's front door, you faced north. Directly across the street our Humvees and a couple of trucks were parked in a row beneath a line of trees and camouflage netting. The armory was just over a hundred yards southwest over open ground, so the trees and vehicles gave good cover to observe what was going on at the armory without being too close. We expected the irhabeen to arrive by truck in the darkness, stop at the armory, and load as many weapons as they could.

We waited across the street from our building—the advisers, Zayn, and Abdallah—spread out among vehicles facing the road. Engines off, lights off. Our plan was to watch the plotters load up on weapons and then swarm them. The advisers thought the irhabeen would have to drive past us to escape through Taji's east gate. I knew they were partly right. The plotters were going to pass between us and the advisers' building. But I expected them to stop there because they planned to get out and kill us while we slept.

We did not know if they were ready to go down shooting. From experience, we knew that when one Iraqi started shooting, the Iraqis around him started shooting. Complicating things further, about eighty yards due west, to our right, two Iraqi guards were outside in the cold night air. They were from the new motor transport brigade—the mostly older unit that had female US advisers. They of course had no idea what was going on. I feared they would shoot indiscriminately if they got excited.

The air got wetter, and the temperature dropped into the forties Fahrenheit. There was a little chatter on the radio, but not much. Then 4 AM came and went, with nothing. Then 4:30 AM. Still nothing.

There were drowsy whispers about calling it off. I began to wonder if the schemers had aborted their plan, but I decided to stay on stakeout until daylight. That was the safest course. We generally expected the Iraqis to be late for everything, and this was no exception.

At 4:50 AM, Johnson's voice came over the comms. He was in a pickup with Warner, closer to the armory than I was.

"Suspects are heading toward the gate. Pickup truck."

I saw a big shadow crawling away from the armory. Its head-lights were off. I had not seen them loading—they must have done it on the other side of the building. The Nissan drove north to the motor transport building, where the two oblivious guards warmed their hands over a barrel fire.

"Looks like four passengers," Johnson said. "Bed's got a tarp on it."

The truck turned right onto the road that would bring them in front of us.

"This is it," I said into my Motorola. "Wait for my command."

The truck stopped directly in front of us, between our position and the advisers' building. They were close. A lumpy tarp lay over the bed, as Johnson said. I could see Omar behind the wheel directly in front of me. A figure stepped from the far passenger side and crept up the walkway toward the door into the advisers' building. He tried the door. It was locked. He tried a second time. Still locked. He moved to a front window and peered inside. Then he looked back over his shoulder at the truck. It felt like a long time went by in the darkness without him moving at all. Then he hurried toward the truck.

"Now!" I shouted into the radio. "Go-go-go-go-go!"

Trucks and Humvees cranked to life and lurched at the little pickup. Johnson and Warner's truck stopped behind it. Another blocked the front. Our vehicles poured light onto the scene, blinding the men in the Nissan. Americans jumped from their vehicles, rifles raised, screaming at the Iraqis to get out of the truck.

Zayn tore off on foot toward the motor transport building, waving his arms and shouting in Arabic. He cut off the guards at their fire barrel before they got involved.

The plotters tried to run from the truck. We closed in on them, shouting down rifle barrels. One of the plotters had a rifle, and I tussled with him for a moment before I recognized Warner's voice behind me screaming that he would kill the man if he didn't get on the ground. The explosion of action frightened them; even Omar was scared. We all were. It all lasted probably ten seconds.

The biggest advisers, Brown and Warner, put the plotters down on their faces in the muddy ground and flex-cuffed them.

Captain Johnson ripped the tarp off the truck bed. It was loaded with weapons, ammunition, body armor, and several pairs of night-vision goggles. They also had Iraqi Army uniforms. Johnson got angrier than I'd ever seen him. Our adrenaline was pumping, and the sight of the weapons and uniforms set off something in him. One of the Iraqis tried to protest his innocence, and Johnson lit up. He grabbed him by the collar and screamed at him: "What the fuck is this? What the fuck *is this*?" He cuffed the plotter hard in the head.

In the confusion, I sought out Omar. The other Americans didn't know what he looked like, and I didn't want him to get hurt. Zayn ran back to us from down the road after ordering the motor transport guards to their posts. He was fired up, yelling at the men on the ground in Arabic. I told him to take Omar away. With the others, we used the US military's Five Ss for taking prisoners: search, segregate, silence, speed, and safeguard.

Somebody alerted the Battalion officer of the day, who in turn got hold of Ahmed Nu'uman. Nobody seemed to know where Sa'ad was. We took the conspirators into separate rooms in the advisers' building. Zayn and Abdallah got Ahmed Nu'uman up to speed with what was going on.

We began to debate whether to call the Iraqi military police (MP). Ahmed Nu'uman and Zayn said we should not. Neither trusted the Taji MPs. Captain Johnson surprised me by loudly agreeing with them. The commander of the military police was a major named Mohammed whom none of us liked. He had a self-important air and a habit of visiting the female advisers' barracks at night to warn about Iraqi soldiers peeking into windows. Nobody, including Major Mohammed, ever caught or otherwise produced any of these supposed peepers. Aside from that, there was bad blood between the MPs and Fifth Battalion already. Shortly after Fallujah, two MPs without a lot to do tried to arrest a Fifth Battalion jundi for cutting in line for chai. A fight broke out, and our veterans of Fallujah ended up taking six MPs into custody and detaining them at Muntaqa Safra. You can bet that sparked a big discussion at the next Taji nightly meeting.

Part of me agreed with Zayn, Abdallah, and Johnson, but I could see no way around Iraqi police protocols now that the plot was exposed. It was an Iraqi matter as much as it was a US matter, and we were guests on their base.

We held four plotters, not including Omar. Two were civilians from off base. A third was a Fifth Battalion jundi whose involvement in the plot surprised me because he was a Kurd I recalled as a good soldier. The fourth was the leader—our irhabi. He was a wiry man in his midtwenties, with a lantern jaw. He was a Sunni, from one of the big insurgent tribes. He sat in his flex-cuffed sequestration and stared at the floor, stunned. His name was Emad al-Dulaimi.

The MP commander, Major Mohammed, showed up with a squad of Iraqi military cops and the new Taji base commander, a sallow-toned colonel named Abbas. He had wide-set eyes and a narrow chin that made him look like a praying mantis. They took the prisoners but said through Abdallah that they would be ours to question later. They also said they needed to confiscate the weapons in the truck, for "evidence."

Chuck Johnson was apoplectic. He took me aside and hissed at me.

"If we give them those weapons, we will never see them again, sir," he said.

But the truth is that I didn't care. In 2004, it would've mattered to me. Not anymore. The weapons were more trouble than they were worth. They had been nothing but trouble almost from the moment we had seized them in Fallujah. The top Iraqis wanted to control them because having them to bestow on others boosted their wasta. Or maybe they just wanted to sell them. I didn't care either way. I told Major Mohammed that we were keeping the night-vision goggles, uniforms, and body armor. Night-vision capability is a big advantage to Marines deployed overseas among enemies who don't have it. We weren't letting them go. As for the weapons, I told Chuck I wanted their serial numbers cataloged and a receipt from Major Mohammed.

There was another reason I didn't care so much about the weapons, of course. I knew, along with Zayn, Abdallah, and Omar, that we advisers had just dodged an assassination attempt. We had captured our would-be killers. And we had done it all without any shots fired. I felt like we had won where it mattered.

Immediately after the night of the stakeout, Zayn took me aside. He told me that he was making me part of his tribe.

Zayn's tribe, the al-Jibouri, is Iraq's biggest. Most Jibouri are Sunni and live north and west of Baghdad in a stretch that reaches beyond Diyala Province all the way up to Kurdistan. Other clans live south of Baghdad, along the Euphrates toward the Persian Gulf. That set is mostly Shiite. Regardless, they are all Jibouri, and tribal loyalty goes a long way in Iraq. It goes further than religion. We do not have a comparable loyalty in the United States, regardless of our race, ethnicity, or beliefs.

Zayn had more than one brother and several cousins in Fifth Battalion. He had been a recruiter, and I don't know if he brought them into the Fifth intentionally during the first recruiting push, or after. But regardless, they were there, in numbers, and I knew it was no coincidence.

Zayn didn't tell just me that I was part of the al-Jibouri. He told everyone. Late at night during our bullshit sessions, he proclaimed it to Shiite and Sunni alike. He told Mohammed Najm and Mohammed Thyab. He told Ahmed Nu'uman. He told them to tell everyone they knew. One night he laid out what it all meant, in terms even I could understand.

"Tell them all that if Raed Zakkiyah is killed, my enemies will owe blood debt to all the Jibouri! Tell them!"

Anyone who hurt me, Zayn was saying, faced prescribed vengeance from Iraq's biggest tribe. The Jibouri, six million strong, also happened to be one of the few Arab tribes in Iraq that included both Sunnis and Shiites. What he was saying was that I was protected, in terms that were unequivocal to any Arab.

Mohammed Najm and Ahmed Nu'uman smiled when they heard Zayn rant, waving his arms with rage over chai.

"Zayn shakhsiyah latifa," Najm said, laughing, not bothering to attempt English for me. He didn't need to. I could understand him: *Zayn is a character.* He switched to English: "The Arab blood is strong in him, Raed Zakkiyah."

But Zayn was serious, and we all knew it. So were his brothers and cousins. For the rest of my time in Iraq, Zayn insisted that I change sleeping quarters on a regular basis. Wherever I slept, even when it was in the American advisers' building, he posted his brothers or his cousins as guards. One or two stood outside my room, and one sat with me while I slept. I was leaving soon. Zayn was making sure I got out alive.

I laughed along with Mohammed Najm and Ahmed Nu'uman and Zayn and Abdallah and Arkan. By mid-January 2005, my mind was like meat coming loose from the bone. But I will forever remember those nights with those Arabs, Shiite and Sunni alike, as some of the best of my life. *That* was my sanctuary in a world where we seemed to have no friends—them and me and our tea and our bullshit about soccer and women and the Apollo moon landing. They were brothers to me.

Sa'ad reappeared from one of his forays to Baghdad and asked me to dinner. Just the two of us, in his quarters. It was still less than a week past Iraqi Army Day. A lot had happened. I agreed to meet him there. Sa'ad had a big place, his own building. It sat midway between the advisers' building and the armory and had several rooms: an office, a bedroom, a shower, a living room where he entertained guests. He had two orderlies who lived with him. I didn't like the concept of orderlies in general—those supposed soldiers who essentially acted as butlers for high-ranking officers. But generals in the US Army have them, and now that Sa'ad was a brigadier, what could I say? It was appropriate, or at least it conformed to US norms for generals. Sa'ad's orderlies were young Shiite junood from his tribe, the al-Harbia.

The tribe, it turned out, was what Sa'ad wanted to talk about. We sat in the living room. I knew something big was coming. We had an excuse to celebrate—he had been promoted, and I had just been awarded the Order of the Lion of Babylon. But I knew he had something else in mind. His orderlies dolloped out sweet rice with raisins. They served chicken sharpened by the grill in that perfect way only Arabs know how to do.

"We have come very far, you and me," he said. He was a big man, a former athlete, and he ate like one. He slapped a heap of saffron rice on his white plate and talked at me while looking at the food. "I have more good news. The al-Harbia will become a brigade in our army."

His tribe. The al-Harbia were prominent in southern Iraq, around Nasiriyah.

"I don't understand, Sa'ad," I said, though I was beginning to understand fully even as the words came out of my mouth. "You're bringing your tribe into the army?"

"Two thousand strong we are!" he said, looking up from his plate. "We are two thousand men, ready to fight for Iraq! We will become a brigade."

"And," he continued, "I will be the commander."

And it all clicked into place. Sa'ad was a sheikh of the al-Harbia. Obviously, they were all Shiite. Now all the males of that tribe would officially be part of the Iraqi Army, meaning they would all be on the government payroll. And I knew—*I knew*—that in return for this favor Sa'ad would deliver two thousand votes for Ayad Allawi. That's why he knew so many people in Allawi's political train. He would deliver the vote in Nasiriyah. That's why he had been running to meetings with the Ministry of Defense in Baghdad for weeks since Fallujah: he had been negotiating.

I had no doubt that Sa'ad could, in fact, produce two thousand fighting-age men. But they would not know how to behave like real soldiers, nor would they learn, nor would anyone try to teach them. They would use the madcap group firearms technique that Hummons once called the "Iraqi death bloom." And they would all be on what the Italian American families from my father's generation in New York used to call the *vig*. Everyone would get a paycheck. And everyone would pay up to the Man, the leader with the wasta, the provider who made those paychecks happen in the first place. The man who knew how to play the Americans, knew how to make their wasta his wasta. That was Sa'ad, the newest brigadier general of the new Iraqi Army. US taxpayer dollars were, indirectly at least, helping to make Sa'ad al-Harbia the top man in a gargantuan, money-making entity in southern Iraq.

"Hodi Jamaal will take command of Fifth Battalion," he continued. "The Ministry has ordered it."

I pondered the man in front of me. How seriously did Sa'ad take the war? This was the guy, I thought, who watched Marines flee their burning AAV at Fallujah and said, "This is war. This is what happens." At the same time, this was the man whose eyes glistened with real tears after I was wounded in Fallujah: *I have seen your blood today*. Trying to gather my thoughts was like trying to catch the wind in a butterfly net.

My mission. What of my mission?

I thought of Hodi, our new CO. Like Sa'ad, he was from the al-Harbia tribe. He was levelheaded and, from what I had seen, capable. But he also invited other thoughts in quick succession: Hodi was being promoted over Ahmed Nu'uman. Hodi was Shiite. Ahmed Nu'uman was Sunni. The Sunni officers would claim that it was anti-Sunni politics. A rising Shiite power structure was systematically marginalizing Sunni officers throughout the Army. Ahmed Nu'uman was the highest-ranking officer in the entire Iraqi Army whom I trusted, and he despaired being on the losing side of religious politics—all the Sunnis did.

And the Sunnis are right to worry.

The scorched hammer rang in my head.

Zayn's tormented face returned to me from a few days before. I could see the pain in his eyes again: *There's no hope for us, is there?*

Sitting at Sa'ad's table, I said none of it. I was processing too much. I was trying to contemplate the leadership of Fifth Battalion, which was what mattered for my mission, just as I was finally seeing the scope of Sa'ad's incredible maneuvering, which was perhaps what really mattered, for all of Iraq. Or didn't. Or did. Or I didn't know.

"Hodi Jamaal is a good officer," I said through a throat full of rice. "I have the utmost faith in his ability."

But . . .

I put down my fork.

"Sa'ad, I know you have been overreporting our battalion numbers. Symons did an audit. I asked him to. I know you have been skimming off the payroll."

We sat in silence, facing each other. An orderly who may or may not have understood English made a quick exit with his jug of ice water.

"It has made it hard for us to get replacement junood," I said. "I need those new troops. You know that; you knew that."

Sa'ad was looking down at his hands lying on either side of his empty plate.

He nodded.

"You are leaving now," I said. "But I hope you will talk to your . . . contacts . . . at the Ministry. I hope you will help me get men. And space. I need both. You know that."

From a purely political perspective, Sa'ad's accomplishments were mind-blowing. He got an appointment to the battalion as CO and arrived without even the American advisers, myself included, knowing he was coming. He earned legitimate honor at Fallujah. He organized a payroll scheme that broadened his influence and amplified his wasta among the other Shiite officers. He successfully marginalized the battalion's highest-ranking Sunnis and in the process ingratiated himself to an incoming Shiite government. He was promoted to brigadier general. Finally, he scored his own, tribe-based brigade in his homeland, thereby boosting his wasta among his own people. He did all this in less than five months. Politically, I had to admit, Sa'ad absolutely killed it.

A day after our dinner, I found myself yelling at him—privately—after I caught men he had hired stealing mattresses and bedsprings from barracks inside Muntaqa Safra. They wanted to take them to Nasiriyah. Like a Lego character, Sa'ad tried to bow his big, blocky head over his big, blocky body and act contrite.

A day after that, Sa'ad and I embraced. We made our good-byes to each other, and he departed for the new battalion that would live in his homeland by the Tigris. The Iraqis take the parting of ways between friends very seriously. Often when an adviser rotated out, Iraqis who were close to him had heartfelt breakdowns. When Reilly left, the cocksure Iskander cried real tears and wailed without shame.

When Sa'ad and I said good-bye to one another, on January 25, we could say a couple of good, true things about our relationship: We shared the worst of combat, and survived. We shared an honest conversation over chicken and rice. But we didn't share tears, not then. His black SUV pulled out of Taji with a trailing escort of white pickups.

Ahmed Nu'uman was put in charge of interrogating the irhabeen plotters. I told him that I would not accept them being mistreated. The Abu Ghraib prison scandal had hit in late 2003, and revelations trickled out about jailers abusing prisoners over the course of 2004. We had once held all-hands meetings with the whole battalion to talk about why the things the Americans did at Abu Ghraib were wrong. We had repeatedly insisted against corporal punishment of junood by NCOs and officers. I told Ahmed Nu'uman that I would disband the battalion if I learned of anything "infamous" about the treatment of our suspects—I used the word specifically, to mean anything that brought shame to us. He was there when I got a medal from Ayad Allawi. He knew that I knew Petraeus. He had every reason to believe I would do it.

The irhabi Emad al-Dulaimi was charged only with theft. He spilled everything. He implicated everyone else we had captured. The Iraqis held a court-martial at the Fifth Battalion officers' building. The two conspirators from outside the battalion were given twenty days confinement on bread and water. The Kurd who was a Fifth Battalion jundi was sentenced to be dismissed from the Iraqi Army after twenty days imprisonment. They brought in Emad al-Dulaimi last. His appearance wasn't what I expected. He carried himself in an almost jaunty way when he walked into the room. Maybe he was happy because he wasn't being tried for conspiracy to commit murder. His eyes were bright. I noticed he was missing a front tooth and wondered if it had been that way before. Emad al-Dulaimi copped to all the charges. I still remember something Arkan said to me in translation during the court-martial: "He says it was nothing personal. It was just an opportunity."

Al-Dulaimi got confinement on bread and water at the battalion; then the plan was that he was to be transferred to the main Taji detention center. I went to check on him at least twice every day while Fifth Battalion still held him. Ahmed Nu'uman was still probing him for information. Al-Dulaimi asked me repeatedly if I could help him. He said he wanted to escape Iraq and live in America. His request stunned me. I never gave him any hope that I'd help him get to America.

We went back to our regular work. I still was determined to carry out missions beyond the Taji perimeter. That had to become a habit. We had to keep the battalion tight, and we had to keep the battalion's leadership in the habit of keeping them tight after I was gone.

Almost every day, Captain Johnson asked me about the status of the captured weapons. He wasn't going to let me forget them. After the court-martial was over, it was no longer necessary for Colonel Abbas and Major Mohammed to hold the weapons for evidence. But they kept putting us off when we asked about them. Not only that, but Colonel Abbas was agitating to take custody of Emad al-Dulaimi early, before Ahmed Nu'uman was done with him. Some of the advisers began to grumble, half within my earshot and half outside it, that it almost seemed like Colonel Abbas wanted to *trade* the weapons for Emad al-Dulaimi. None of the Americans could understand why. But the Iraqi officers virulently opposed the irhabi being transferred to Colonel Abbas.

Emad al-Dulaimi asked me again, directly, if I could help him migrate to America. Having failed to kill me or steal weapons for the insurgency, he was trying to squeeze a new benefit out of the whole affair. He raised his eyebrows and held up his palms:

"Please, Raed Zakkiyah." He seemed to genuinely believe that I would see him as a fellow combatant and perhaps extend assistance as I would to a peer. He didn't anger me, though. I was beyond being surprised at what I would hear people say or do in Iraq.

The last time I saw Emad al-Dulaimi, he was still asking the same question. I visited with Zayn and the battalion surgeon, Adnan Naji, just before evening chow. Emad was dropping weight fast. Otherwise, he seemed to be in good health. Satisfied that the Iraqis were taking proper care of him, we concluded our visit and went to the dining facility. I never responded to Emad's request that I help him migrate to the States.

An hour later, Zayn and I had left chow and were walking toward the advisers' building. Johnson ran up to us. He was yelling and very animated, pushing his wire-rimmed glasses against the bridge of his nose so they didn't fly off his face.

"He's gone! Emad is gone!"

In that hour that I was away with Zayn, the irhabi Emad al-Dulaimi had somehow disappeared, despite the guards posted at the room where he was detained, despite guards around the battalion area, despite guards at the perimeter of Taji. I activated the battalion reaction force and formed search parties. We called the Taji military police. We spread out. We turned things upside down. But Taji was immense. We found no trace of Emad al-Dulaimi. As usual, nobody had seen anything.

A day or two went by. Johnson was livid. So was Zayn. So was I. I went to see Hodi Jamaal, the new battalion commander, and told him I wanted an internal investigation. I listed, bullet-point style, all the reasons we needed an inquiry. I gave a briefing that would have been convincing to, say, an American like Lieutenant Colonel Symons. I explained to Hodi the principles at stake: the veracity of our authority, the legitimacy of our battalion, the very concept of effective criminal justice in Iraq.

It was quiet and warm in his office. Hodi Jamaal was a tall man, crisp for an Iraqi officer. A swirl of steam rose from his tea. I thought that maybe the idea of an escape by Emad, a Sunni insurgent, would agitate him. I even thought that maybe he would suspect that the Sunni Colonel Abbas had a hand in things, and perhaps that suspicion would spur him to action. But he was calm. He listened to me, and as I talked, I got the idea that he was just patiently waiting for me to finish.

Hodi looked at me with frank, placid eyes. As I talked, he was communicating to me with that calm silence. The composure and half smile of the Shiite officer across from me was conveying something important about Emad al-Dulaimi. And in the split-second after I was done speaking, just before Hodi finally spoke, I realized what he was trying to say to me. I realized it with as much clarity as if I had witnessed the irhabi on his knees in the desert while the pistol barrel came down behind his head.

Emad al-Dulaimi had not escaped. Emad al-Dulaimi was dead.

"Raed Zakkiyah," Hodi said to me, as level as the tea he lifted to his lips, "I would not look too closely into this."

20

GOING TO SEE
THE WIZARD

IN THE US MILITARY, psychologists and psychiatrists are called wizards. Visiting one is called going to see the wizard. The military is decades behind the rest of society when it comes to the way mental-health treatment is perceived. There's still a stigma attached to it that most of America dropped in the 1970s.

After the assassination plot, I needed to go see the wizard. I put it off too long. I had been, and still was, deeply afraid of what the other Americans would think. It's hard to make a civilian understand how anxious I was that people would think me unfit for command. Psychological injury is not accorded the respect in the military that physical injury is—far, far from it. It's accepted that our flesh cannot withstand bullets and shrapnel, but to many in the Marine Corps—and especially officers—there is a perceived weakness in failing to withstand the stresses of hardship and combat. For most officers, there is no humiliation that could be worse than to have your superiors decide you can't lead men because your mind is weak. It is dishonor.

The stigma kept me pushing ahead without help. This was unsustainable. I could not eat. From the time before Fallujah until February 2005, I lost at least twenty-five pounds. I could not sleep.

I lay down at night, and the terrors waited for me on the other side in ghoulish ambush. They shocked me back to screaming wakefulness. And the longer I went without sleep, the more my wakeful moments lost their integrity. My senses veered from near collapse to sudden agitation. I lived a bright, daytime obscurity. My ability to form memories weakened. I didn't understand that at the time as I do now. People still tell me stories about myself from then that are totally unfamiliar to me, like the animations of a blackout drunk.

I got into an SUV and drove to the American side of Taji without knowing where the wizard was. I needed to find the combat-stress clinic. I started at a building called the Mayor's Cell, which housed Taji's utilities and similar services—waste disposal, electricity, firefighting, and the like. I pulled the truck up to an Army sergeant major on the street who seemed to belong there, and pretended to be asking about the clinic for somebody else. It was a cliché, but I couldn't think of what else to do. He looked at me through the driver's-side window and gave me directions. I felt like a stranger stopping a townie, and that made me think about how I was more comfortable with the Iraqis on "our" side of the base. I didn't mind when the Iraqi officers like Zayn or Ahmed Nu'uman saw my stress. I didn't fear their sympathy.

The combat-stress clinic turned out to be close to the barbershop where I went once a week to get my head shaved. I had just been there a couple of days earlier. I didn't want anyone, not even a barber, catching me in the area when I didn't need a haircut. Then I worried that someone would recognize the SUV. I parked the big vehicle close to a high cement Texas barrier nearby, thinking that may conceal it. I speed-walked to the doorway.

The clinic interior was spare, with walls of bare plywood. Thankfully, nobody was waiting inside. An Air Force sergeant at a steel desk raised his eyes behind thick-rimmed spectacles. He asked if he could help me.

"I need to see a doctor," I said.

He gave me a clipboard questionnaire and disappeared behind a door. The ten minutes before he returned seemed like an hour. I wanted to walk through the door behind him. Thankfully, nobody walked into the clinic. He returned to the room and reviewed my paperwork. He told me to wait a minute and went back through his door. *Please, Sergeant, do not make me wait again.* Then he popped back.

"Sir, would you like to step this way with me?"

The inner room held a framed diploma, two steel chairs, and a canvas cot, the most spartan version of a shrink's office imaginable. He asked if I'd be more comfortable sitting or lying down. I decided to lie down. The sergeant asked me open-ended questions, and I told him briefly about the events of the past few months, culminating with the assassination plot. He finished his notes and asked me to wait. I nodded, my fingers laced across my chest. I was still wearing my combat boots.

Sometime later—I don't know how long it was—an Army captain entered with the clipboard. He was tall and lean, his skin sun darkened and his head shaved. He wore gold-rimmed glasses. He introduced himself as the duty psychiatrist.

"You've had quite a few months," he said.

I agreed. He asked me about it. I gave him an abbreviated description of my deployment. He listened. It took about an hour.

"So you've been here since March of 2004," he said. "Have you been home yet?"

No, I told him. I had not taken leave. There was never any time. Something was always going on. We seemed to career from one critical event to the next. I listened to the captain's ballpoint pen make its official scratchings on the clipboard.

"That is not supposed to happen," he finally said, and the pen clicked. "Do you want to get some R & R? I will talk to your command, if you want me to."

I told him I did not want him to talk to my command. I did not want them to know that I went to see the wizard.

"I understand that, sir," he said, and the pen returned to its clipboard etchings. "I won't do anything you don't want. But meanwhile, you can come here, anytime. In fact, I'd like to see you every day if your schedule allows it. If it does not, then come when you can. Even if it's just to get away from the demands of your mission for a little while."

"And if you change your mind—if you need to get out of Iraq for a while—you come see me," he said.

We agreed that I would check in with him every other day, more often if necessary. As I worked it out with him, I could feel myself negotiating with an interior expectation that I should not be there at all. I was torn between a wish to feel better and a shame for wishing it. As it would turn out, I was going to start visiting daily.

It did not occur to me that what I was feeling, the way I was reacting to the events of the previous months, was natural. They were to be expected. I did not think that then; I was not going to think that way until after Iraq was long behind me.

Back on our side of Taji, Zayn stayed close. He found excuses to talk. We shot the shit about my fiancée, my family, his wife, his family. His father sold his beloved Chevy Malibu without his permission, Zayn said, but he shrugged it off. His father had a right to all of his property, so it was OK for him to sell the Malibu. Like Zayn, his father was a devout Sunni, but unlike Zayn, he opposed the Americans. Zayn told me that he kept a photograph of the two of us framed on the wall of his home near Mosul. When he was on duty with the battalion, his father visited the house and told Zayn's wife to take the picture down. Then Zayn returned on leave and hung it back up again.

He kept trying to draw me out. Sometimes he succeeded. One day, out of nowhere, he told me he was thinking about taking a second wife.

"What?" I said. It genuinely surprised me. "Where is this coming from? You're barely home for the wife you've got."

"She is very beautiful, this woman," he said. She was a grammar school teacher. "Ten years younger than me."

Zayn and I were the same age, so that meant she was twenty-six. Zayn's father was against her, though. First, she had a limp. Second, she could speak English. Zayn's father didn't want English entering the family any more than a limping daughter-in-law. But that was part of the reason Zayn liked her—he wanted his children to learn English.

There was hope in January 2005 that Iraq may move into a new era that would outlast the war, and most of that feeling stemmed from the elections scheduled for the end of the month. Interim Prime Minister Ayad Allawi was Shiite, but he used secular rhetoric that was designed to draw support from Shiites, Sunnis, and Kurds alike. All the other political parties were built around religious or ethnic identity. Naturally, Allawi was favored by the United States. He had already shown a willingness to play ball with the Americans and their imposed power structure. And we didn't want to see Saddam Hussein replaced by Islamists. That would be a sick joke.

Voices in Iraq and beyond were calling for the election to be delayed, even with only weeks left before it was to occur, on the grounds that most of Iraq's Sunnis planned to boycott the vote. It would not be representative, those voices argued, of the entire population. Besides, security was nonexistent in much of the country. I did not have a good sense of which political party would win the election, but I did know who was going to win the debate about when the election would happen. The vote was going to go ahead. The White House demanded it. The United States needed to show progress in its grand remaking of Iraq. The insurgency did not make the United States less likely to push for elections; the insurgency made the elections an absolute necessity for the Americans.

Fifth Battalion was still manning all of the forty-four guard towers that ringed Taji. Given our low numbers and other security responsibilities, that meant each jundi worked twelve hours in the tower and had twelve hours off. Manning towers meant we could not train and could not go on missions. But taking the towers was what we had to do to earn our living space—that's why I talked Sa'ad into the idea in the first place.

My next step was to lobby Americans and Iraqis in daily briefings and behind the scenes to get the battalion partially relieved of tower duty. Eventually, it was decided that half the towers would go to mercenaries from Lebanon and Macedonia. The Lebanese were Druze who were too quick to open fire when they were out on the berms. They hated the Muslim Iraqis but liked the American advisers. The Macedonians were Eastern Orthodox Christians who were even quicker on the trigger than the Lebanese. They hated both the Iraqis and the Americans. (Just six years before, the US was bombing their Eastern Orthodox friends, the Serbs.) The Macedonians had hashish and alcohol and started luring female coalition soldiers to join them at underground parties in crumbling nighttime corners of Taji. Faulkner and Brown went to a few of those too, bringing food for the party. I freaked them out by dropping in on one myself. I didn't much care about Lebanese dinners or Macedonian hashish though. I cared about getting Fifth Battalion back into the field. After we turned some of the security work over to mercenaries, we were able to deploy one rifle company at a time outside the wire. I was finally able to put a blooded, battle-toughened Iraqi battalion out on missions.

And that is how it came to pass that, starting in late January and rolling into February 2005, just when I was feeling the most psychologically shredded, and only weeks before I hoped to leave, the Fifth Battalion reached its apex as a professional military unit. We had the battalion back up to about six hundred men, though that was a fluid number. As usual, our numbers were impossible to nail down at any given time. The roster was riddled with question marks. Despite that, Fifth Battalion had excellent unit integrity by Iraqi standards. It had coalesced around a core of Sunni and Shiite officers like Zayn and Mohammed Najm who remained after a monthslong weeding-out process. The same was true for the NCOs, who were mostly Kurdish, former Peshmerga fighters like Iskander. The al-Insaharin foundation of the battalion also included 100 to 150 dedicated, enlisted junood. As new soldiers joined the battalion, that core set an example. Many replacement junood had no real desire to be soldiers and did not follow the example set for them by the al-Insaharin, but some of them did try to emulate their senior comrades. The battalion's better habits began to self-perpetuate, and the solid core slowly grew.

The battalion's field missions around Taji involved establishing tactical control points. We took control of a designated area and set to our work. We set up checkpoints, patrolled villages, and undertook cordon-and-search missions. Our goals were to disrupt insurgents, deny them the chance to operate freely, seize their weaponry, gather intelligence, and create a high profile in the eyes of civilians. It was critical that enemies and friends alike see that we were establishing order.

The battalion also carried out raids, acting on tips or other intelligence. In just weeks, we seized hundreds of weapons, including rockets, mortars, and bomb-making materials. We captured suspected insurgents and transferred them to Iraqi and American intelligence. In our first predawn mission to al-Muzerfa village, we scored a weapons cache but nothing huge. In our second mission, we seized a huge cache: small arms, rockets, mortars, and crates of ammunition that dated back to the Saddam Hussein era. In February, we successfully raided an enemy training camp. We began to range south beyond al-Muzerfa. We coordinated with American units. Accidents declined. Vehicles stayed in running condition. Rifles remained in operating order. Civilians began cooperating. The battalion soldiers started to sense that their status was rising in the eyes of the people. We were clicking.

It turns out there was no single formula for motivating the Iraqis. Every man who remained by 2005 had his own reasons. Each officer, each NCO, each jundi had his own story that drove him. And those stories could be brutal.

A big reason Fifth Battalion was clicking was that one of its rifle companies—Third Rifle Company—was clicking. And Third Rifle Company was running well because of the newly promoted Capt. Mohammed Ahmed. He was the officer from Mosul who in late December planted his ID on a corpse for the insurgents to find. Capt. Mohammed Ahmed's ruse probably helped him escape Mosul and get back to Taji when his leave was over. But it did not save his family. Somehow, the insurgents got wind of what he had done. A month after Fallujah, they slaughtered his family. All of them—his fiancée and immediate family members, everyone they could find. When his next leave came, Capt. Mohammed Ahmed stayed in Taji. He had nowhere to go, no one to see. He spent his time on a lawn chair in his quarters and watched movies. The advisers walked past his door and saw him entranced by *The Godfather.*

When leave was over, Mohammed Ahmed plunged into his job. He trained himself mercilessly and pushed the men of Third Rifle Company just as hard. The Kurd who cocommanded the company with him, Captain Bakr Saleh, followed his example. Mohammed Ahmed launched himself into physical training every morning, and slowly, his riflemen began to follow his example. He and his junood were an instant anomaly—up until that point, all of the Iraqis hated PT. Mohammed Ahmed was not perfect. Sometimes he was lazy, and he carried himself among his men in an entitled, superior way, even during missions. Worse, he began to take unnecessary risks. More than once, he disarmed an IED on his own. Worse than that, and for reasons I absolutely could not understand, he began to transport disarmed IEDs inside his vehicle back to base. This was hugely dangerous and completely unnecessary. During missions around Taji, he directed his men from the middle of the street with an ostentatious flair that inspired the junood but made him an obvious target for insurgent snipers. More than once, Faulkner or Brown or Fryar tried to rein him in a little—"We love what you're doing, man, but don't get yourself killed, OK?"

Capt. Mohammed Ahmed did not listen. He took to wearing mirrored aviator sunglasses while on missions, a cigarette hanging at the corner of his mouth. Mohammed Ahmed did not have real wasta—he didn't have anything to bestow on anybody else—but he tried to look the part anyway. The men changed under Mohammed Ahmed's command. His NCOs spent their own money to have armbands made for all of Third Rifle Company. A white scorpion staked itself on the black armband across each man's bicep, with gold Arabic script underneath. Third Rifle Company began to refer to itself as Scorpion Company, and they showed a level of professionalism that I had never seen among Iraqis.

Scorpion Company exhibited an arrogant esprit de corps that as a Marine I immediately welcomed. They considered themselves superior to the other rifle companies of Fifth Battalion, and they did not hesitate to show it.

And then something even more amazing happened. The other company COs, maybe out of envy, maybe out of some built-in sense of straightforward competition, began to follow Capt. Mohammed Ahmed's lead.

"I am convinced," Faulkner said, "that the battalion is now as good as a US National Guard unit." It didn't sound like a compliment, but it was. And it was amazing how suddenly it seemed to happen. The Fifth Battalion, now formed around a core of al-Insaharin Fallujah veterans, was behaving like a group of professional soldiers. It was only years later, long after I left Iraq, that I understood that Capt. Mohammed Ahmed became a good officer when he stopped caring if he died.

Everyone's motivation was different. Personal. Not always ideal, and rarely idealistic. In the predawn hours before one mission, Faulkner set out with Capt. Mohammed Ahmed's Scorpion Company, and he saw Iskander. The Kurdish NCO had slipped into a state of placid focus, as he always did during missions. His normally tremulous hand steadied itself.

"Iskander, why does a Kurd like you keep fighting in this Iraqi Army?" Faulkner asked, teasing the sergeant major.

Iskander looked at Faulkner with half-lidded eyes and spoke flatly:

"Because they let us kill Arabs."

Zayn kept his brothers and cousins rotating in and around my quarters as my security detail. I thought more than once about the irony of the situation. I had deployed to Iraq to help its people build a safe and free society only to find myself secured where I slept by one faction of Iraqis who were protecting me from other Iraqis. We had not changed them. The country's preexisting rules prevailed. Even Iraqi factionalism came into play—it was one tribe, the al-Jibouri, that acted as my guardians. And I was letting them do it. Zayn ensured their loyalty to me by making me one of them. He had given up on the dream of working with me to make Iraq into America. He settled instead on making me more like an Iraqi. That was how I'd get out of Iraq alive. The battalion administrative officer, Mohammed Thyab, said it to me one night: "You have become Iraqi, Raed Zakkiyah."

My al-Jibouri guardians didn't make it any easier for me to sleep. I could not find a restful state. When I drifted, the ghouls chased me back into the half-wakeful middle. Migraines nearly incapacitated me. There were days I couldn't stand to see light. In 2005, some doctors believed that posttraumatic stress disorder could not develop from events that coincided with traumatic brain injuries (TBIs), because memories couldn't imprint on the mind when the brain's consciousness was impaired. I was hit by two head injuries: the truck crash on the berms in Taji that injured the front of my head, and the RPG in Fallujah that injured the back of my head.

The brain is complex, and medical professionals really know little about how it works. PTSD is a mental disorder. TBI is a neurological disorder. Or at least that's how they're categorized now—as separate, discrete things. Since the wars in Iraq and Afghanistan began, there's been more research than ever on PTSD and TBI. And it looks more and more like PTSD can in fact form during events that are traumatic to the brain. It may even make PTSD worse. And anyway, it wasn't any one event in Iraq that somehow burned PTSD into my brain. I did not know any of this in February 2005. I was concerned not with understanding my condition but with hiding it. My war was going to end before I would try to learn more.

The consequences of letting Zayn and the Iraqis know the truth about my state seemed less threatening to my career and others' esteem for me than letting Americans see it. I still think I was right about that—the negative consequences *were* fewer. When I was alone with Iraqis during our nighttime talks, I dropped the pretense of unsmiling, stoic determination that I wore with the Americans. Unable to sleep, I found myself staying up with the Iraqi officers later and later. The Iraqis genuinely wanted to help. Arkan advised me to take salt to relieve the pressure in my head. The administrative officer Mohammed Thyab, who had been with the battalion from day one, told me virtually every day that something in me had changed. I wasn't the man he knew when we began many months before. I remember I told him that I had seen a lot that was bad, but it was the betrayals that had hurt me most.

"But in Iraq, such things are commonplace. We know to expect such things," he said in his fluent English. "You are too good for Iraq."

One day I sat with Zayn and the interpreters Abdallah and Sala'am, drinking chai in the small officers' mess. They decided to give me their version of therapy, which amounted to encouragement, plain and simple. Zayn said he did not want me to leave Iraq, but he hoped I would return to the United States soon, to my family and to safety. He grasped my arm and pressed his forehead to my shoulder.

"Raed Zakkiyah, we all believe you are a very good man," Sala'am said. "Your name comes from Allah, and He has given you a good heart. Nothing can change that."

Abdallah took his turn: "We have not told you this before, but the soldiers brag about you. They are all very proud of you. They call you our lion—the lion of Taji and Fallujah. They tell their families about you. You are famous in Iraq."

I was humbled and a little embarrassed. I thanked them.

During the day, I continued to surreptitiously visit the psychiatrist captain. Otherwise, among the other advisers, I worked like hell to keep the strains hidden. I didn't even think of them as injuries at the time. I couldn't think of them as anything but weakness. And weakness is not to be shown. For the most part, I think I put on a good front. The other advisers at least seemed to maintain their confidence in me. But I did sometimes get hints that they thought something was amiss. One dim, predawn morning, as Iraqi NCOs shouted orders and grim junood clambered into trucks for a tactical control point south of Taji, I caught Faulkner watching me sideways. I looked at him, and he smiled.

"You OK to head out this morning, Major?"

"Yes," I said blankly. Neither Faulkner nor the others had seen me smile for weeks. He nodded.

"You know major, I've really come to like you," he said. "And I really don't feel like writing a letter home to your fiancée."

I stopped what I was doing and looked at him. He looked away. He checked the action on his rifle, busying himself to let me know that he was going to leave it alone if that's what I wanted.

I didn't say anything. I checked my own rifle. And then Faulkner and I went out together on the tactical control point with the junood.

The first national elections in Iraqi history took place on January 30, 2005, exactly six months after the country regained its sovereignty from the United States. It was also six months to the day since the al-Insaharin finished recruit training. On voting day, the battalion secured the village of Assiriyah near Taji and set up a perimeter to protect Iraqi soldiers from other units while they waited in line to vote.

Allawi did not win. The secular, Westernized Shiite simply could not defeat parties built around religion and ethnicity. A Shiite named Ibrahim al-Jaafari was victorious, with his party taking 48 percent of the vote. Al-Jaafari was seen as a moderate, but most members of his party were hardline Shiite Islamists. He believed the Koran should form the basis for civil law. The main Kurdish party came in second place with 26 percent of the vote. Allawi's party carried 14 percent of voters. The best-performing Sunni party won only 1.8 percent. In Sunni Anbar Province, home to Fallujah, almost no one cast a ballot.

In just a couple of months, al-Jaafari would align himself with Muqtada al-Sadr, the leader of Baghdad's deadliest Shiite insurgent group, the Mahdi Militia. The secularist Allawi would never again hold real power. His defense minister, Hazem al-Sha'alan, the man who gave me a medal, would be convicted in 2007 of embezzling $1 billion from the Iraqi government.

But that was all yet to come. Back in the United States, most people experienced the January 2005 Iraq elections as a set of televised images that portrayed happy Iraqis with purple fingertips. The stain, designed to prevent voters from casting more than one ballot, became a symbol of hope and democracy. For a little while, it even became a symbol of transformation. Most people who weren't in Iraq got to feel good about the war, temporarily at least. It almost seemed like the invasion of Iraq was working.

Toward the end, for me, there was no place like home. I don't remember it now, but my fiancée—who is now my ex-wife—told me after the war that in every e-mail, every letter, every phone conversation, I kept saying the same thing: "I gotta get home. I gotta get out of here. I gotta get home."

The date for my departure remained elusive. The American officer who was now top adviser for the base at Taji mentioned that he'd like to have me on for another six months. He said it in an offhand way, as if he was feeling me out. I had done such a good job with my battalion, he said. The other advisers could learn from me.

He scared the hell out of me. I skipped channels at Taji and went straight to the administrative support network run by the Marine Corps. A Marine at Taji—a captain who was one of the cocky advisers with me at Quantico a year earlier—was tasked with making travel arrangements for himself, me, and two other Marines. He was advising the Iraqi mechanized brigade and was as eager to get out of Iraq as I was. The logistics proved difficult, of course. Arranging the trip home is always a catch-as-catch-can affair that surprises people who aren't in the military. You hitch rides. The captain was trying to arrange our return for the beginning of March.

Zayn and I kept my departure secret from the other Iraqis. Most knew it would come sometime soon—it had been about a year since we started, and the Marines were not going to leave one of their own downrange in the war zone for more than a year. I asked Hodi Jamaal and Mohammed Najm not to discuss my departure with anyone. It wasn't the sort of information we wanted to have leak out to the irhabeen. They agreed.

News like that travels though. In the middle of February, I was in my office doing paperwork when I saw out of the corner of my eye a large, dark figure walked through the door. I looked up. It was Sa'ad.

The big Iraqi flashed white teeth below his furry black mustache. He wore a black lambskin jacket, a black silk shirt, and gray slacks. I realized that I had not seen him in civilian clothes since the day I met him, when he showed up and told everyone he was the new boss. In my office all those months later, he looked like he was loving the role of successful, upwardly mobile Iraqi military alpha male. He walked in with a light step.

Sa'ad asked if I would accompany him to Hodi Jamaal's office, which had been his office only a month earlier. Hodi was out. The Iraqi orderly assigned to Hodi, who like Hodi and Sa'ad was from the al-Harbia tribe, snapped to attention. Sa'ad ordered a pot of chai and two cups. We chatted about the battalion. He told me about his new brigade at Nasiriyah. I wasn't surprised to see Sa'ad because Hodi had warned me he may come to say good-bye before I left. It was customary for friends to exchange gifts after long stretches apart. I could only shop at the post exchange in Taji, but I went there and picked items for Sa'ad that conveyed status: Wiley X sunglasses, an American combat knife, and a portable DVD player. Sa'ad presented me with a silver Saddam Hussein watch. It had a picture of the dictator in military uniform smack in the middle of the face. I half expected Saddam's arms to move, like a Mickey Mouse watch.

"He gave it to me himself," Sa'ad said. "Before the Americans invaded, he promised the battalion and brigade commanders that he would not forget their loyalty. He said more gifts would come after."

He also gave me a small ziggurat in a plastic case, a replica of one of the ancient stepped towers near his tribal lands. It was like a tiny Tower of Babylon. We sipped the last of our tea.

Sa'ad got to what was really on his mind. In the past, he had shared pictures of his family with me, which I recognized was a serious honor. I had actually met two of his younger sons, boys in their early teens whose eyes flashed like their father's, but who were too young to grow mustaches. Sa'ad also had two daughters, whom I'd seen in photos.

"You remember my daughter Zahra?" he asked.

"Yes, of course," I said, meaning I remembered her pictures. His youngest was a dark-haired girl with chubby cheeks and deep eyes that shone even through photos.

Sa'ad put his hand on my arm and pulled close enough that I could smell the sweetness of chai on his breath. He produced a family picture from his lambskin jacket. He pointed her out to me. She was the smallest and shiest, standing in front but looking like she wanted to fade into the background. She held one hand behind her skirt.

Sa'ad stared at it with me for a moment.

"Do you know any doctors in New York?" he asked. "When Zahra was born, she . . . her . . ." He cast about for words in English for a second before giving up. He raised his left hand. "Her hand never popped out. When she was born. Understand?"

No, I did not.

"Like this," Sa'ad said, and he pulled his left hand up into the sleeve of his lambskin jacket. He raised the empty cuff before by eyes. "When she was born, her left hand didn't pop out. Like when you wear a glove and pull it off, and the fingers are inside, and you have to pull them out."

I involuntarily popped my head back so I could better look him in the face.

"Oh. I see."

"We tried to find doctor who could help to pull out her hand. None of the doctors in Iraq can do this. Maybe doctors in America can. Could you help us find one? Could you help Zahra?"

I did see. This poor little girl—born without a left hand. In Iraq, she would always be unclean. Hers would be a lifetime of eating with the same hand that she used to clean herself. She would be shunned by the other children. The education opportunities that should open for the daughter of a brigadier general would remain closed to her. She would never marry. No son's mother would accept her for marriage. She would never move into a husband's household, would never have children. She faced a lifetime sequestered in Sa'ad's household, and he knew it. He hoped that I had the wasta to help him help his daughter.

At that moment, my heart broke. After everything—after all the pain and stupidity and broken lives and death, after the lunacy and the courage and the hate and the love that had shaken my very foundations but had never made me crumble—a fissure finally split somewhere deep in me.

I did not have the strength to tell Sa'ad al-Harbia that his daughter did not have a hand. I could not tell him that it was not there, that it was never going to be there. The silence drew out as we stared at each other, wide-eyed, each of us helpless in his own way.

Embarrassed, a little panicked at my hesitation, Sa'ad stammered at me.

"I'm sure it's not a big operation," he said. "Probably in America—probably they do this all the time."

He blinked, and after a moment he added:

"I can pay! Whatever they want, Raed Zakkiyah. No problem, I can pay!"

"Yes, I know you can. I'm sorry, Sa'ad. I'm . . . I'm just thinking this through."

I gotta get home.

I looked back into his eyes. Six months earlier, I would have told him that I was sorry, that there was nothing to be done. I would have felt that being honest was the most important thing. That time was gone.

"I will do my best for your little girl," I said and, stumbling a bit, added the next thing that popped into my mind: "Insha'Allah."

What did I just say?

I gotta get home.

Sa'ad vigorously embraced me. He kissed me on each cheek, pulled away, and examined my face for a moment. He stood and smiled. I stood. We shook hands. I turned to the door. The noon sun lit me like a carbon arc lamp.

I never saw Sa'ad again.

21

DELIVERED

ZAYN AND I did our best to keep the date of my departure secret. Even when the advisers brought up the subject, I was intentionally vague about things. But I had a firm date by then. I was leaving on the last day of February.

Symons told me that my replacement was an Army Reservist, a major who, like me, was a Long Islander. The major had been activated from the Individual Ready Reserve. The IRR is a category of reservists who are former soldiers but who usually no longer drill, conduct training, or do anything military. They're typically unpaid until they're activated. It's possible for IRR personnel to go years without putting on a uniform or firing a rifle; there were even cases during the Iraq War of former active-duty personnel who were in the IRR and not even aware of it until they were called up.

I couldn't imagine why they tapped someone from the IRR. The new senior adviser probably didn't have the proper command of the military culture that he needed in his dealings with the Iraqis. The Americans basically took a civilian with some military history, plucked him out of his world, and dropped him into the middle of a cultural immersion mission in Iraq. His very survival was going to depend on everything he did or said, and he usually would be doing his job without close supervision.

I drove to Samarra with Zayn and a squad of Iraqis to pick up the Long Island major. We got shot at going there; we got shot at coming back. I told him that I wanted the Iraqis to have the impression that he was replacing Captain Johnson, not me. He agreed to tell no one that he was taking over my billet.

Aside from me, three other veteran advisers left the battalion that month to be replaced by new Army Reservists. On February 16, Capt. Chuck Johnson and the sergeants Eric Warner and Richard Fryar rotated out. Johnson had been an indispensable officer, bringing an even-keeled personality to the battalion just as I most needed stability around me. Warner and Fryar were both part warrior, part workhorse, risking their lives when the battalion was fighting, and taking on the toughest tasks when it wasn't. Their departure was a real loss. Johnson was close to Ali Ghali, the Iraqi major who was wounded with Lombard at al-Hadra mosque. Ali Ghali wept as they said their good-byes, and I could see emotion in the steady American captain as well. For me, seeing the three Americans leave made my own looming end seem more real.

The Iraqis became increasingly anxious about my departure. They asked about it, often in roundabout ways. I told the officers over our dinners that I'd be departing sometime in the spring. I didn't counter rumors that some of the Americans wanted me around an extra six months. Zayn, who knew exactly when I was going away, played along and continued to insist that I sleep in alternating rooms, always with his brothers or cousins posted guard. I still wasn't sleeping well. I worked feverishly to get things ready for the transition to the Long Island major. At night, I handled endless administrative tasks for the turnover. During the day, the major bird-dogged Zayn and me, asking questions and taking notes. People continued to assume that I was teaching him the deputy senior adviser role that Captain Johnson held. Or at least they acted as if that was their assumption.

In the meantime, there was still a war on. We remained an active unit. Fifth Battalion kept up its pace of missions and instruction. I arranged for a mobile US Army training team to teach operational planning techniques to the battalion staff. It was a weeklong course designed to culminate in a mock staff exercise. It required a big time commitment from the officers. But Iraqi attendance dwindled until one morning, after a break, the only people who showed up were Zayn, Ali Ghali, and me.

I told Zayn and Ali Ghali to go out and gather up every officer in the battalion they could find, immediately. The Army trainers cleared their throats and waited. I was embarrassed and furious. Again, I implored the Iraqis to understand the importance of what I wanted them to do. Again, I explained that our mission was on the line. I kicked a wooden chair into the wall. The chair shattered. I stormed out. Again, after I raged, they did as I asked. The course came together.

Intelligence started to come in from the US Seventh Cavalry Regiment that the insurgents were training fighters north of Taji, near a farming town called Tarmiya. The American cavalry regiment was going home soon and didn't seem eager to take on new fights. I asked if I could develop a plan to raid the camp, and they were more than happy to give Fifth Battalion permission. I told the Army trainers running the operations course that I wanted the Iraqi officers to develop a real working plan, rather than a mock one, based on the intelligence from Seventh Cavalry. I didn't want a planning exercise—we were going to build a real plan, and then the battalion was going to carry it out.

We executed a raid on Tarmiya in mid-February. It went very well. We seized a significant amount of IED-making material and caught a handful of insurgents alive. After Fifth Battalion's successful strike, Second Battalion, Seventh Cavalry, did their own mission in Tarmiya. This time the insurgents were ready. They had laid out a daisy-chain IED, which is a long line of explosives wired together to go off at the same time. They're designed to hit an entire convoy at once. Three American soldiers were killed.

I was determined to keep doing missions. The Fifth was going to remain sharp only if it was in the field. The rifle companies were building a real esprit de corps, and we needed to foster that as much as we could. Separately, I believed it was good to create the impression that I would be with the battalion several months more. The irhabeen had already proved that they could infiltrate the battalion, had already promised I would die "like the other dogs," and had already tried to kill the advisers. I didn't want our enemies to feel pressure to accelerate the time frame on any more assassination attempts. And finally, combat takes on a logic of its own. A body in motion tends to stay in motion. A body at rest tends to stay at rest. I was a body in motion, and the motion made sense to me. *Keep doing missions.*

We stayed busy out beyond Taji's berms for a week or two. Then the day came. February 28.

That morning, only hours before I was to head to Baghdad International Airport and fly out of the country, I announced to the officers and advisers that I was leaving. We were at a regular battalion command meeting.

"I'm doing it today," I said. "Almost immediately. Early this afternoon."

I looked at the faces in the room. Americans and Iraqis alike wore stunned expressions.

"I've prepared some remarks for later," I said, trying to head off any emotional farewells there at the morning meeting. I dreaded saying good-bye and didn't know how well I would hold up when I did. I felt unsteady as it was, even before any final partings. I was also torn—I desperately wanted to leave but felt guilty doing it. And of course, I had deceived everyone about when I was going. I hoped they'd understand why it was necessary. "I'll be delivering an address at formation this morning."

The battalion formed up at 11:30 AM, just before lunch. Everyone was there. CO Hodi Jamaal and his XOs Ahmed Nu'uman and Mohammed Najm stood at front. The rank and file presented themselves on our patch of parade ground, five or six hundred men in their brown-and-green uniforms. Arkan, Abdallah, and the other interpreters waited off to both sides. Iskander stood erect as a post at front with his scabbarded dagger and beret, presenting the junood. The staff officers—Zayn and the rest—were arrayed before the troops, their green-and-gold epaulets bright in the high sun. Company commanders stood at front of their riflemen. Mohammed Ahmed squinted in the sun, his mirrored sunglasses hanging from a chest pocket, and ranks of sun-bronzed men in white-scorpion patches upright behind him. The battalion was sharp and primed.

Hodi Jamaal gave a short speech in Arabic. He told them the news. As he spoke, his words almost seemed to soften the features on the junood's faces. Ahmed Nu'uman spoke next, and men began to wipe their eyes. My hands shook holding my handwritten speech, and my fingertips went cold.

This is it. This is good-bye.

Ahmed Nu'uman must have told the junood to draw closer, because they broke formation and gathered in a massive semicircle around me. Abdallah and Arkan mixed into the crowd to begin translating. I was surprised by the press of men and didn't want anyone to see me shaking.

Just start. Just do it.

"My dear friends," I said, "at long last God has delivered us to this sad day, when we must part. I have been here for a year, and I am going home to my family."

My voice broke, and I stopped. The 'terps finished my sentence. The men pressed in, too close as always. After a moment, I reclaimed my composure.

"I want to take this opportunity to tell you that I have the greatest respect and admiration for your courage and sacrifice in this war. You know I believe that we must win this war and deliver Iraq from the wicked men who would rule it. You know I believe absolutely and utterly in the rightness of our cause. Without this belief, and absent God's will, none of our successes would have been possible.

"I know how dangerous it is for you to join the army, to travel here, and to bring your pay home to your families. I understand the danger your families face. I understand that the wicked men, the irhabeen, seek to win by destroying the bonds that hold us together. But those of you who have been with us from the beginning, the al-Insaharin who went through the Crucible training in Kirkush, understand that these bonds are unbreakable. That you are here, now, and have faced the very worst the irhabeen could throw at you proves the truth of my words."

My hands relaxed. I told myself to project louder. I wanted them to hear my voice, even if it was only Arkan and Abdallah's translation that they could understand.

"I brag to all my friends, to everyone who will listen, about this battalion. I tell them about the hard times, when we had nothing. I tell them about all that we have shared and endured together. About your courage in combat in the face of the enemy, about the crucible of Fallujah, about our soldiers who have been wounded and killed."

I named the killed and wounded, starting with Abdel-ridha Gibrael and including those who were murdered on leave, some of whom I never knew, never exchanged a word with. Then I named many there near me who had not been injured physically but whose hardship I witnessed: Mohammed Ahmed. Iskander. Adnan Naji.

The battalion was quiet. I took a deep breath.

"I say to you today, each of you is my brother. I wish for each of you all of God's blessings, and for your families, only peace and prosperity. It is my fondest wish that you should be delivered from war and the wicked men who would rule Iraq. It is my fondest wish that you should all be free."

I folded my small sheet of paper.

The soldiers crowded in further, some in tears. Hundreds of men. Many I did not know, a dozen I considered friends. They hugged me and kissed me good-bye. It went on like that for almost half an hour. It exhausted me.

Finally, Sergeant Brown and the other advisers pulled up in two Humvees. Hodi Jamaal shouted for the soldiers to back off. They had to take me to the airport. The NCOs repeated the order and waded into the mob, arms outstretched. Someone organized an Iraqi escort. The junood parted. I separated myself from the loosening throng and took my seat in a Humvee.

I looked at Fifth Battalion for the last time. Some of the men waved. All of them, in their berets and chocolate-chip camouflage, seemed to look at me at once. And I hated what I thought at that moment. I knew that Fifth Battalion would not survive. And I knew the new Iraq would not survive either.

We pulled out.

The Humvee rumbled over the road to Baghdad International Airport. Steel rasped with the bounding suspension. A pungency of burned garbage announced itself through the open windows.

The closer I got to home, the more anxious I became. Roadsides snapped past. I sat in the death seat. My journals, photos, and other belongings were bundled into a huge seabag. I was hypervigilant, terrified that catastrophe would strike my last convoy. I just wanted to get out of there. I swayed from hope to fear and back again.

This is actually ending. It's been a year and it's ending right now.

That road to the airport was the final gauntlet of a twelve-month passage, one that had never failed to deliver the unexpected. I knew the meaning of vigilance. I had learned that anything coming our way, seen or unseen along our route, had the potential to detonate.

I glanced back at the other Humvee and white Nissan pickups trailing us. Arkan sat in the backseat as always, and his eyes caught mine. They were rimmed red. He attempted a half smile. Iraq's dry, flat landscape sailed behind him through a rear window. I tried a half smile back at him. My loyal, clean-shaven interpreter, my Arabic voice, was never going to realize his dream of immigrating to America. At the end of 2005 and the beginning of 2006, he would survive two assassination attempts less than a month apart. He did not survive a third. The civilian who braved bullets and shrapnel with me at Fallujah was gunned down by irhabeen on March 12, 2006.

After I left, assassination would hit Fifth Battalion again and again. In classic Middle Eastern fashion, it would often be unclear who the assassins were. That would be especially true of Ahmed Nu'uman, the youthful Sunni who served as Fifth Battalion XO to three different commanding officers, and who briefly was CO himself. Ahmed Nu'uman became commander yet again after I left Iraq, when Hodi Jamaal departed the battalion to join Sa'ad and the al-Harbia tribe at their new Shiite brigade in Nasiriyah.

In 2005, Ahmed Nu'uman turned up dead on the side of the road, shot in the back of the head on his way back from a payroll run to Baghdad. Another Sunni officer was executed with him. The payroll was stolen. Ahmed Nu'uman had become increasingly vocal about Shiite efforts to marginalize the Sunnis like himself who were still loyal to the Iraqi Army. Nobody knows who killed Ahmed Nu'uman, and, of course, it will never be investigated. It could have been the irhabeen. It could have been an organized ring of thieves. Or, as the war morphed into a genocidal power struggle between Shiites and Sunnis in 2005 and 2006, it could have been Shiites in the Iraqi Army and Ministry of Defense.

It's an ironic constant of warfare that the most dedicated officers—the believers who actually lead men to victory—are also the ones who are most likely to get killed. It's simple: they willingly place themselves in greater danger than the officers who don't care. That was the case with Capt. Mohammed Ahmed, the hard-driving commander of Scorpion Company who lost his entire family to insurgent slaughter. Captain Ahmed was fearless, but he flaunted his Iraqi machismo by taking unnecessary risks. In 2005, he discovered an IED on the roadside and, rather than blow it up in place, he put it in his vehicle and tried to transport it to base. Maybe he planned to dissect it later; maybe he wanted some kind of trophy. I don't know his motivation. The IED exploded in the Humvee, killing Mohammed Ahmed and three of his men from Scorpion Company.

The fate of Fifth Battalion followed the destiny of the new Iraq itself. From around the time of the first democratic elections and for a year or so after I left, Fifth Battalion experienced its apex, becoming one of the best units in the Iraqi Army. It had just enough cohesive power to stay together and successfully operate as a religiously and ethnically diverse unit. In June 2006, the Fifth supported the US operation that killed Abu Musab al-Zarqawi, the Jordanian who murdered Armstrong, Hensley, and Bigley and whom the Marines and Fifth Battalion chased like a ghost at Fallujah. I got e-mails from Zayn, Mohammed Najm, and some of the new advisers describing the strike, celebrating the elimination of our enemy. Zarqawi was killed on June 7 at Baqubah, only twenty miles northeast of Taji.

The Fifth Battalion briefly became, in microcosm, something close to the inclusive Iraq it was supposed to represent: Shiites, Sunnis, and Kurds fighting together for a new idea that was bigger than religion and ethnicity. Notice I said it came close. It never made it all the way. And the progress it made did not last.

The day after Zarqawi was killed in 2006, a new prime minister named Nouri al-Maliki finished forming his government. The previous leader brought in by Iraq's successful elections of 2005, Ibrahim al-Jaafari, stepped aside under pressure from the Bush White House, which considered him ineffectual. His replacement, al-Maliki, was even more pro-Shiite, more anti-Sunni, and more anti-Kurd than al-Jaafari had been.

The inclusiveness and unity that we hoped would undergird Fifth Battalion and Iraq itself did not survive, but the sectarian bias of al-Maliki and religious fanaticism of Zarqawi did. In fact, they flourished, to extremes that even the harshest critics of the American war in Iraq never predicted. After Zarqawi's death, his surviving followers went on to form the Islamic State of Iraq and Syria, which was more murderous and depraved than anything seen in the Middle East for centuries. Today, we know that group as ISIS.

The Iraq War devolved into interreligious slaughter, and the ethnic and religious seams of Fifth Battalion, fragile to begin with, frayed and finally came apart. Sunni Arabs like Lt. Col. Ahmed Nu'uman and Kurds like Sergeant Major Iskander weren't being paranoid when they told me that the majority Shiites, led by men like Sa'ad, were disenfranchising the others and accumulating power for themselves. Sectarian divisions deepened throughout 2006 and 2007, throughout Iraq. General Petraeus temporarily achieved détente with the Sunni Arab tribes and rallied them to fight alongside the Americans in 2006—the so-called Sunni

Awakening. But Sunni Arabs' faith in a free, inclusive Iraq and the army that would protect it were on a downward trajectory. Many Sunnis, alienated by the regime of al-Maliki and sick of hoping for a voice in government that never came, supported ISIS with open arms.

As for the Kurds, they grew increasingly aware that the free Kurdistan they aspired to was within their grasp. The dream of my warrior messenger Abdel-ridha Gibrael survived, even if he did not. The Kurds lost interest in a unified Iraq. Iskander finally followed through on his threats to leave the Iraqi Army. He returned north and rejoined the Peshmerga.

Fifth Battalion and the Iraqi Army as a whole fell victim to the competing political agendas of the three sects. Sunni junood were moved over time to predominantly Sunni units, Shiites to mostly Shiite units. The Kurds were put in Iraqi Kurdish units until they decided to just quit the Iraqi Army. No longer recognizable as al-Insaharin who had persevered through the Crucible and Fallujah, Fifth Battalion was reflagged in 2007 and finally disbanded altogether in 2011. That same year, the administration of President Barack Obama withdrew US forces from Iraq.

In the end, Fifth Battalion was a nearly perfect allegory for Iraq. But it wasn't a symbol of Iraq as the Americans wanted to see the country. It was a symbol of Iraq as it really was. Like a mirage, the Americans' illusory notions for Iraq disappeared. The dream dissolved, just as the battalion that was meant to embody it evaporated like water under a vertical sun. All that remained in Iraq were the religions and ethnicities and tribes that were already in place before the Americans got there.

In April 2004, General Eaton told us that, ten years hence, we would look back and see the results of our work and sacrifice. He proved prophetic.

In January 2014, ISIS swept out of Syria and seized Fallujah. The city where thousands of Americans and Iraqis risked their lives and for which hundreds of men like Abdel-ridha Gibrael died ended up under the control of Zarqawi's demented offspring. ISIS drove the collapsing Iraqi Army before it, seized millions of dollars in American weapons and other equipment, and charged forward under a black flag. In June 2014, a mere one thousand ISIS fighters stormed Mosul, a walled city that was supposedly defended by twenty thousand soldiers and police. The defenders cast aside their weapons and ran.

Or almost all of them did. At least one man did not abandon his post. Zayn was from Mosul, and most of his family became instant refugees as ISIS closed in. Zayn's brother, a man I never met but whom Zayn talked about often, was the chief of police of Mosul. He continued to fight as the ISIS irhabeen—the "violent criminals" that Zayn refused to acknowledge as Muslims—closed in. In July 2014, Zayn sent me a message via Facebook: "Dear brother. I am safe. My brother you remember was the chief of police. He remained faithful when the Irhabi came. They beheaded him in the square."

You understand another culture only after you live in it. You also understand your own culture only after you live in another. It's only by learning about another culture that you even grasp what culture *is*: that sum of thinking and living and believing that evolves in a place over generations. It pervades all. It preempts all. It can't be remade by bullets, barter, or bribes.

The United States has made a habit of trying to remake the Muslim world. It's been one of our primary compulsions so far this century. We're terrible at it, but we keep trying anyway.

We do so because that's a trait of our own culture. We think we know what the world wants. We're certain that the rest of the world will adopt our traditions if given a chance. That assumption is beyond question for most of us, regardless of where we fall on the political spectrum. How could anyone *not* want freedom for individuals? How could anyone *not* want prosperity for their nation? Such desires are *universal*, right? It's astounding the assumptions we'll make and the actions we'll take in the name of sharing our American bounty, whether it comes in the form of inclusive democracy or unfettered markets. Sometimes our actions are effective, and sometimes they're not. (In the Middle East, they never are.) Regardless, we share our beliefs like missionaries. Like no other country does, anywhere. Coming from our American culture, we did not have it within us to recognize that maybe our assumptions about what Iraq wanted were really just assumptions about what we wanted for Iraq and the wider Middle East.

We overthrew Iraq, and we assumed it would rise again in our image, a beacon of fair elections and minority rights and rules-based commerce in the center of the Middle East. Amazingly, there were people in the White House who thought this would occur. They even thought our way of thinking and living would spread out of Iraq, transforming the entire Middle East. Instead, a fractured, multifaceted Middle Eastern war broke out. The American task then became to reestablish the stability it had destroyed and hope that Iraq would hold together long enough to morph into some sort of Middle Eastern America. For the advisers on the ground, that meant giving the Iraqis an entirely new set of priorities and aspirations to live by. Our job even required us to try to make them willing to *die* for those new ideas. As if they did not already have notions in place that they were living for—concepts about religion and tribe, yes, but also traditions we Americans didn't even know existed, like wasta and baksheesh and a thousand others. And why did we think we could magically supplant those ancient ideas? Why did we think they would drop everything they knew and adopt new modes of thinking? Simple: because we didn't understand that they already had ideas of their own. In our haste to get them on board with our culture, we never bothered to learn anything about theirs.

To be sure, some of the Iraqis did want an Iraq that looked more like America. Like Arkan. Even some of the deeply religious ones bought into what we were preaching, like Zayn. Maybe some do still. But it's not possible for a nation of people to adopt a new way of living, embracing it as if they come from within a vacuum. They're bringing their own culture and assumptions with them. Acknowledging that lesson was hard for me. It is hard for a lot of Americans—most will never learn it. And our great, flawed experiment was very hard indeed on regular Iraqis.

It took a while for me to comprehend that only so much change was going to be possible in Iraq, and the price I paid for that comprehension was high. I do not believe the United States has learned that there are limits to how much it can change other people, other places, other religions, even after fourteen years of dying and killing in Iraq. I've written this book to teach Americans about those constraints—those cultural checks on how much can be accomplished, *especially through the use of armed force alone.* I learned it so you don't have to. For me, the puzzle came together over one brutal year, shown to me in fragments, each one imparted to me piecemeal by men with names like Arkan, Ahmed Nu'uman, Iskander, Abdel-ridha Gibrael, Sa'ad, and, of course, Zayn.

I never thanked any of the Iraqis of Fifth Battalion for what I learned when I lived among them. I did not do so when I was in Iraq because I still didn't see things clearly. I did not after I got home either. I never did. But I am trying to now. I am trying to say thank you.

I would like to write here that on that last day of February 2005, I shared a thoughtful, reflective good-bye with Zayn. I did not. I want to say that we commiserated on our tragic, shared journey. We did not. I am ashamed and still confused about why, on that final day, I did not even care very much whether I said good-bye to Zayn at all. I can't explain it. I can make excuses, but I can't explain it. What I can say is that our final moment was more fitting for that world anyway, more in keeping with the impromptu, unpredictable nature of that country and my friendships there.

The small convoy pulled away and left me there at Baghdad International, next to the gate that was going to take me back to *the world.* I collapsed onto my seabag, my back against the trailer. I tried to take a deep breath, but my clenched chest refused to let anything more in. I had three seconds of asthmatic solitude before I vaguely heard the high yelp of brakes and the sound of truck tires sliding on the gravelly tarmac. A voice shouted something indecipherable around the corner, and as I turned my head down the length of the trailer to look in the direction the convoy had gone, Zayn appeared there.

He had come at a run. His narrow face was twisted with grief. He sobbed uncontrollably. I pushed up off the seabag on stiff legs, and he came at me with long, quick strides, arms outstretched. He almost knocked me over. Zayn gave me three kisses, alternating on each cheek in the Arab tradition. His tears were hot on my neck as he sobbed into my shoulder.

"I love you, my brother," he said.

And then, as if he could not bear being close anymore, he pushed away. He faced me for a moment: the man who more than anyone was the human face of everything I hoped for from my mission in Iraq. Then he turned and ran back around the corner to the waiting convoy. He never looked back. Those were the last words anyone from Fifth Battalion spoke to me.

I sat down carefully on the seabag, stunned.

I love you too, brother.

I put my head into my hands and closed my eyes. For the first time in more than a year, I felt alone. Truly alone. I would feel that way for a long time.

ABOUT THE AUTHORS

Lieutenant Colonel Michael Zacchea (USMC-ret.) led the Kurds, Shiites, and Sunnis of the Iraqi Fifth Battalion and their US advisers. He was awarded two Bronze Stars, the Purple Heart, and Iraq's Order of the Lion of Babylon. In 2006 Zacchea helped form a nonprofit organization of military advisers, now known nationally as Netroots: the List Project, to help Iraqi interpreters immigrate to the United States. He has testified before a joint field session of the House and Senate Armed Forces Committee on the Iraqi military and holds a high profile as a veterans' advocate with VoteVets.org and elsewhere, appearing widely as a public speaker; in the documentaries *Thank You for Your Service* (2016), *Eleven: From WWII to the Present Day* (2012), *The Road to Fallujah* (2009), and *Odysseus in America* (2005); and in the *New York Times* and on NPR and CBS News, among other news outlets. Zacchea is director of the UConn Entrepreneur Bootcamp for Veterans with Disabilities. He holds an MBA from the University of Connecticut, an MA from Hawaii Pacific University, and a BA from Notre Dame University. He lives in Connecticut.

Ted Kemp is a journalist who has worked as an editor, writer, and field correspondent overseas and in the United States, principally for CNBC. He has managed projects and overseen writers working in Iraq, Iran, Jordan, and the United Arab Emirates, and has covered events ranging from maritime piracy in the Singapore Strait to the 2011 London riots. Most recently, he helped create a television documentary on slavery and illegal commercial fishing in Southeast Asia. Kemp was an undergraduate degree at North Carolina State University and received his journalism degree from the University of Illinois at Urbana-Champaign. He is a passionate reader, a boxing